4 JiUn Yun

"A TRAVELER'S MIDNIGHT SENTIMENTS"
BO DOO

A BREEZE BLOWS THROUGH THE GRASSES ON THE
RIVERBANK.
I ALONE CANNOT SLEEP BENEATH THE HIGH MAST
OF THE SHIP.
STARS TWINKLE ABOVE THE SPRAWLING FIELDS
AS THE YANGTZE RIVER FLOWS AND RIPPLES
UNDER THE MOONLIGHT.
HOW CAN SOMEONE REVEAL HIMSELF IN THE
WORDS OF A POEM?
IT IS ONLY NATURAL TO WITHDRAW WHEN ONE IS
OLD AND SICK.
WHAT AM I WHO FLUTTERS IN THE WIND?
I AM A LONELY SEAGULL, WANDERING THE WORLD.

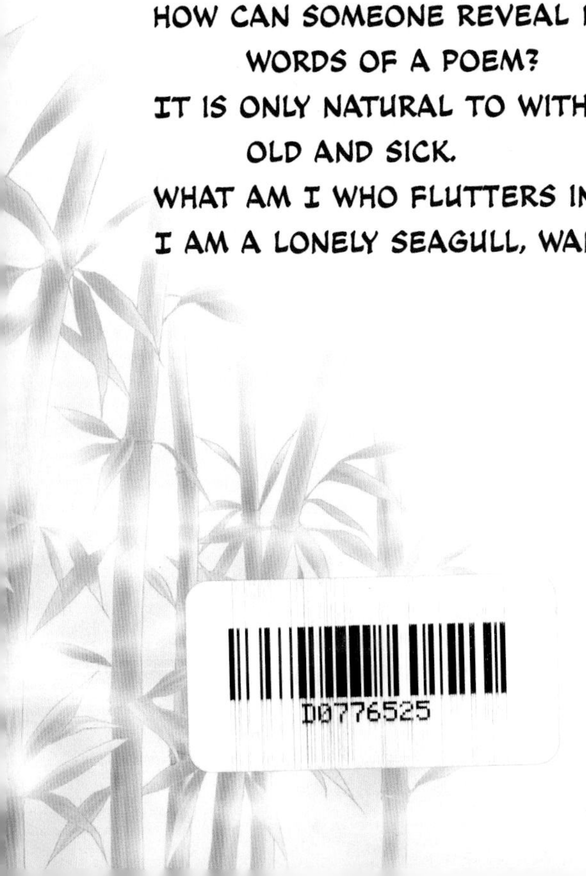

TIME
AND
AGAIN

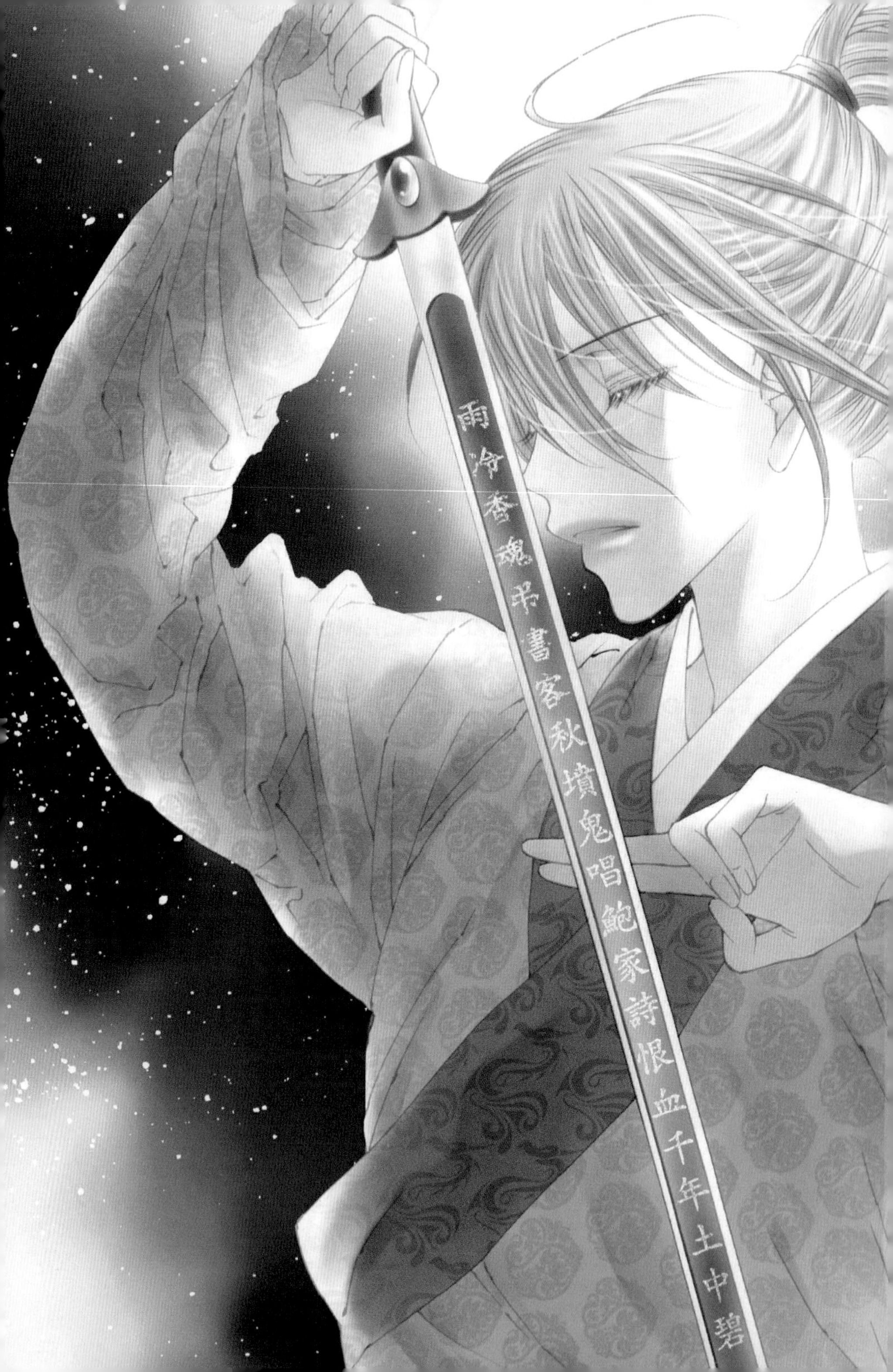
雨冷香魂弔書客秋墳鬼唱鮑家詩恨血千年土中碧

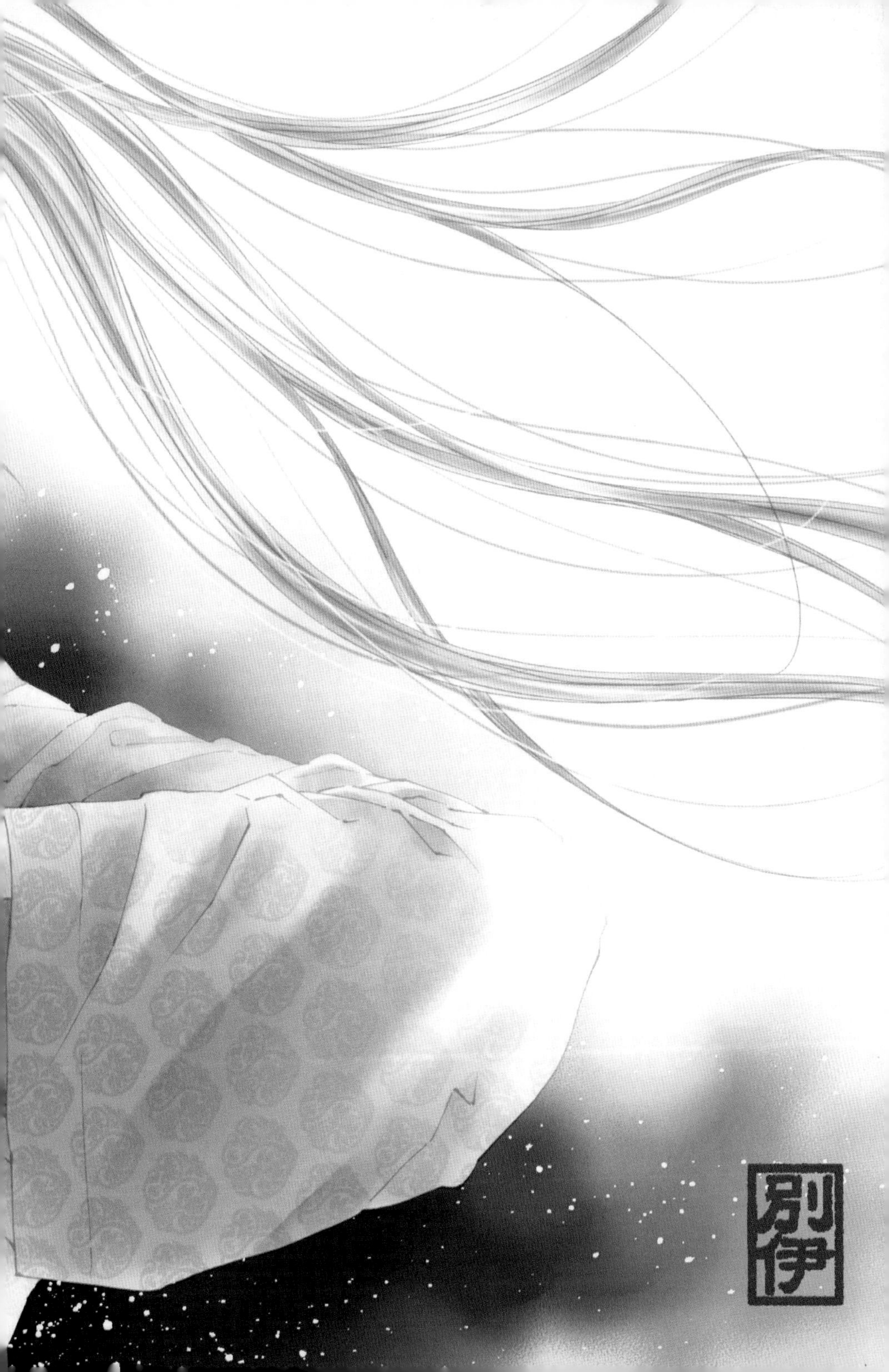
別伊

CONTENTS

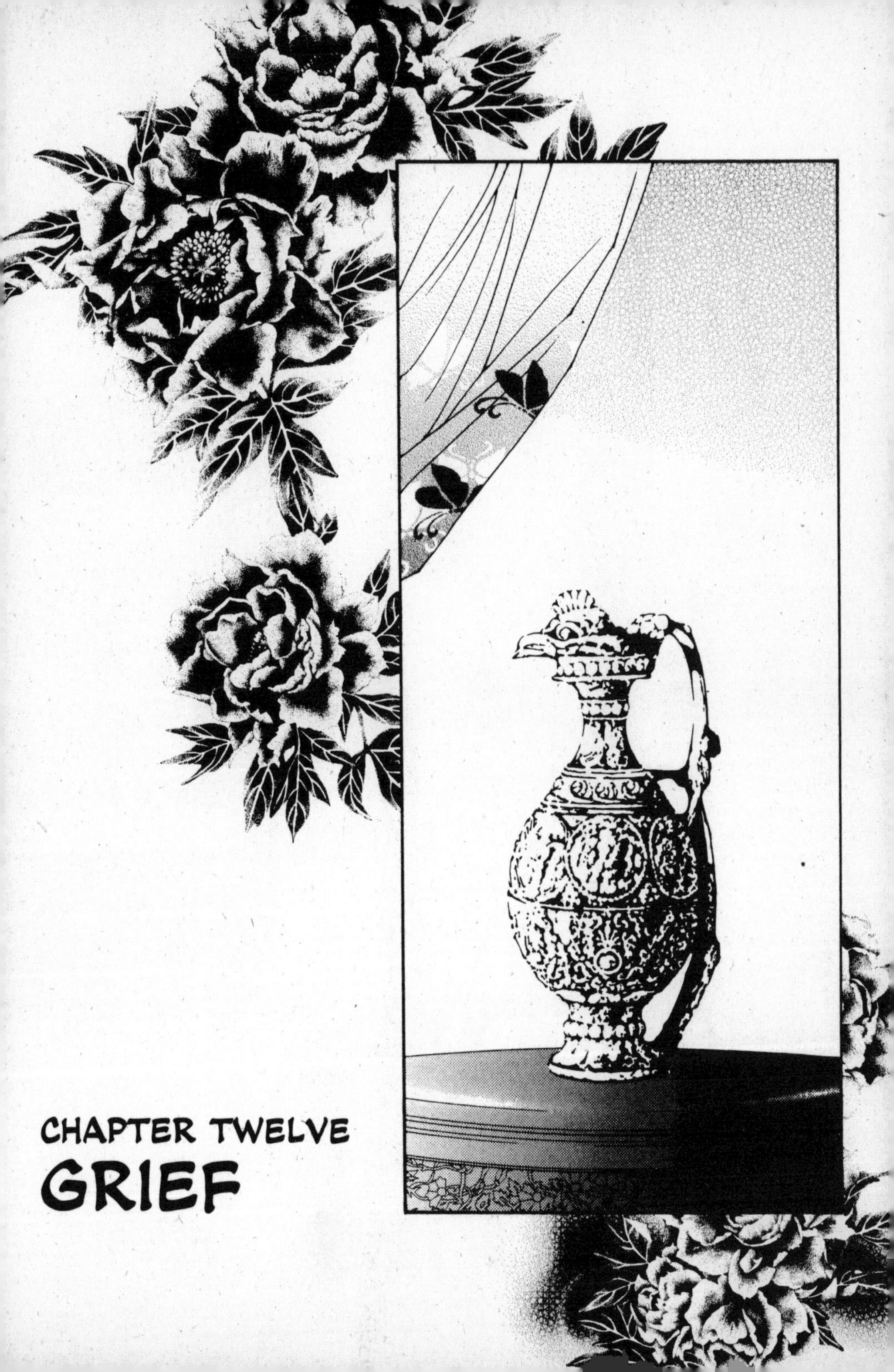

CHAPTER TWELVE

GRIEF

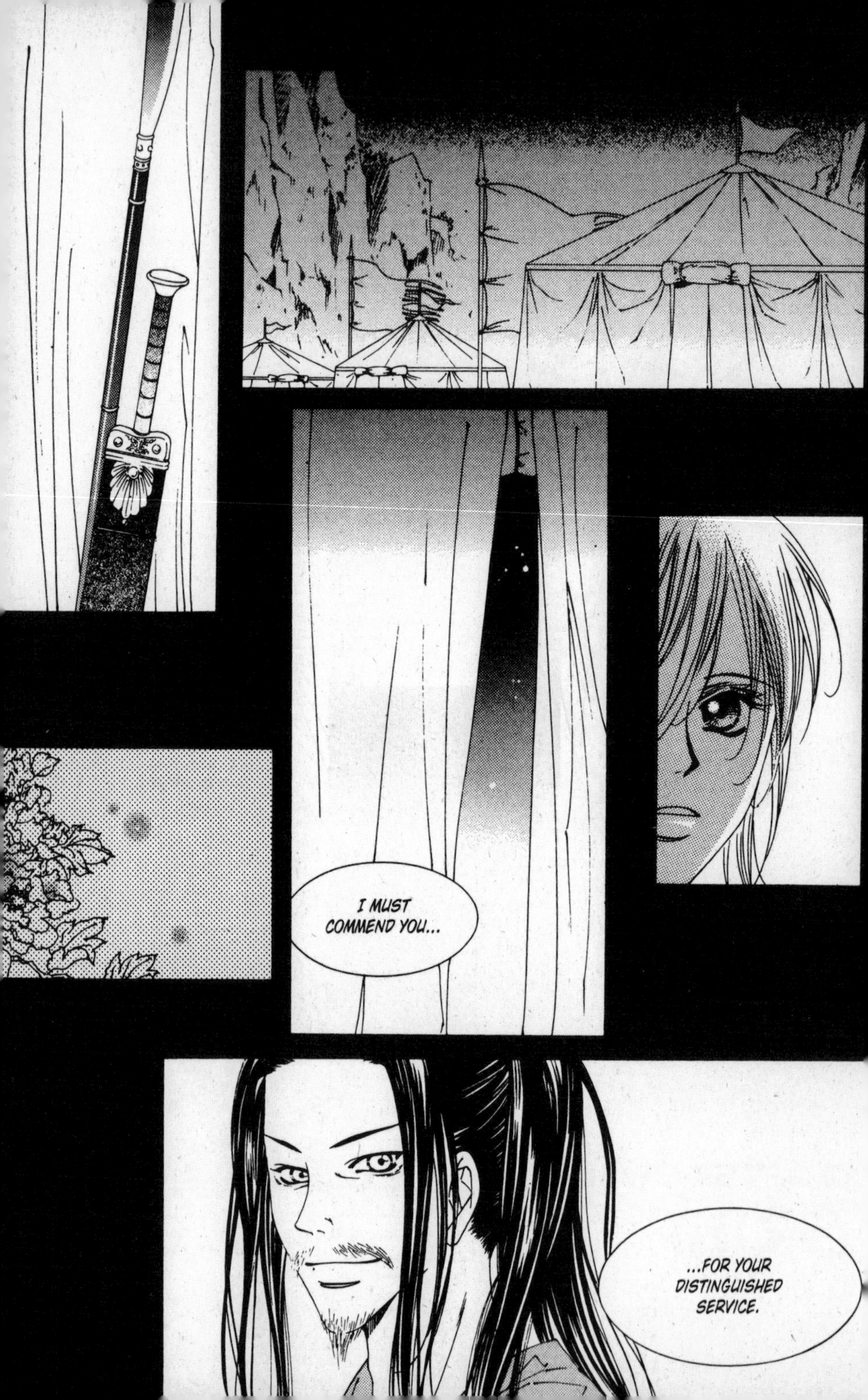
I MUST COMMEND YOU...
...FOR YOUR DISTINGUISHED SERVICE.

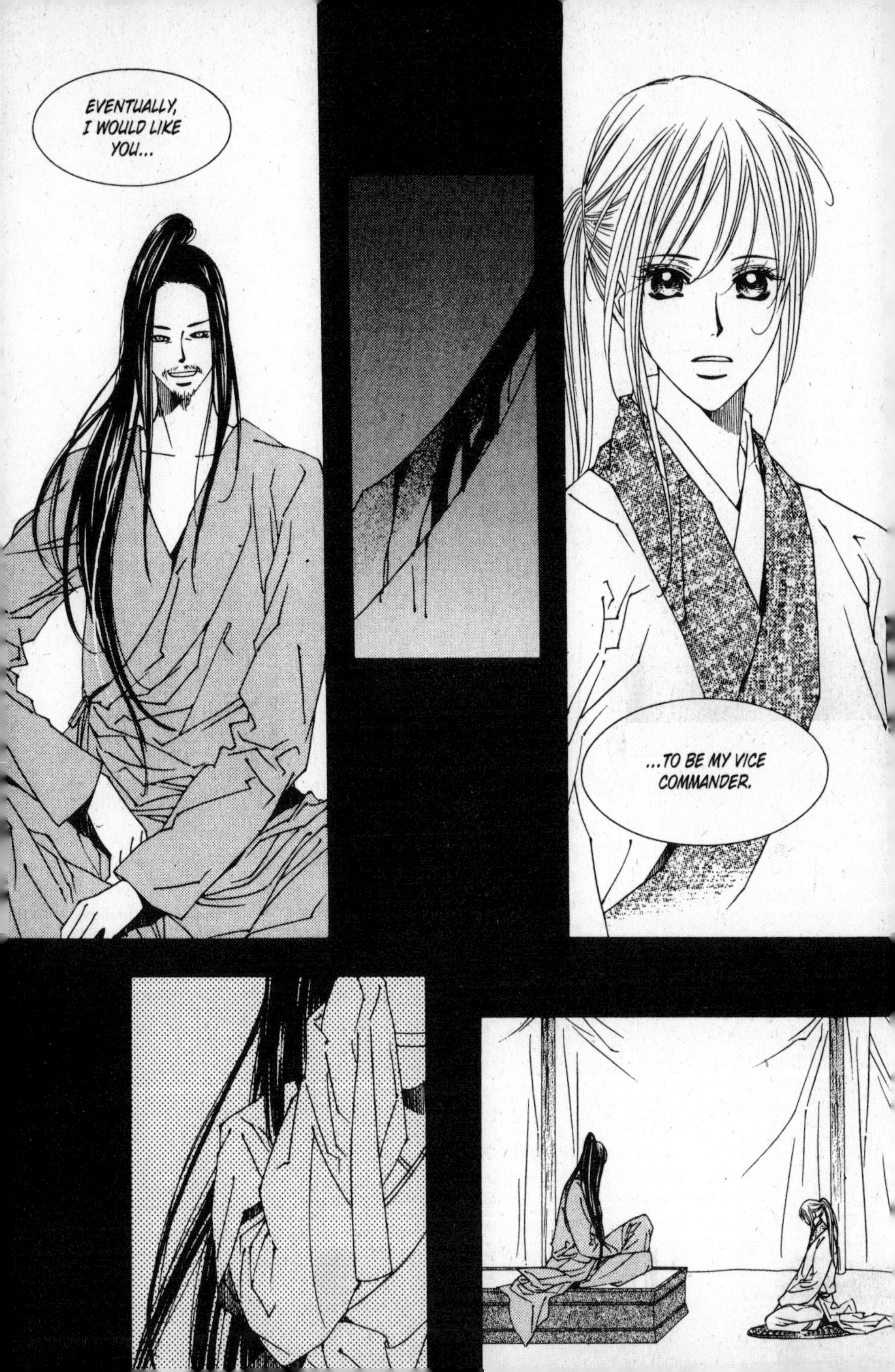
EVENTUALLY, I WOULD LIKE YOU...
...TO BE MY VICE COMMANDER.

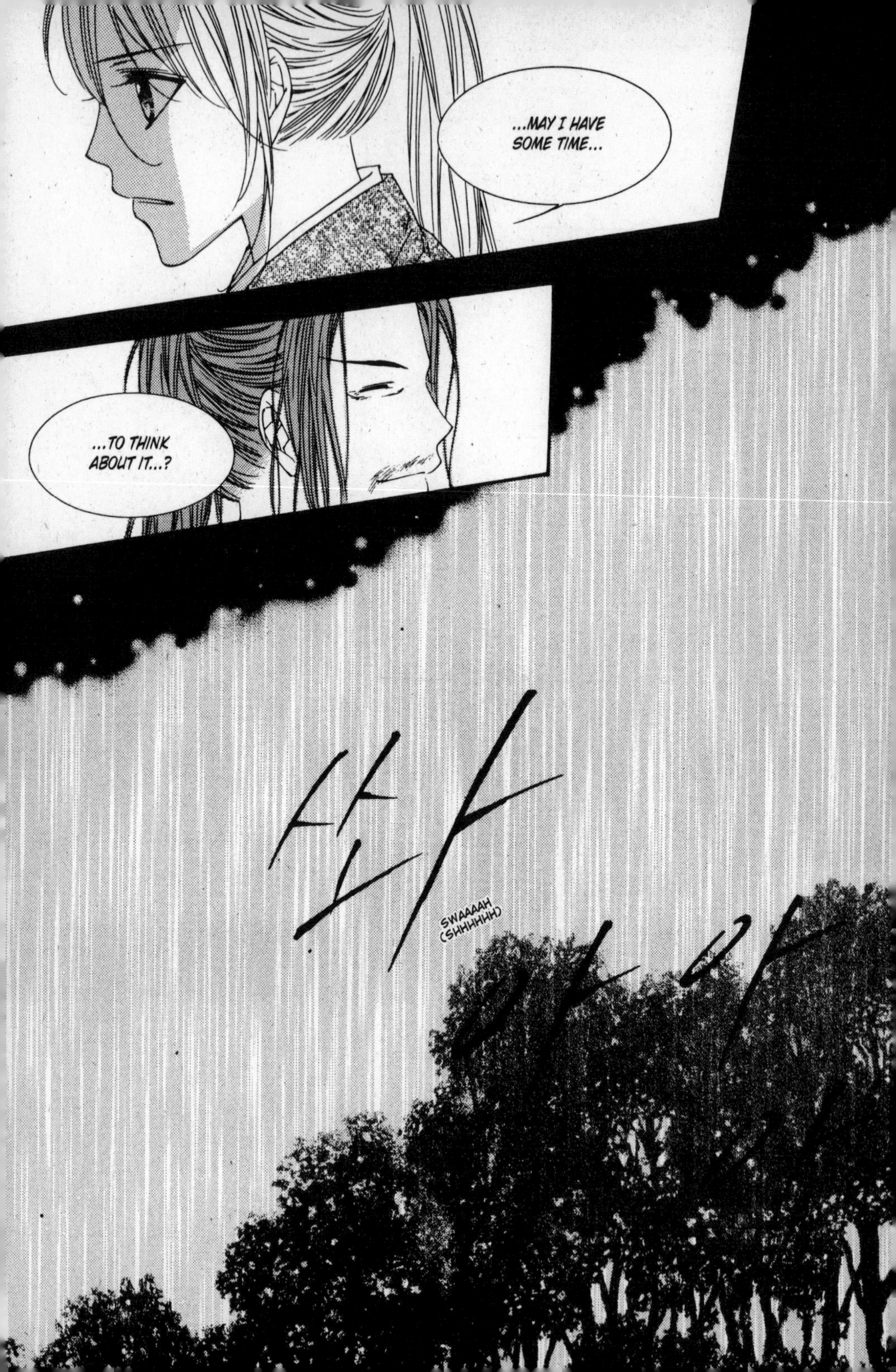
...MAY I HAVE SOME TIME...
...TO THINK ABOUT IT...?
SWAAAAH (SHHHHHH)

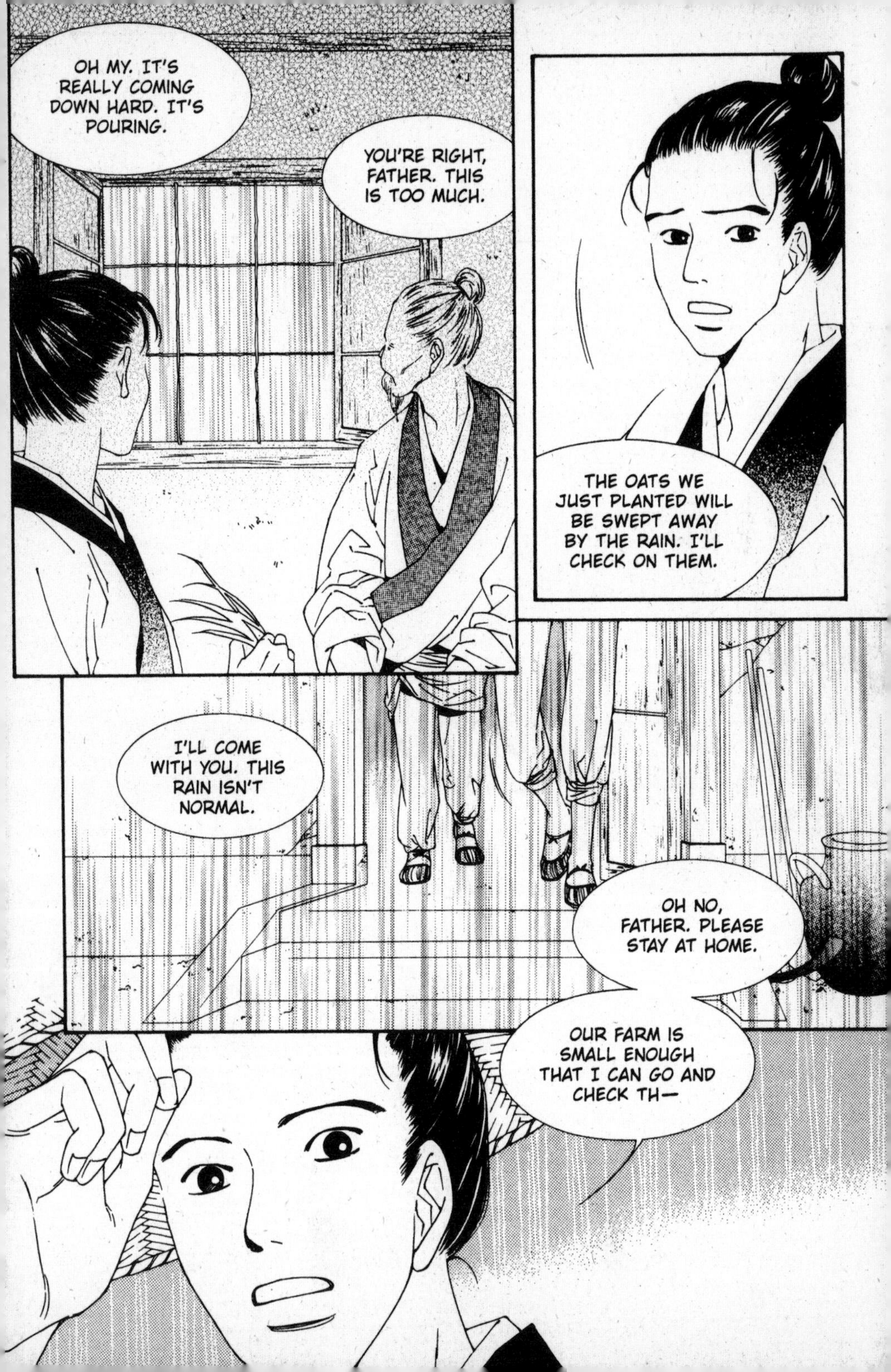
OH MY. IT'S REALLY COMING DOWN HARD. IT'S POURING.
YOU'RE RIGHT, FATHER. THIS IS TOO MUCH.
THE OATS WE JUST PLANTED WILL BE SWEPT AWAY BY THE RAIN. I'LL CHECK ON THEM.
I'LL COME WITH YOU. THIS RAIN ISN'T NORMAL.
OH NO, FATHER. PLEASE STAY AT HOME.
OUR FARM IS SMALL ENOUGH THAT I CAN GO AND CHECK TH—

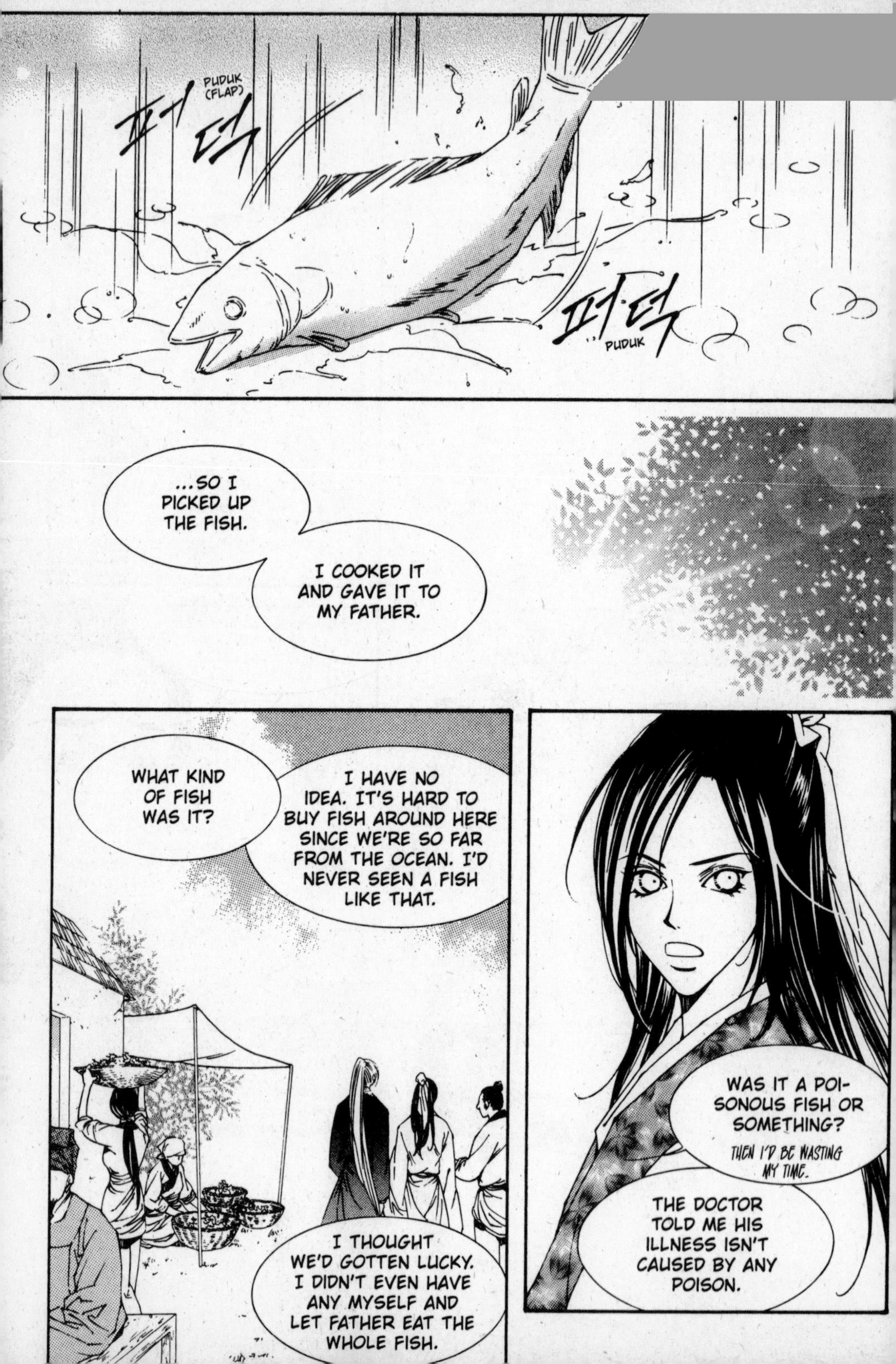
퍼덕
PUDUK (FLAP)
퍼덕
PUDUK
...SO I PICKED UP THE FISH.
I COOKED IT AND GAVE IT TO MY FATHER.
WHAT KIND OF FISH WAS IT?
I HAVE NO IDEA. IT'S HARD TO BUY FISH AROUND HERE SINCE WE'RE SO FAR FROM THE OCEAN. I'D NEVER SEEN A FISH LIKE THAT.
I THOUGHT WE'D GOTTEN LUCKY. I DIDN'T EVEN HAVE ANY MYSELF AND LET FATHER EAT THE WHOLE FISH.
WAS IT A POI-SONOUS FISH OR SOMETHING?
THEN I'D BE WASTING MY TIME...
THE DOCTOR TOLD ME HIS ILLNESS ISN'T CAUSED BY ANY POISON.

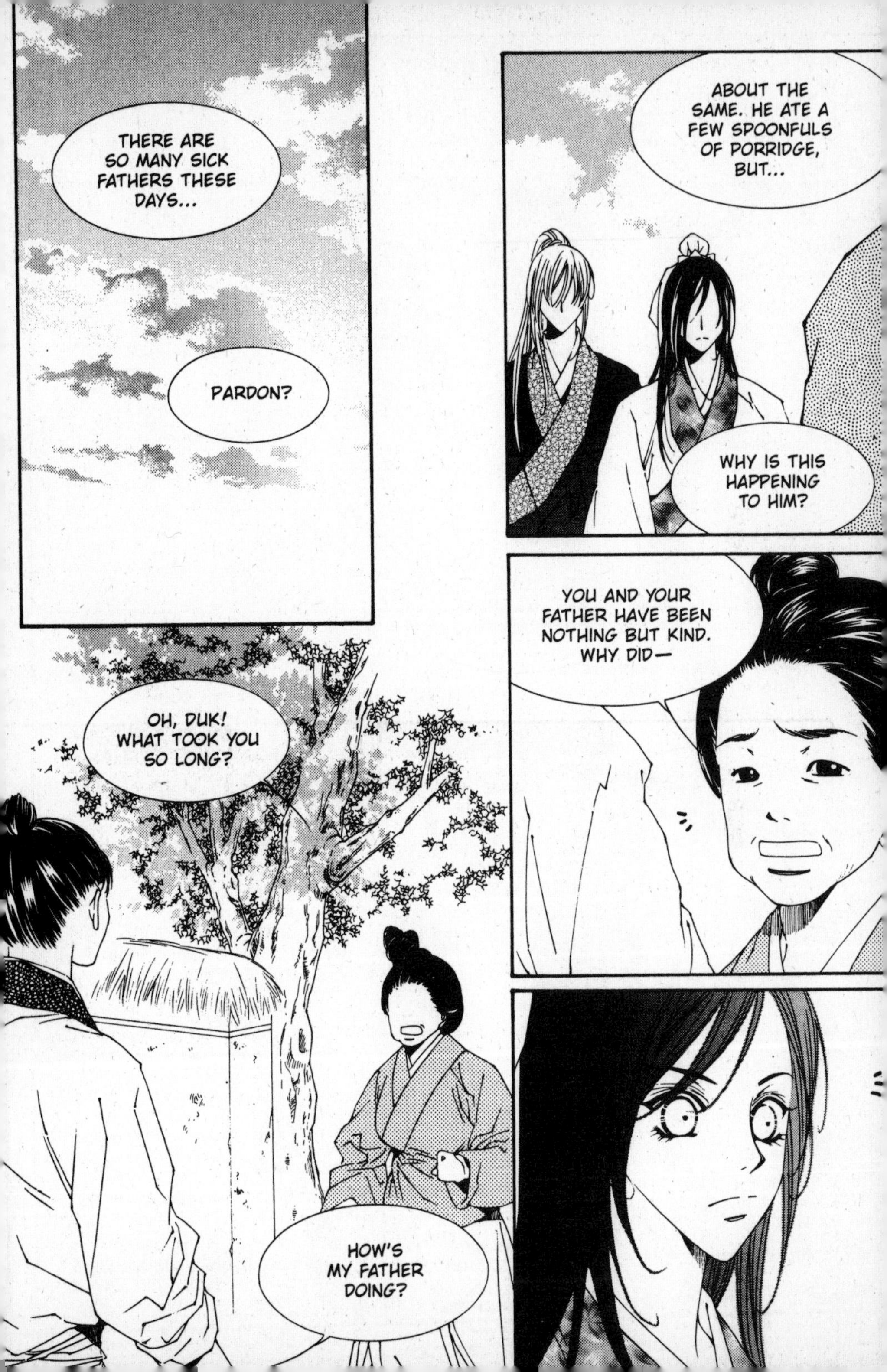
THERE ARE SO MANY SICK FATHERS THESE DAYS...
PARDON?
OH, DUK! WHAT TOOK YOU SO LONG?
HOW'S MY FATHER DOING?
ABOUT THE SAME. HE ATE A FEW SPOONFULS OF PORRIDGE, BUT...
WHY IS THIS HAPPENING TO HIM?
YOU AND YOUR FATHER HAVE BEEN NOTHING BUT KIND. WHY DID—

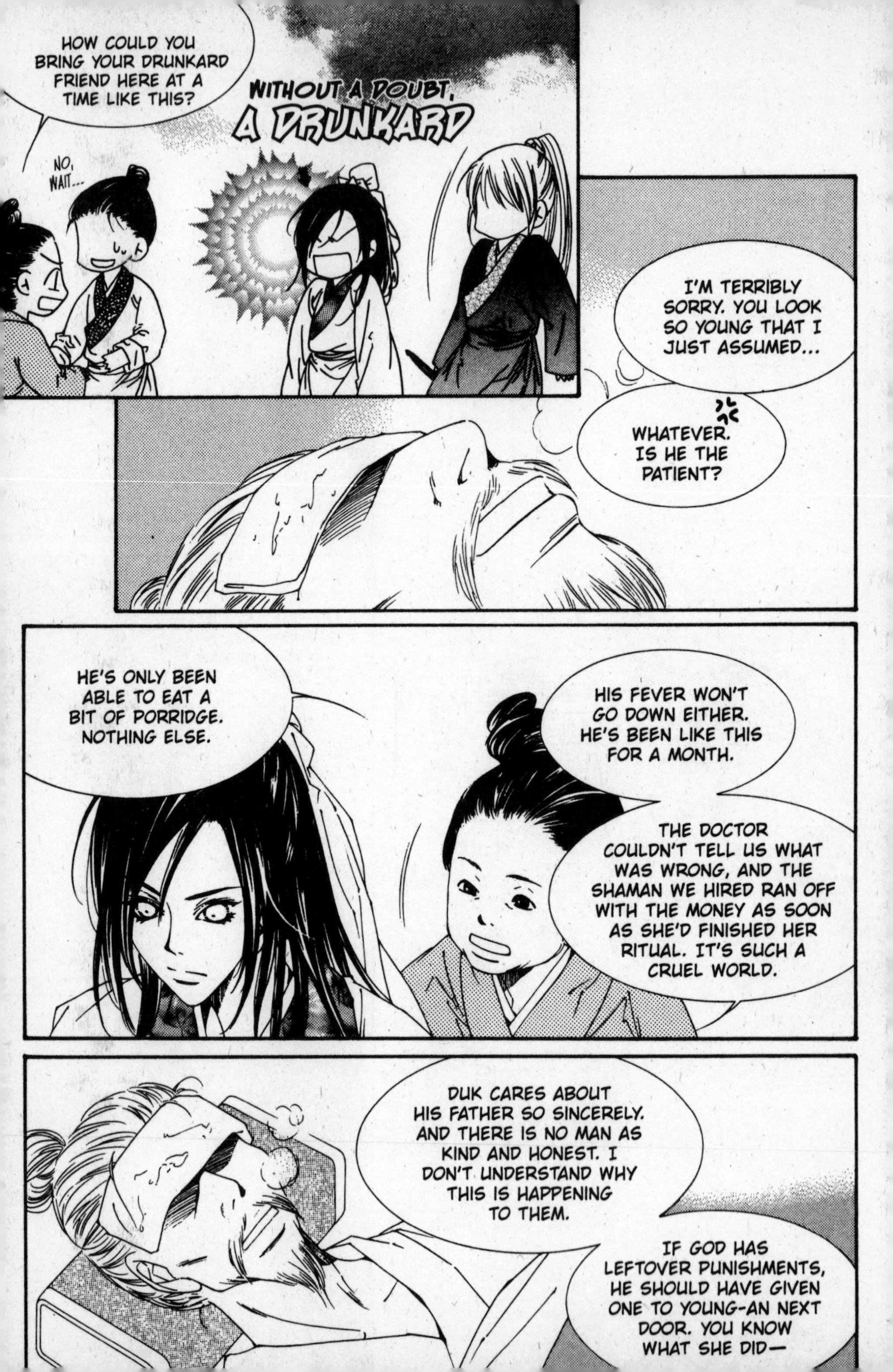
HOW COULD YOU BRING YOUR DRUNKARD FRIEND HERE AT A TIME LIKE THIS?
WITHOUT A DOUBT, A DRUNKARD
NO, WAIT...
I'M TERRIBLY SORRY. YOU LOOK SO YOUNG THAT I JUST ASSUMED...
WHATEVER. IS HE THE PATIENT?
HE'S ONLY BEEN ABLE TO EAT A BIT OF PORRIDGE. NOTHING ELSE.
HIS FEVER WON'T GO DOWN EITHER. HE'S BEEN LIKE THIS FOR A MONTH.
THE DOCTOR COULDN'T TELL US WHAT WAS WRONG, AND THE SHAMAN WE HIRED RAN OFF WITH THE MONEY AS SOON AS SHE'D FINISHED HER RITUAL. IT'S SUCH A CRUEL WORLD.
DUK CARES ABOUT HIS FATHER SO SINCERELY. AND THERE IS NO MAN AS KIND AND HONEST. I DON'T UNDERSTAND WHY THIS IS HAPPENING TO THEM.
IF GOD HAS LEFTOVER PUNISHMENTS, HE SHOULD HAVE GIVEN ONE TO YOUNG-AN NEXT DOOR. YOU KNOW WHAT SHE DID—

THOUGH IF WE'RE TALKING ABOUT DESERVING PUNISHMENT, JI-CHUN FROM THE NEXT VILLAGE—

YOU TALK TOO MUCH! GET OUTTA HERE, LADY!!

I JUST WANTED TO EXPLAIN—

PLEASE...

WHY ARE YOU YELLING?

I GOT IT! FATHER IS SICK! SON IS KIND! YOUNG-AN IS A BAD WOMAN! RIGHT?!!

GEEZ, I WAS ABOUT TO LOSE MY MIND. MAYBE SHE'S A GHOST...

TAK (CLICK)

...HUH?

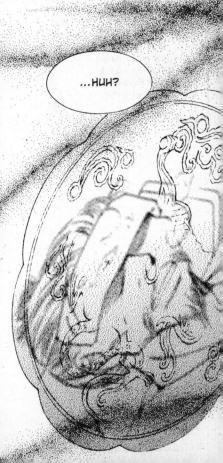

SO, IN SHORT, THIS OLD MAN GOT SICK FROM EATING A FISH THAT FELL FROM THE SKY...

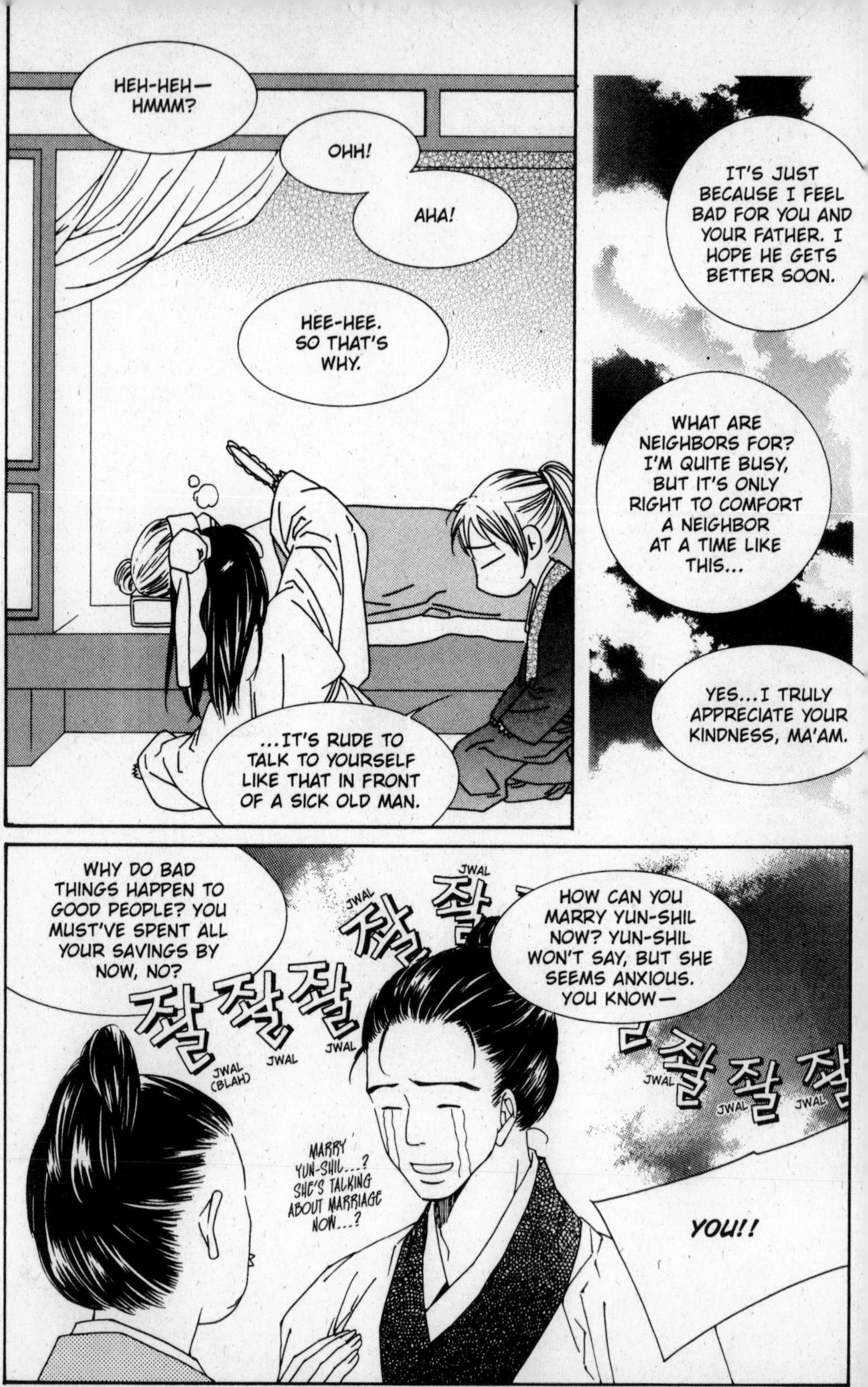
HEH-HEH— HMMM?
OHH!
AHA!
HEE-HEE. SO THAT'S WHY.
...IT'S RUDE TO TALK TO YOURSELF LIKE THAT IN FRONT OF A SICK OLD MAN.
IT'S JUST BECAUSE I FEEL BAD FOR YOU AND YOUR FATHER. I HOPE HE GETS BETTER SOON.
WHAT ARE NEIGHBORS FOR? I'M QUITE BUSY, BUT IT'S ONLY RIGHT TO COMFORT A NEIGHBOR AT A TIME LIKE THIS...
YES...I TRULY APPRECIATE YOUR KINDNESS, MA'AM.
WHY DO BAD THINGS HAPPEN TO GOOD PEOPLE? YOU MUST'VE SPENT ALL YOUR SAVINGS BY NOW, NO?
JWAL (BLAH)
JWAL
JWAL
JWAL
JWAL
HOW CAN YOU MARRY YUN-SHIL NOW? YUN-SHIL WON'T SAY, BUT SHE SEEMS ANXIOUS. YOU KNOW—
JWAL
JWAL
JWAL
MARRY YUN-SHIL...? SHE'S TALKING ABOUT MARRIAGE NOW...?
YOU!!

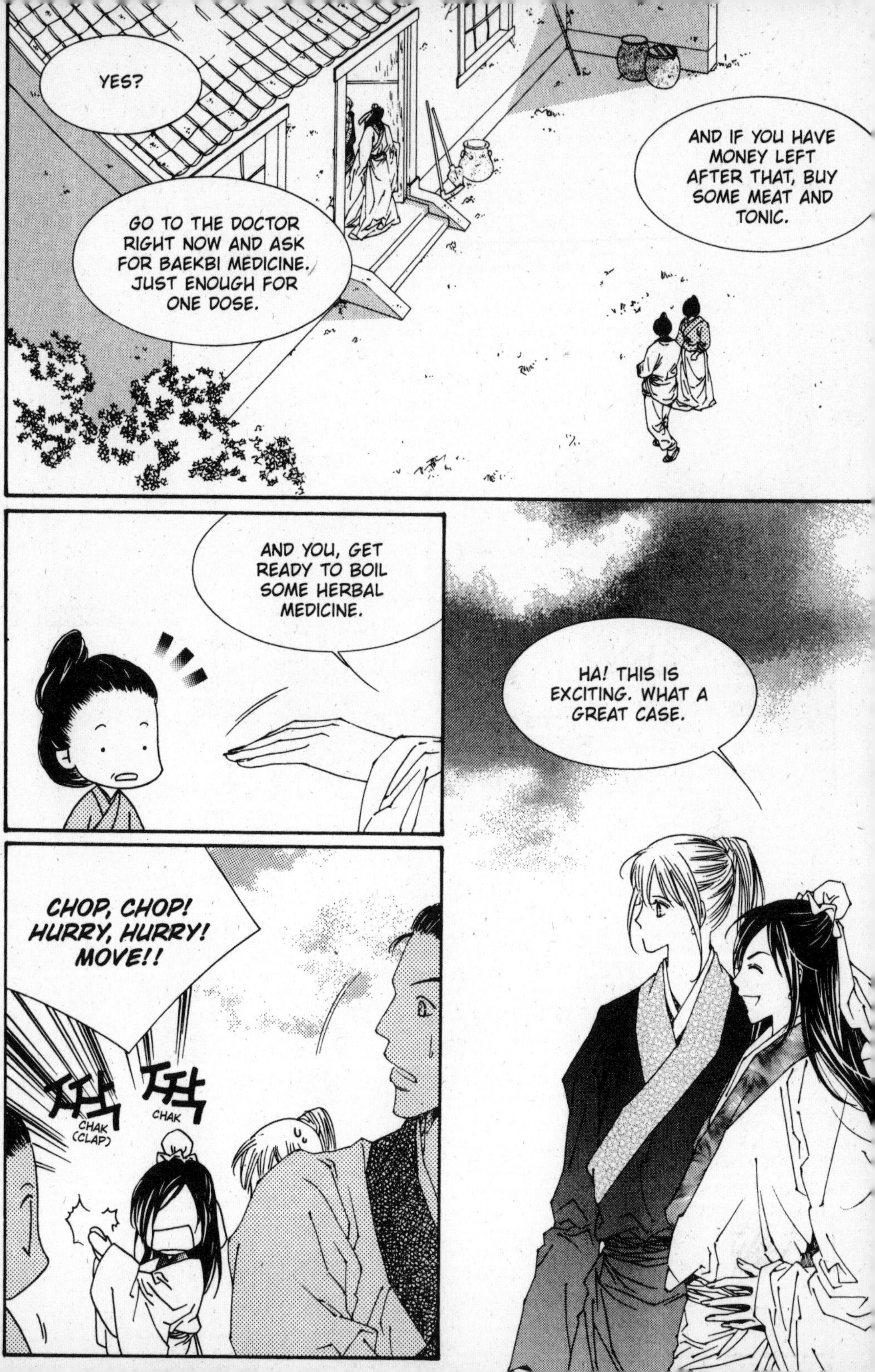
YES?
GO TO THE DOCTOR RIGHT NOW AND ASK FOR BAEKBI MEDICINE. JUST ENOUGH FOR ONE DOSE.
AND IF YOU HAVE MONEY LEFT AFTER THAT, BUY SOME MEAT AND TONIC.
AND YOU, GET READY TO BOIL SOME HERBAL MEDICINE.
CHOP, CHOP! HURRY, HURRY! MOVE!!
CHAK (CLAP)
CHAK
HA! THIS IS EXCITING. WHAT A GREAT CASE.

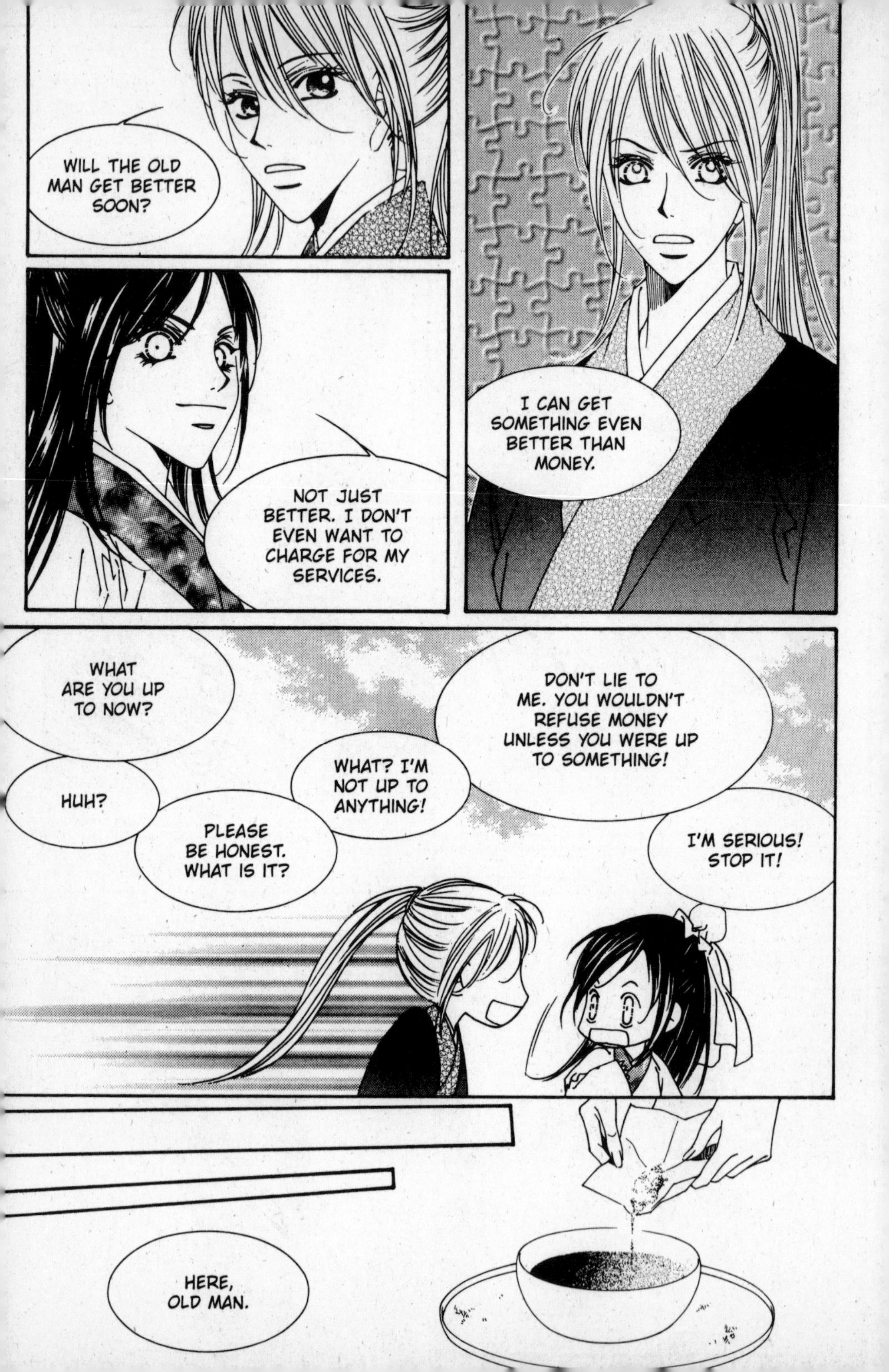
WILL THE OLD MAN GET BETTER SOON?
NOT JUST BETTER. I DON'T EVEN WANT TO CHARGE FOR MY SERVICES.
I CAN GET SOMETHING EVEN BETTER THAN MONEY.
WHAT ARE YOU UP TO NOW?
HUH?
PLEASE BE HONEST. WHAT IS IT?
WHAT? I'M NOT UP TO ANYTHING!
DON'T LIE TO ME. YOU WOULDN'T REFUSE MONEY UNLESS YOU WERE UP TO SOMETHING!
I'M SERIOUS! STOP IT!
HERE, OLD MAN.

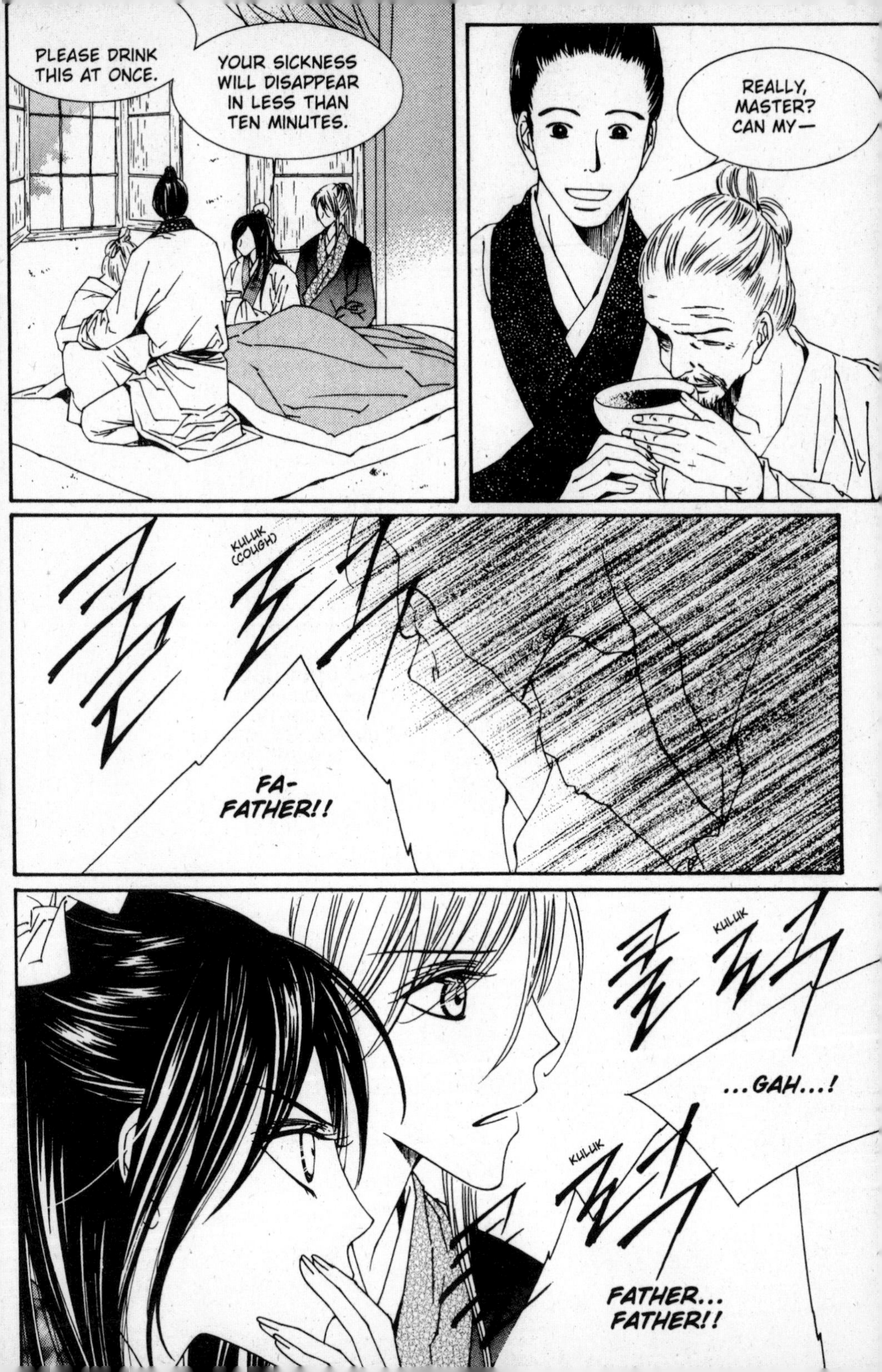
PLEASE DRINK THIS AT ONCE.
YOUR SICKNESS WILL DISAPPEAR IN LESS THAN TEN MINUTES.
REALLY, MASTER? CAN MY—
KULUK (COUGH)
FA- FATHER!!
KULUK
...GAH...!
KULUK
FATHER... FATHER!!

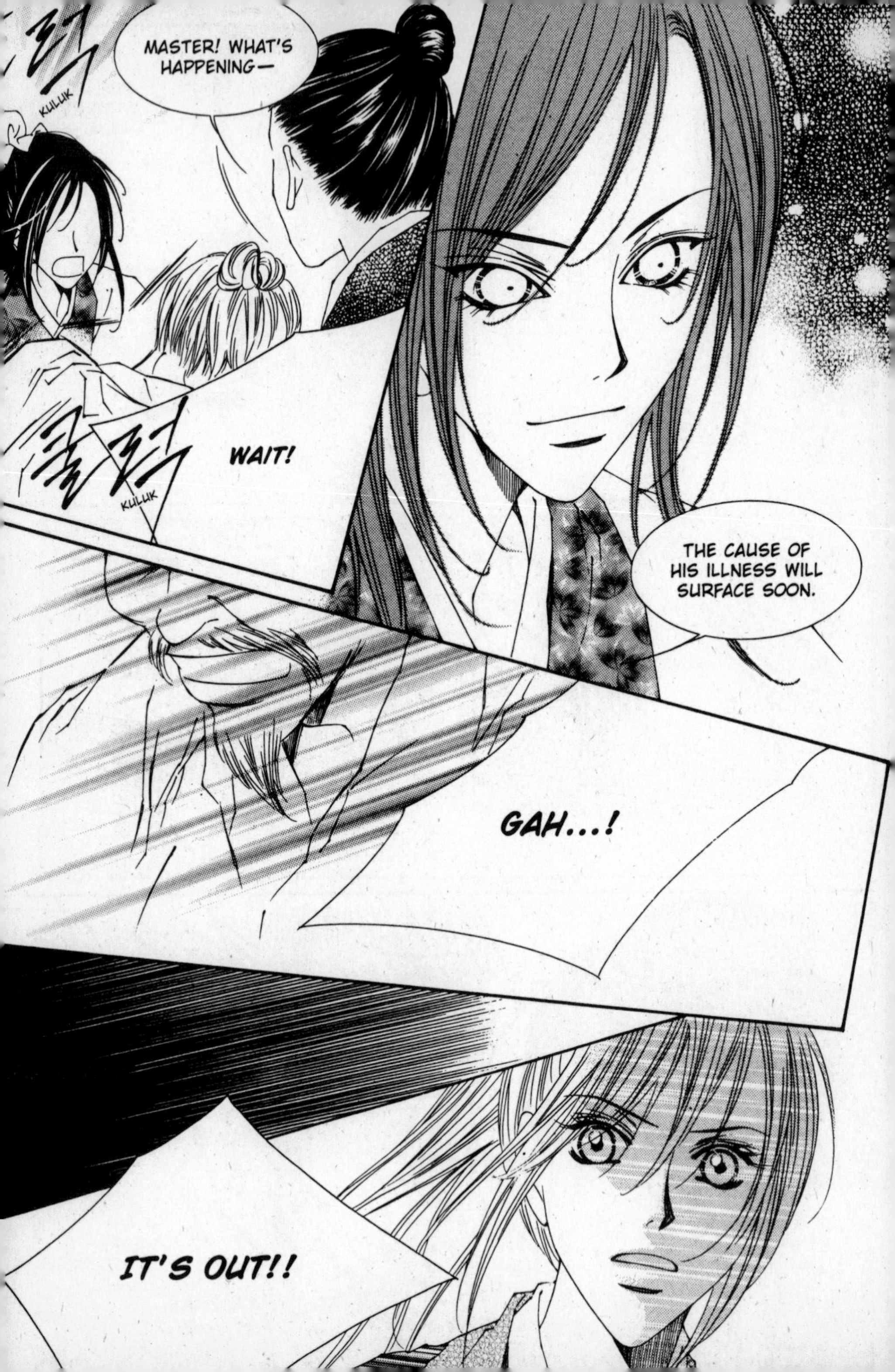

KULUK
MASTER! WHAT'S HAPPENING—
KULUK
WAIT!
THE CAUSE OF HIS ILLNESS WILL SURFACE SOON.
GAH...!
IT'S OUT!!

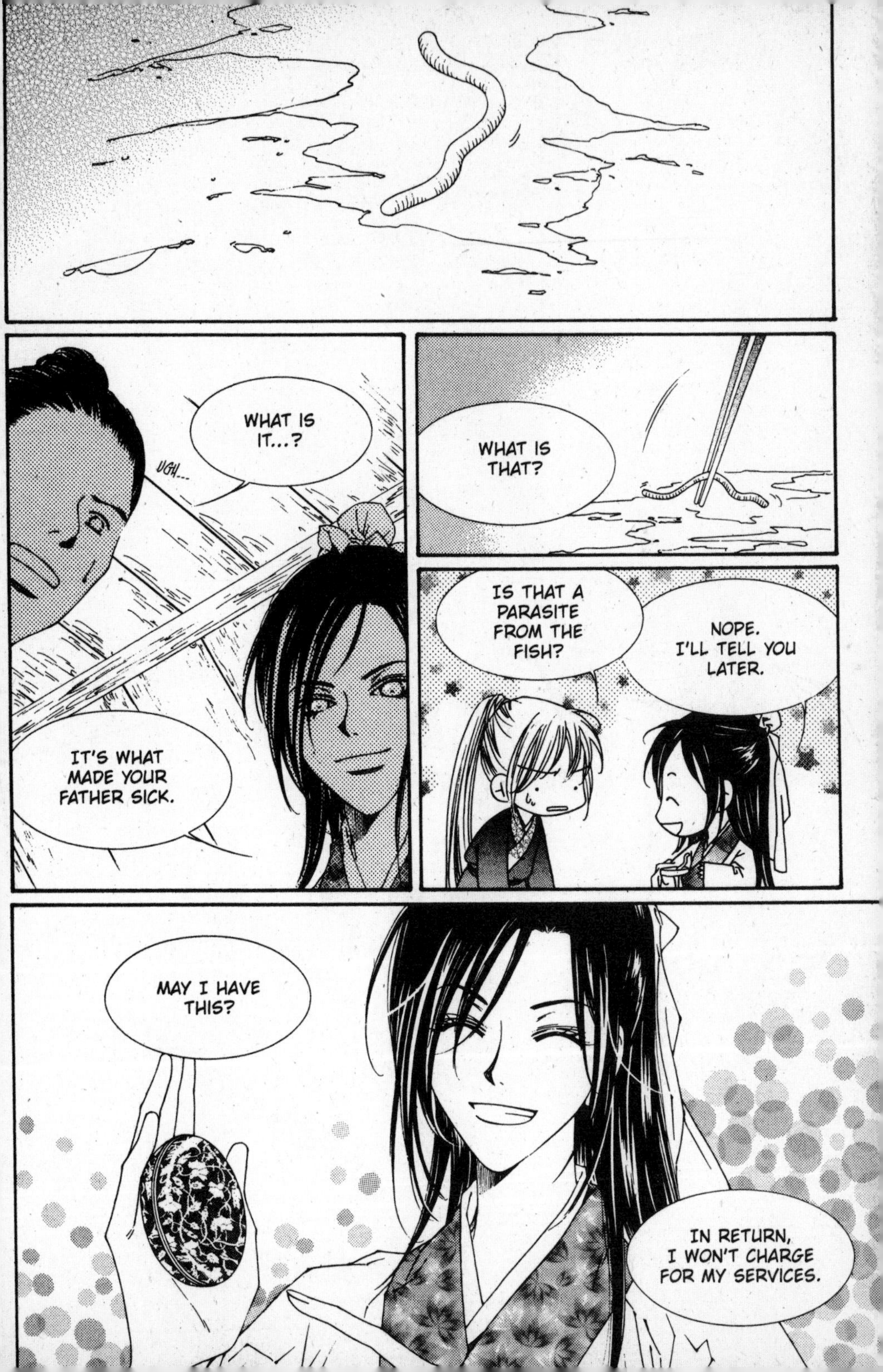

UGH...
WHAT IS IT...?
IT'S WHAT MADE YOUR FATHER SICK.
WHAT IS THAT?
IS THAT A PARASITE FROM THE FISH?
NOPE. I'LL TELL YOU LATER.
MAY I HAVE THIS?
IN RETURN, I WON'T CHARGE FOR MY SERVICES.

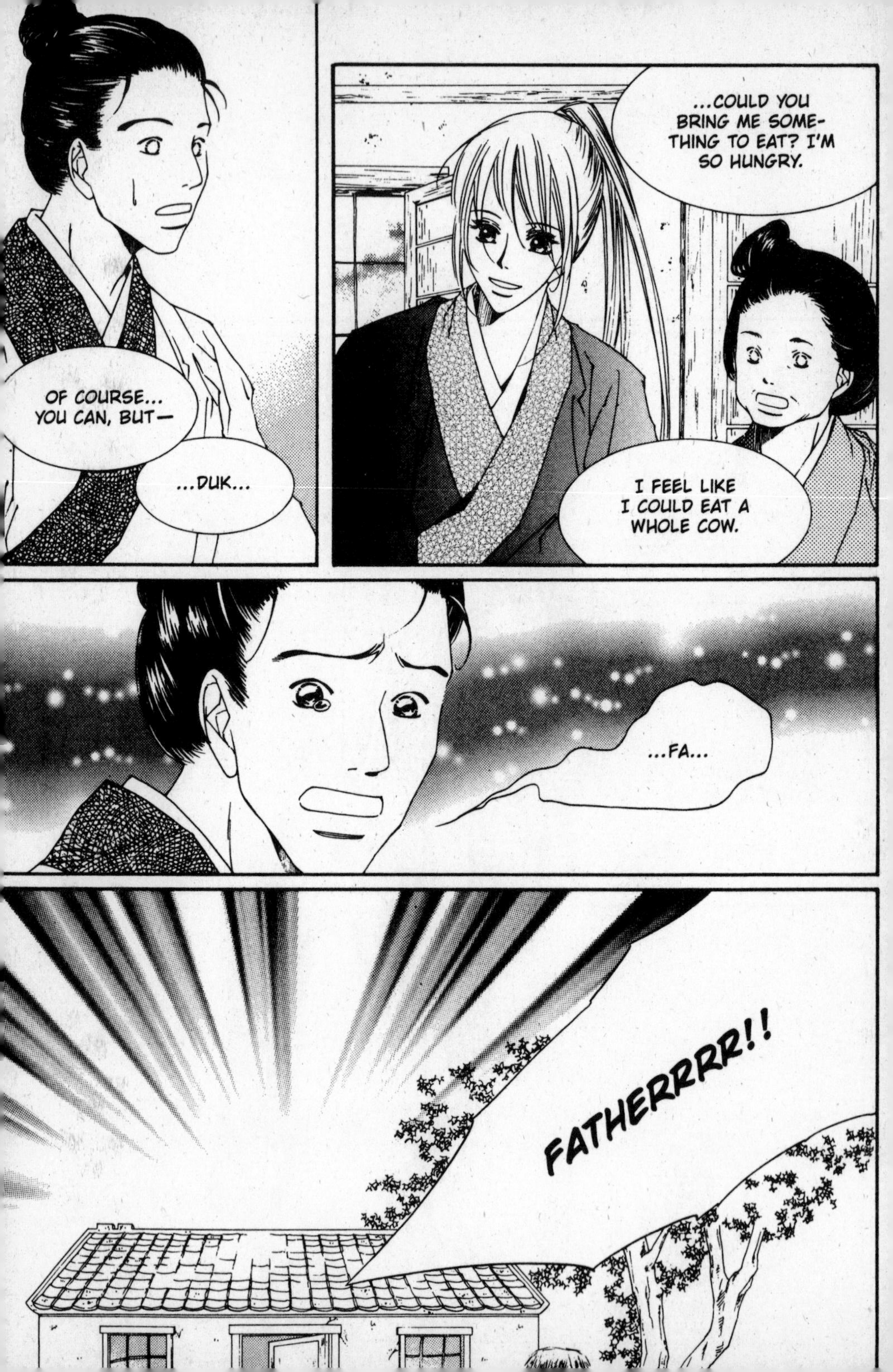
OF COURSE... YOU CAN, BUT—
...DUK...
...COULD YOU BRING ME SOME-THING TO EAT? I'M SO HUNGRY.
I FEEL LIKE I COULD EAT A WHOLE COW.
...FA...
FATHERRRR!!

THANK YOU, THANK YOU, MASTER!!

OH MY! INCREDIBLE! YOU'RE WELL AGAIN!

WHAT A NICE VIEW...

IF YOU'RE CURIOUS ABOUT THIS, YOU CAN COME WITH US.

I PRAYED OVER CLEAN WATER FOR YOU. ON THE WAY TO THE WELL I MET MR. YANG'S DAUGHTER. SINCE HER SISTER-IN-LAW IS CAUSING SO MUCH TROUBLE, SHE WON'T LISTEN TO... AND MR. YANG... LOST HER LAMB MEAT... SO MR. YANG AND MR. JIN... HAD A FIGHT OVER WHO LOST... THE CAT. BUT MR. JIN HAPPENED TO... DAYS LIKE A FIEND. AFTER... HONEY, IT WAS... WHEN HE... HIM THAT HER CATCH... AND THAT YOUNG WOMAN WAS SUPPOSED TO BE YOUR DAUGHTER-IN-LAW.

PARDON? MAY I?

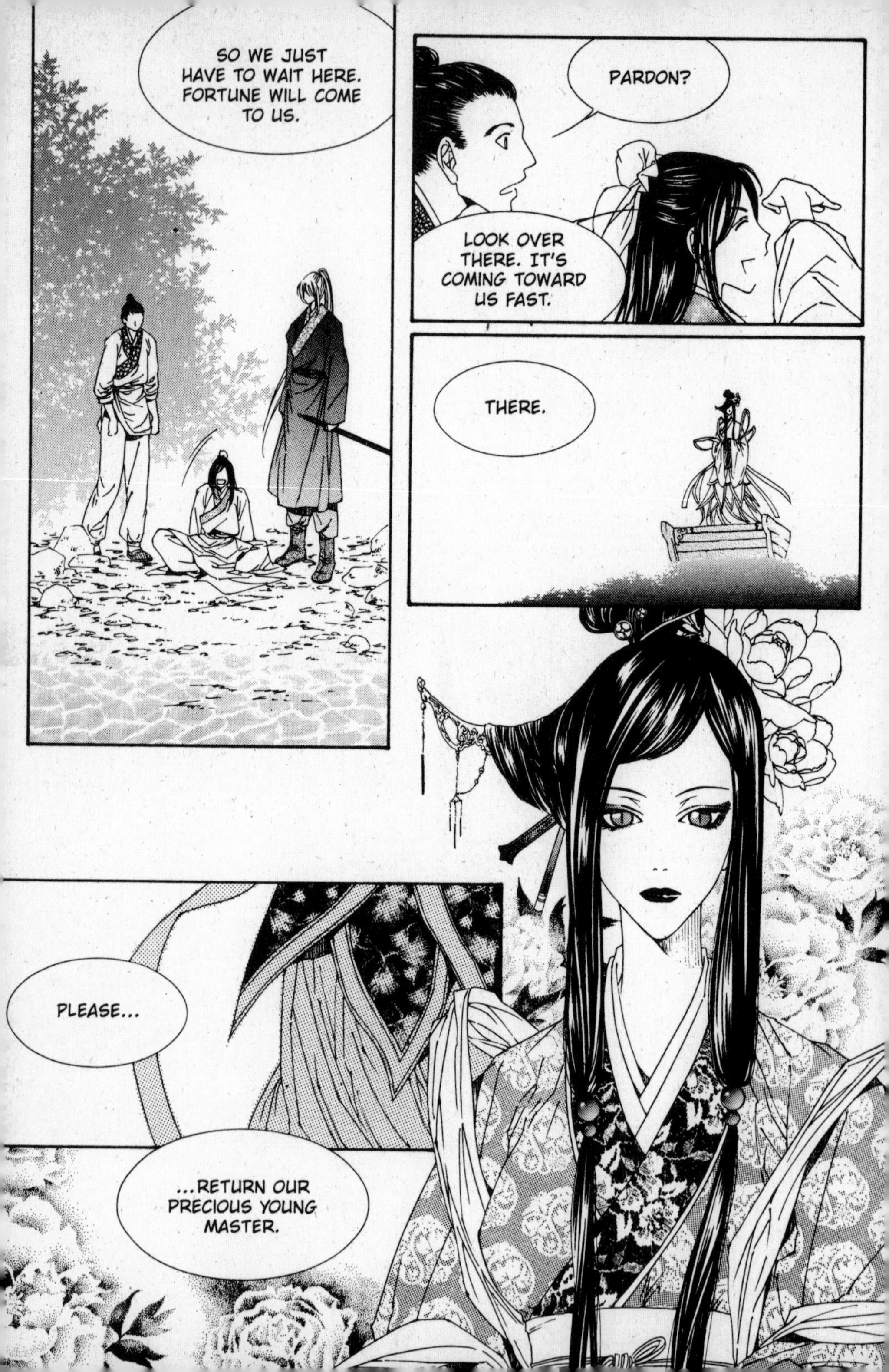
SO WE JUST HAVE TO WAIT HERE. FORTUNE WILL COME TO US.
PARDON?
LOOK OVER THERE. IT'S COMING TOWARD US FAST.
THERE.
PLEASE...
...RETURN OUR PRECIOUS YOUNG MASTER.

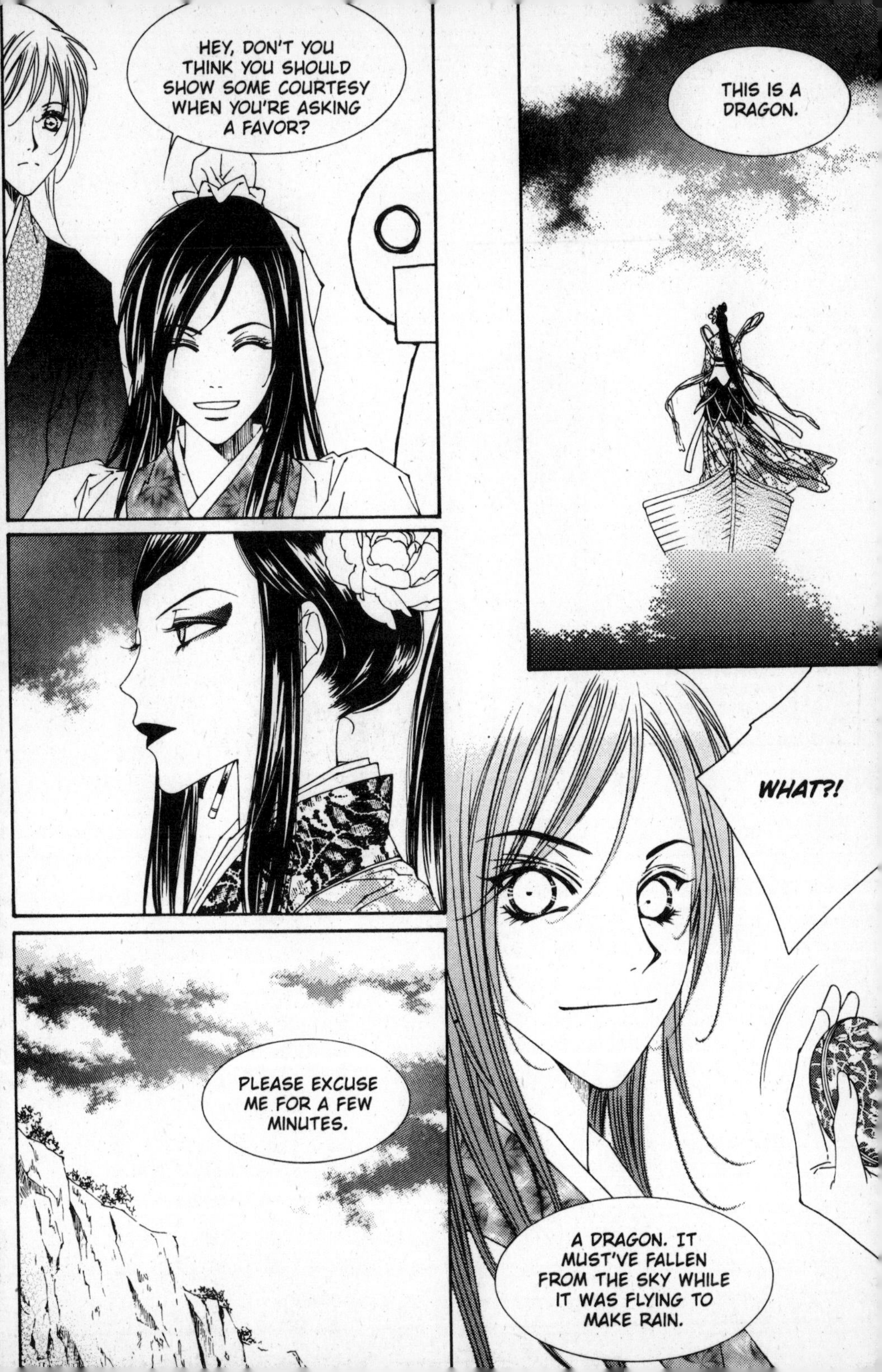
HEY, DON'T YOU THINK YOU SHOULD SHOW SOME COURTESY WHEN YOU'RE ASKING A FAVOR?
PLEASE EXCUSE ME FOR A FEW MINUTES.
THIS IS A DRAGON.
WHAT?!
A DRAGON. IT MUST'VE FALLEN FROM THE SKY WHILE IT WAS FLYING TO MAKE RAIN.

YOUNG DRAGONS SOMETIMES MAKE MISTAKES LIKE THAT.

OHH...

RIGHT?

I SAW FOUR TWITCHING CLAWS WHEN I EXAMINED YOUR FATHER WITH MY MIRROR.

IT MUST'VE CHANGED INTO A FISH BECAUSE IT DIDN'T KNOW WHAT TO DO AFTER IT HIT THE GROUND.

AH.

HERE COMES THE LADY WITH OUR FORTUNE.

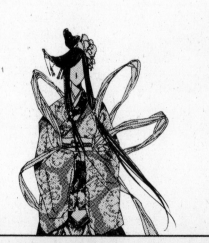

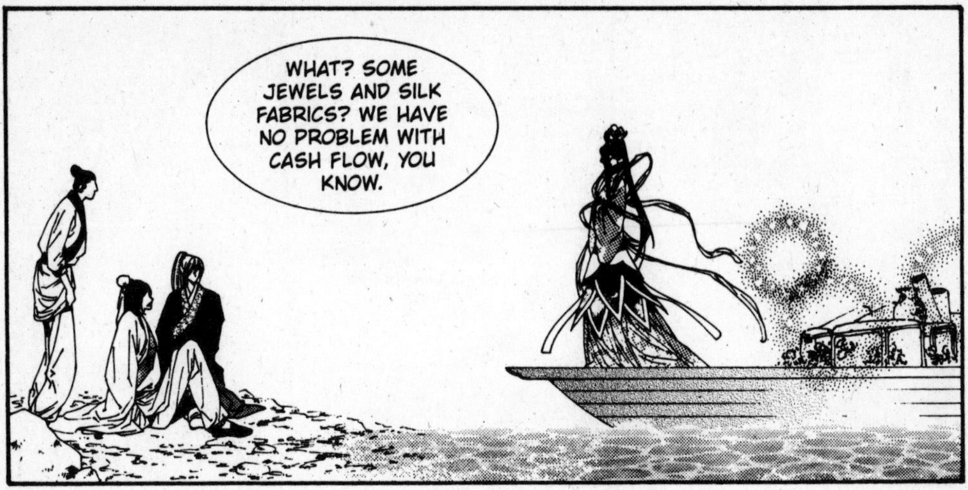
WHAT? SOME JEWELS AND SILK FABRICS? WE HAVE NO PROBLEM WITH CASH FLOW, YOU KNOW.

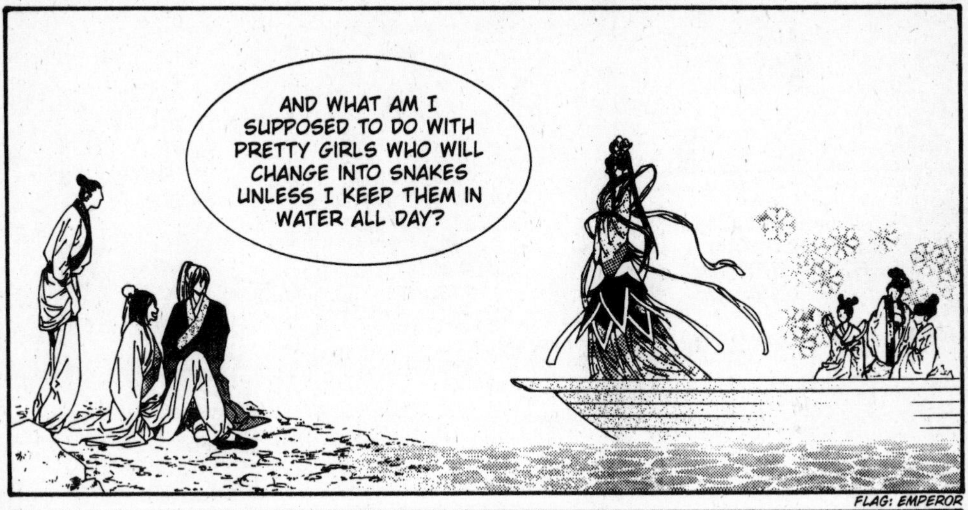
AND WHAT AM I SUPPOSED TO DO WITH PRETTY GIRLS WHO WILL CHANGE INTO SNAKES UNLESS I KEEP THEM IN WATER ALL DAY?

FLAG: EMPEROR

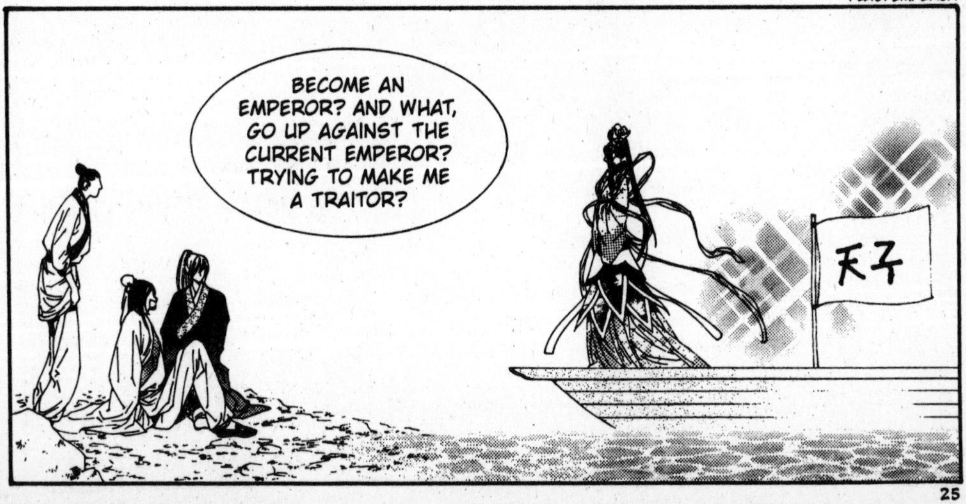
BECOME AN EMPEROR? AND WHAT, GO UP AGAINST THE CURRENT EMPEROR? TRYING TO MAKE ME A TRAITOR?
天子

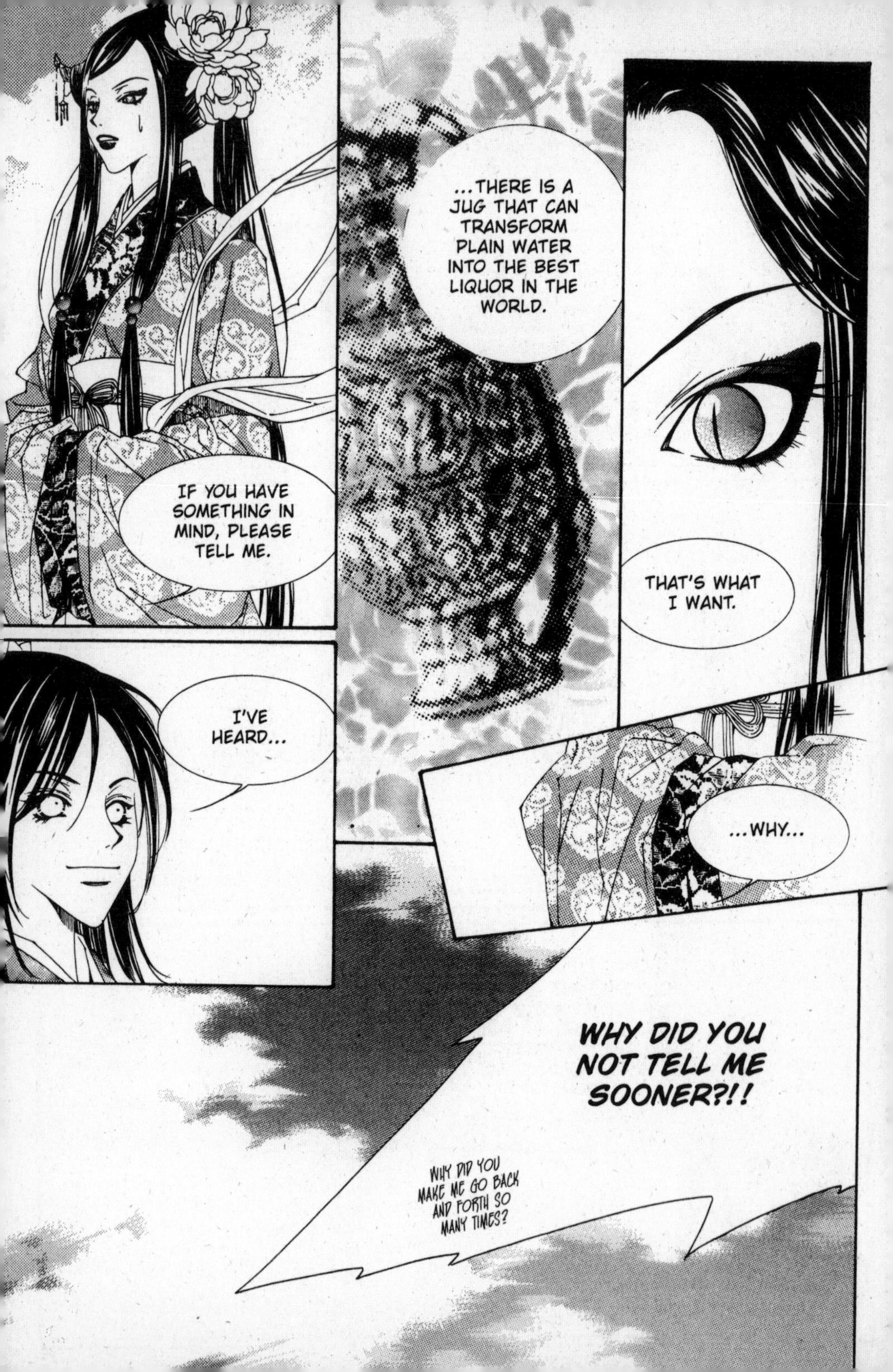
IF YOU HAVE SOMETHING IN MIND, PLEASE TELL ME.
I'VE HEARD...
...THERE IS A JUG THAT CAN TRANSFORM PLAIN WATER INTO THE BEST LIQUOR IN THE WORLD.
THAT'S WHAT I WANT.
...WHY...
WHY DID YOU NOT TELL ME SOONER?!!
WHY DID YOU MAKE ME GO BACK AND FORTH SO MANY TIMES?

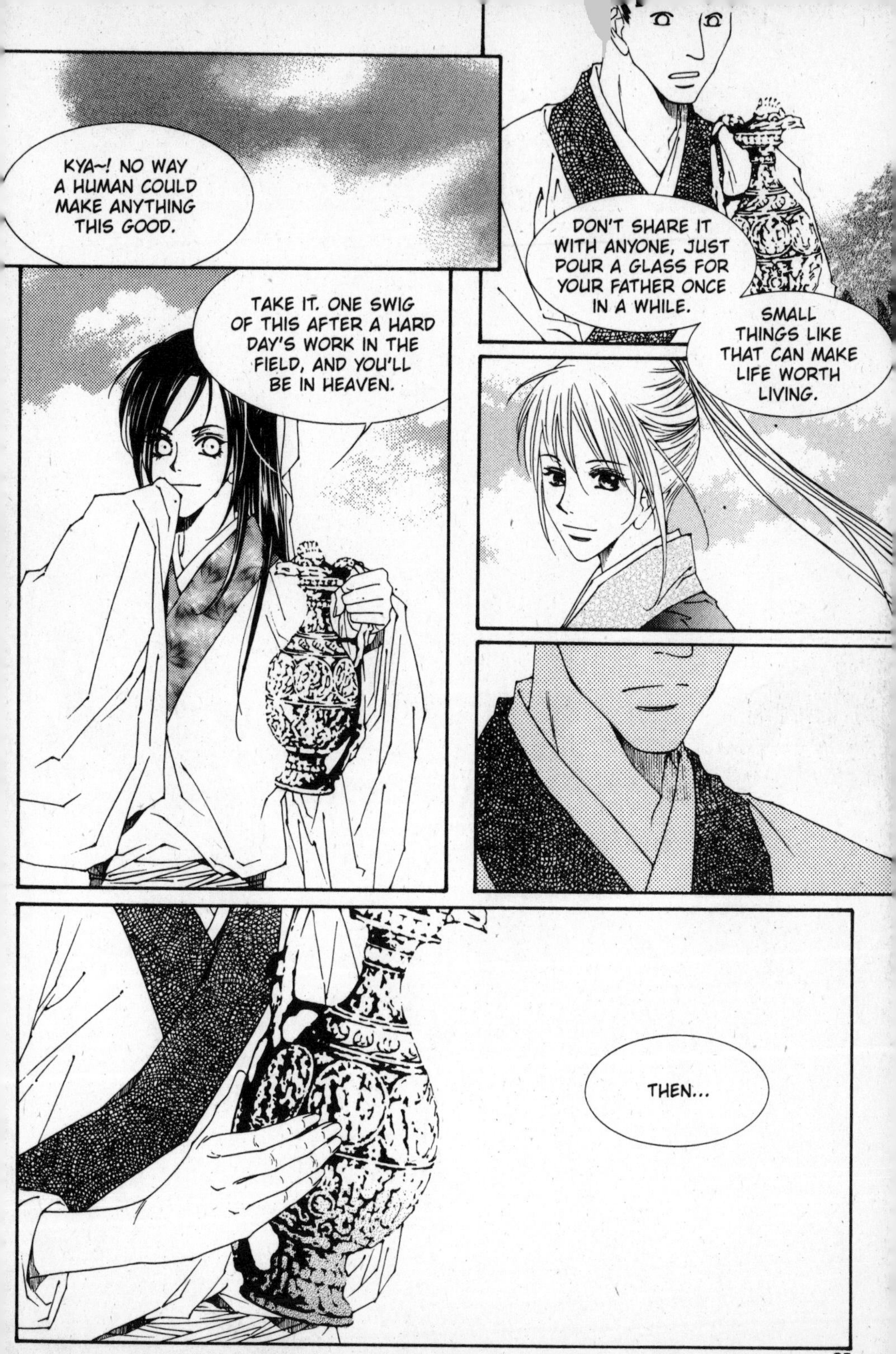
KYA~! NO WAY A HUMAN COULD MAKE ANYTHING THIS GOOD.
DON'T SHARE IT WITH ANYONE, JUST POUR A GLASS FOR YOUR FATHER ONCE IN A WHILE.
TAKE IT. ONE SWIG OF THIS AFTER A HARD DAY'S WORK IN THE FIELD, AND YOU'LL BE IN HEAVEN.
SMALL THINGS LIKE THAT CAN MAKE LIFE WORTH LIVING.
THEN...

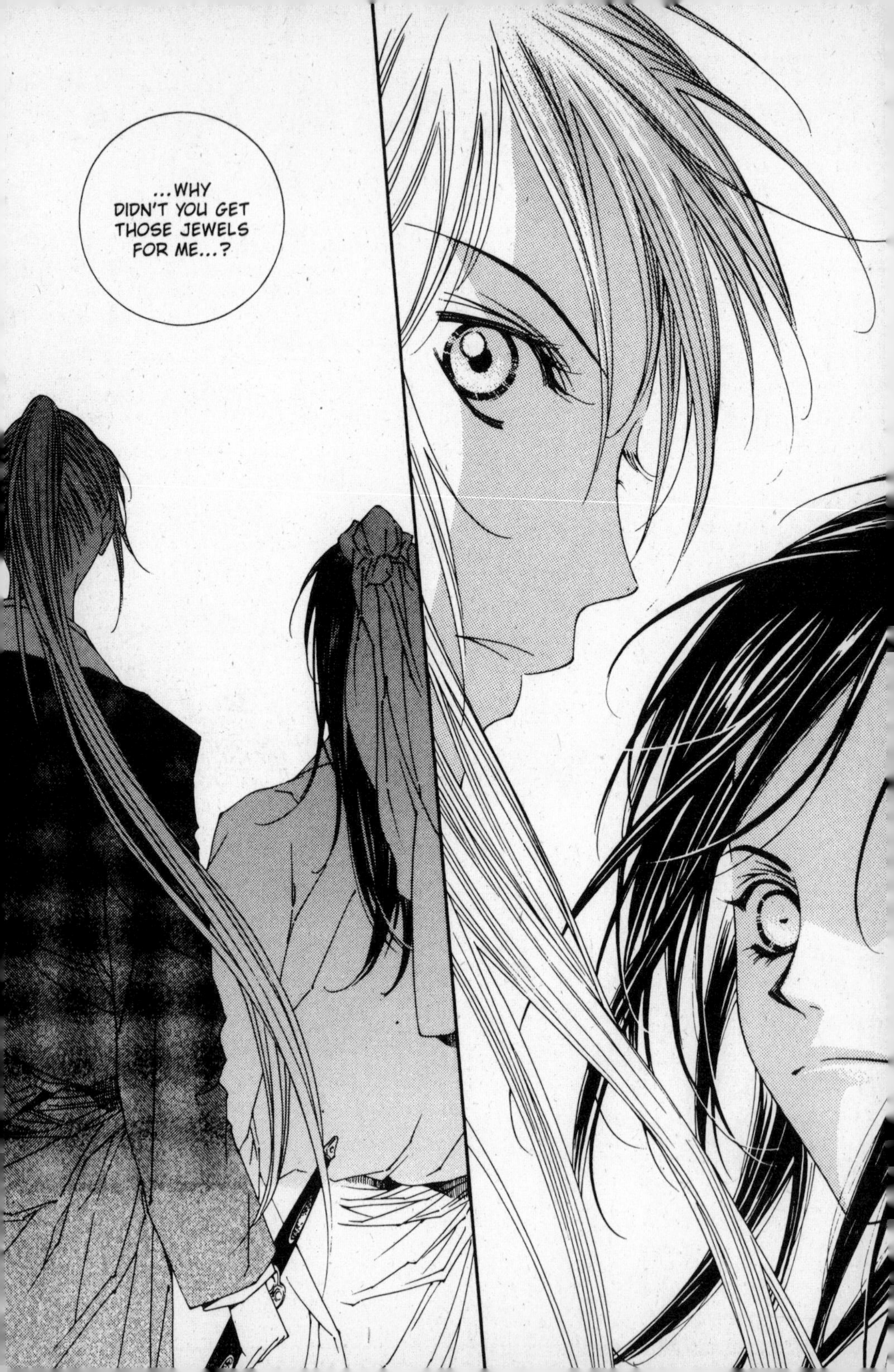
...WHY DIDN'T YOU GET THOSE JEWELS FOR ME...?

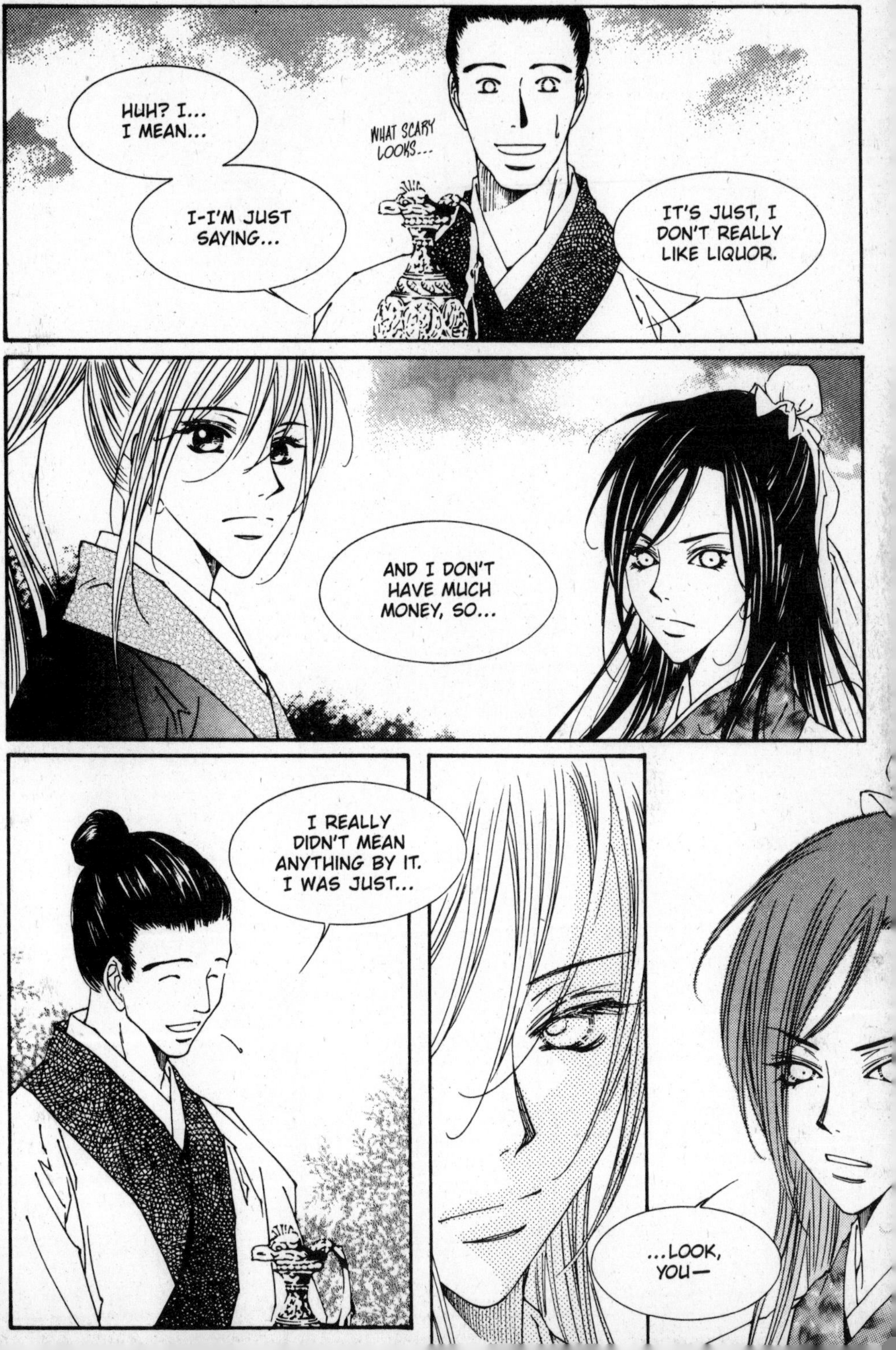
HUH? I... I MEAN...
I-I'M JUST SAYING...
WHAT SCARY LOOKS...
IT'S JUST, I DON'T REALLY LIKE LIQUOR.
AND I DON'T HAVE MUCH MONEY, SO...
I REALLY DIDN'T MEAN ANYTHING BY IT. I WAS JUST...
...LOOK, YOU—

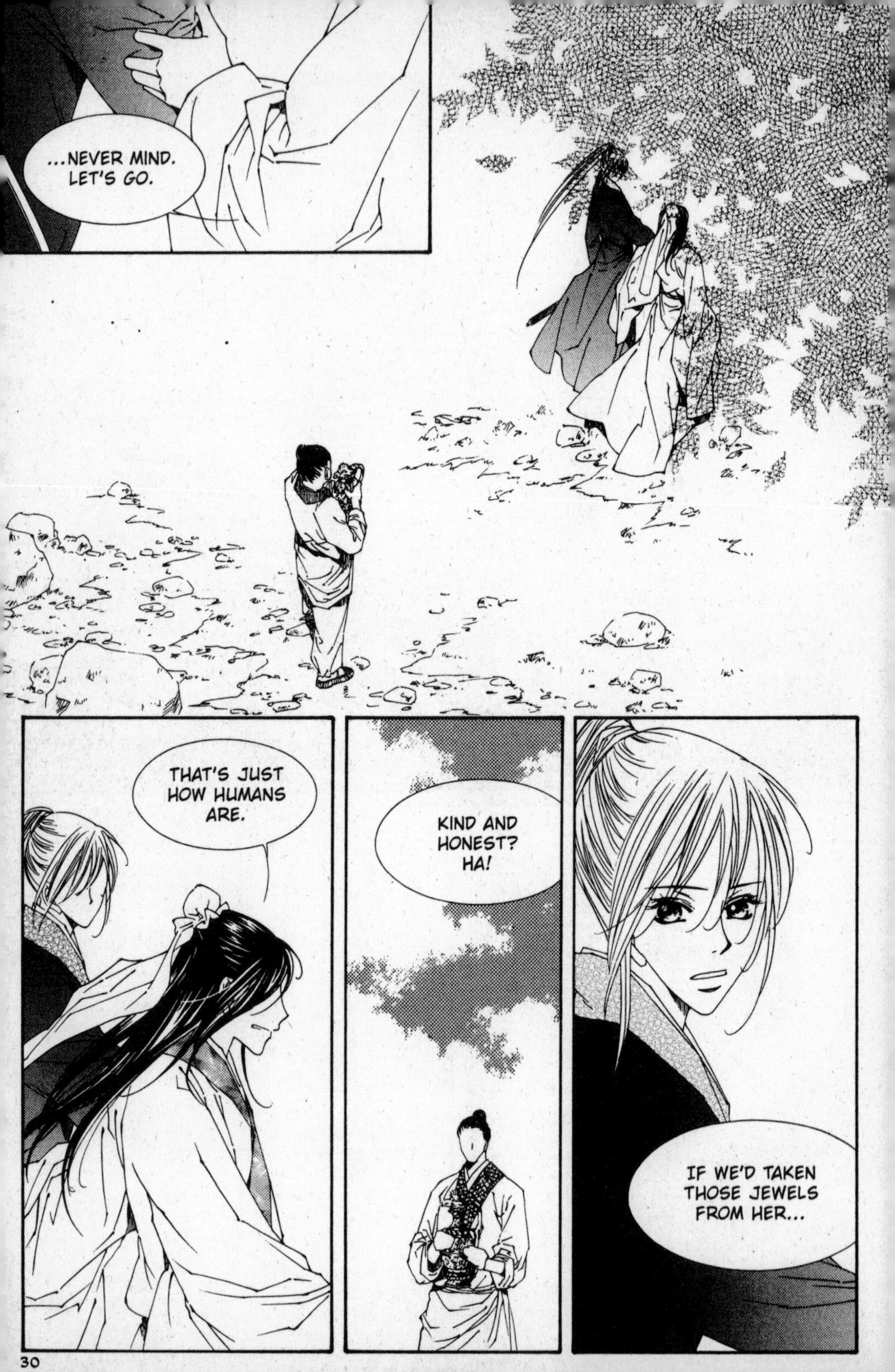
...NEVER MIND. LET'S GO.
THAT'S JUST HOW HUMANS ARE.
KIND AND HONEST? HA!
IF WE'D TAKEN THOSE JEWELS FROM HER...

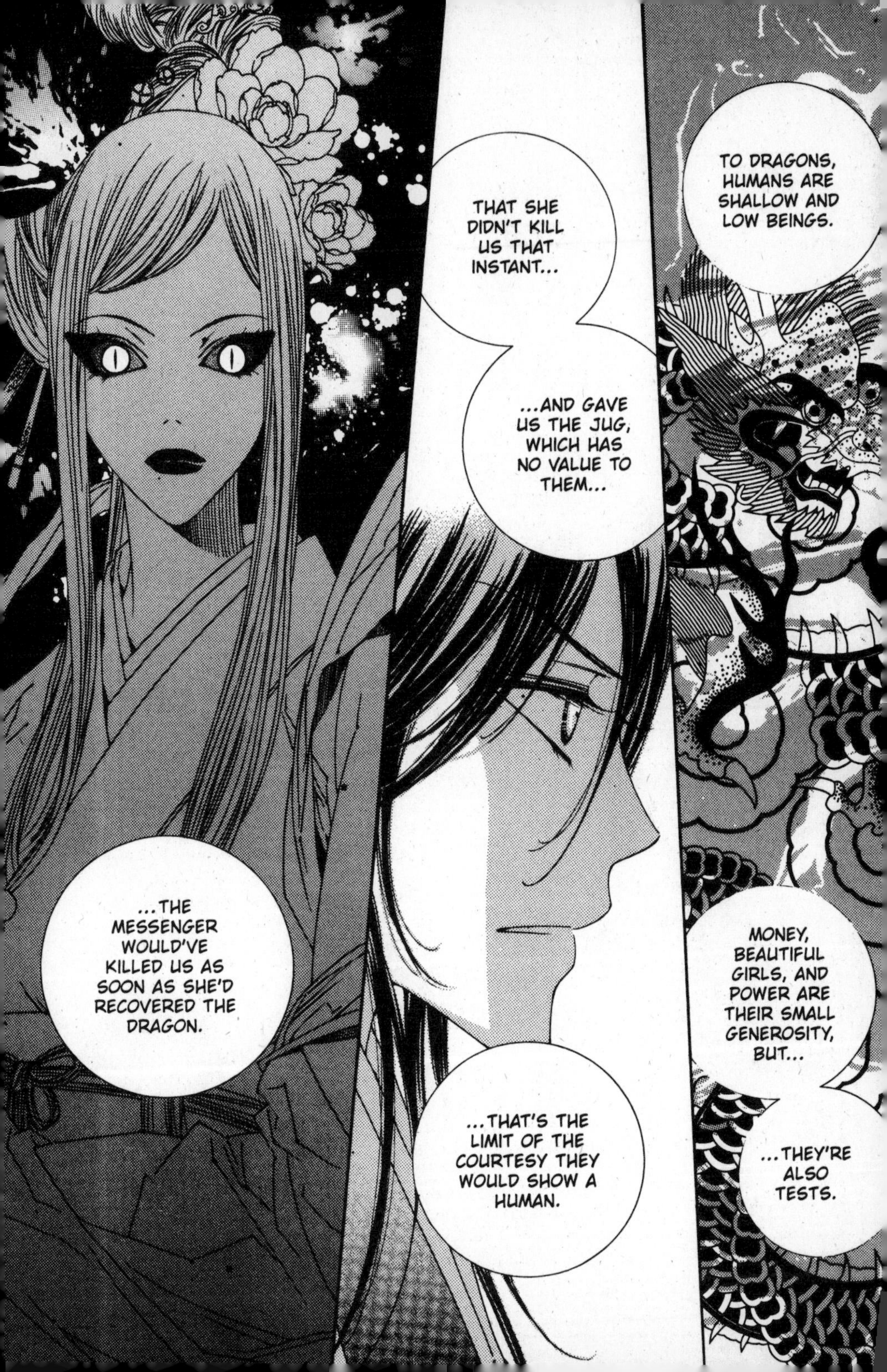
...THE MESSENGER WOULD'VE KILLED US AS SOON AS SHE'D RECOVERED THE DRAGON.
THAT SHE DIDN'T KILL US THAT INSTANT...
...AND GAVE US THE JUG, WHICH HAS NO VALUE TO THEM...
...THAT'S THE LIMIT OF THE COURTESY THEY WOULD SHOW A HUMAN.
TO DRAGONS, HUMANS ARE SHALLOW AND LOW BEINGS.
MONEY, BEAUTIFUL GIRLS, AND POWER ARE THEIR SMALL GENEROSITY, BUT...
...THEY'RE ALSO TESTS.

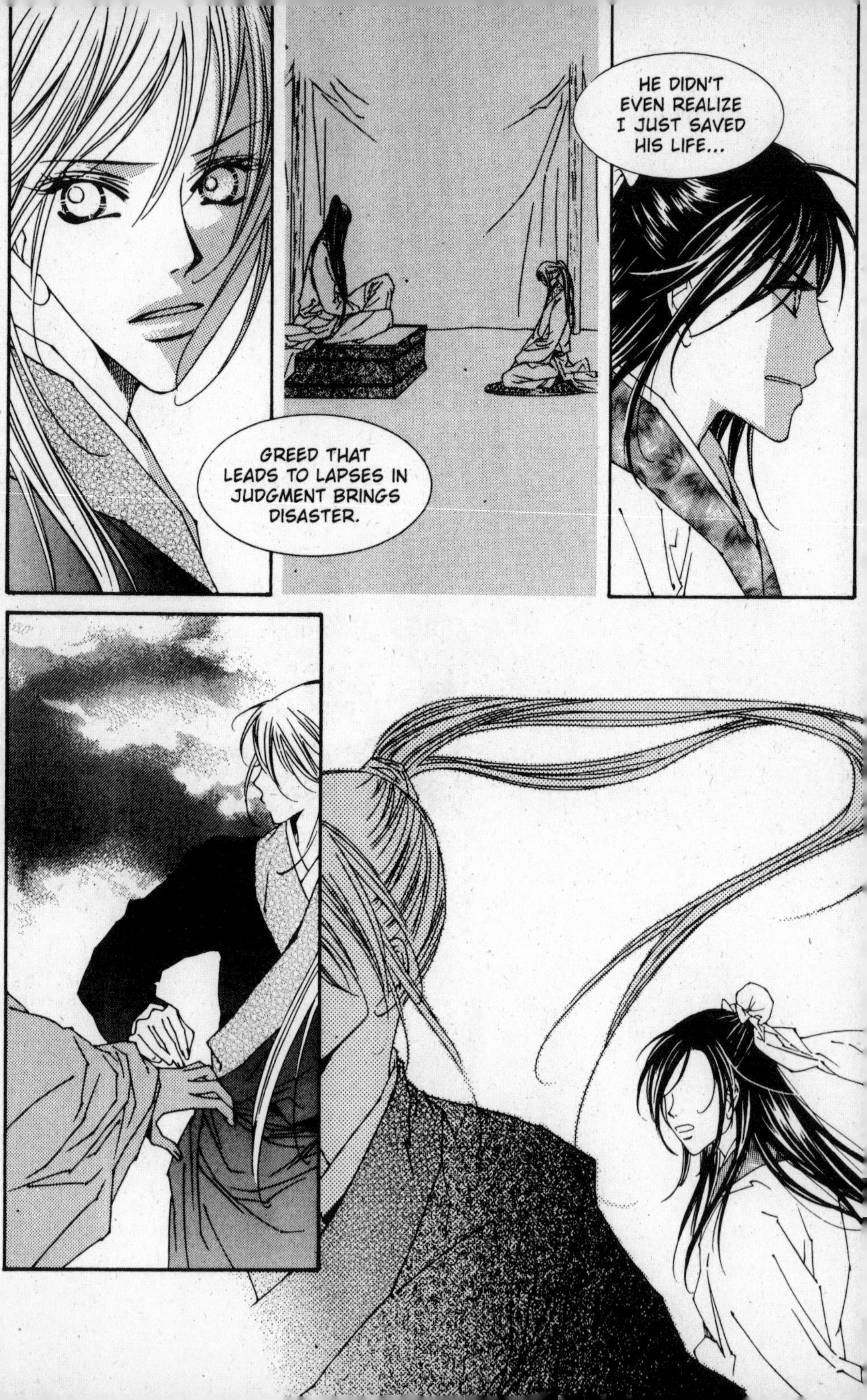
GREED THAT LEADS TO LAPSES IN JUDGMENT BRINGS DISASTER.
HE DIDN'T EVEN REALIZE I JUST SAVED HIS LIFE...

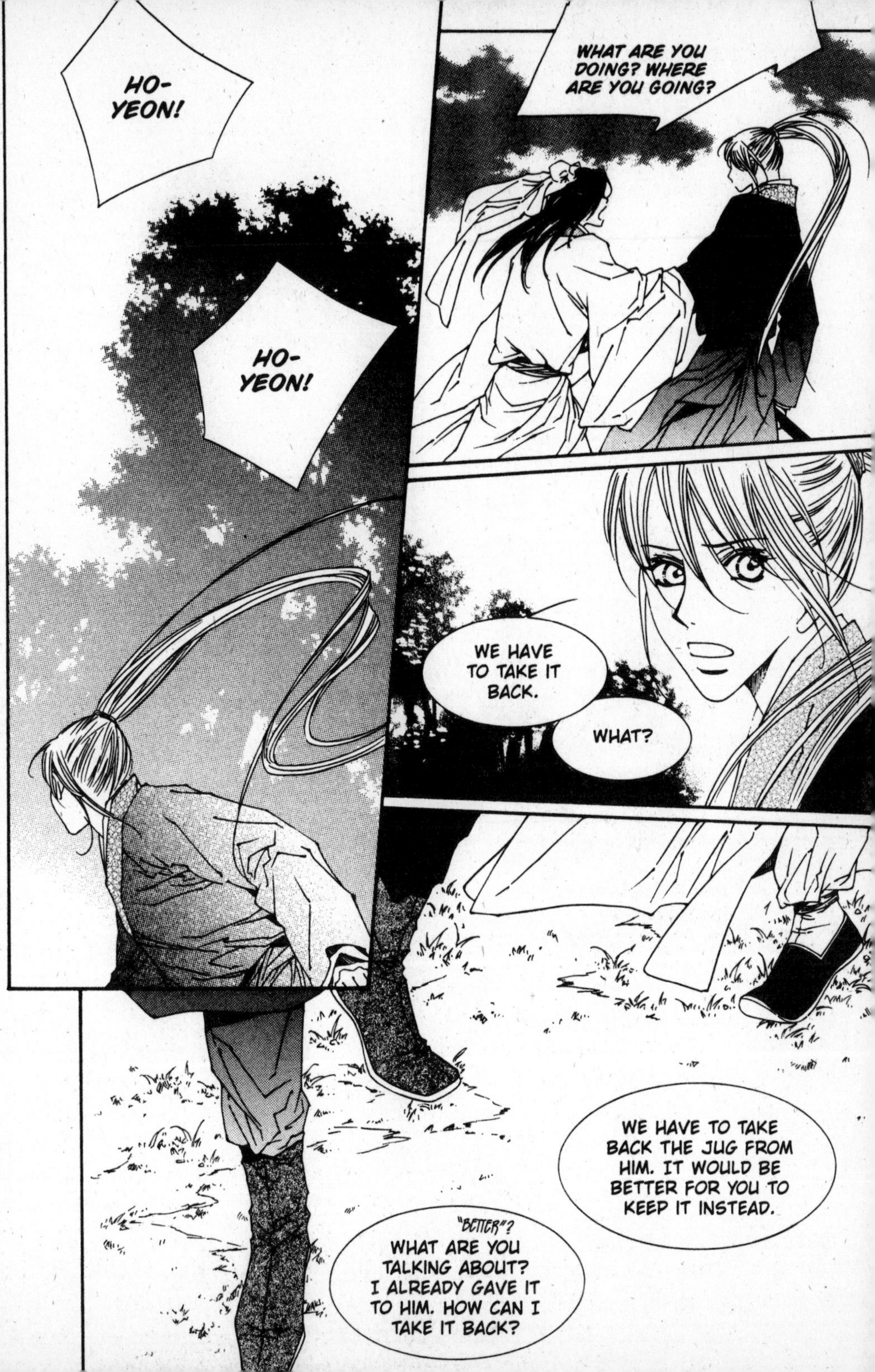
HO-YEON!
HO-YEON!
WHAT ARE YOU DOING? WHERE ARE YOU GOING?
WE HAVE TO TAKE IT BACK.
WHAT?
WE HAVE TO TAKE BACK THE JUG FROM HIM. IT WOULD BE BETTER FOR YOU TO KEEP IT INSTEAD.
"BETTER"? WHAT ARE YOU TALKING ABOUT? I ALREADY GAVE IT TO HIM. HOW CAN I TAKE IT BACK?

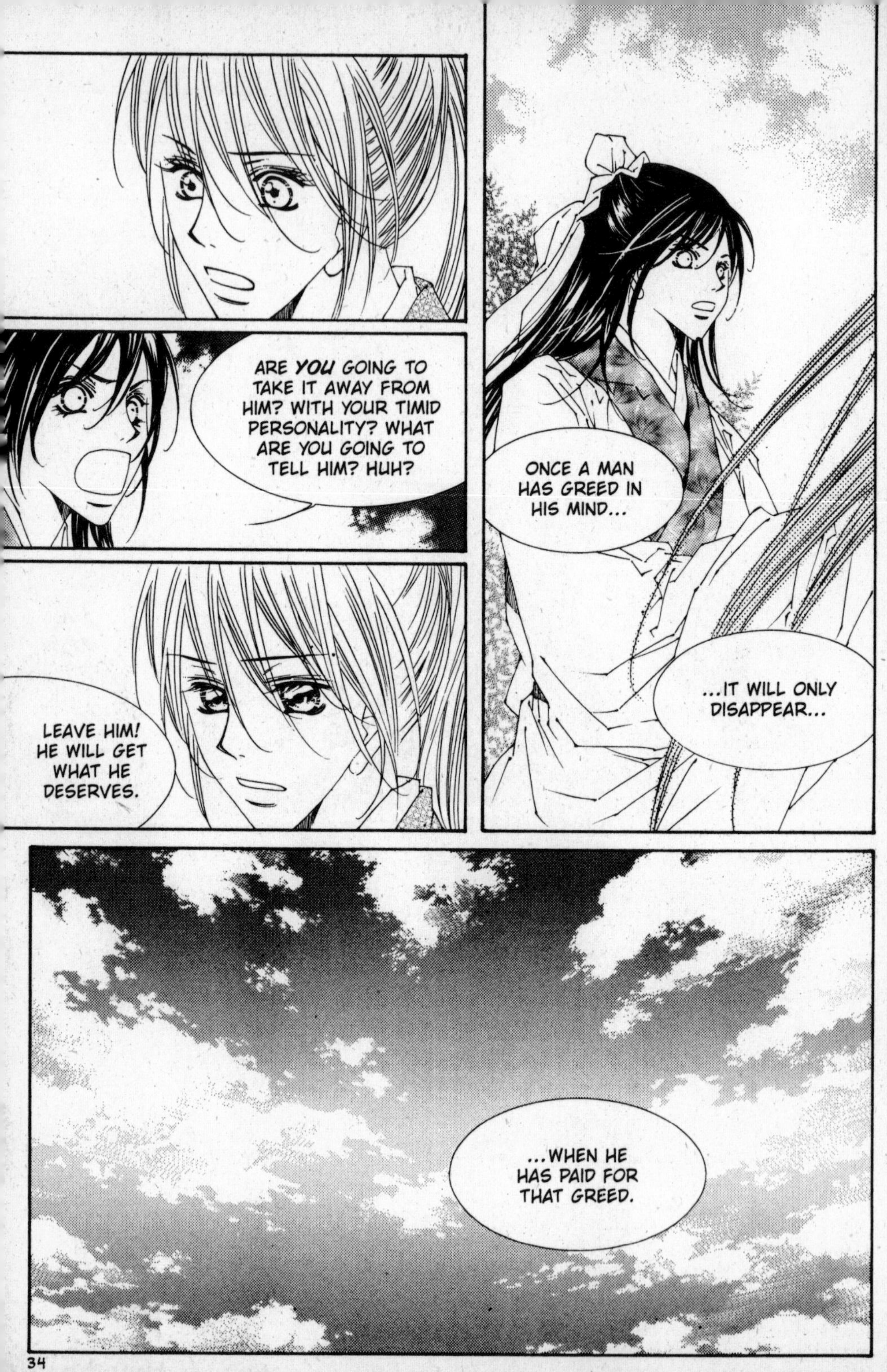
ARE YOU GOING TO TAKE IT AWAY FROM HIM? WITH YOUR TIMID PERSONALITY? WHAT ARE YOU GOING TO TELL HIM? HUH?
LEAVE HIM! HE WILL GET WHAT HE DESERVES.
ONCE A MAN HAS GREED IN HIS MIND...
...IT WILL ONLY DISAPPEAR...
...WHEN HE HAS PAID FOR THAT GREED.

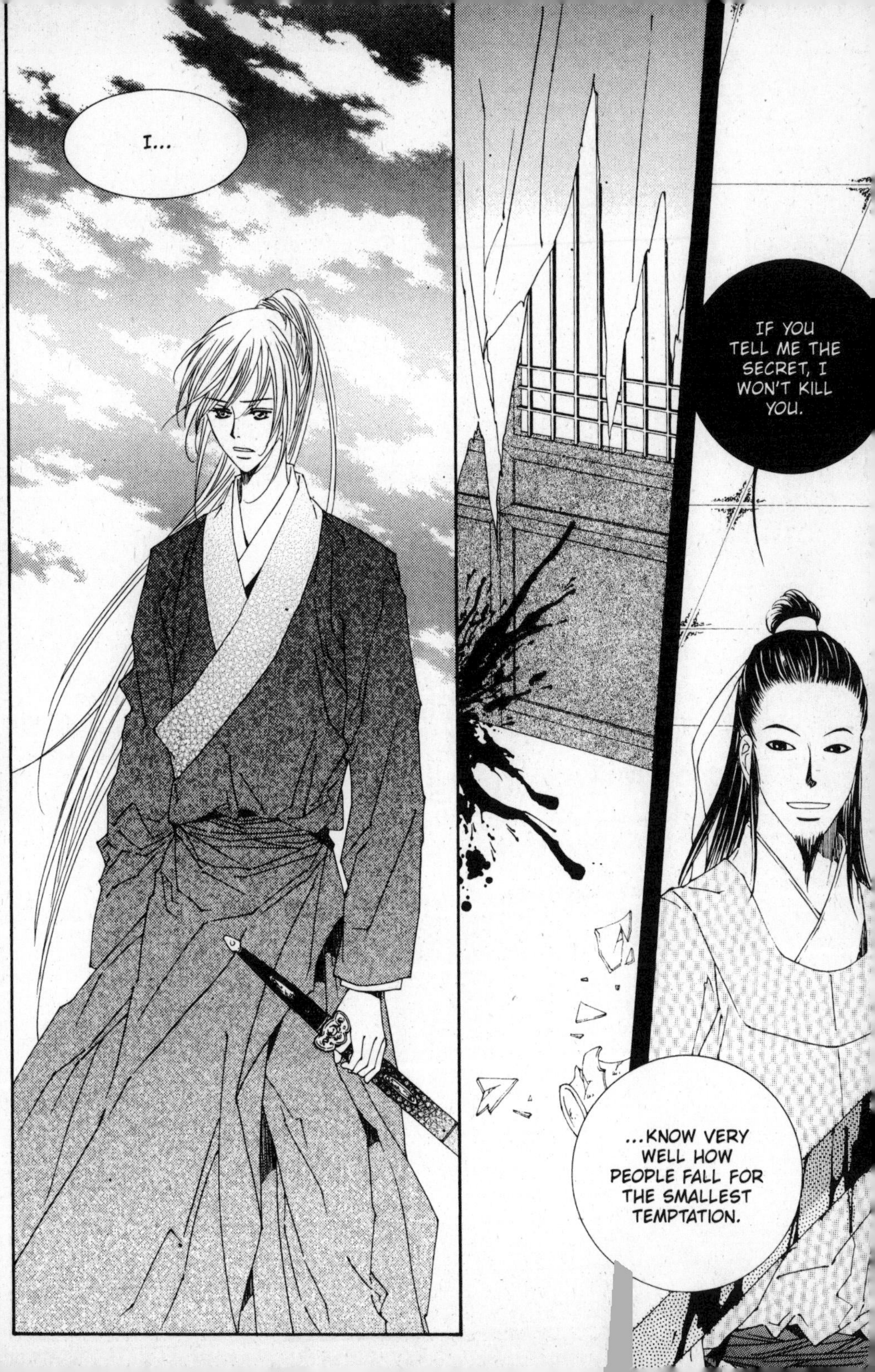
I...
IF YOU TELL ME THE SECRET, I WON'T KILL YOU.
...KNOW VERY WELL HOW PEOPLE FALL FOR THE SMALLEST TEMPTATION.

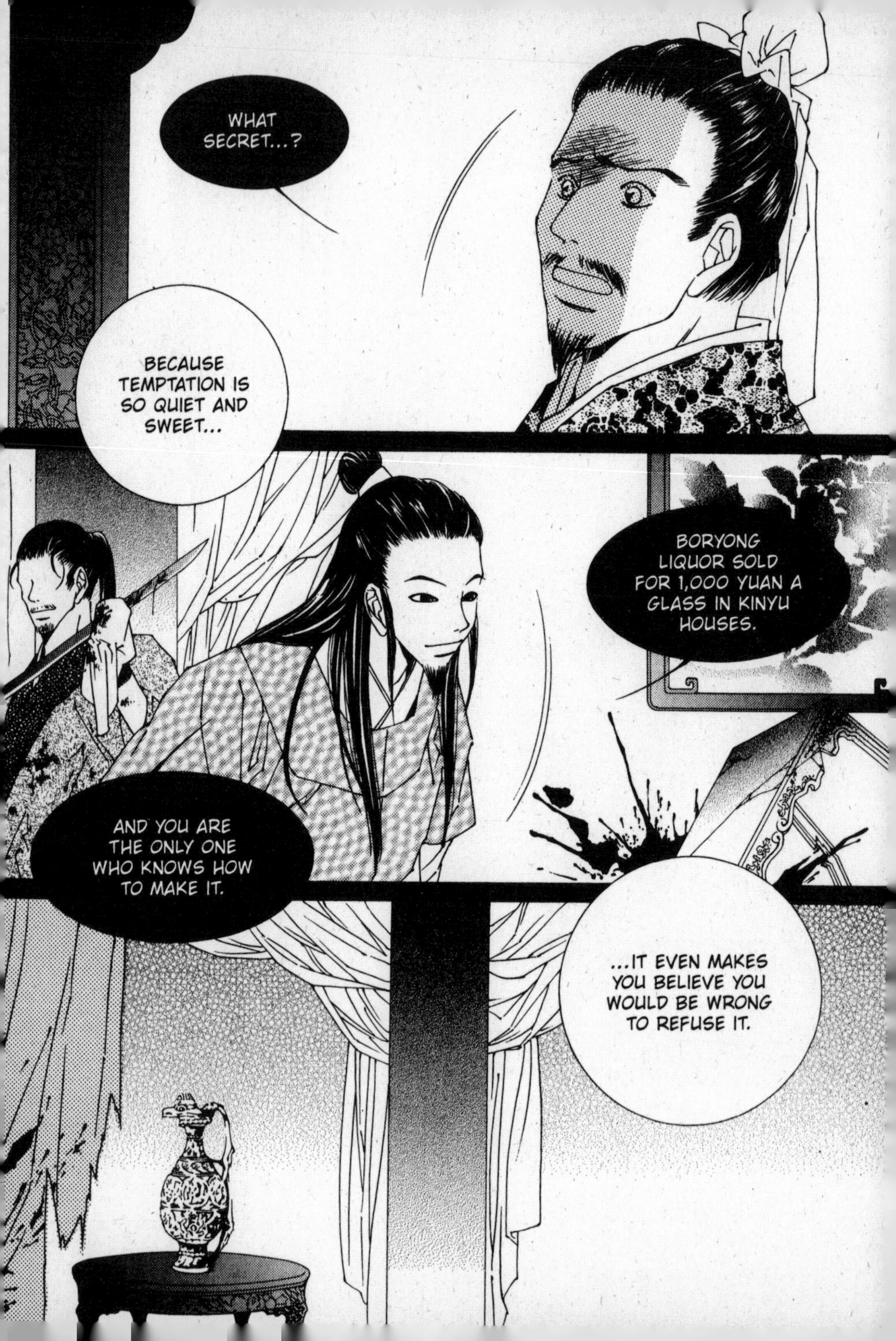
WHAT SECRET...?
BECAUSE TEMPTATION IS SO QUIET AND SWEET...
BORYONG LIQUOR SOLD FOR 1,000 YUAN A GLASS IN KINYU HOUSES.
AND YOU ARE THE ONLY ONE WHO KNOWS HOW TO MAKE IT.
...IT EVEN MAKES YOU BELIEVE YOU WOULD BE WRONG TO REFUSE IT.

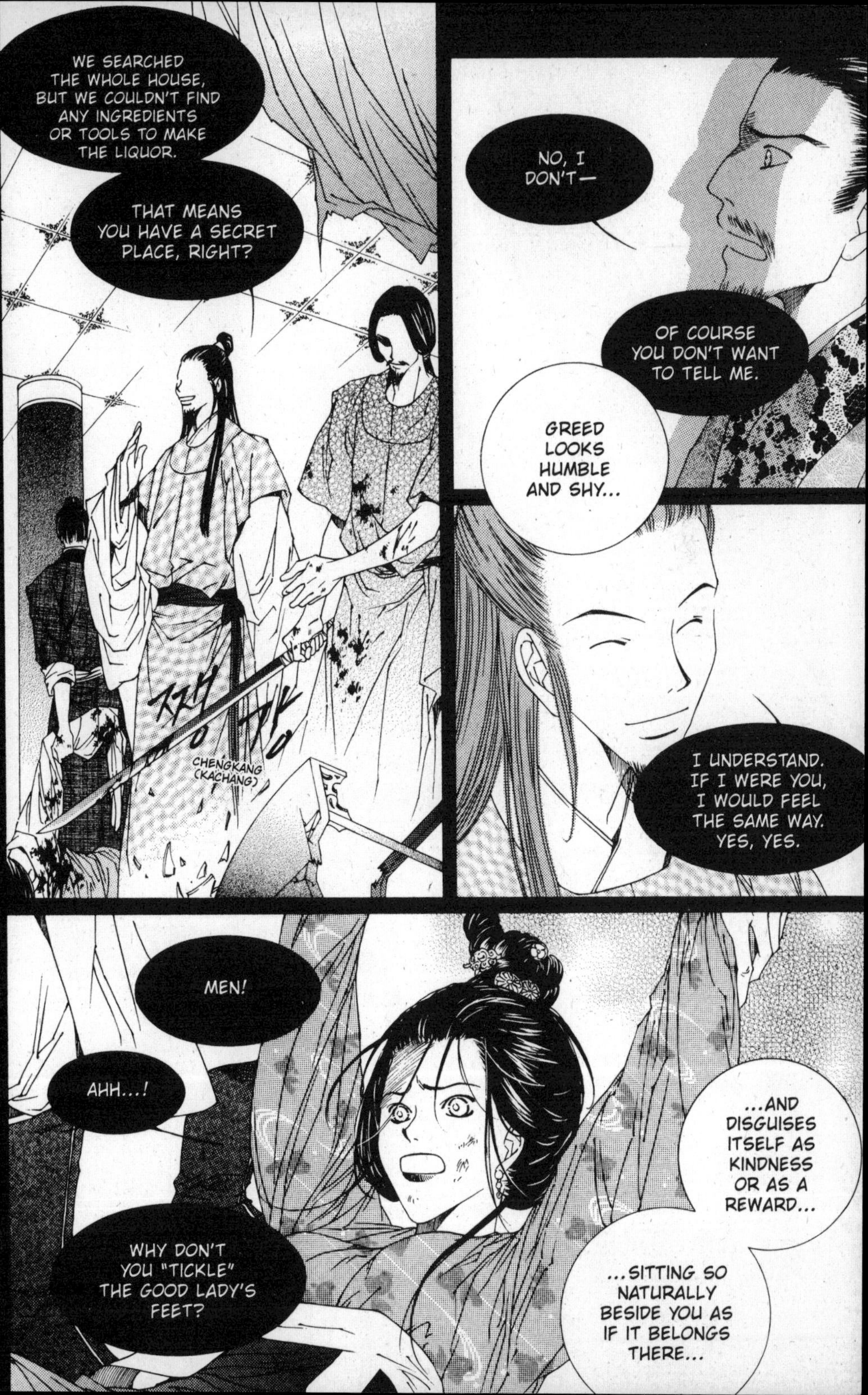
WE SEARCHED THE WHOLE HOUSE, BUT WE COULDN'T FIND ANY INGREDIENTS OR TOOLS TO MAKE THE LIQUOR.
THAT MEANS YOU HAVE A SECRET PLACE, RIGHT?
CHENGKANG (KACHANG)
NO, I DON'T—
OF COURSE YOU DON'T WANT TO TELL ME.
GREED LOOKS HUMBLE AND SHY...
I UNDERSTAND. IF I WERE YOU, I WOULD FEEL THE SAME WAY. YES, YES.
MEN!
AHH...!
WHY DON'T YOU "TICKLE" THE GOOD LADY'S FEET?
...AND DISGUISES ITSELF AS KINDNESS OR AS A REWARD...
...SITTING SO NATURALLY BESIDE YOU AS IF IT BELONGS THERE...

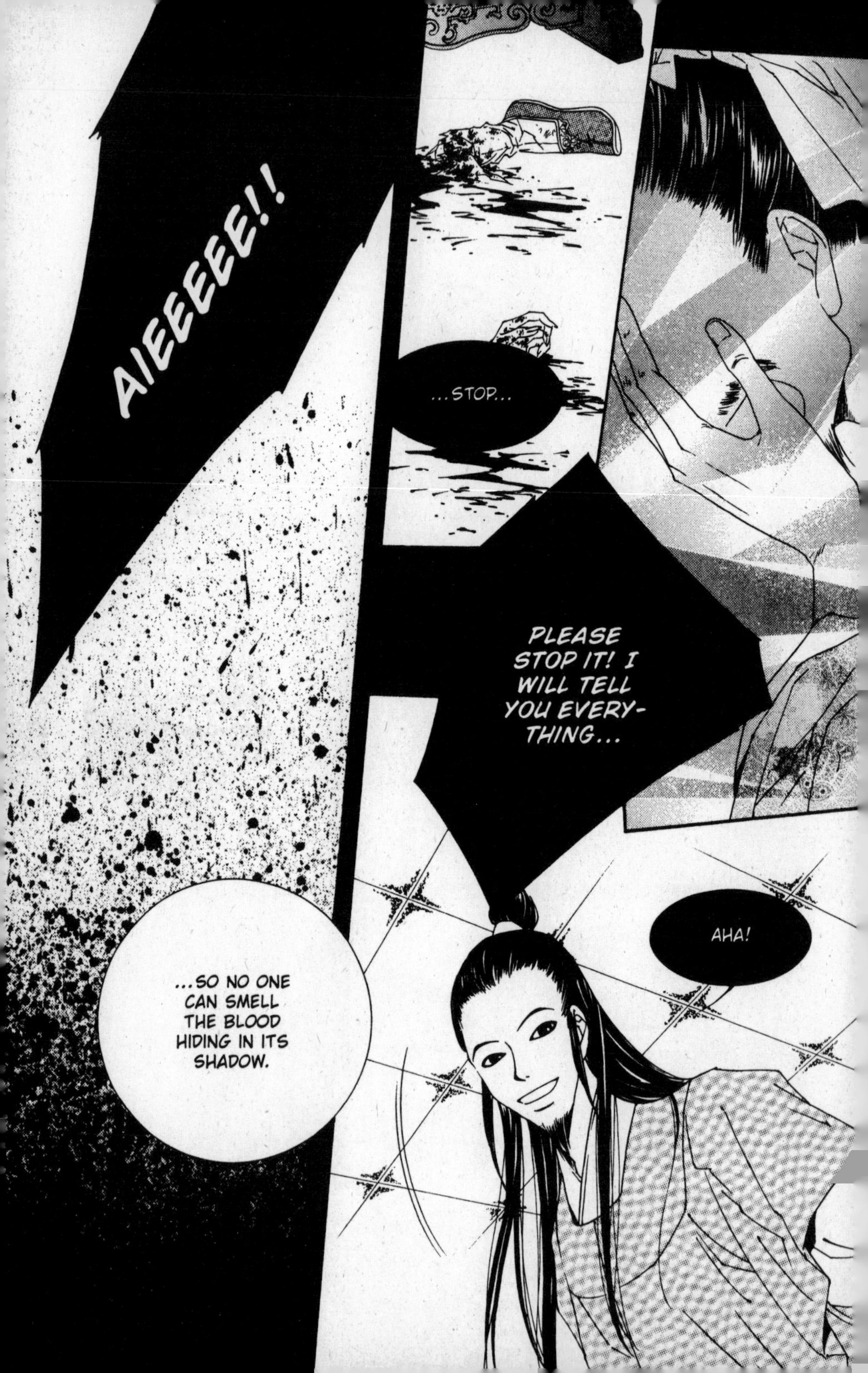
AIEEEEE!!
...STOP...
PLEASE STOP IT! I WILL TELL YOU EVERY-THING...
...SO NO ONE CAN SMELL THE BLOOD HIDING IN ITS SHADOW.
AHA!

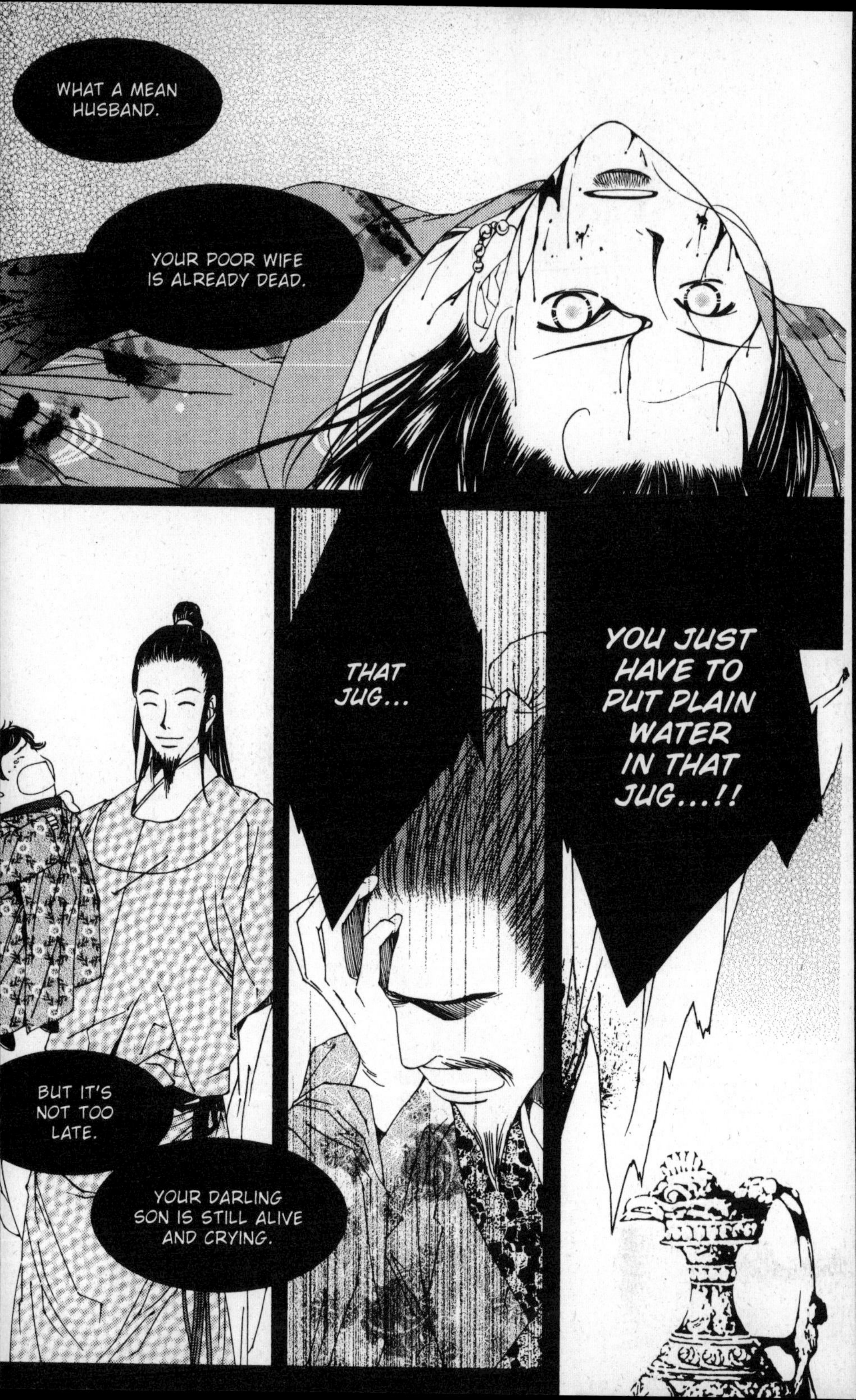
WHAT A MEAN HUSBAND.
YOUR POOR WIFE IS ALREADY DEAD.
BUT IT'S NOT TOO LATE.
YOUR DARLING SON IS STILL ALIVE AND CRYING.
THAT JUG...
YOU JUST HAVE TO PUT PLAIN WATER IN THAT JUG...!!

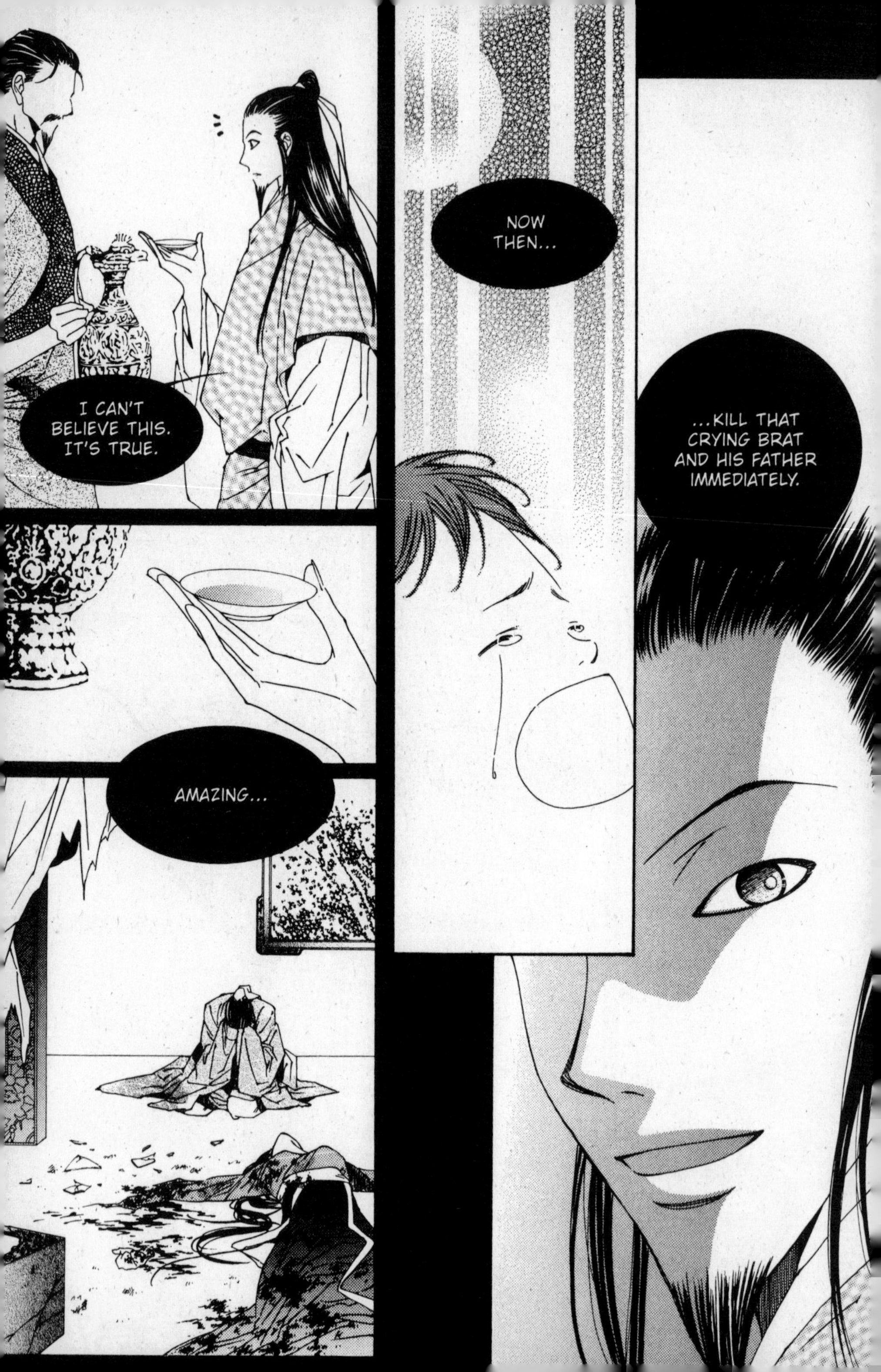
I CAN'T BELIEVE THIS. IT'S TRUE.
AMAZING...
NOW THEN...
...KILL THAT CRYING BRAT AND HIS FATHER IMMEDIATELY.

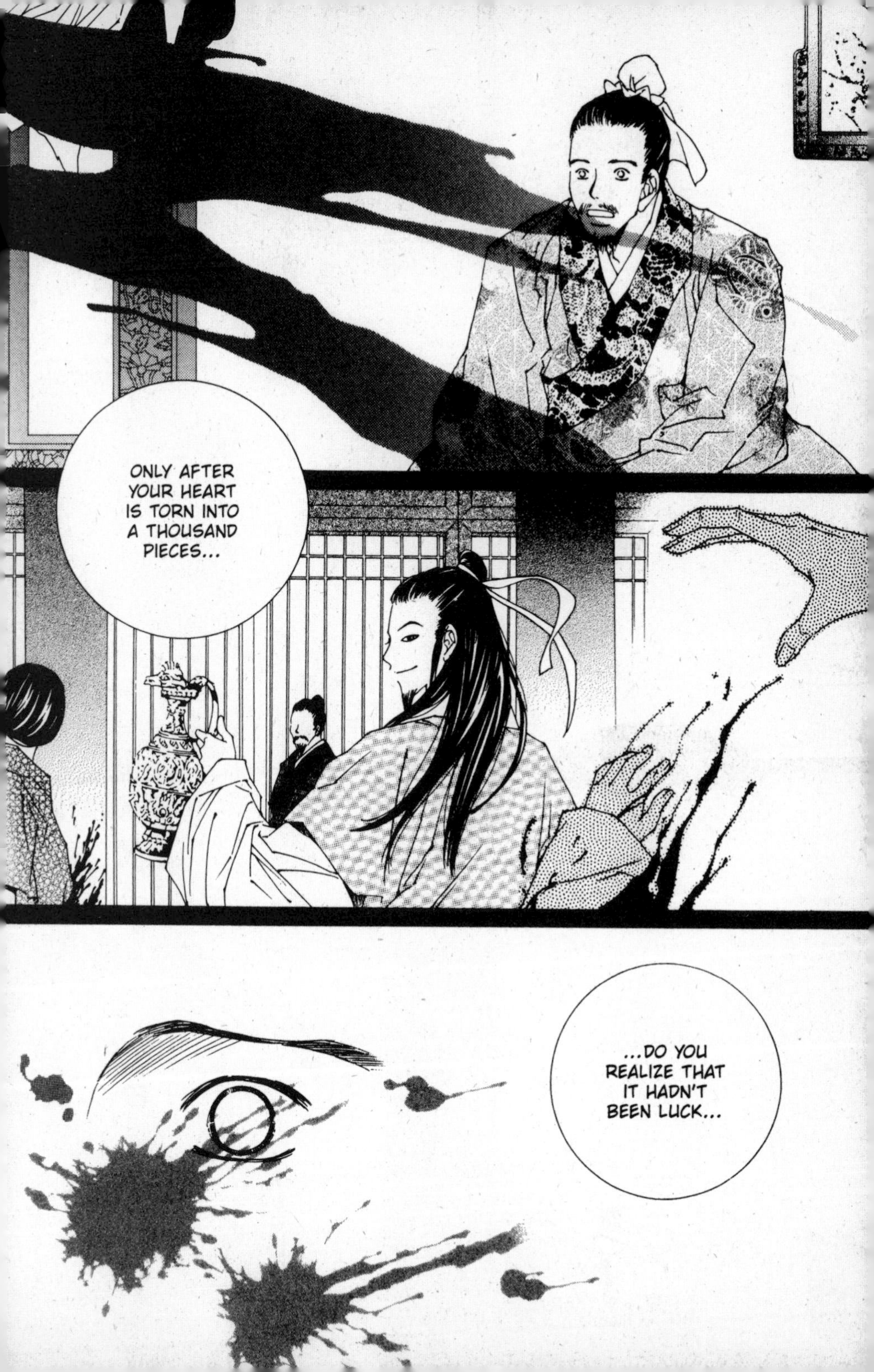
ONLY AFTER YOUR HEART IS TORN INTO A THOUSAND PIECES...
...DO YOU REALIZE THAT IT HADN'T BEEN LUCK...

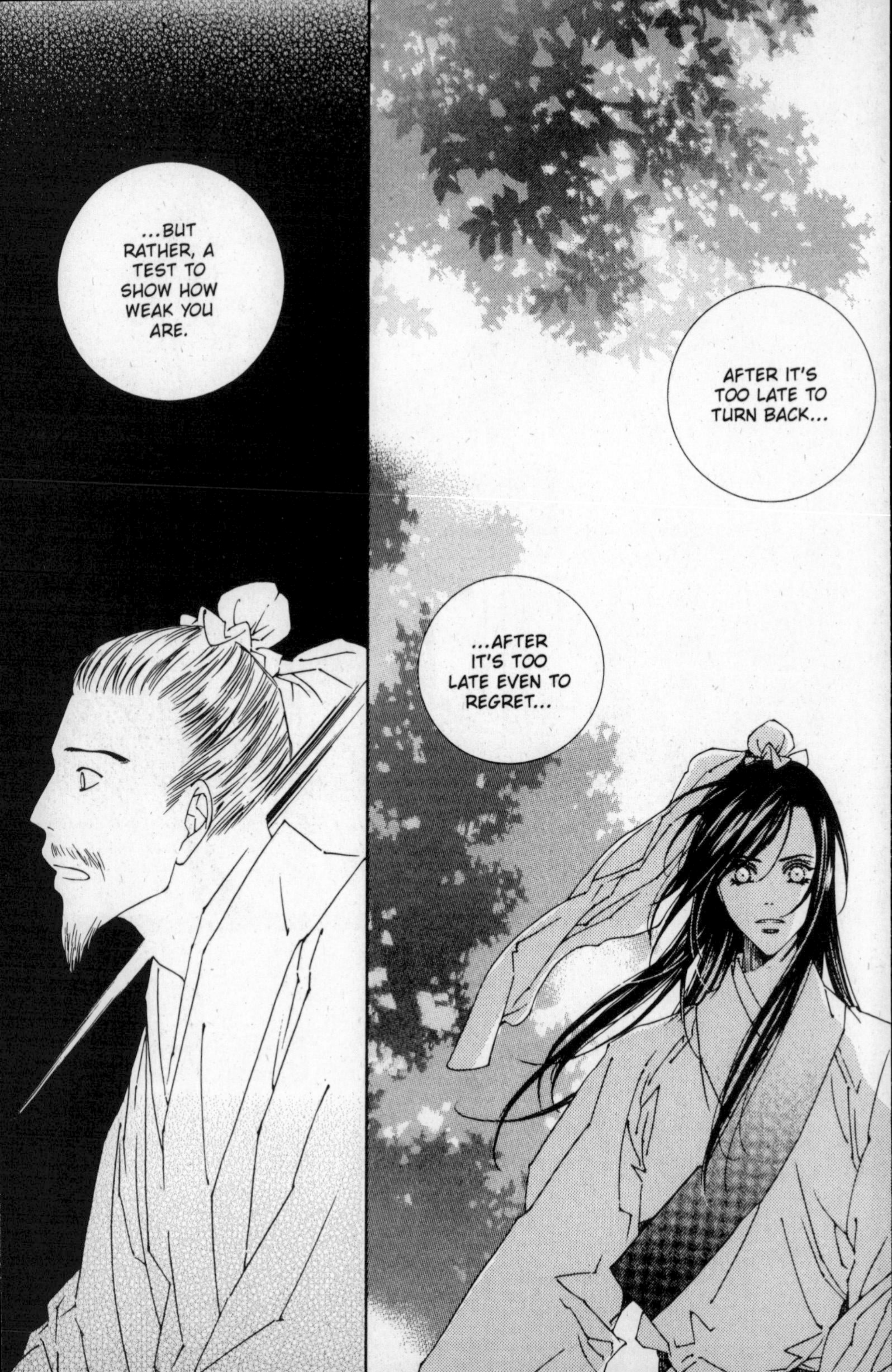
...BUT RATHER, A TEST TO SHOW HOW WEAK YOU ARE.
AFTER IT'S TOO LATE TO TURN BACK...
...AFTER IT'S TOO LATE EVEN TO REGRET...

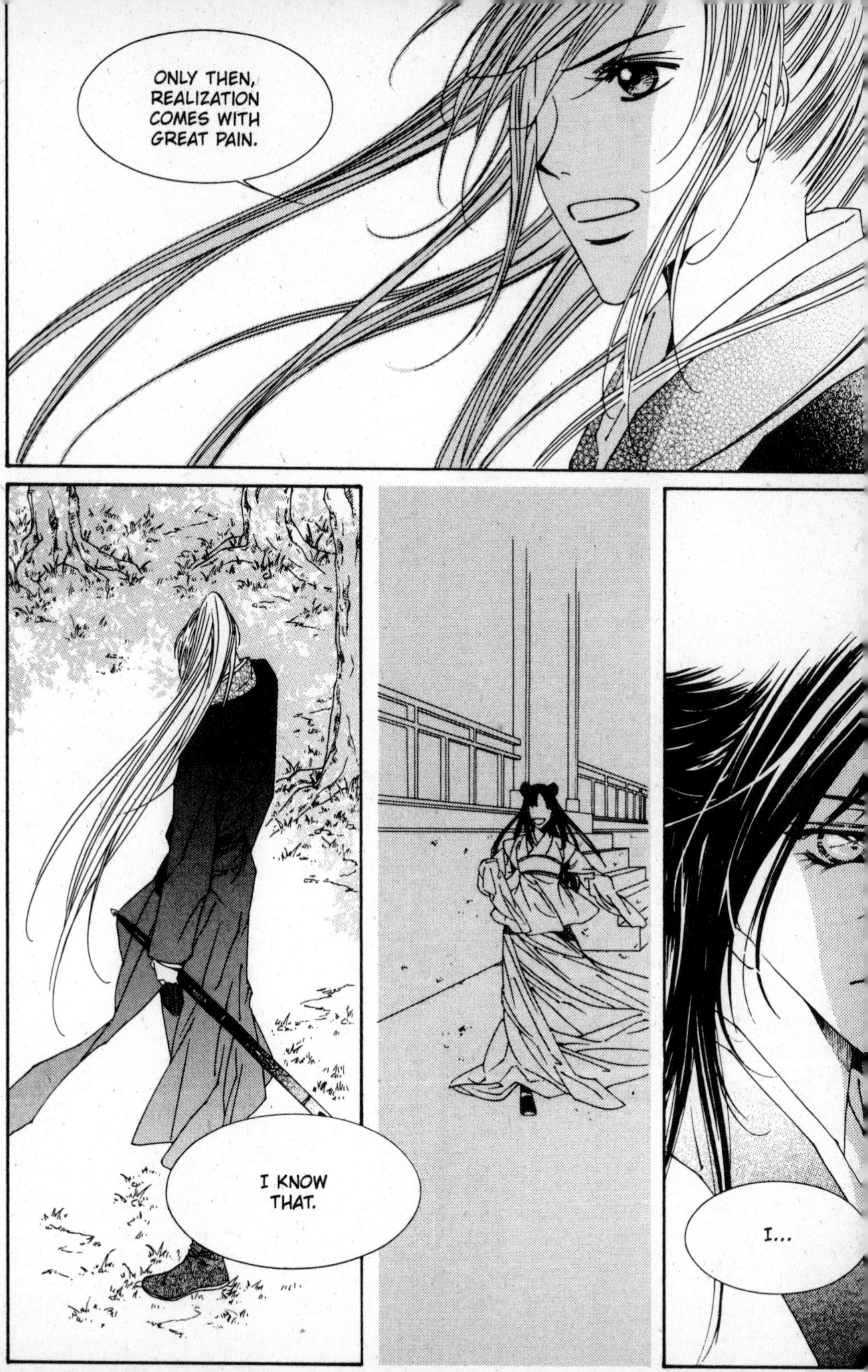
ONLY THEN, REALIZATION COMES WITH GREAT PAIN.
I KNOW THAT.
I...

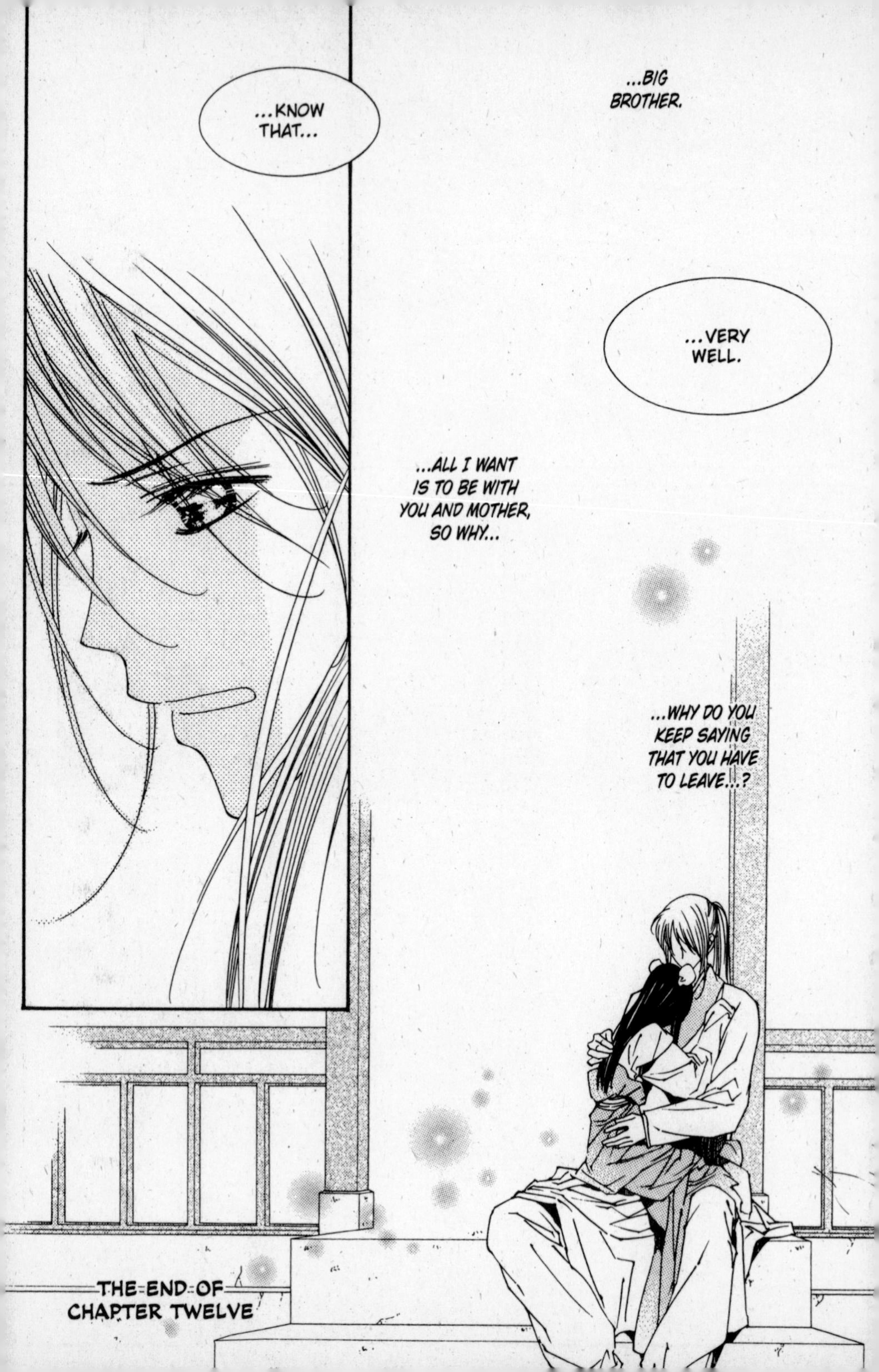
...KNOW THAT...
...BIG BROTHER.
...VERY WELL.
...ALL I WANT IS TO BE WITH YOU AND MOTHER, SO WHY...
...WHY DO YOU KEEP SAYING THAT YOU HAVE TO LEAVE...?
THE END OF CHAPTER TWELVE

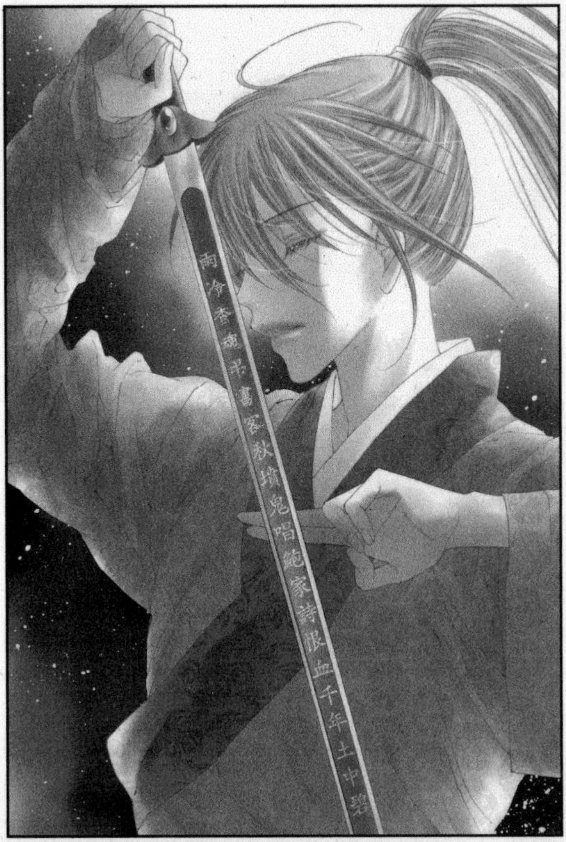
雨冷香魂弔書客秋墳鬼唱鮑家詩恨血千年土中碧

TIME
AND
AGAIN

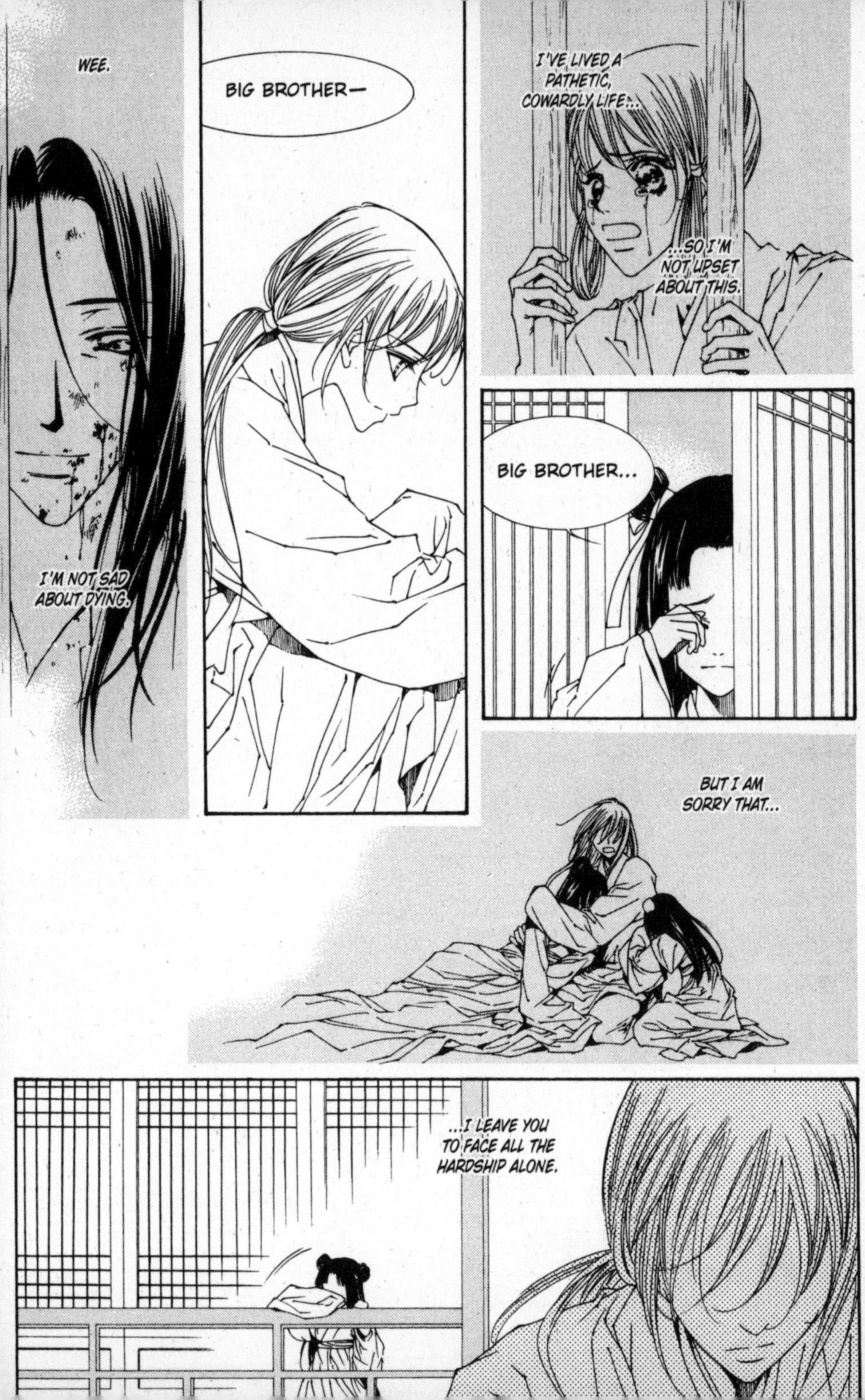
WEE.
I'M NOT SAD ABOUT DYING.
BIG BROTHER—
I'VE LIVED A PATHETIC, COWARDLY LIFE...
...SO I'M NOT UPSET ABOUT THIS.
BIG BROTHER...
BUT I AM SORRY THAT...
...I LEAVE YOU TO FACE ALL THE HARDSHIP ALONE.

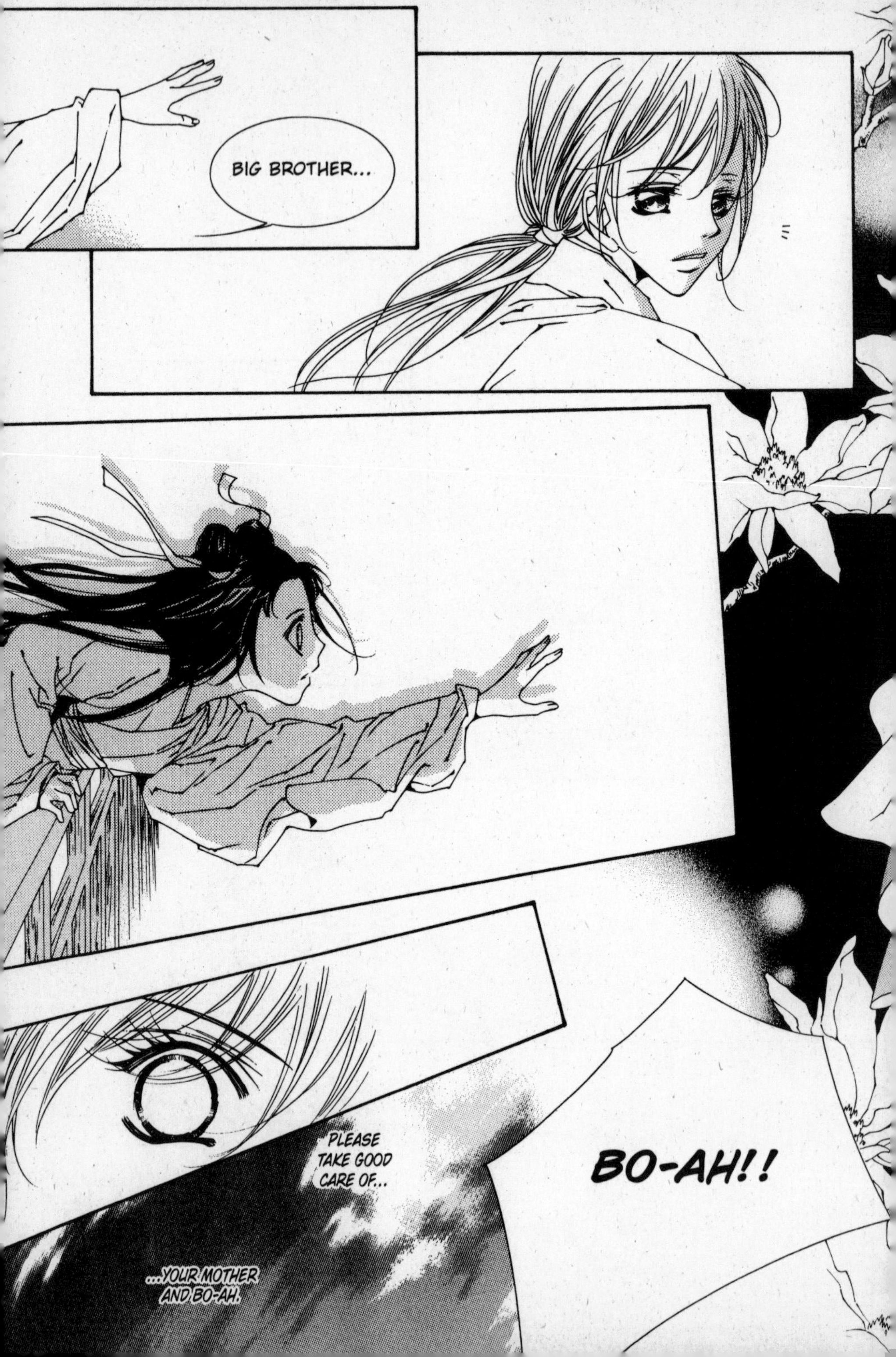
BIG BROTHER...
PLEASE TAKE GOOD CARE OF...
BO-AH!!
...YOUR MOTHER AND BO-AH.

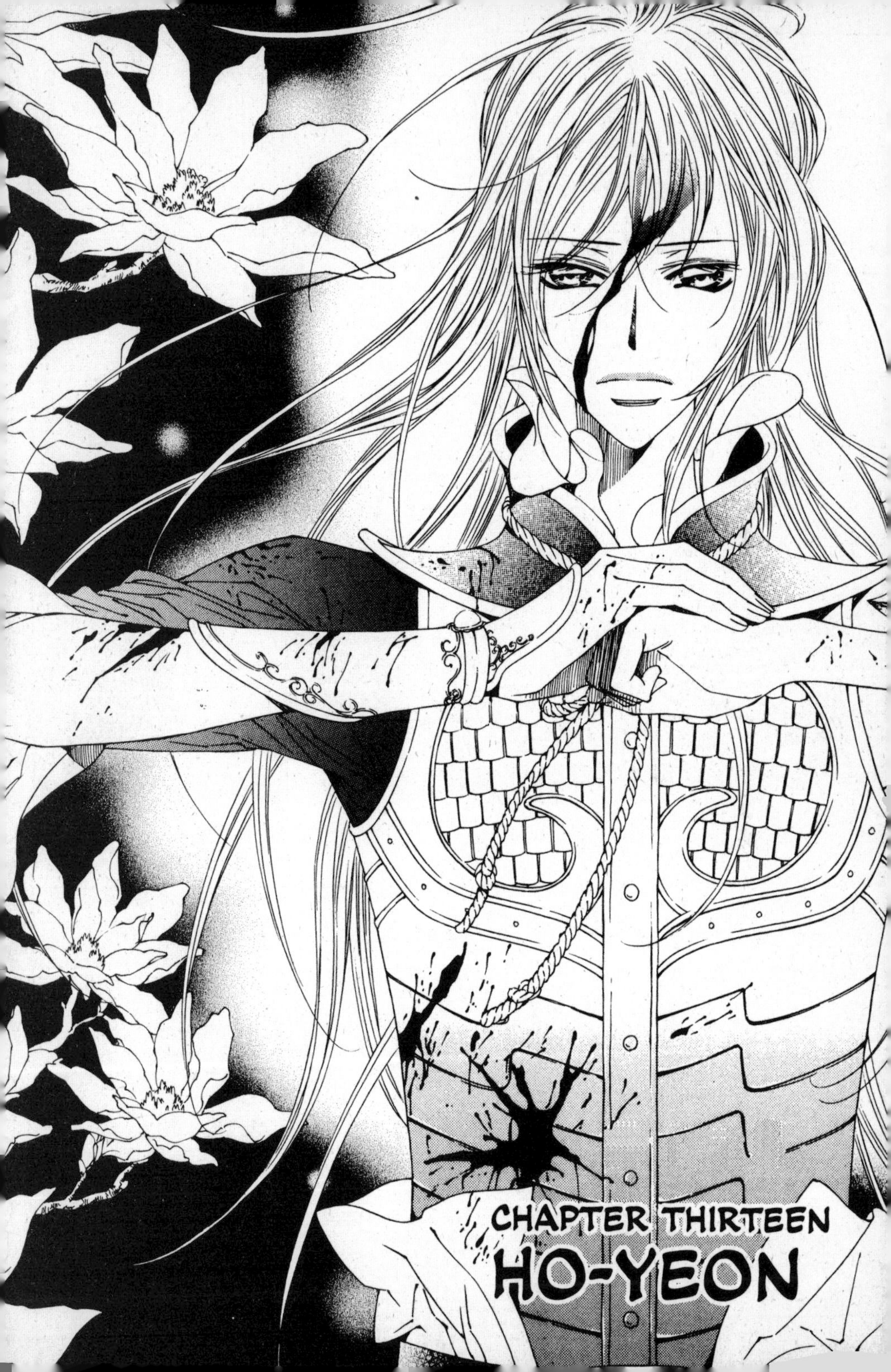
CHAPTER THIRTEEN
HO-YEON

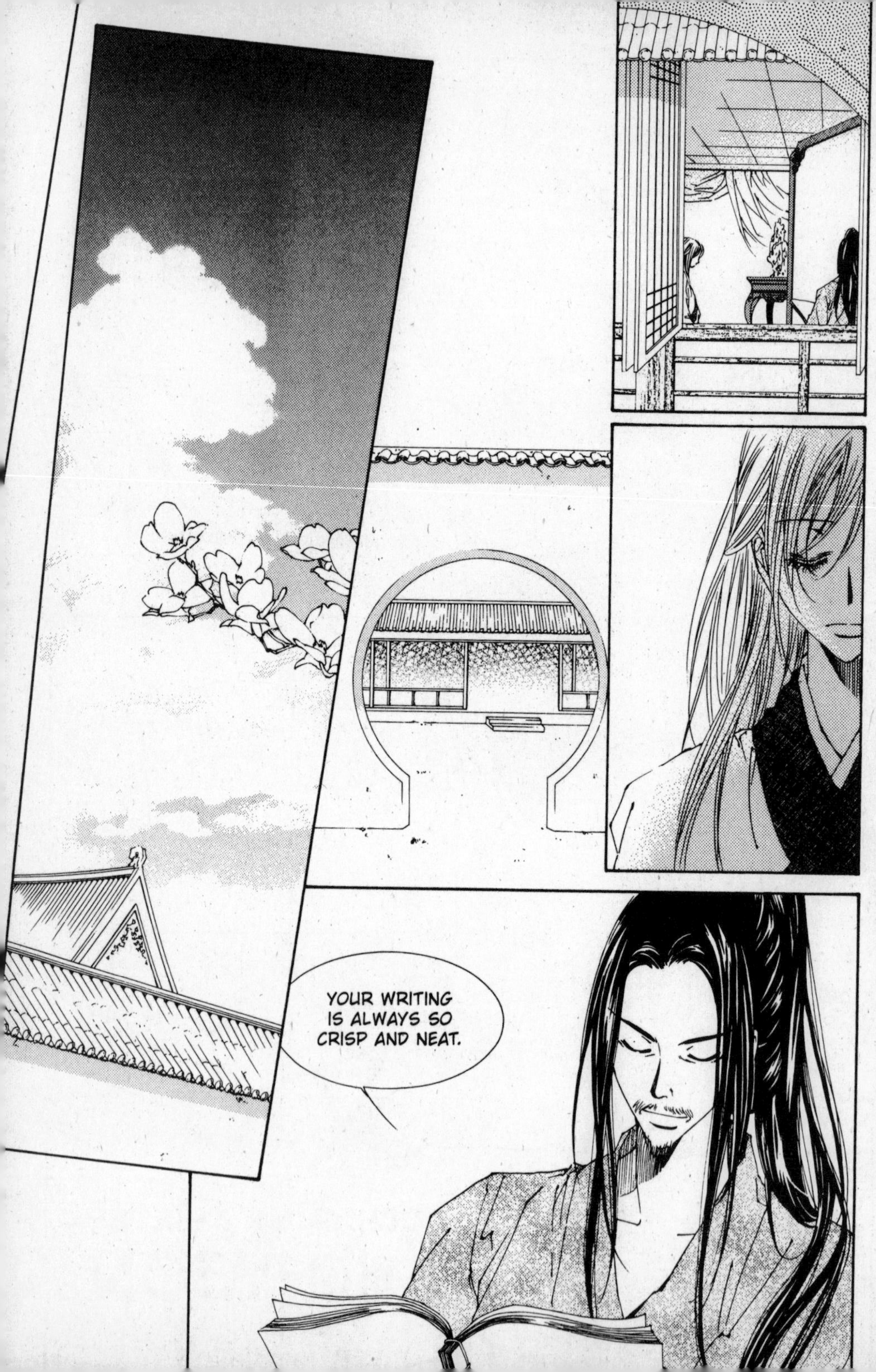
YOUR WRITING IS ALWAYS SO CRISP AND NEAT.

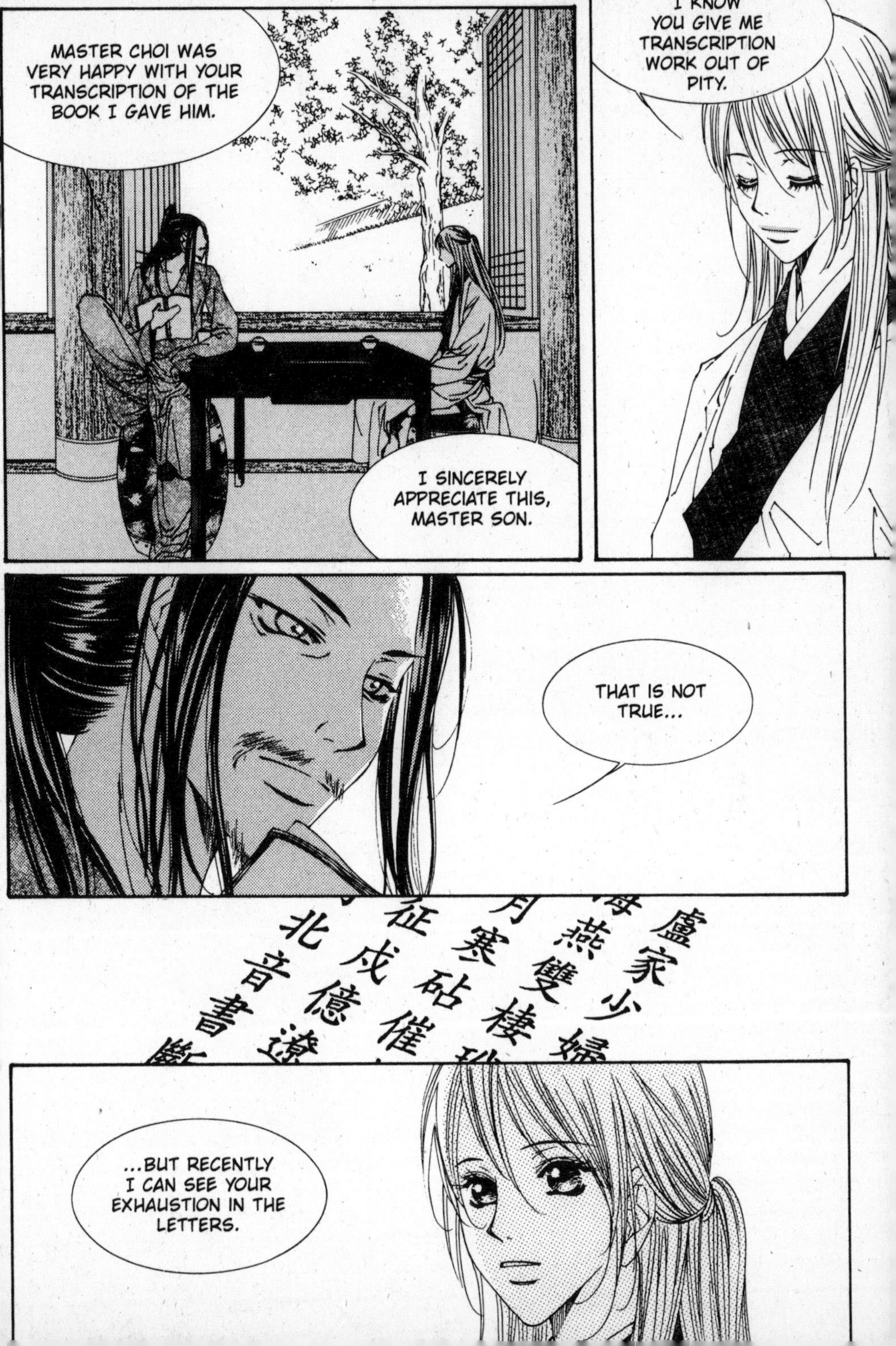
MASTER CHOI WAS VERY HAPPY WITH YOUR TRANSCRIPTION OF THE BOOK I GAVE HIM.
I SINCERELY APPRECIATE THIS, MASTER SON.
I KNOW YOU GIVE ME TRANSCRIPTION WORK OUT OF PITY.
THAT IS NOT TRUE...
盧家少婦
海燕雙棲
月寒砧催
征戍憶遼
北音書
...BUT RECENTLY I CAN SEE YOUR EXHAUSTION IN THE LETTERS.

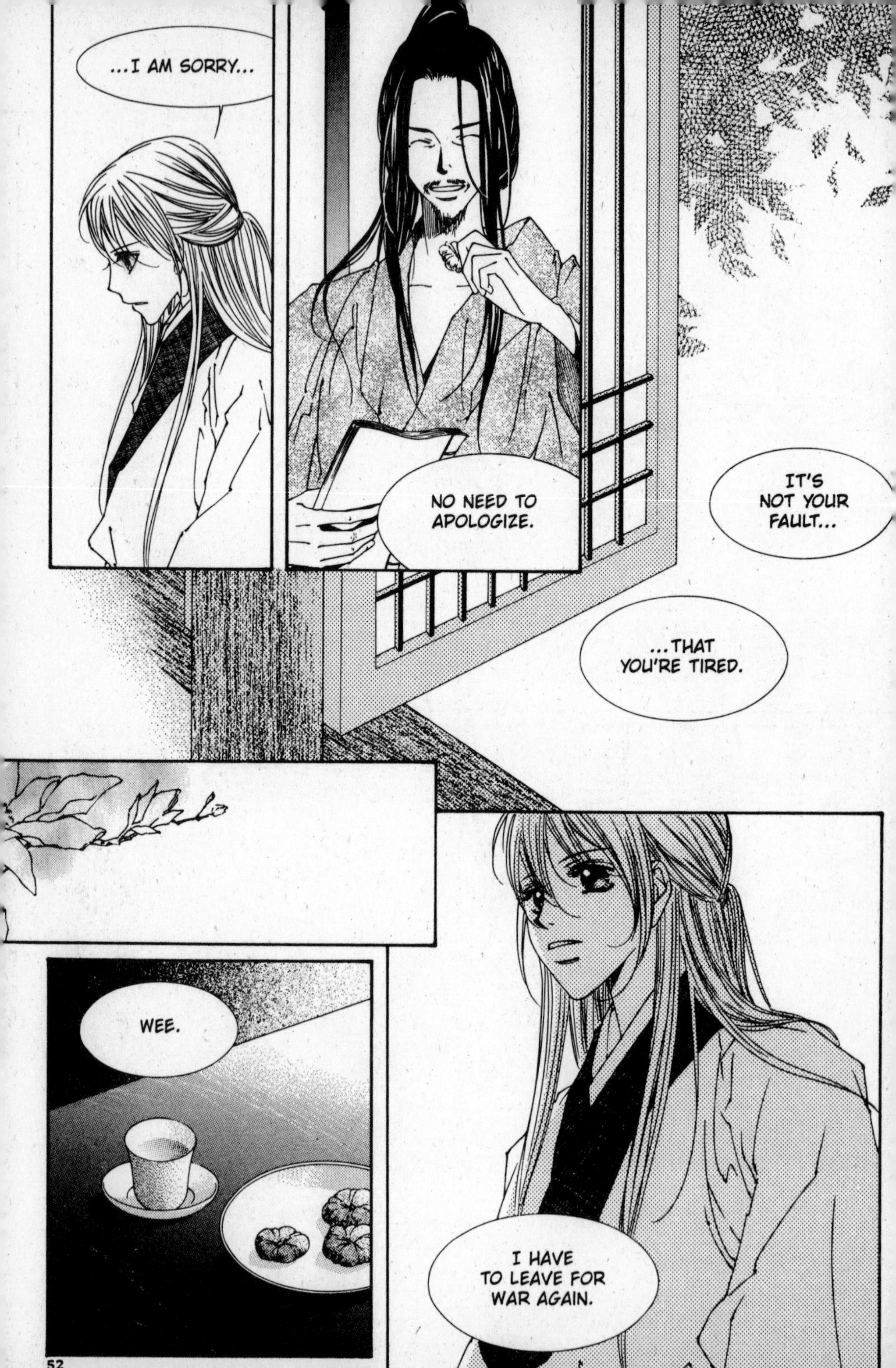
...I AM SORRY...
NO NEED TO APOLOGIZE.
IT'S NOT YOUR FAULT...
...THAT YOU'RE TIRED.
WEE.
I HAVE TO LEAVE FOR WAR AGAIN.

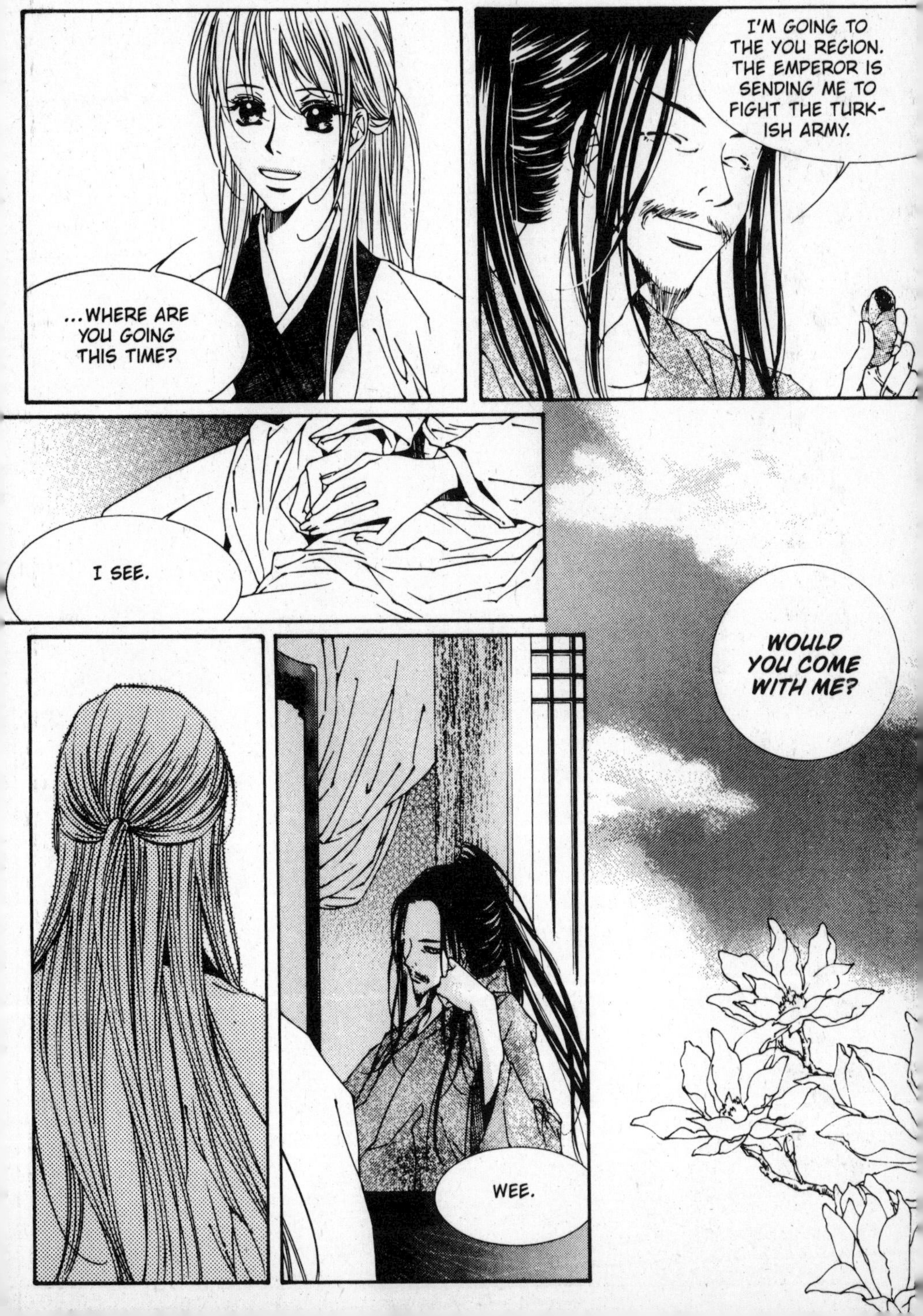
...WHERE ARE YOU GOING THIS TIME?
I'M GOING TO THE YOU REGION. THE EMPEROR IS SENDING ME TO FIGHT THE TURK-ISH ARMY.
I SEE.
WOULD YOU COME WITH ME?
WEE.

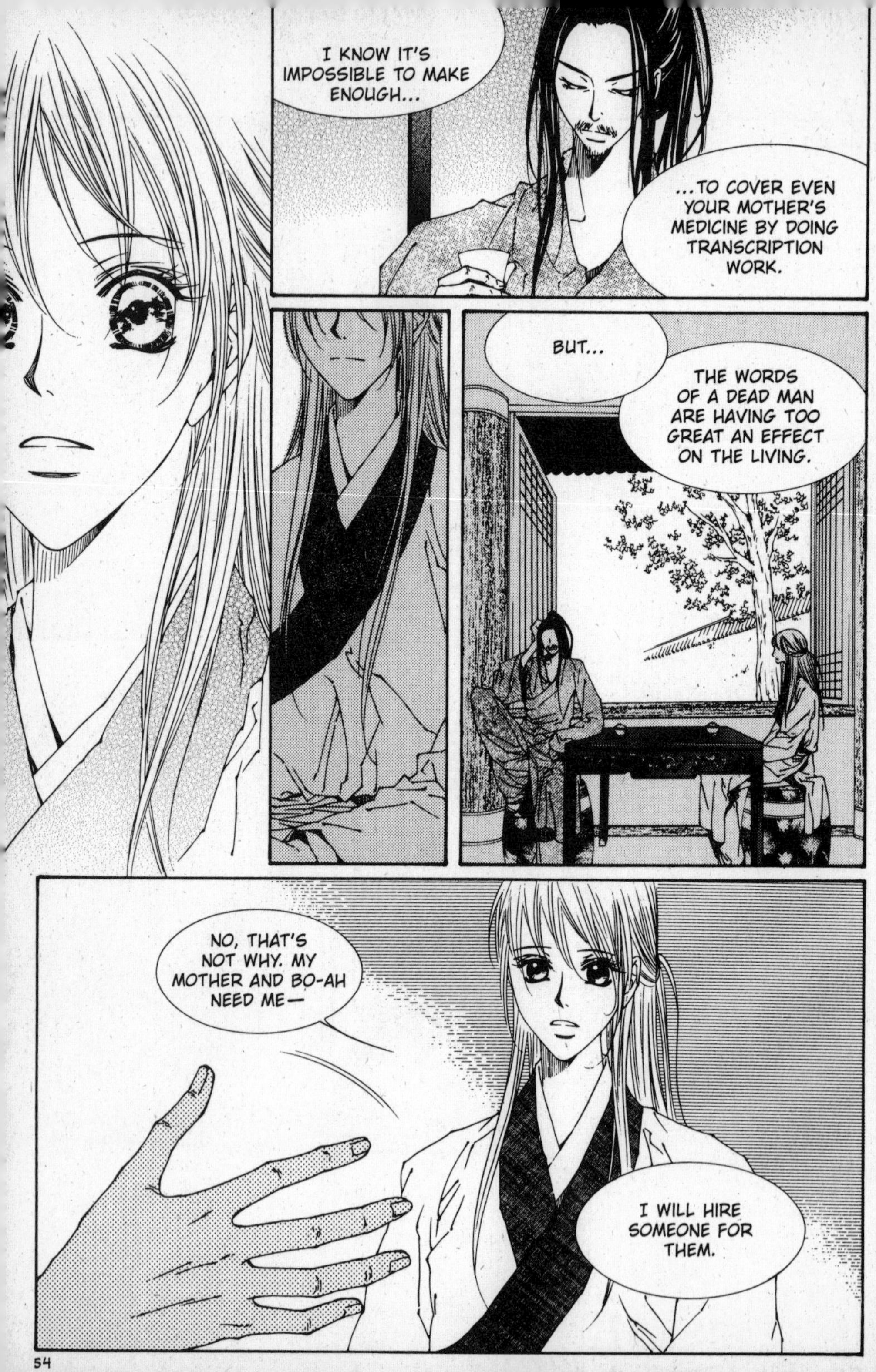
I KNOW IT'S IMPOSSIBLE TO MAKE ENOUGH...
...TO COVER EVEN YOUR MOTHER'S MEDICINE BY DOING TRANSCRIPTION WORK.
BUT...
THE WORDS OF A DEAD MAN ARE HAVING TOO GREAT AN EFFECT ON THE LIVING.
NO, THAT'S NOT WHY. MY MOTHER AND BO-AH NEED ME—
I WILL HIRE SOMEONE FOR THEM.

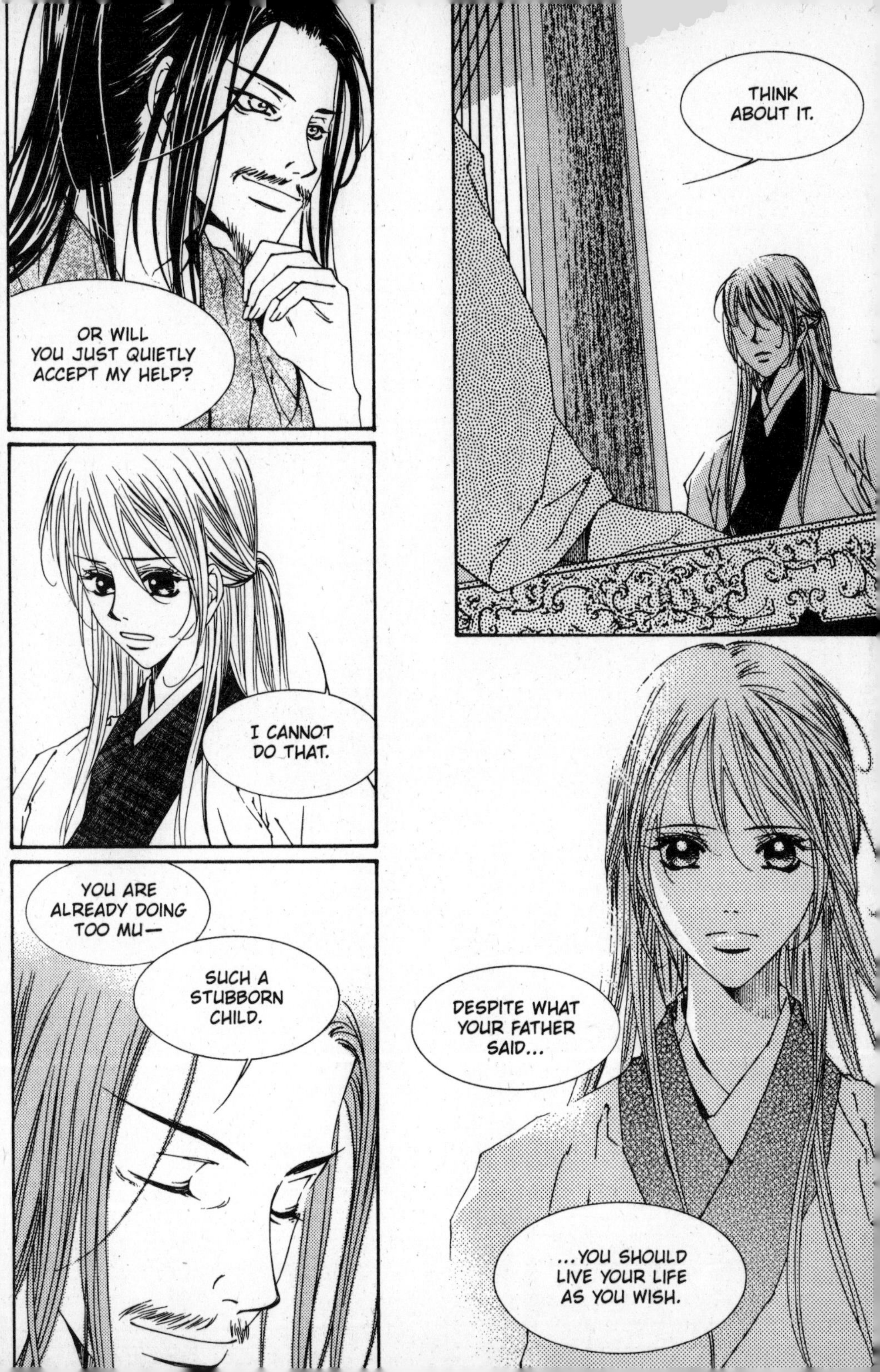
OR WILL YOU JUST QUIETLY ACCEPT MY HELP?
I CANNOT DO THAT.
YOU ARE ALREADY DOING TOO MU—
SUCH A STUBBORN CHILD.
THINK ABOUT IT.
DESPITE WHAT YOUR FATHER SAID...
...YOU SHOULD LIVE YOUR LIFE AS YOU WISH.

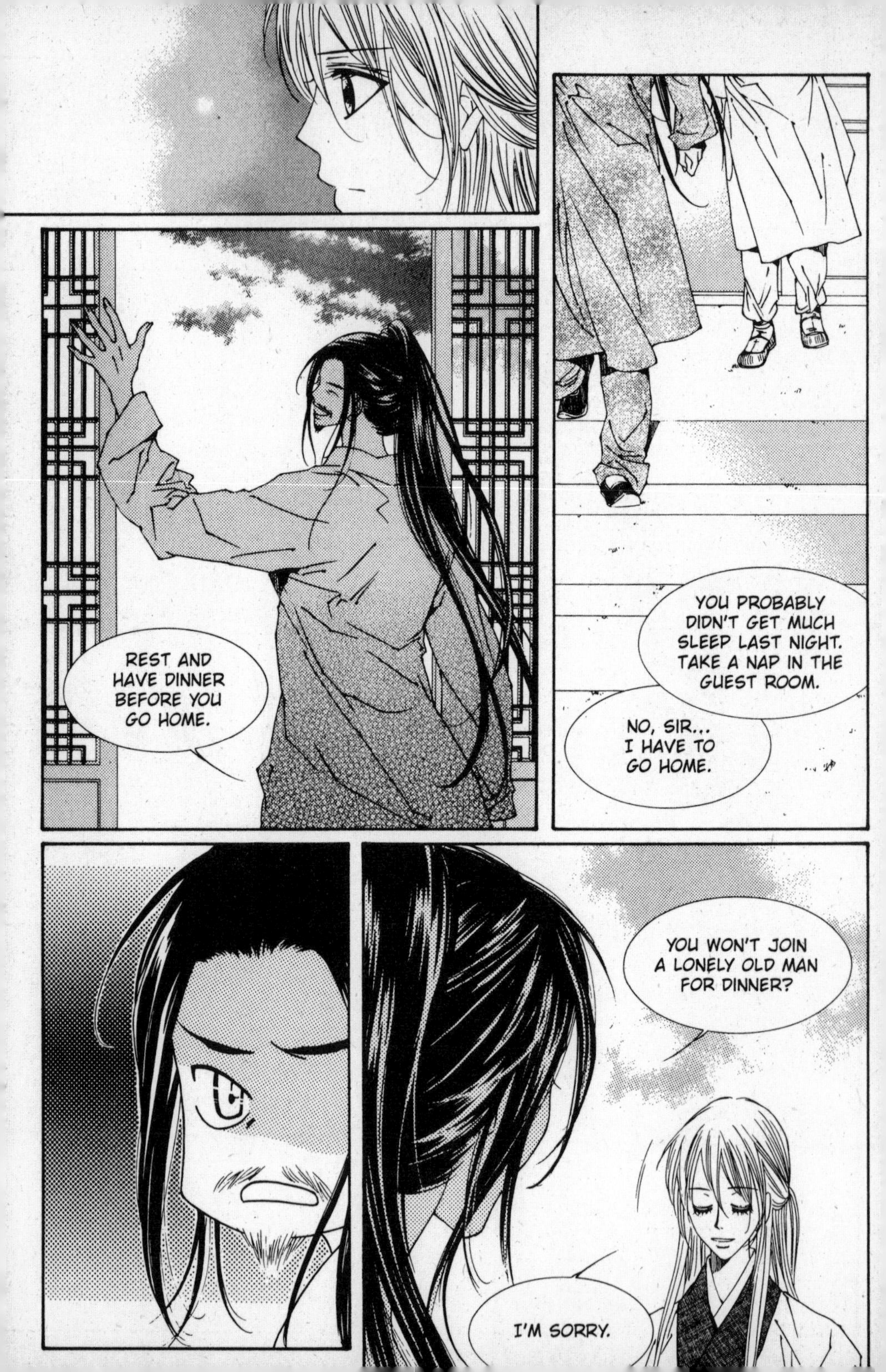
REST AND HAVE DINNER BEFORE YOU GO HOME.
YOU PROBABLY DIDN'T GET MUCH SLEEP LAST NIGHT. TAKE A NAP IN THE GUEST ROOM.
NO, SIR... I HAVE TO GO HOME.
YOU WON'T JOIN A LONELY OLD MAN FOR DINNER?
I'M SORRY.

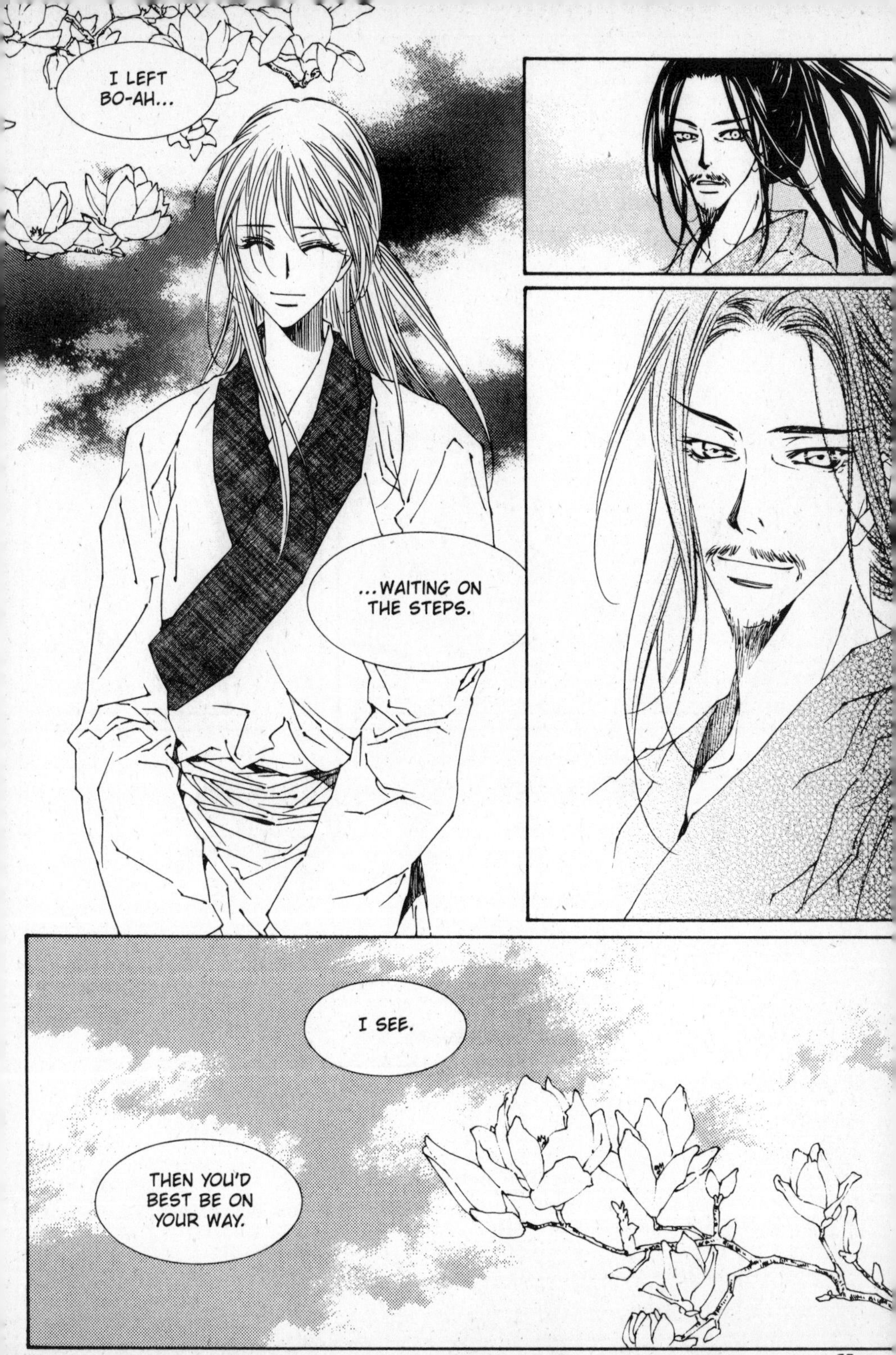
I LEFT BO-AH...
...WAITING ON THE STEPS.
I SEE.
THEN YOU'D BEST BE ON YOUR WAY.

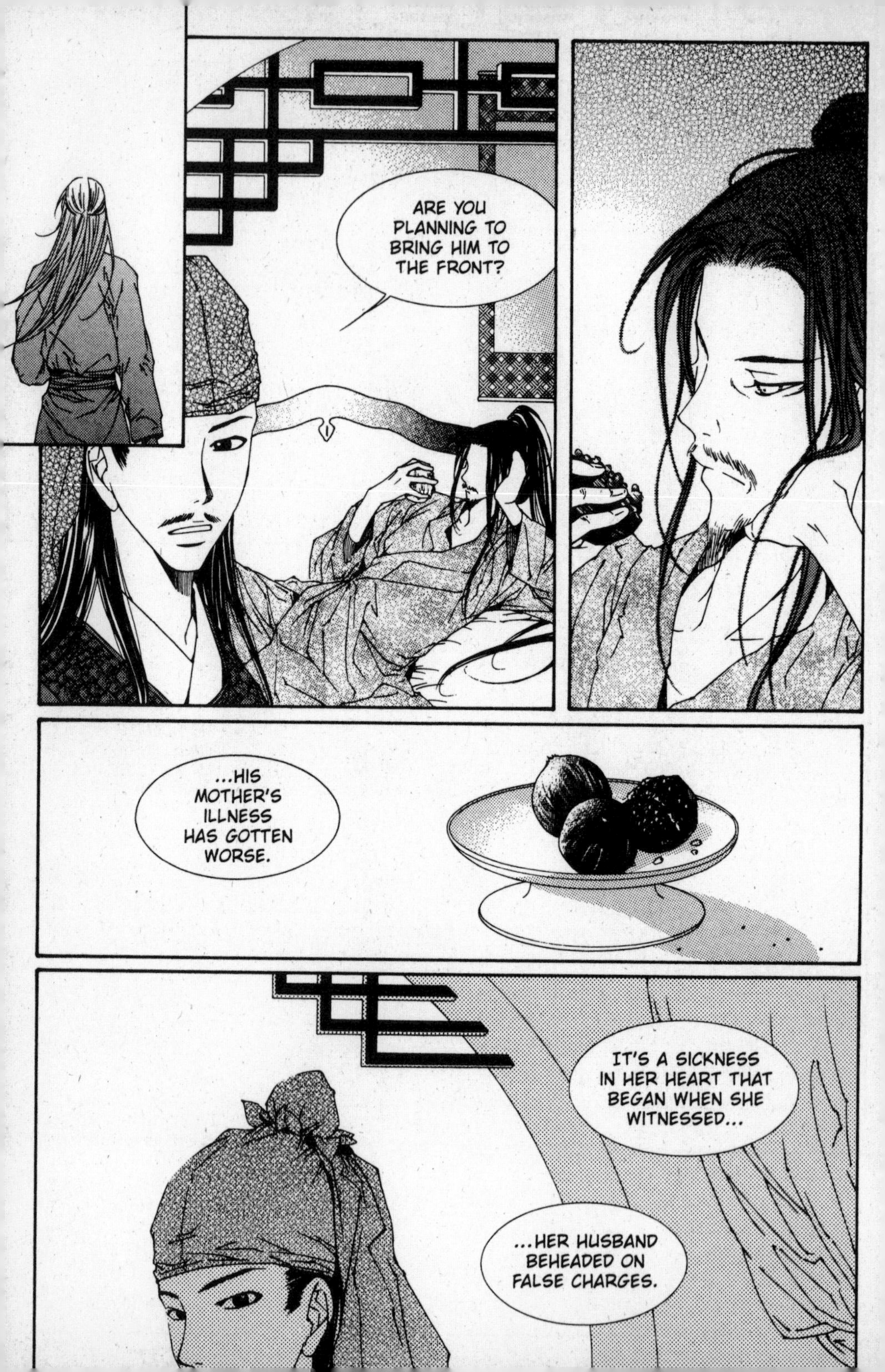
ARE YOU PLANNING TO BRING HIM TO THE FRONT?
...HIS MOTHER'S ILLNESS HAS GOTTEN WORSE.
IT'S A SICKNESS IN HER HEART THAT BEGAN WHEN SHE WITNESSED...
...HER HUSBAND BEHEADED ON FALSE CHARGES.

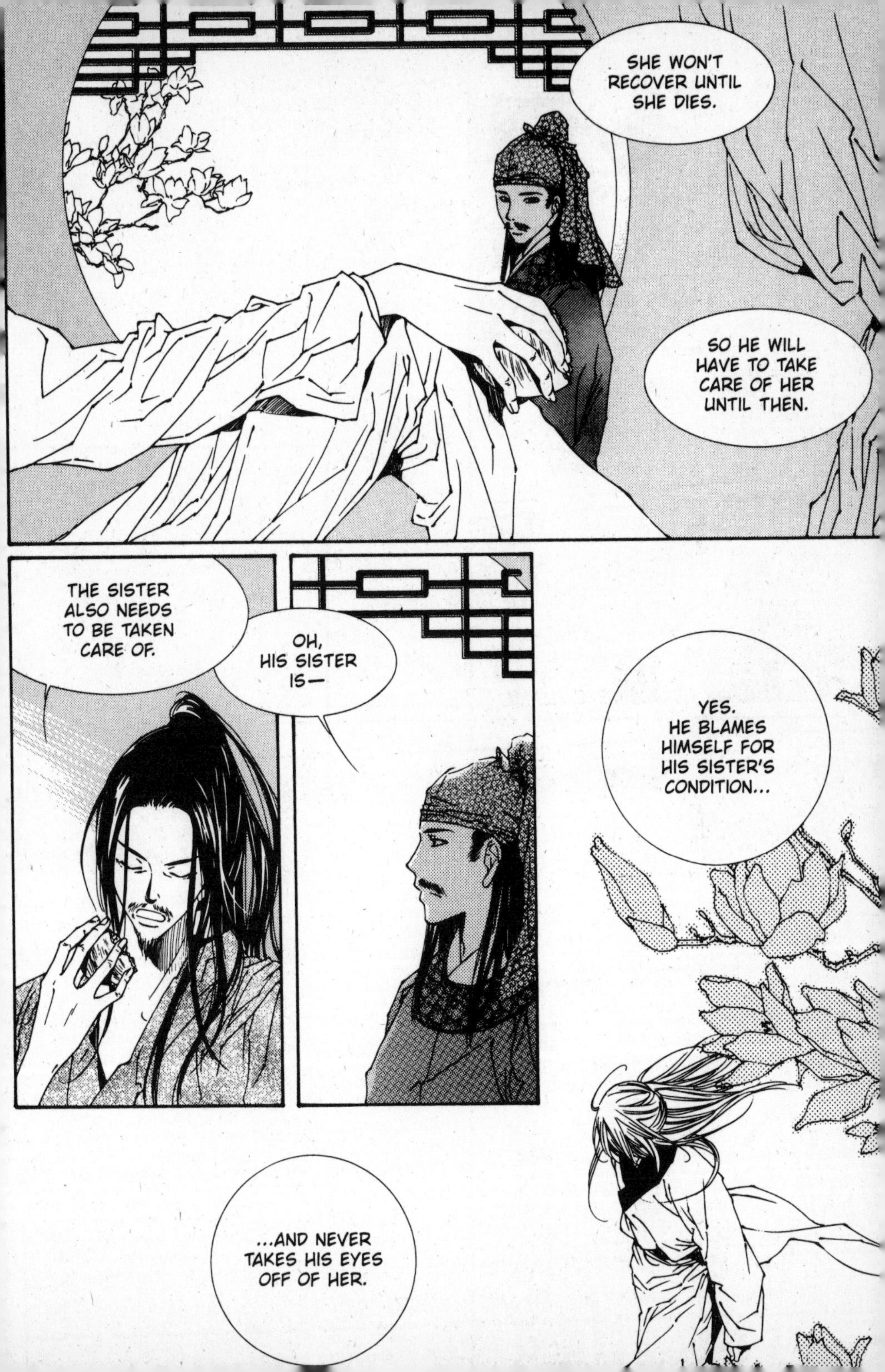
SHE WON'T RECOVER UNTIL SHE DIES.
SO HE WILL HAVE TO TAKE CARE OF HER UNTIL THEN.
THE SISTER ALSO NEEDS TO BE TAKEN CARE OF.
OH, HIS SISTER IS—
YES. HE BLAMES HIMSELF FOR HIS SISTER'S CONDITION...
...AND NEVER TAKES HIS EYES OFF OF HER.

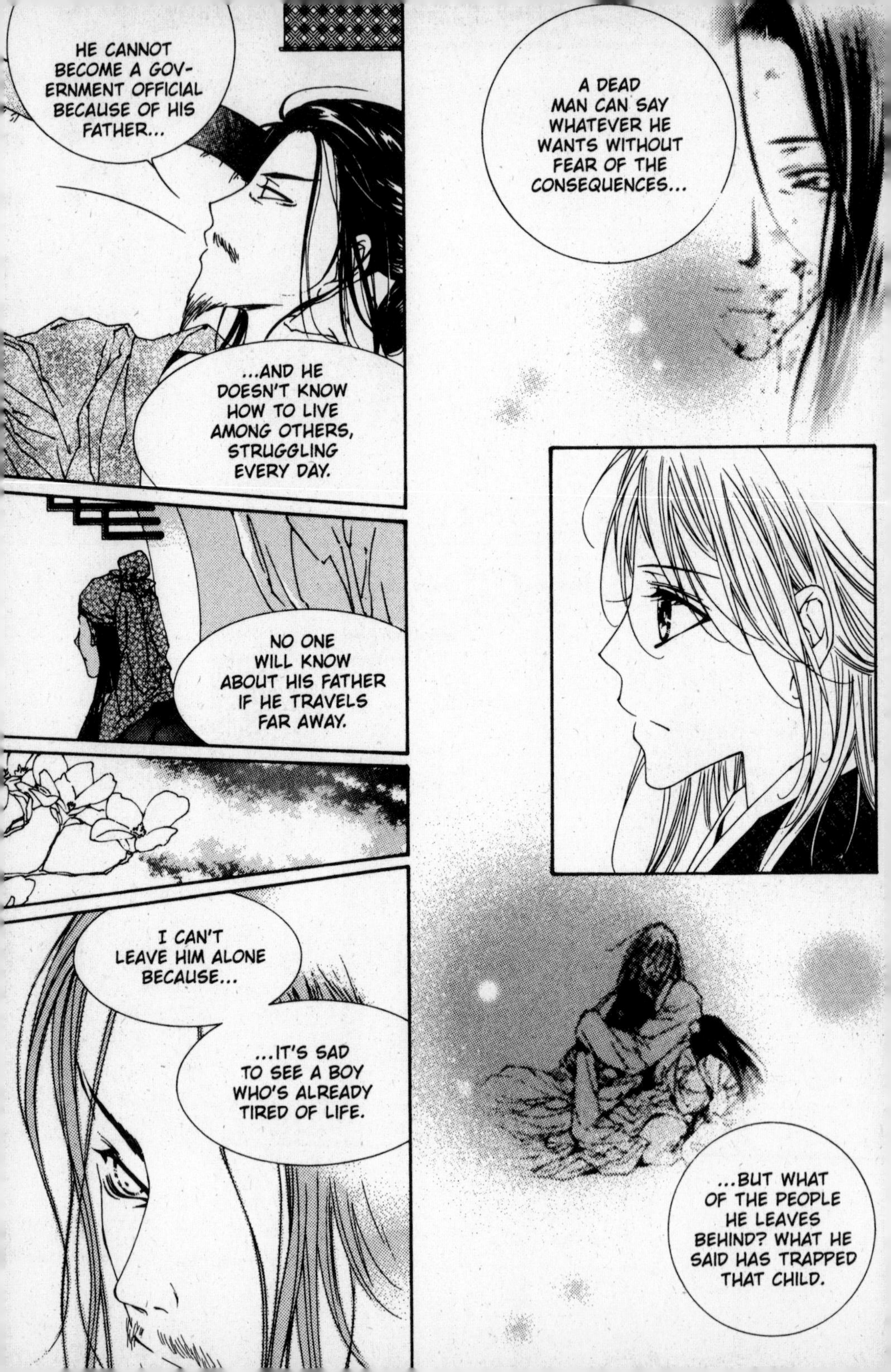
HE CANNOT BECOME A GOVERNMENT OFFICIAL BECAUSE OF HIS FATHER...
...AND HE DOESN'T KNOW HOW TO LIVE AMONG OTHERS, STRUGGLING EVERY DAY.
NO ONE WILL KNOW ABOUT HIS FATHER IF HE TRAVELS FAR AWAY.
I CAN'T LEAVE HIM ALONE BECAUSE...
...IT'S SAD TO SEE A BOY WHO'S ALREADY TIRED OF LIFE.
A DEAD MAN CAN SAY WHATEVER HE WANTS WITHOUT FEAR OF THE CONSEQUENCES...
...BUT WHAT OF THE PEOPLE HE LEAVES BEHIND? WHAT HE SAID HAS TRAPPED THAT CHILD.

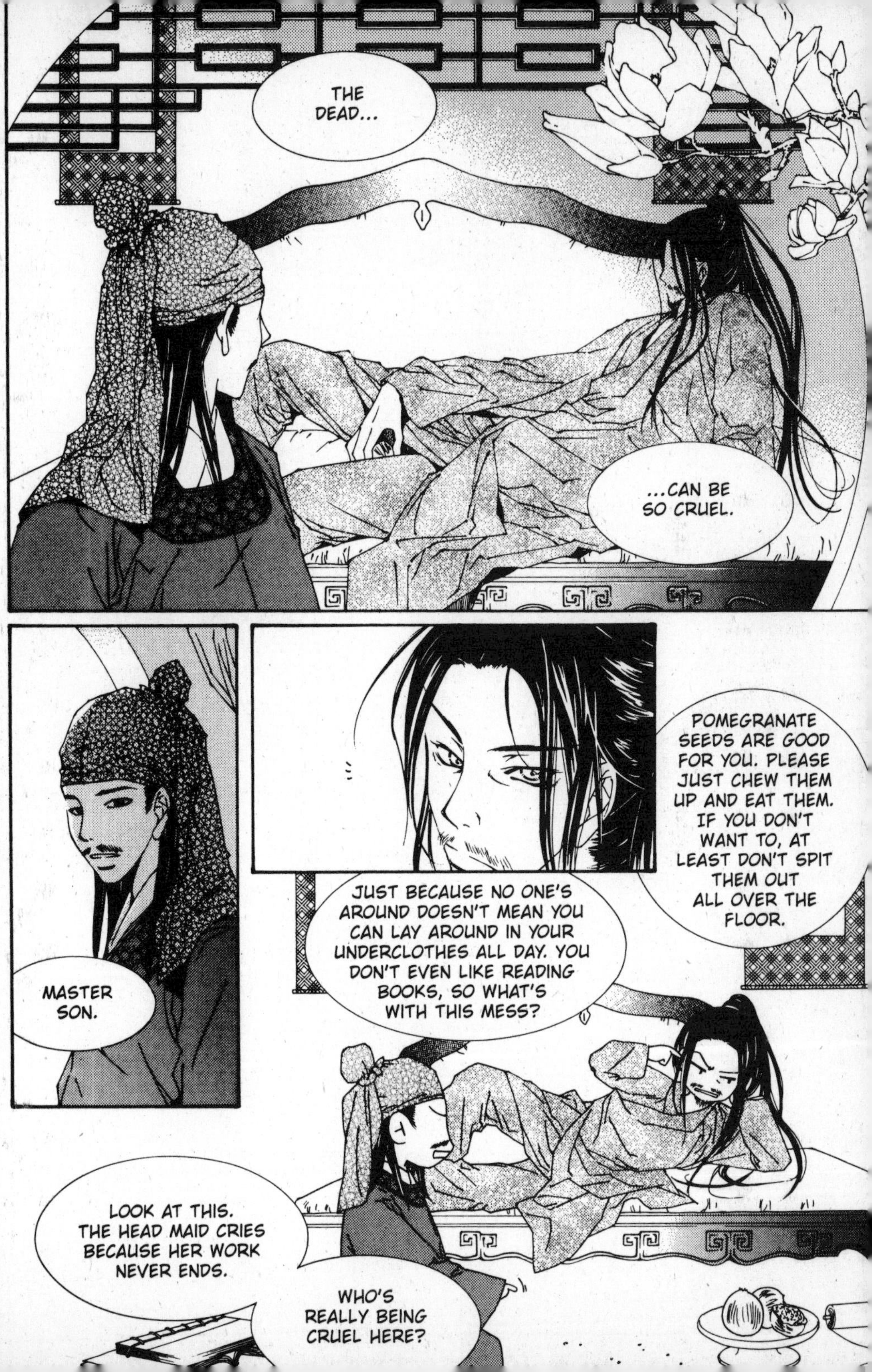
THE DEAD...
...CAN BE SO CRUEL.
MASTER SON.
POMEGRANATE SEEDS ARE GOOD FOR YOU. PLEASE JUST CHEW THEM UP AND EAT THEM. IF YOU DON'T WANT TO, AT LEAST DON'T SPIT THEM OUT ALL OVER THE FLOOR.
JUST BECAUSE NO ONE'S AROUND DOESN'T MEAN YOU CAN LAY AROUND IN YOUR UNDERCLOTHES ALL DAY. YOU DON'T EVEN LIKE READING BOOKS, SO WHAT'S WITH THIS MESS?
LOOK AT THIS. THE HEAD MAID CRIES BECAUSE HER WORK NEVER ENDS.
WHO'S REALLY BEING CRUEL HERE?

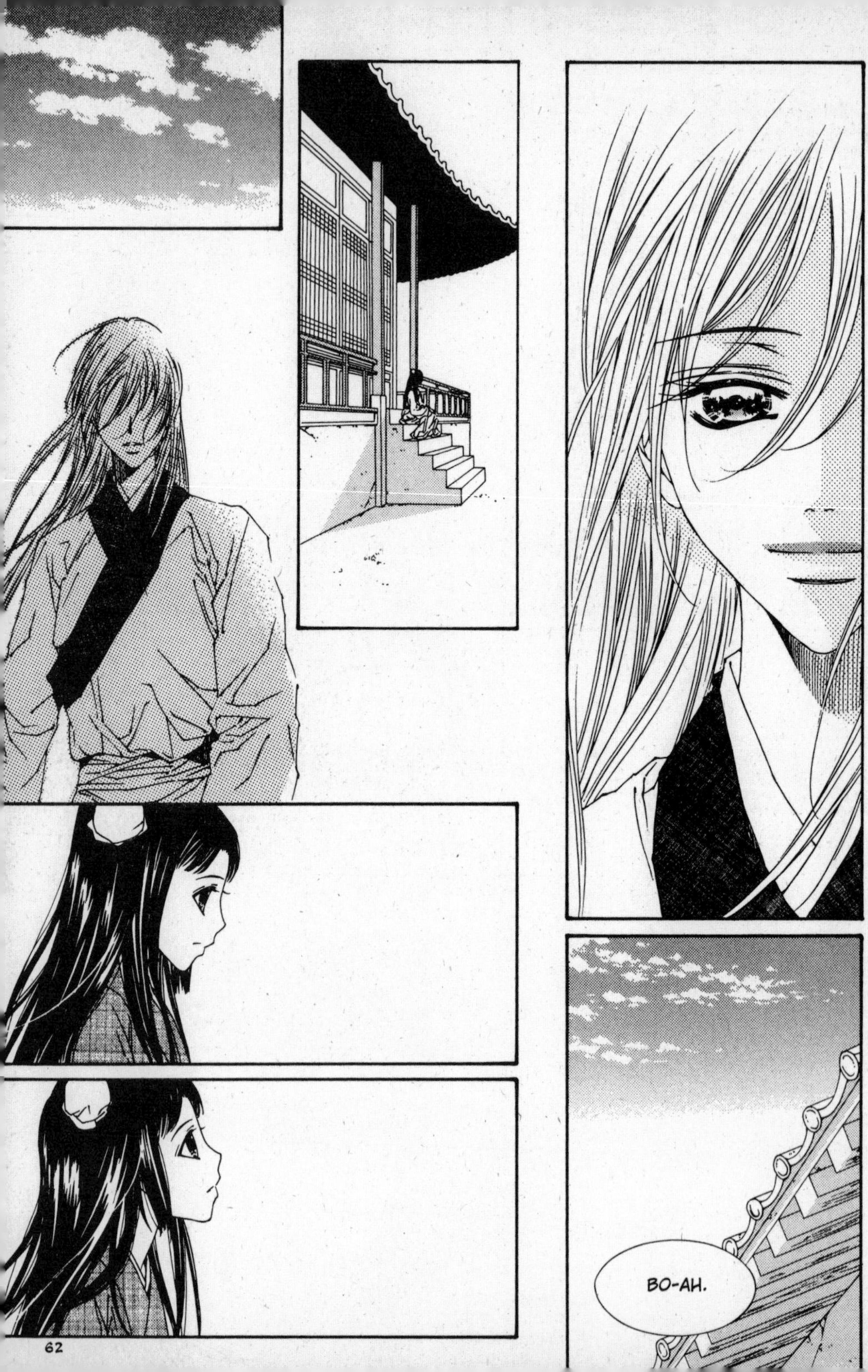
BO-AH.

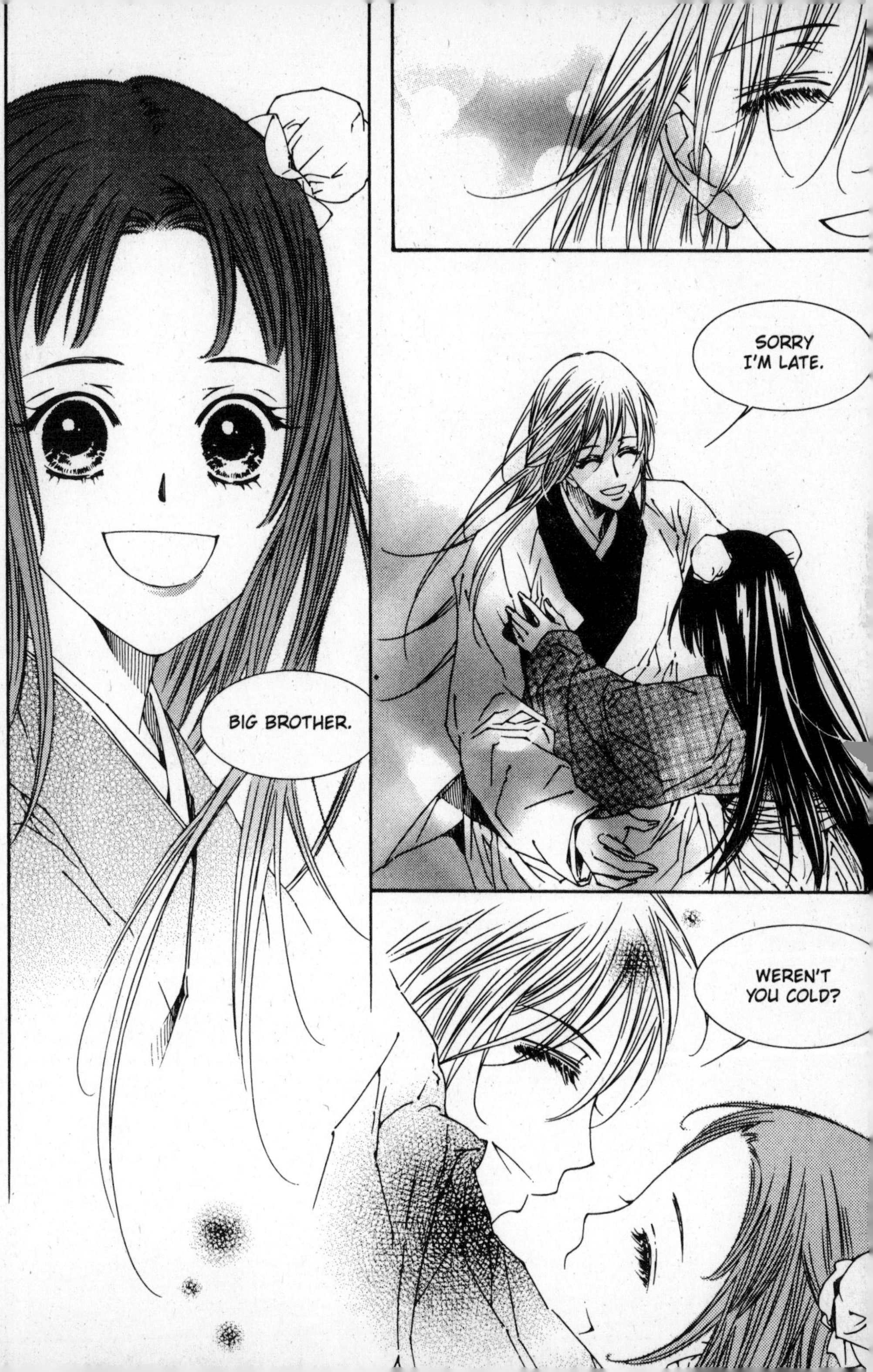
BIG BROTHER.
SORRY I'M LATE.
WEREN'T YOU COLD?

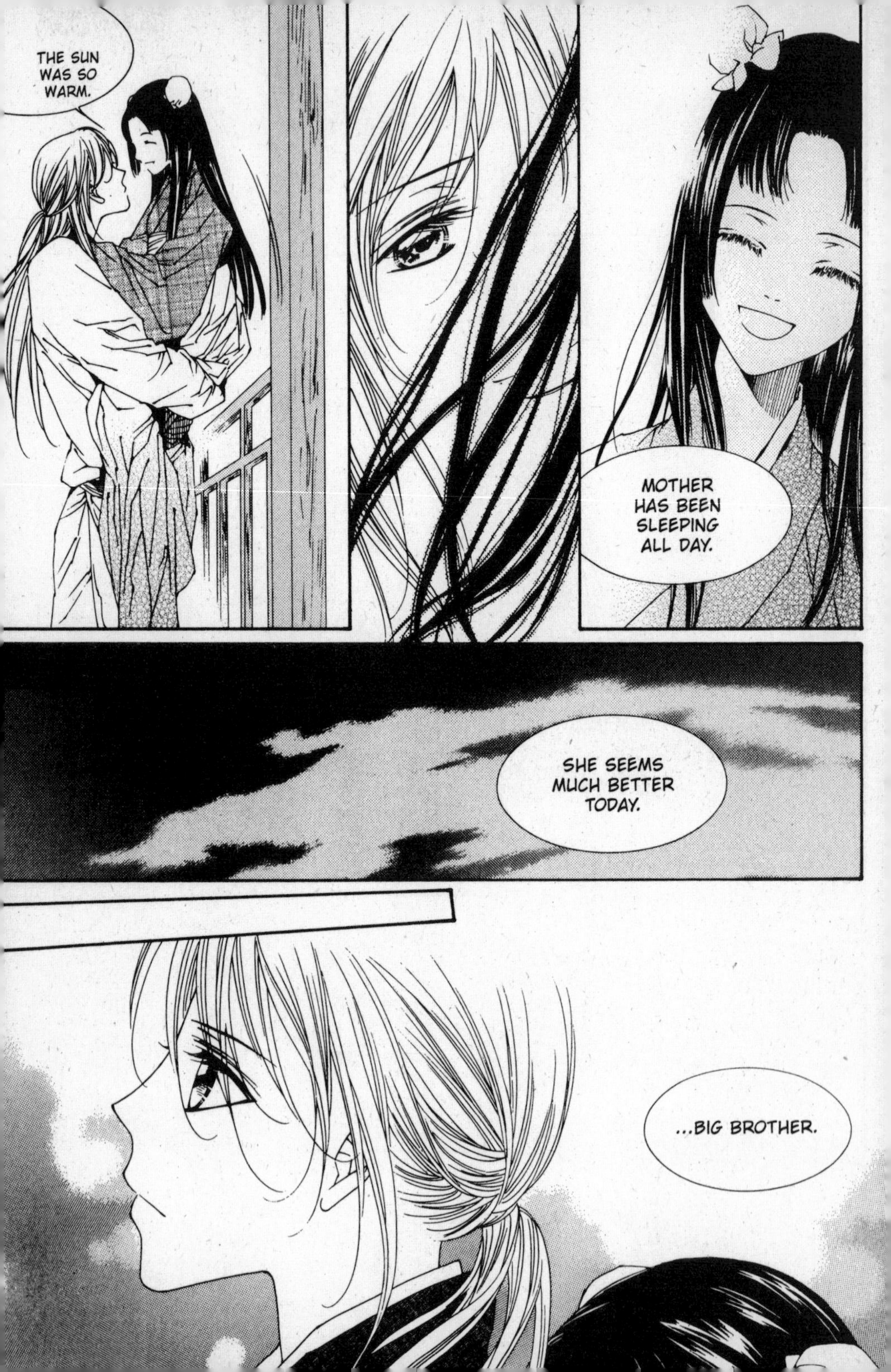
THE SUN WAS SO WARM.
MOTHER HAS BEEN SLEEPING ALL DAY.
SHE SEEMS MUCH BETTER TODAY.
...BIG BROTHER.

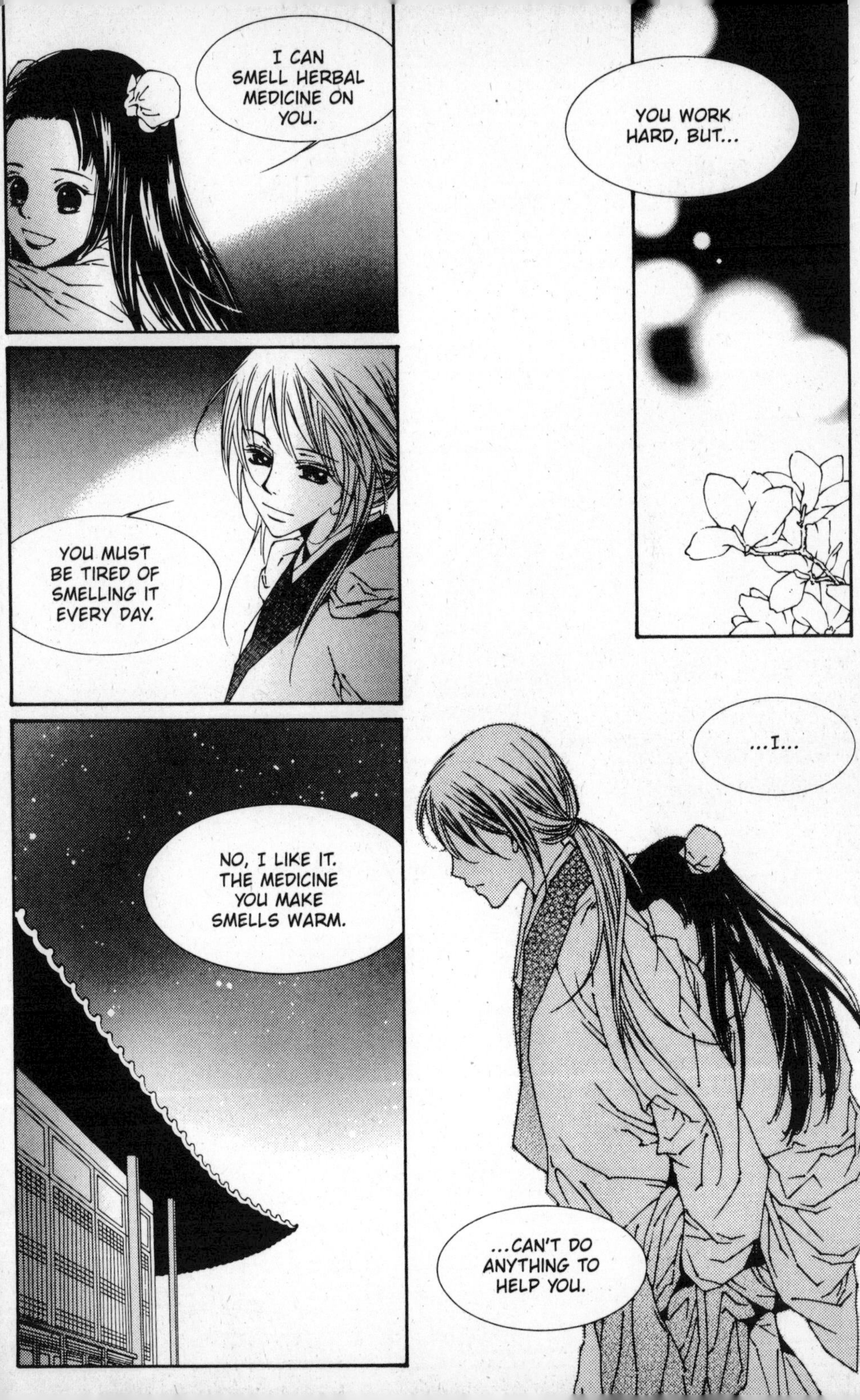
I CAN SMELL HERBAL MEDICINE ON YOU.
YOU MUST BE TIRED OF SMELLING IT EVERY DAY.
YOU WORK HARD, BUT...
NO, I LIKE IT. THE MEDICINE YOU MAKE SMELLS WARM.
...I...
...CAN'T DO ANYTHING TO HELP YOU.

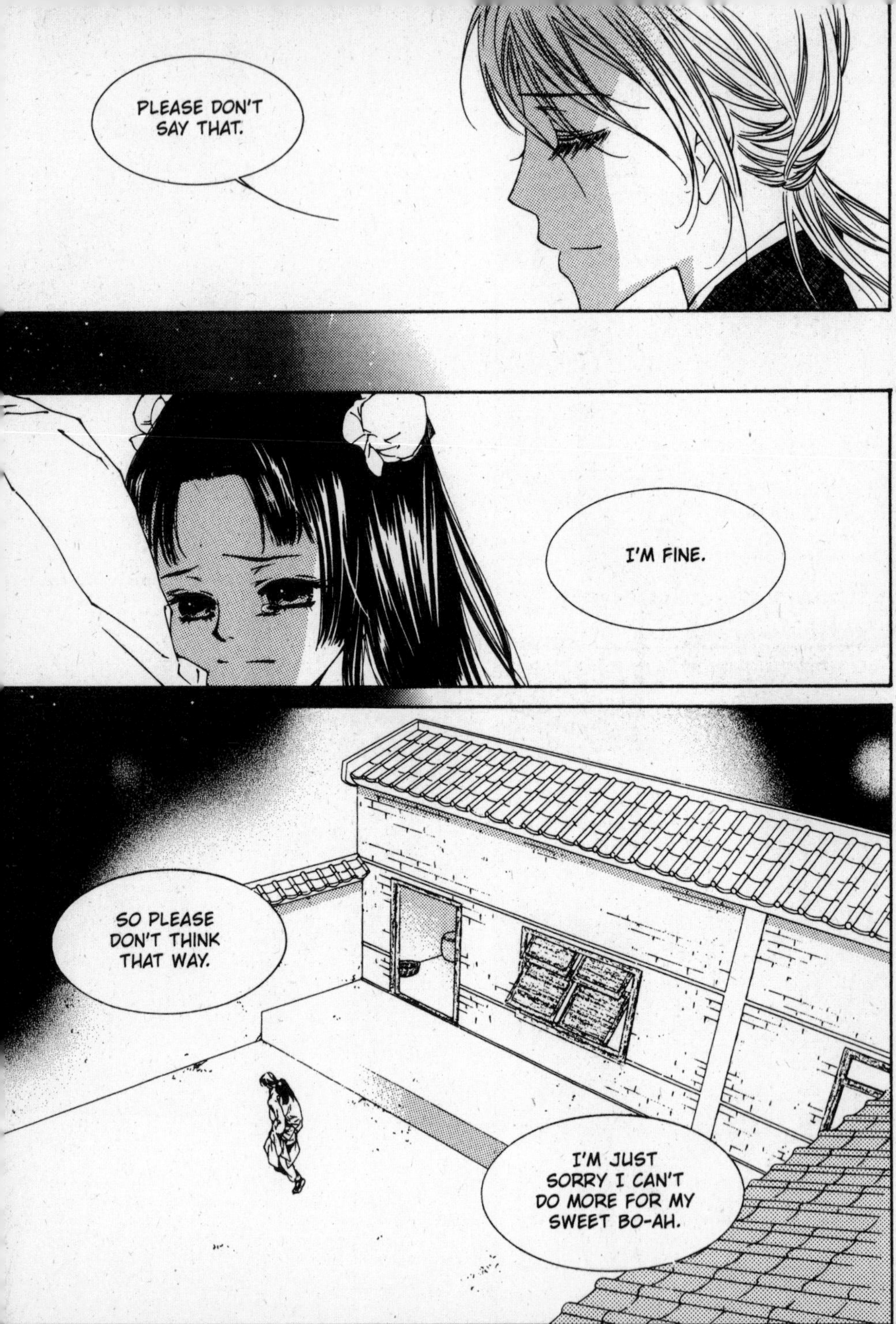
PLEASE DON'T SAY THAT.
I'M FINE.
SO PLEASE DON'T THINK THAT WAY.
I'M JUST SORRY I CAN'T DO MORE FOR MY SWEET BO-AH.

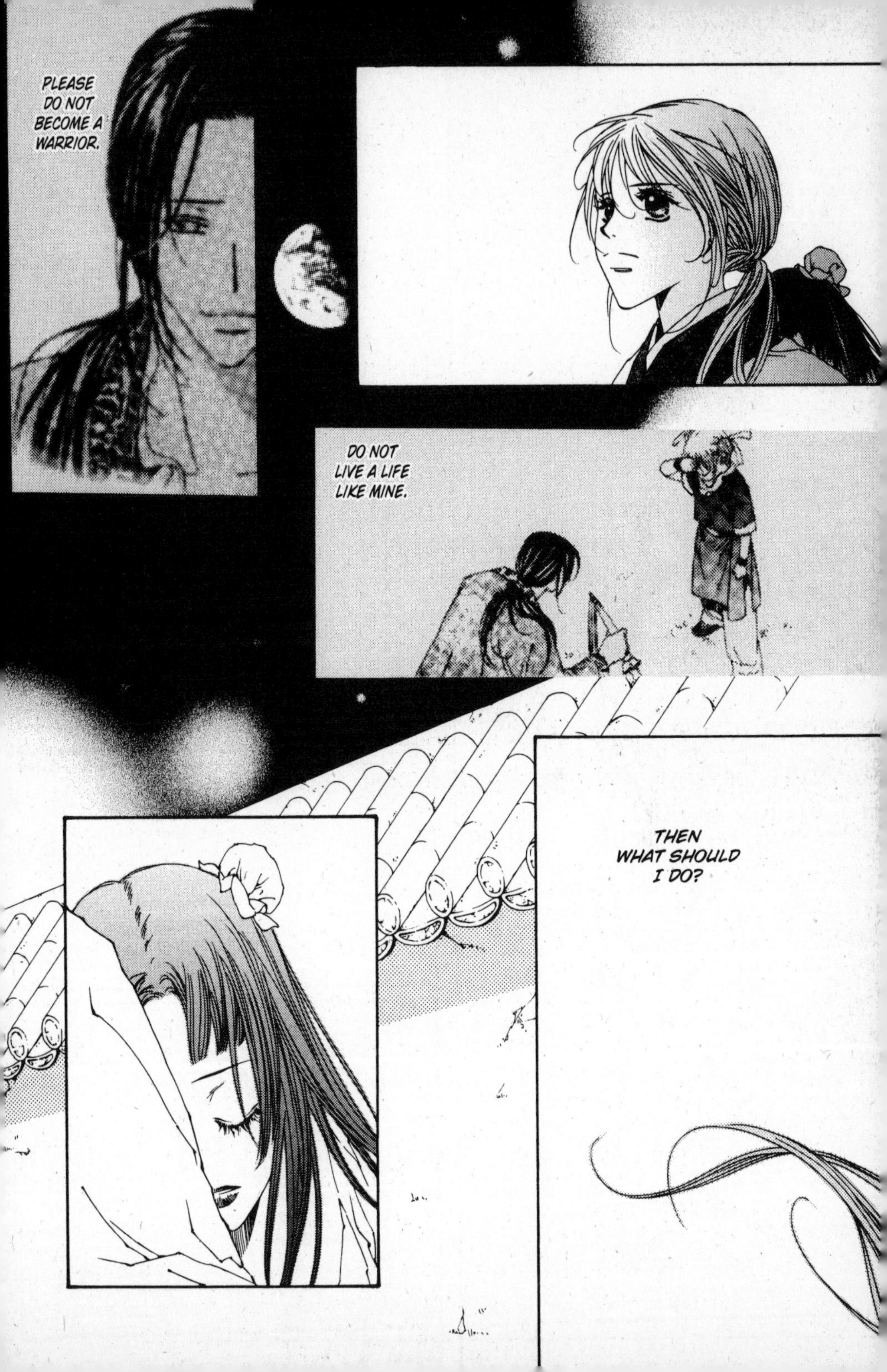
PLEASE DO NOT BECOME A WARRIOR.
DO NOT LIVE A LIFE LIKE MINE.
THEN WHAT SHOULD I DO?

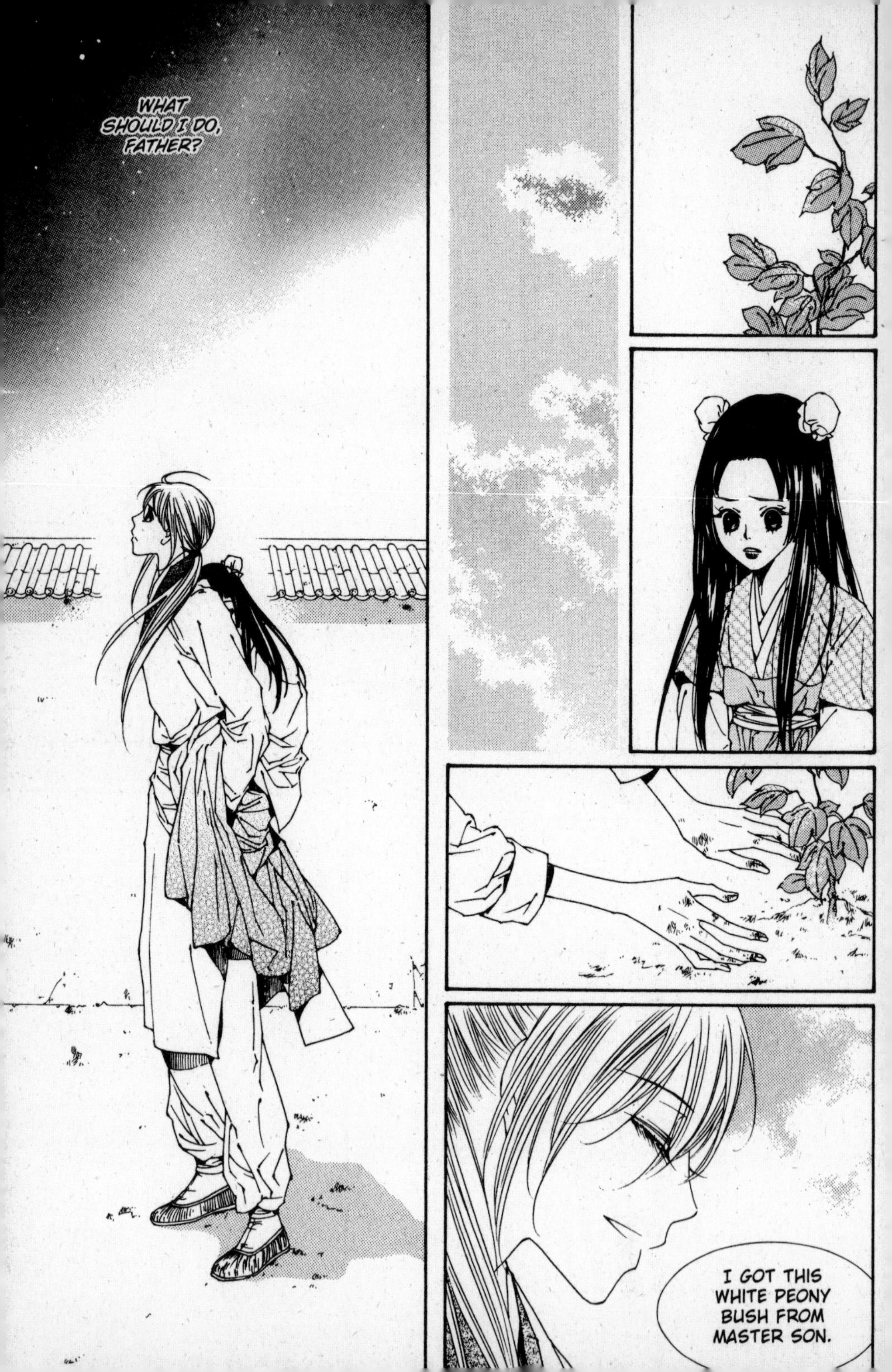
WHAT SHOULD I DO, FATHER?
I GOT THIS WHITE PEONY BUSH FROM MASTER SON.

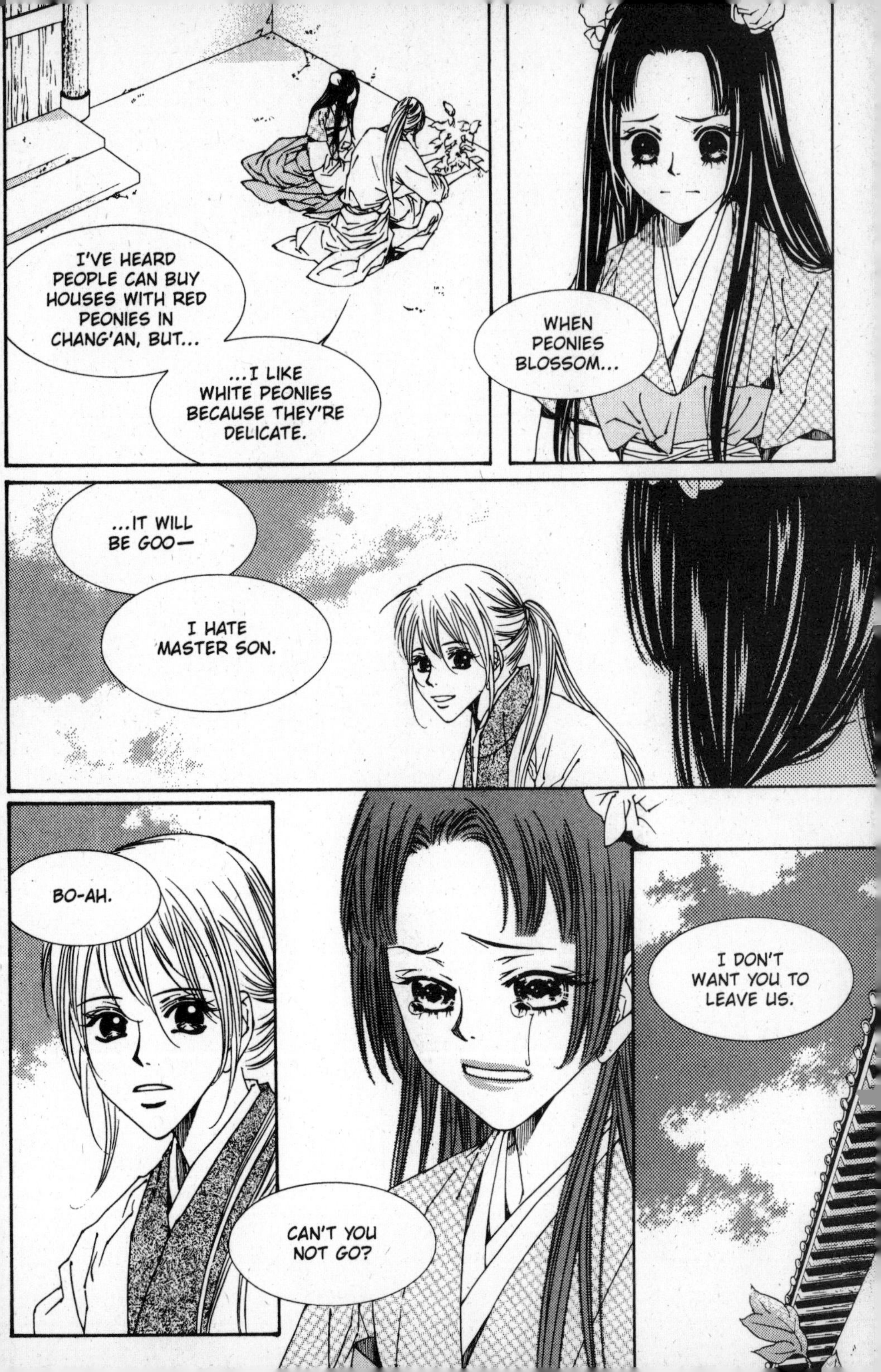
I'VE HEARD PEOPLE CAN BUY HOUSES WITH RED PEONIES IN CHANG'AN, BUT...
...I LIKE WHITE PEONIES BECAUSE THEY'RE DELICATE.
WHEN PEONIES BLOSSOM...
...IT WILL BE GOO—
I HATE MASTER SON.
BO-AH.
CAN'T YOU NOT GO?
I DON'T WANT YOU TO LEAVE US.

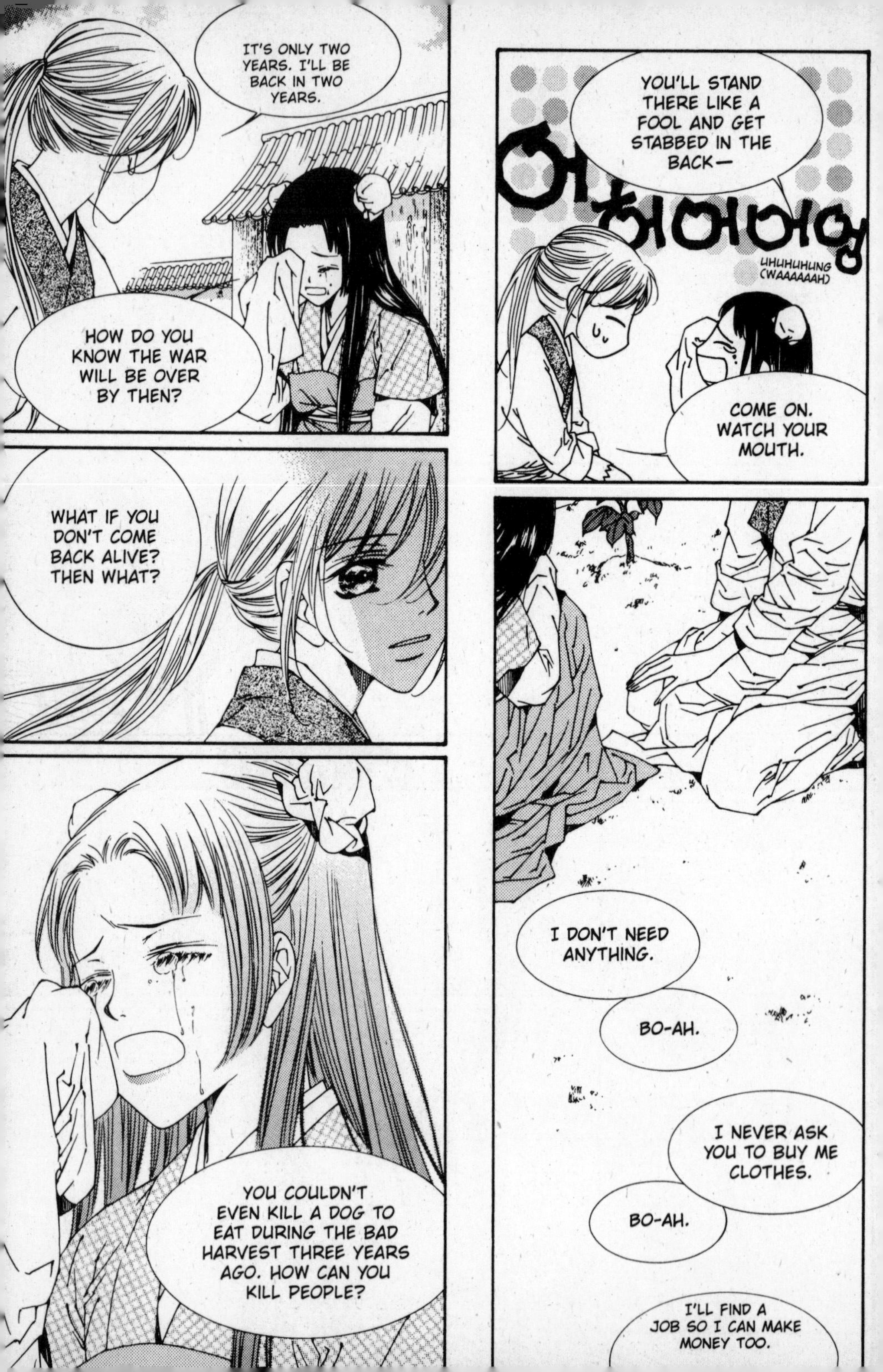

IT'S ONLY TWO YEARS. I'LL BE BACK IN TWO YEARS.
HOW DO YOU KNOW THE WAR WILL BE OVER BY THEN?
WHAT IF YOU DON'T COME BACK ALIVE? THEN WHAT?
YOU COULDN'T EVEN KILL A DOG TO EAT DURING THE BAD HARVEST THREE YEARS AGO. HOW CAN YOU KILL PEOPLE?
YOU'LL STAND THERE LIKE A FOOL AND GET STABBED IN THE BACK—
UHUHUHUNG (WAAAAAAH)
COME ON. WATCH YOUR MOUTH.
I DON'T NEED ANYTHING.
BO-AH.
I NEVER ASK YOU TO BUY ME CLOTHES.
BO-AH.
I'LL FIND A JOB SO I CAN MAKE MONEY TOO.

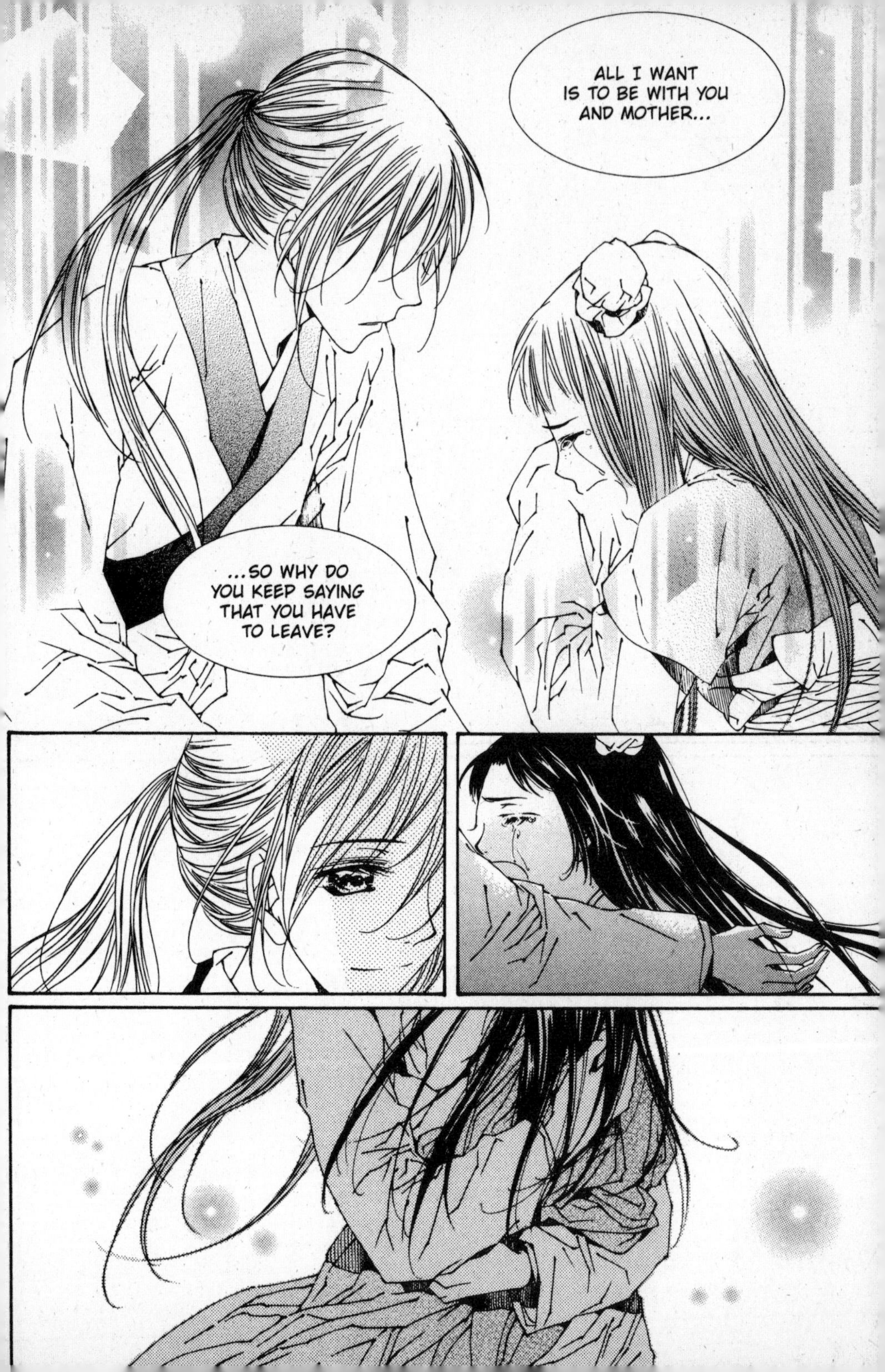
ALL I WANT IS TO BE WITH YOU AND MOTHER...
...SO WHY DO YOU KEEP SAYING THAT YOU HAVE TO LEAVE?

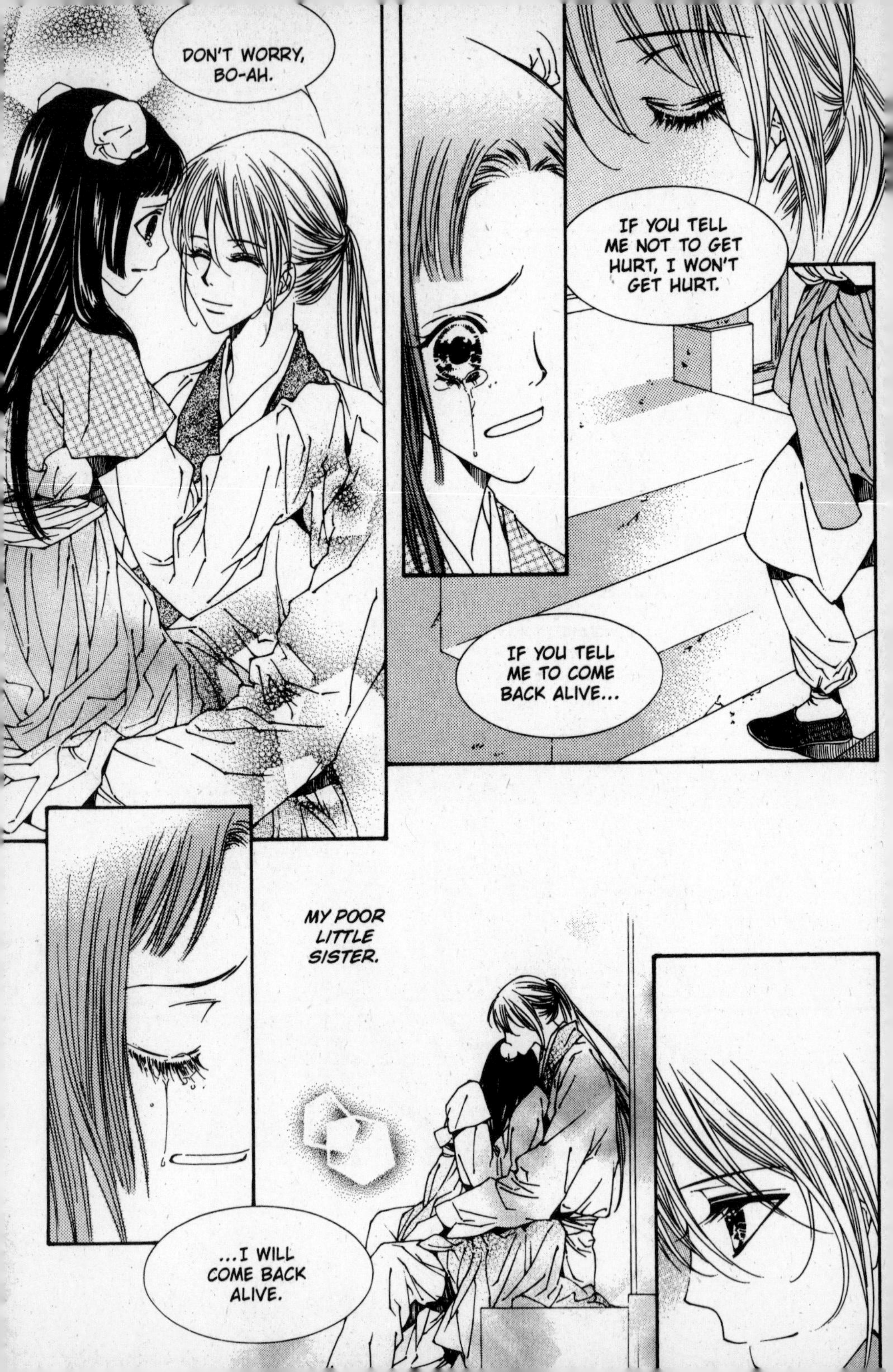
DON'T WORRY, BO-AH.
IF YOU TELL ME NOT TO GET HURT, I WON'T GET HURT.
IF YOU TELL ME TO COME BACK ALIVE...
MY POOR LITTLE SISTER.
...I WILL COME BACK ALIVE.

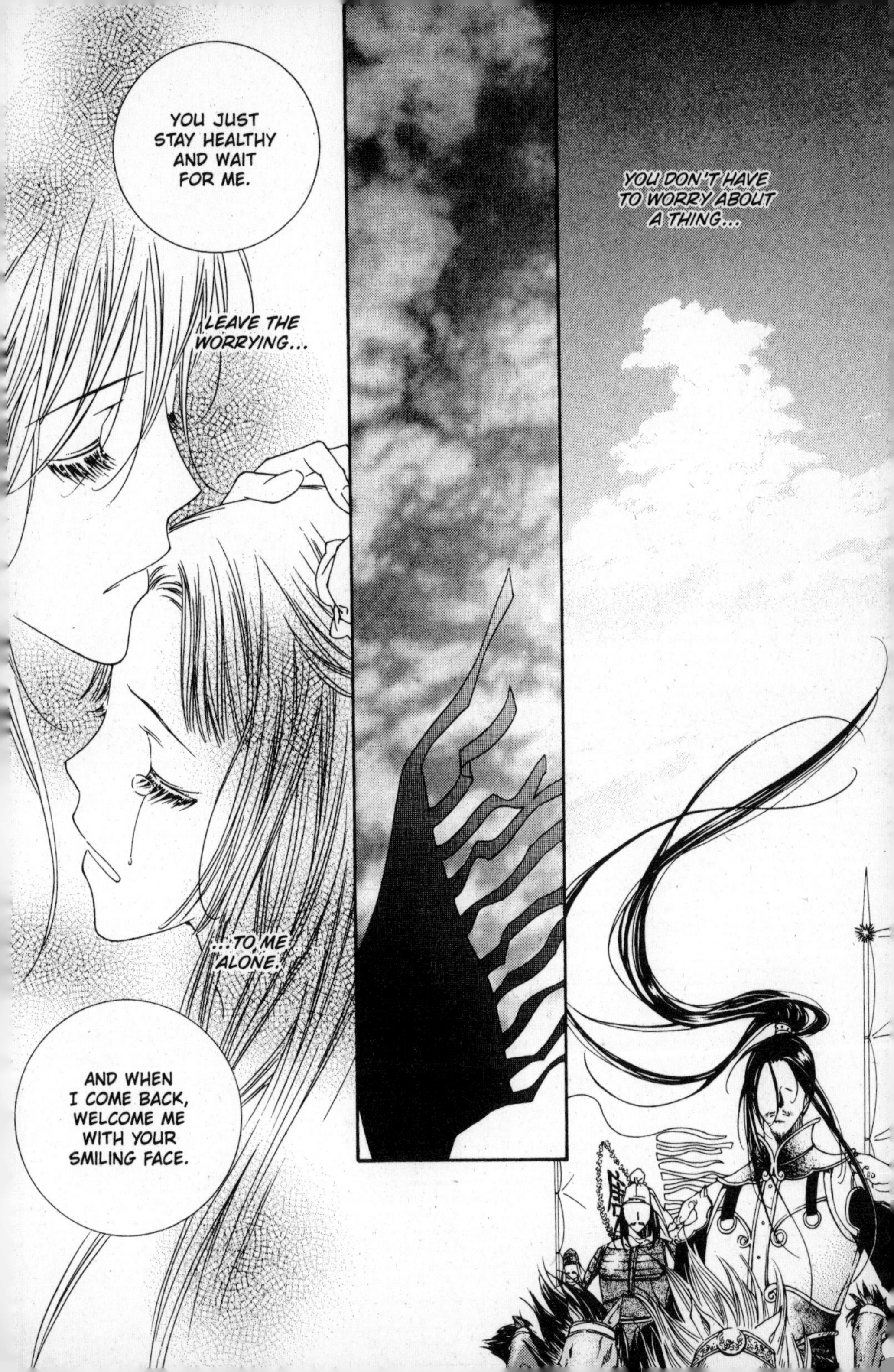
YOU JUST STAY HEALTHY AND WAIT FOR ME.
LEAVE THE WORRYING...
...TO ME ALONE.
AND WHEN I COME BACK, WELCOME ME WITH YOUR SMILING FACE.
YOU DON'T HAVE TO WORRY ABOUT A THING...

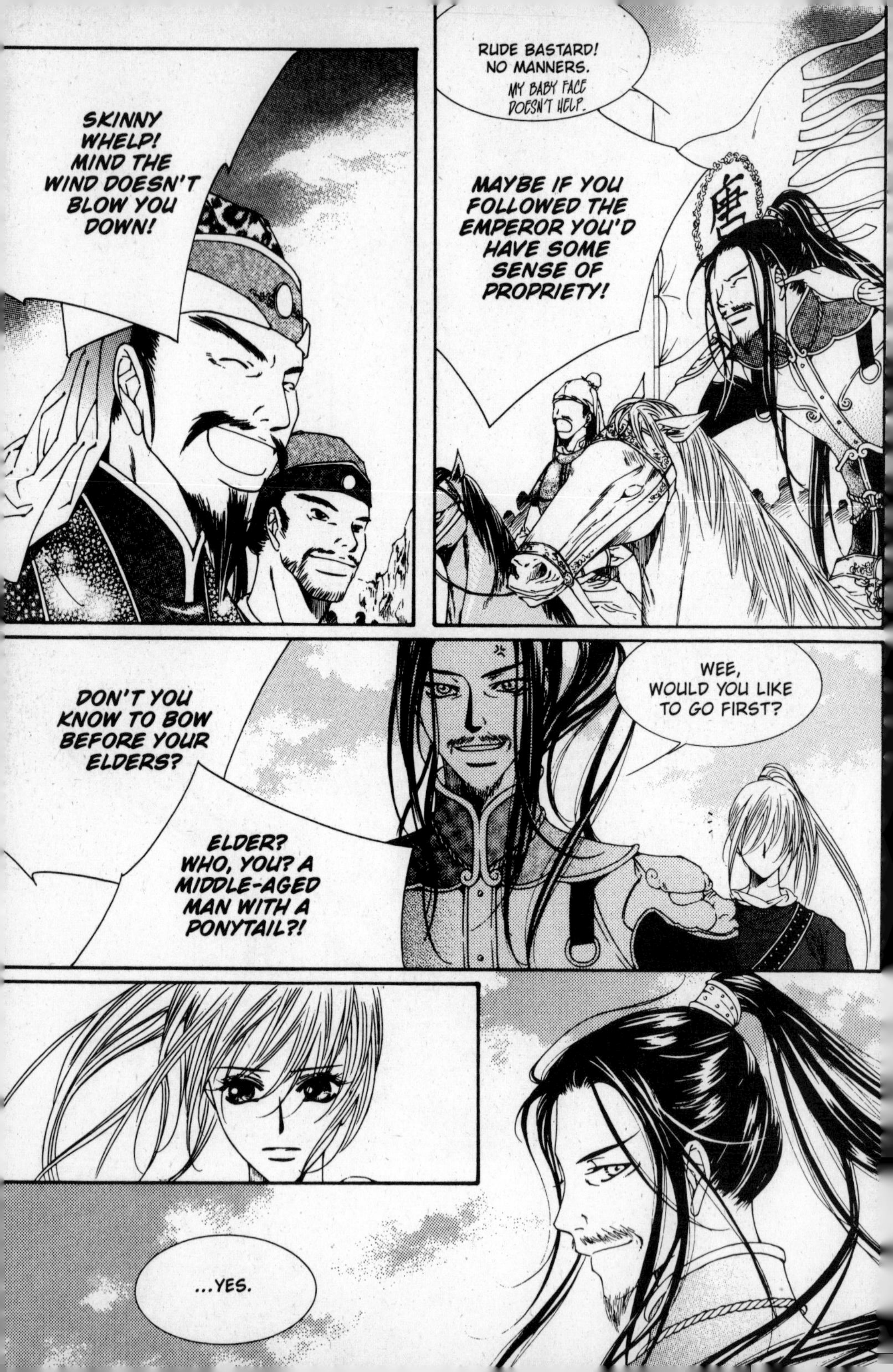
SKINNY WHELP! MIND THE WIND DOESN'T BLOW YOU DOWN!
RUDE BASTARD! NO MANNERS.
MY BABY FACE DOESN'T HELP.
MAYBE IF YOU FOLLOWED THE EMPEROR YOU'D HAVE SOME SENSE OF PROPRIETY!
DON'T YOU KNOW TO BOW BEFORE YOUR ELDERS?
ELDER? WHO, YOU? A MIDDLE-AGED MAN WITH A PONYTAIL?!
WEE, WOULD YOU LIKE TO GO FIRST?
...YES.

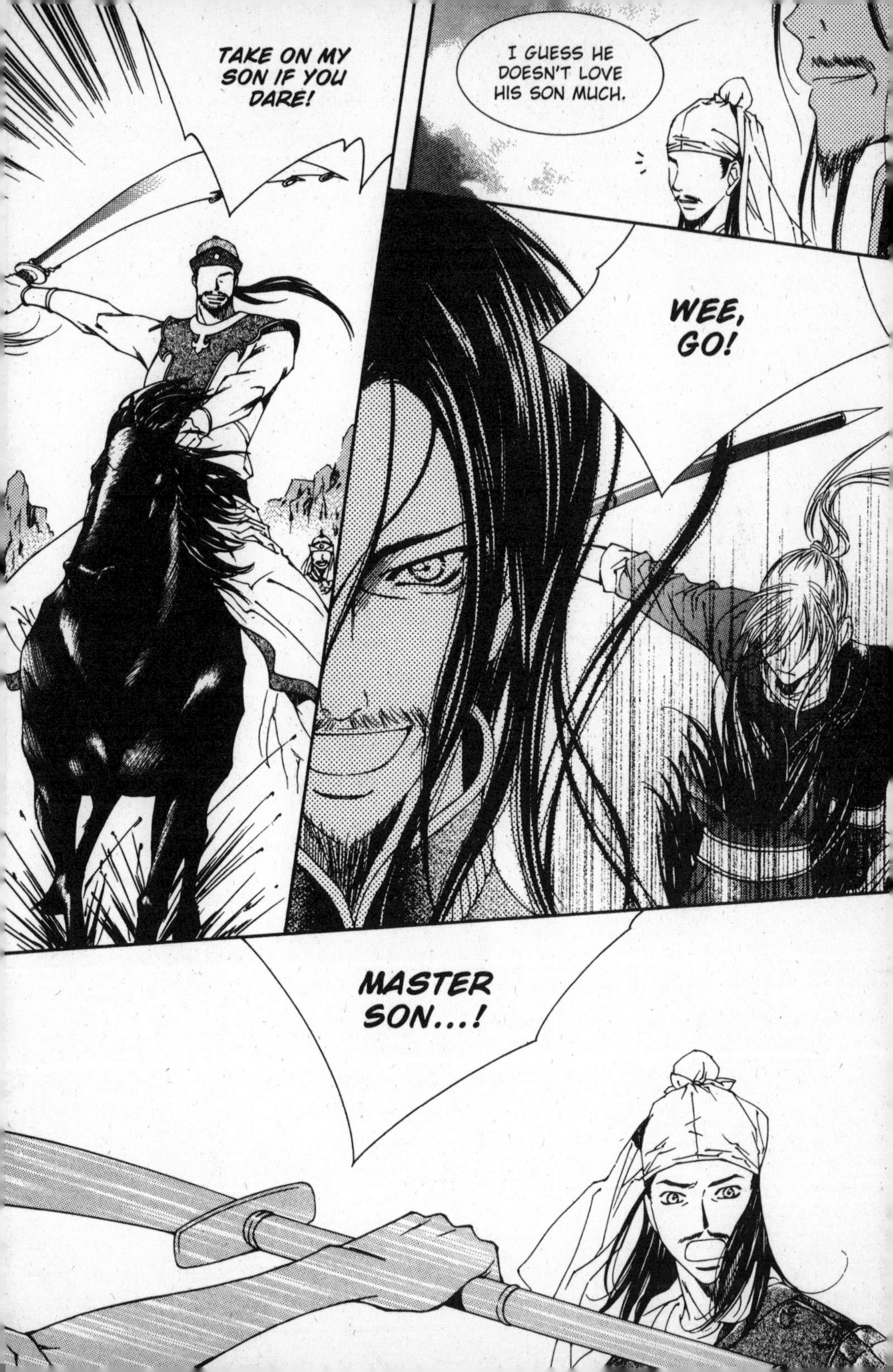
TAKE ON MY SON IF YOU DARE!
I GUESS HE DOESN'T LOVE HIS SON MUCH.
WEE, GO!
MASTER SON...!

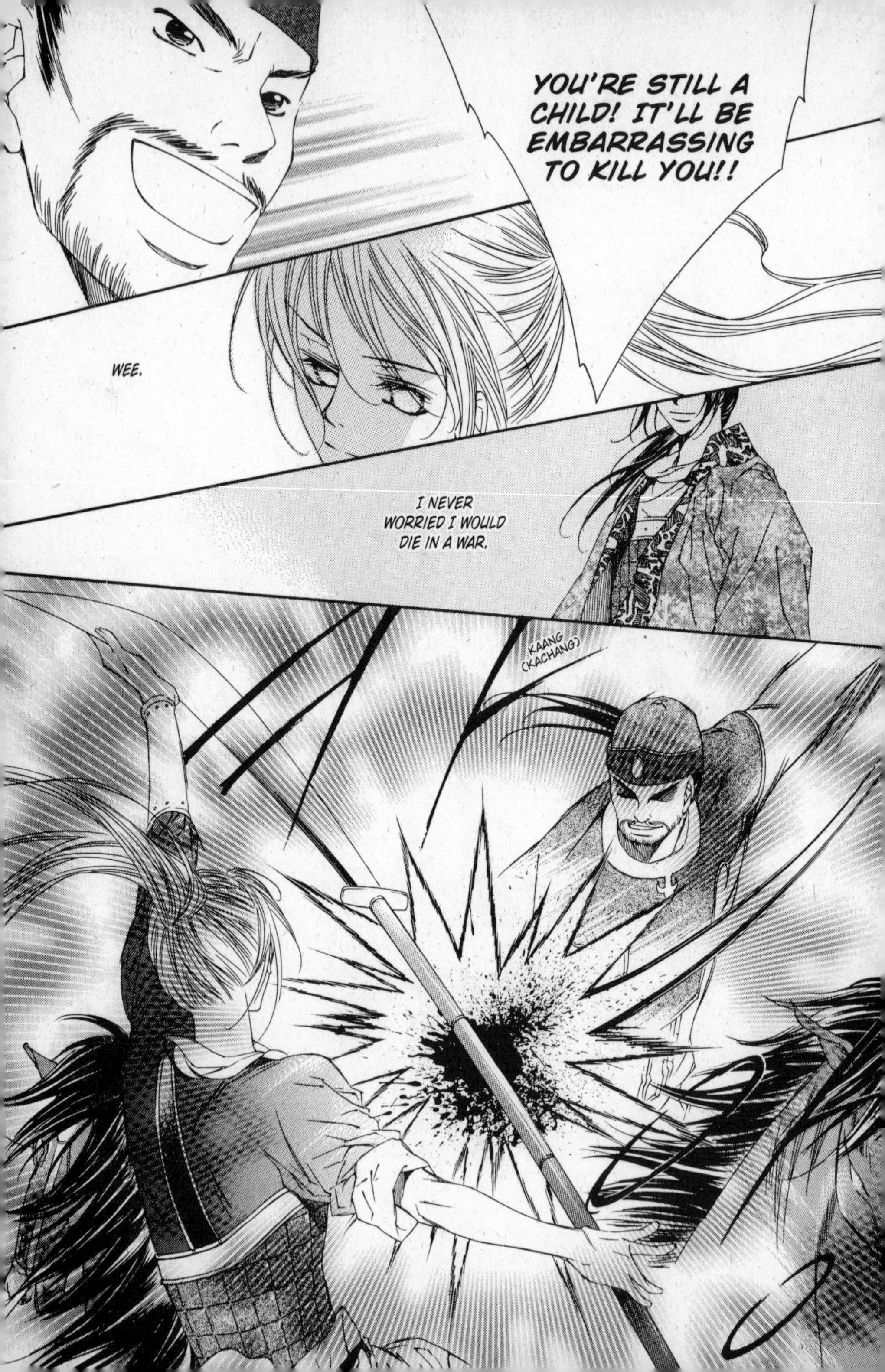

YOU'RE STILL A CHILD! IT'LL BE EMBARRASSING TO KILL YOU!!
WEE.
I NEVER WORRIED I WOULD DIE IN A WAR.
KAANG (KACHANG)

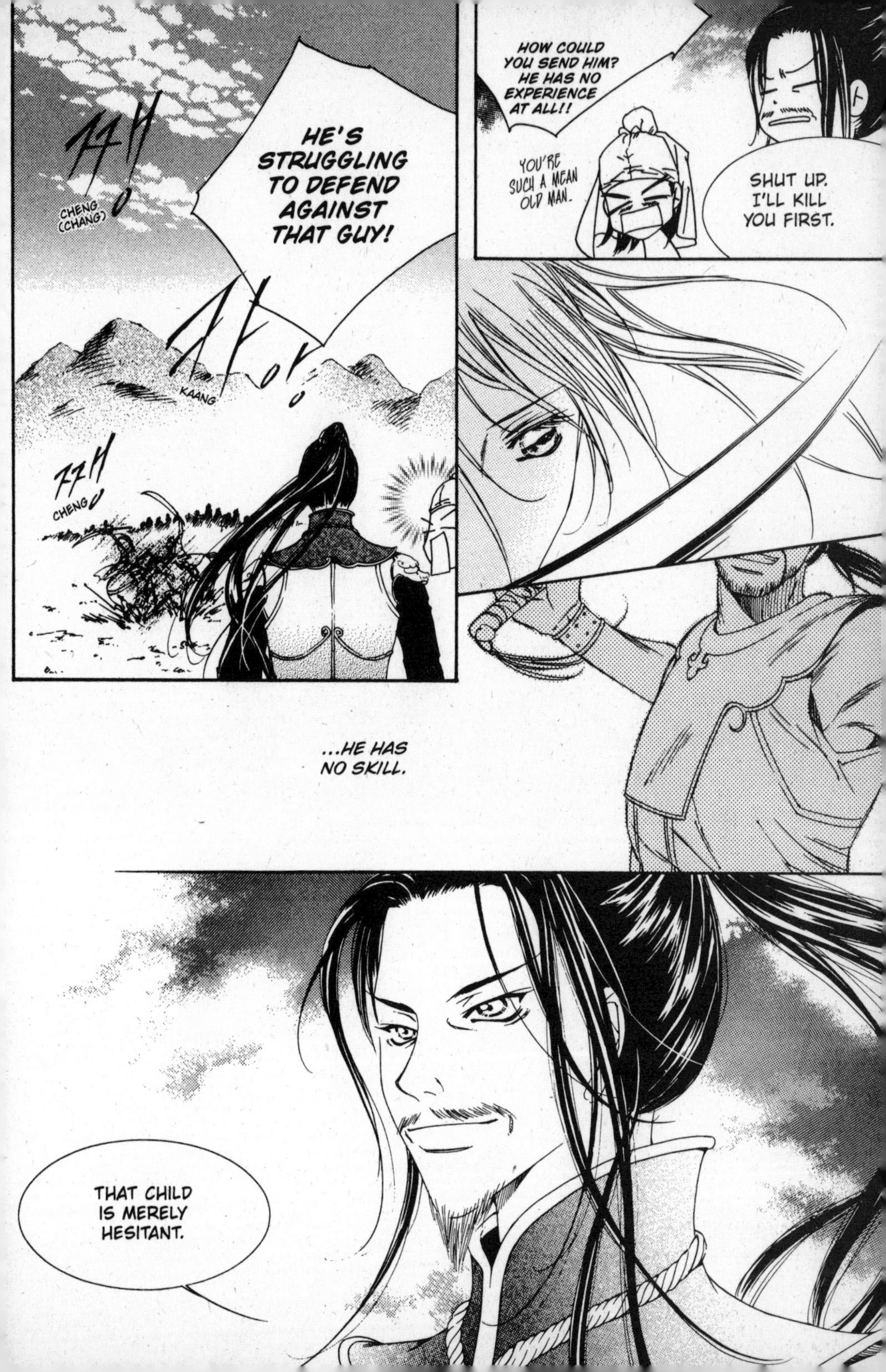
HE'S STRUGGLING TO DEFEND AGAINST THAT GUY!
CHENG (CHANG)
KAANG
CHENG
HOW COULD YOU SEND HIM? HE HAS NO EXPERIENCE AT ALL!!
YOU'RE SUCH A MEAN OLD MAN.
SHUT UP. I'LL KILL YOU FIRST.
...HE HAS NO SKILL.
THAT CHILD IS MERELY HESITANT.

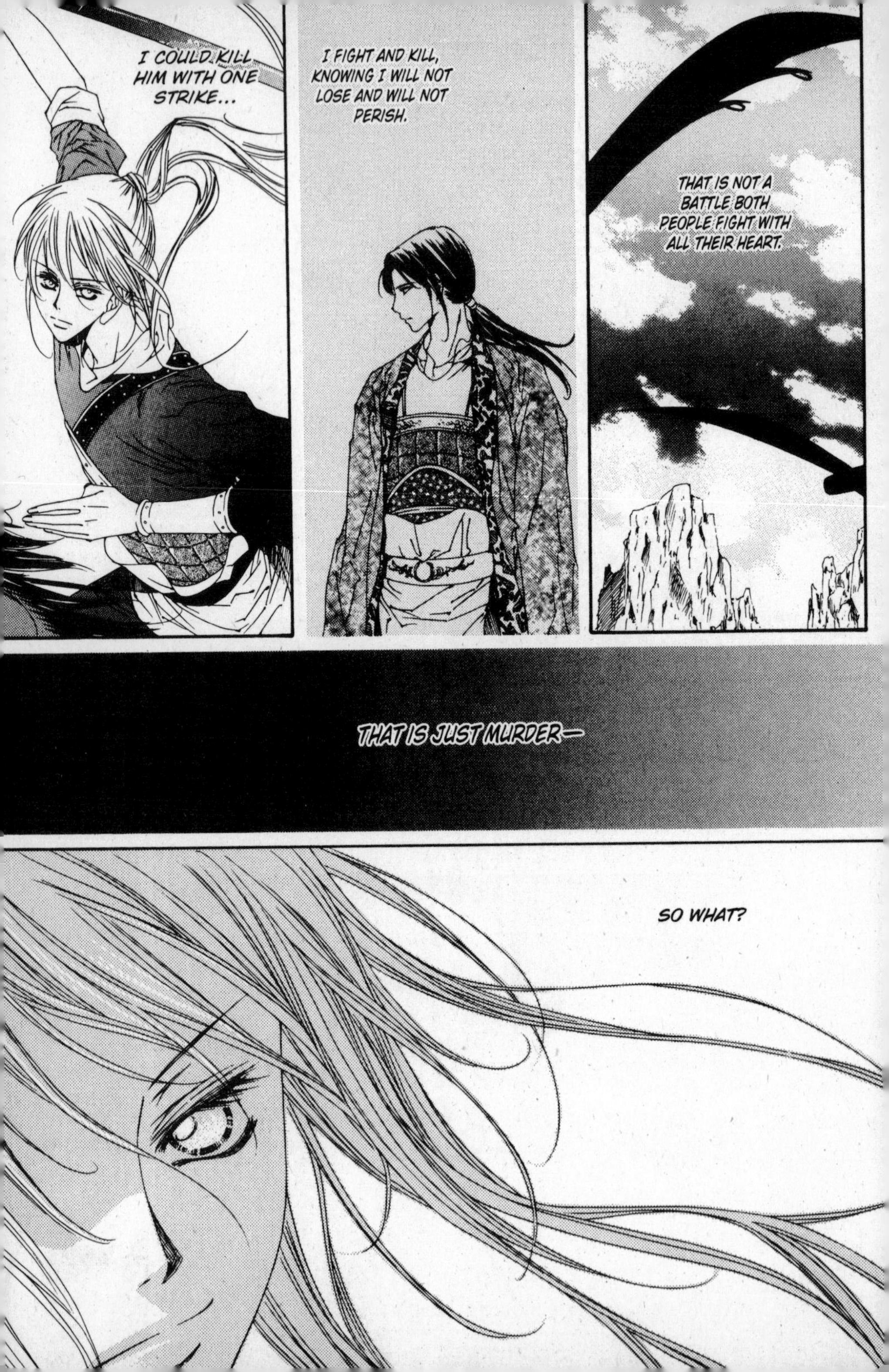
I COULD KILL HIM WITH ONE STRIKE...
I FIGHT AND KILL, KNOWING I WILL NOT LOSE AND WILL NOT PERISH.
THAT IS NOT A BATTLE BOTH PEOPLE FIGHT WITH ALL THEIR HEART.
THAT IS JUST MURDER—
SO WHAT?

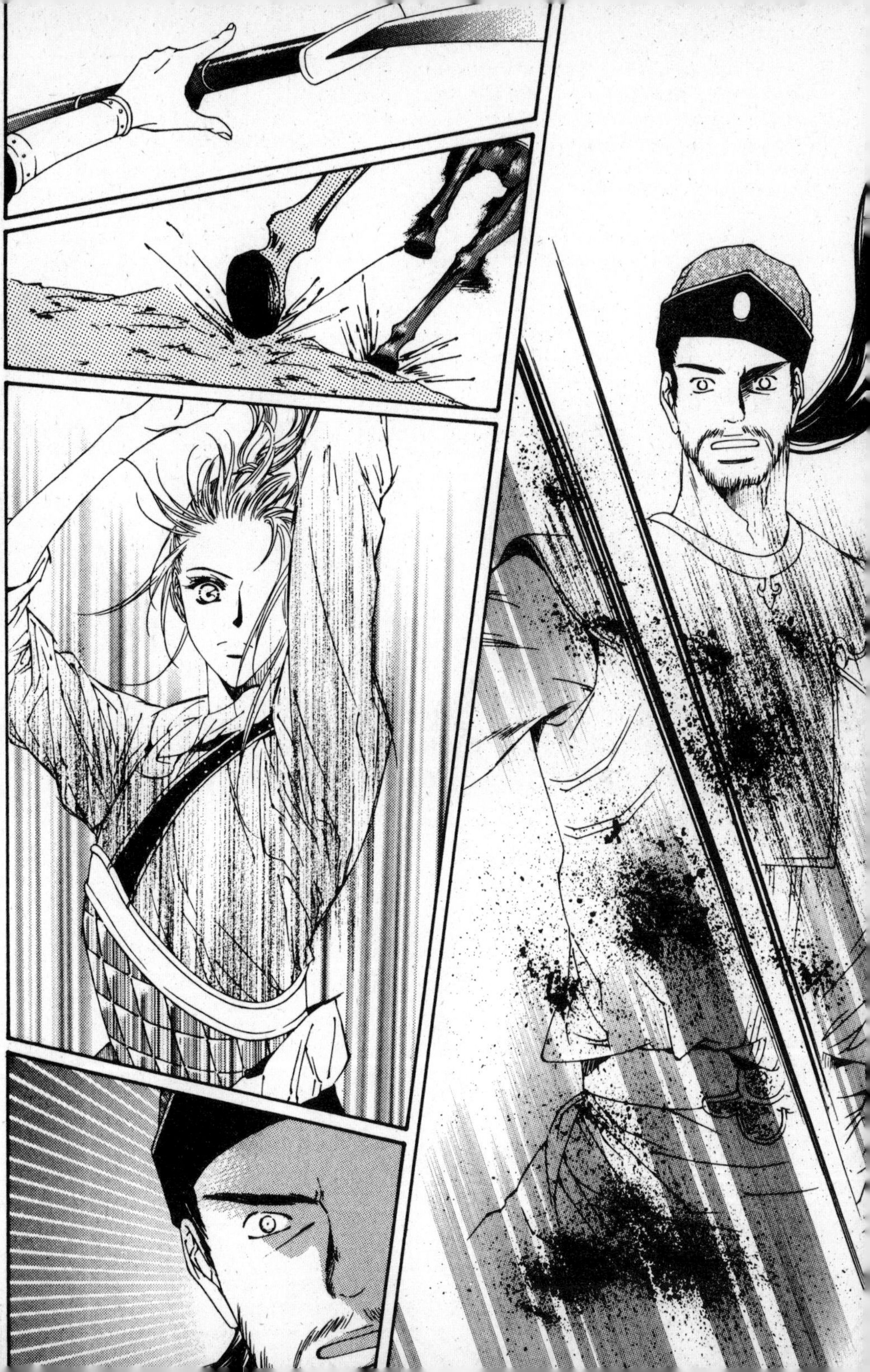

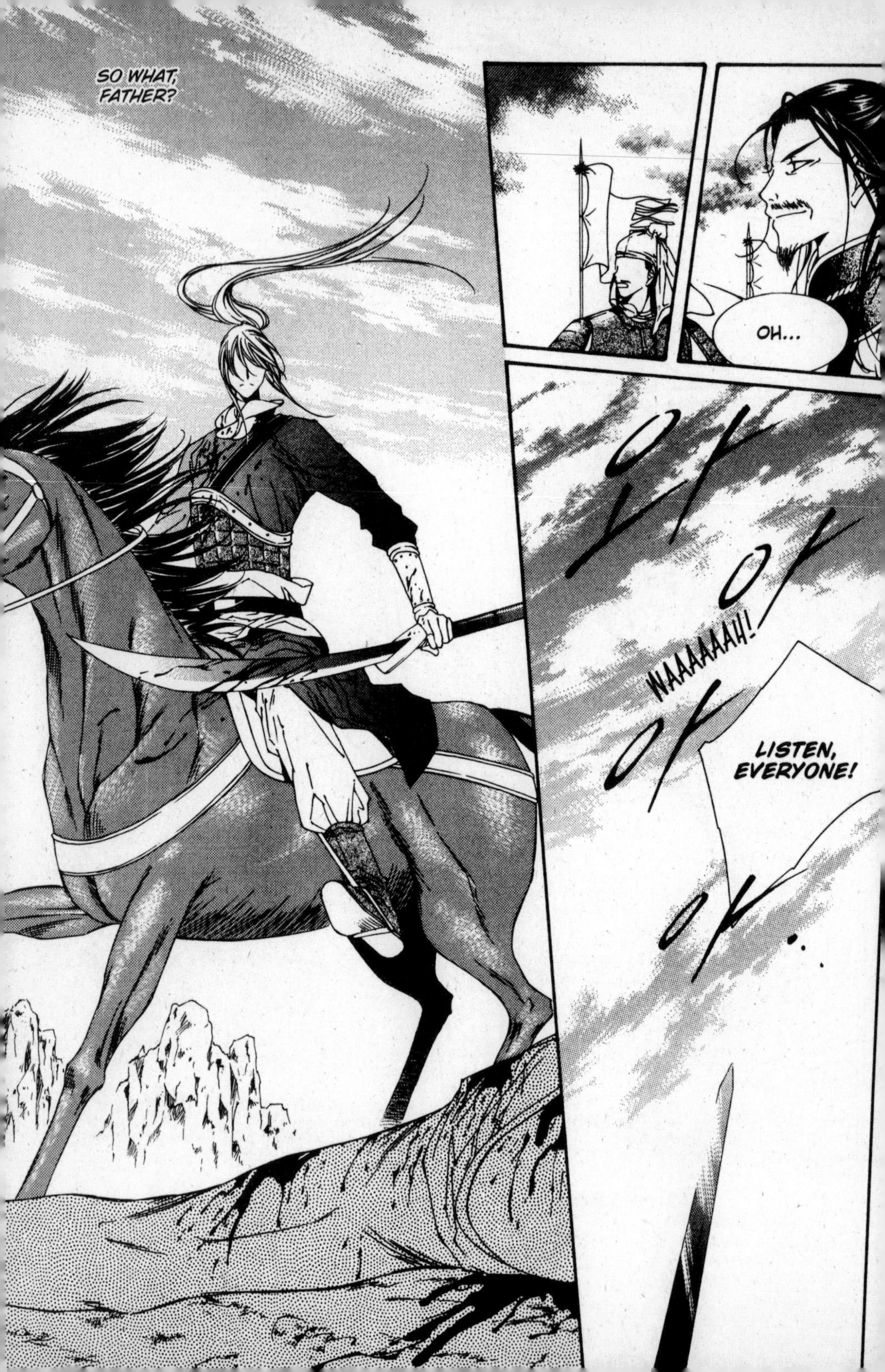
SO WHAT, FATHER?
OH...
WAAAAAAH!
LISTEN, EVERYONE!

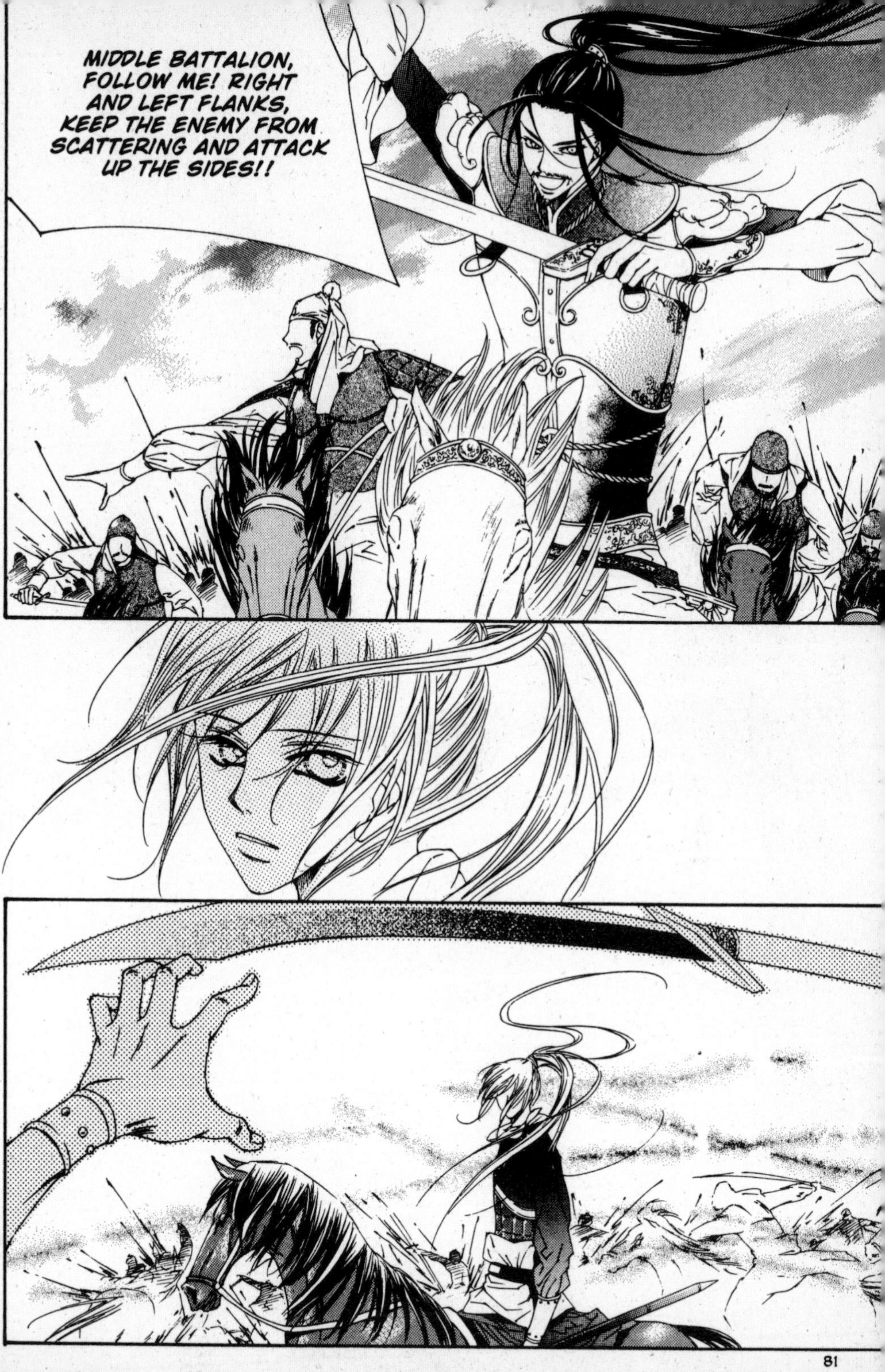
MIDDLE BATTALION, FOLLOW ME! RIGHT AND LEFT FLANKS, KEEP THE ENEMY FROM SCATTERING AND ATTACK UP THE SIDES!!

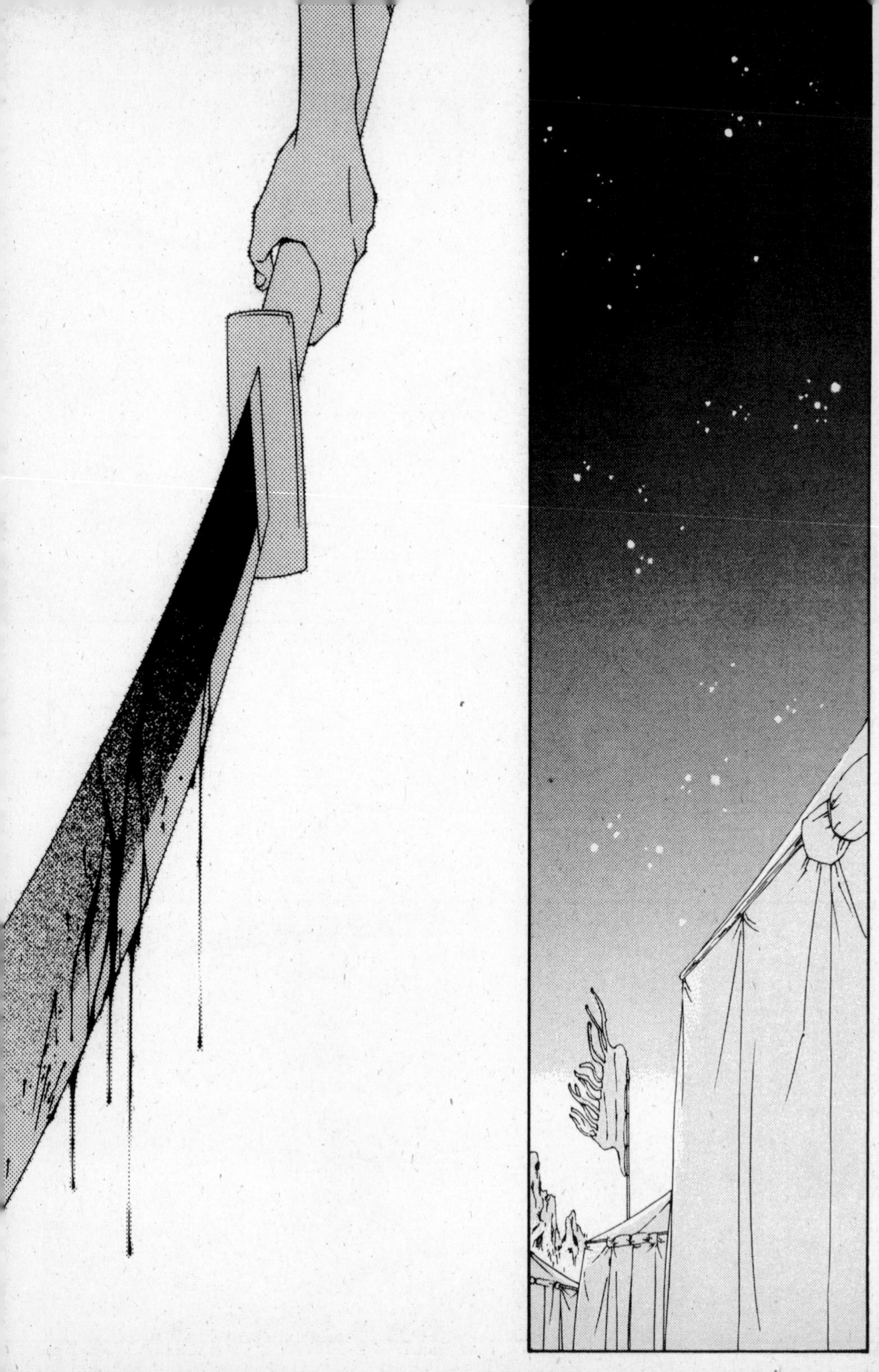

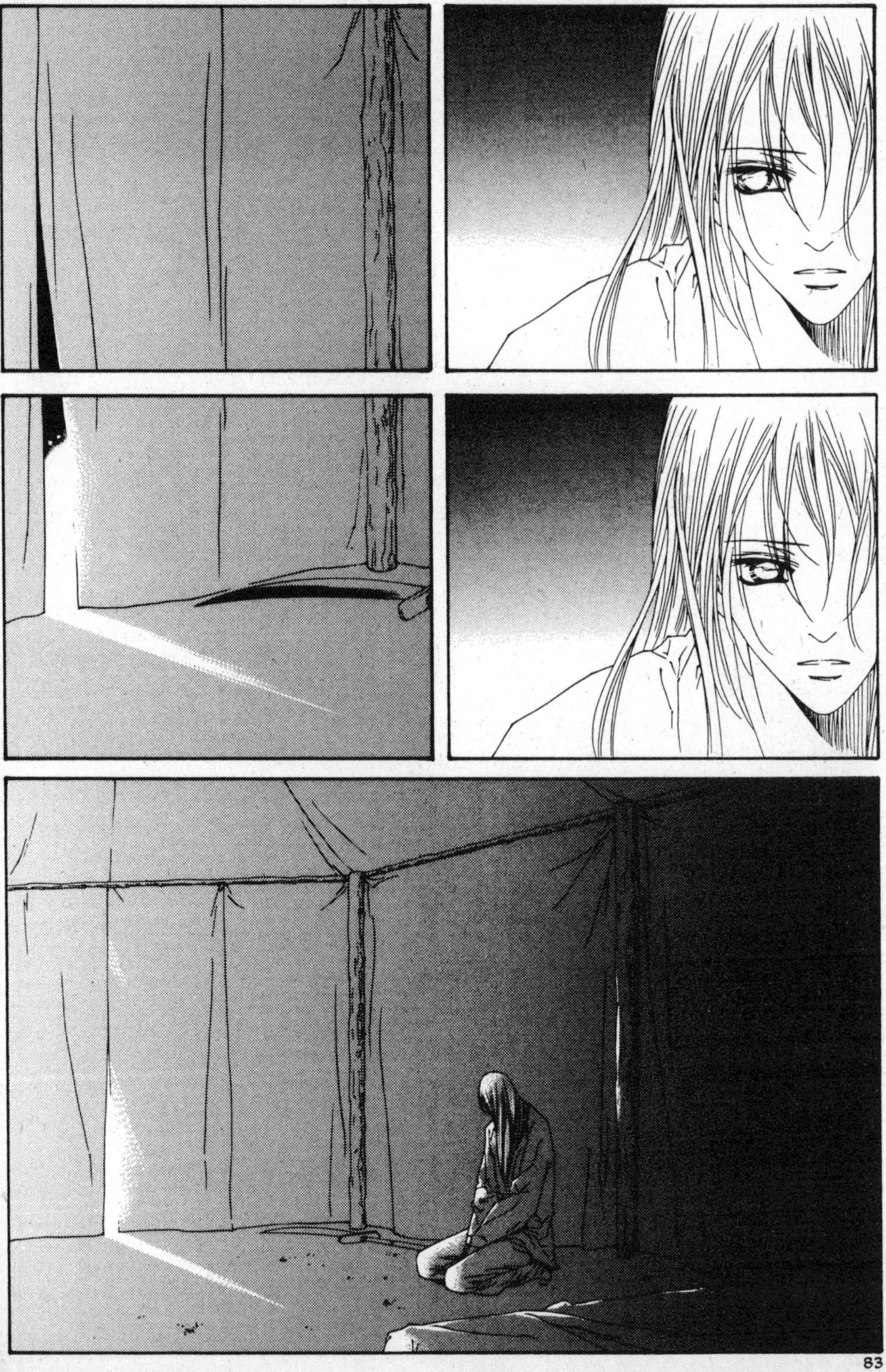

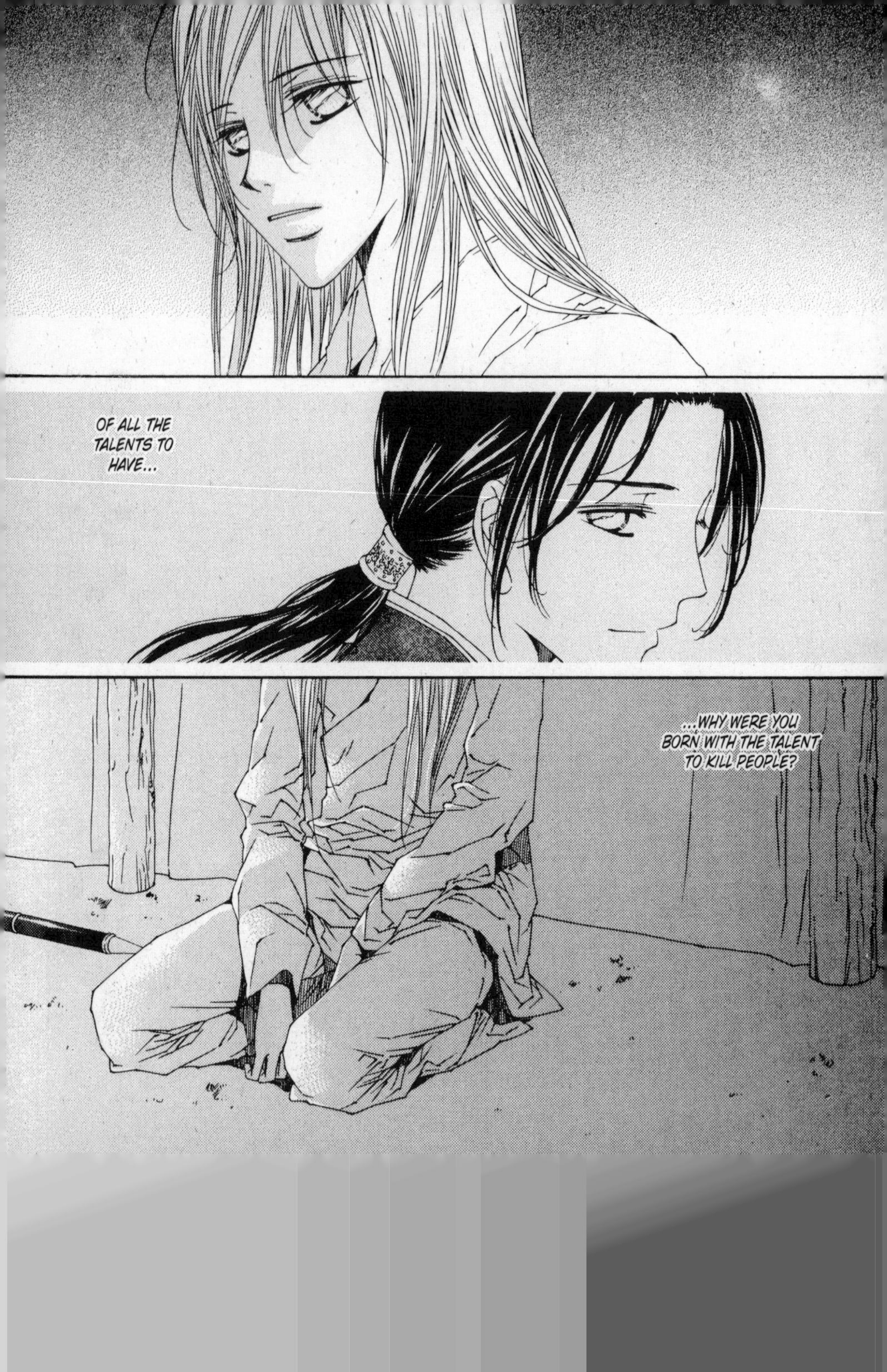
OF ALL THE TALENTS TO HAVE...
...WHY WERE YOU BORN WITH THE TALENT TO KILL PEOPLE?

I MADE MY FORTUNE KILLING PEOPLE. THERE IS NO LIFE MORE WRETCHED THAN THIS.

NEVER SEEK TO IMPROVE THE COMFORTS OF YOUR LIFE BY TAKING THE LIVES OF OTHERS.

WHAT ELSE CAN I DO?

I'M JUST TRYING TO SURVIVE.

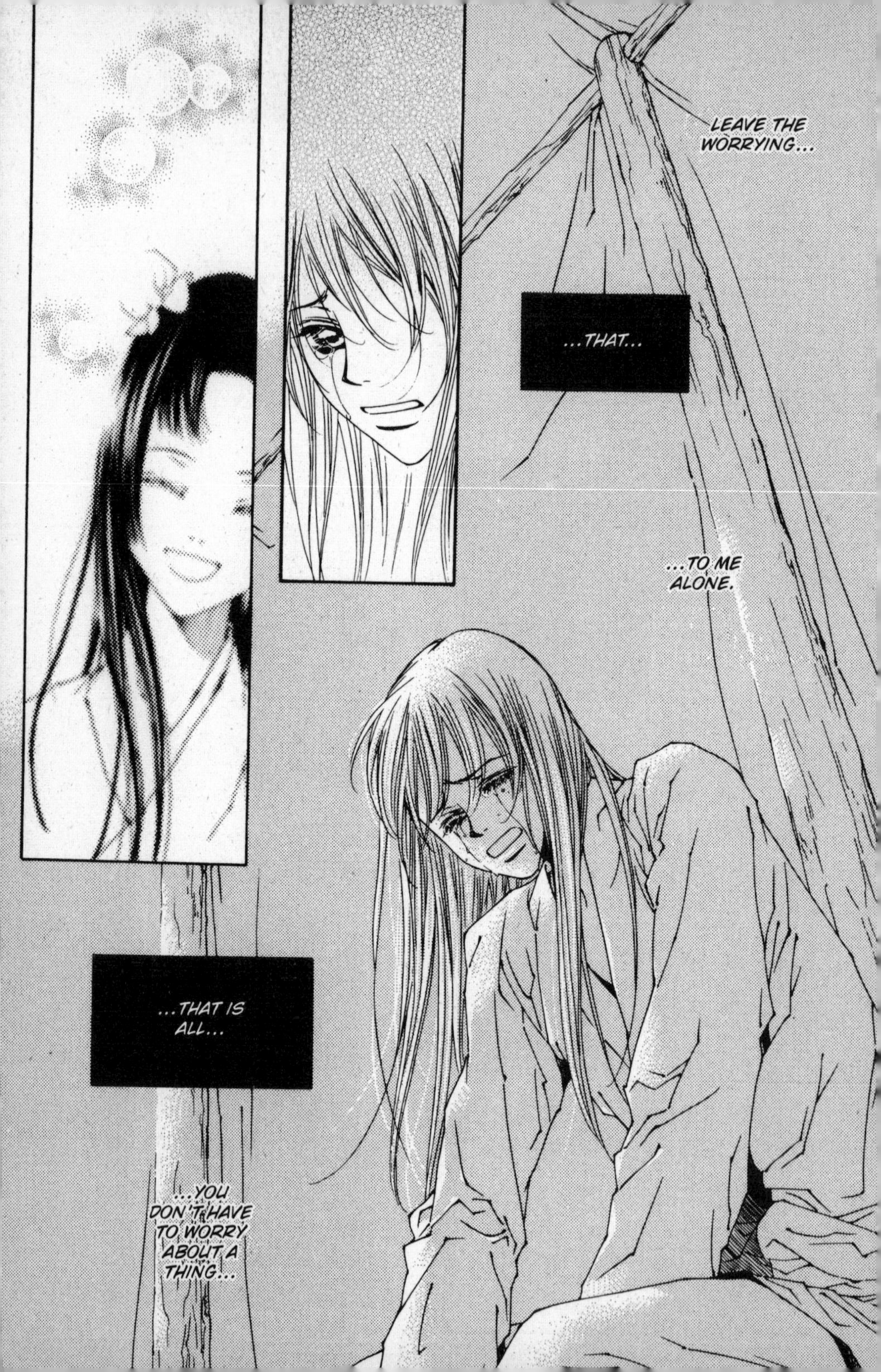

LEAVE THE WORRYING...
...THAT...
...TO ME ALONE.
...THAT IS ALL...
...YOU DON'T HAVE TO WORRY ABOUT A THING...

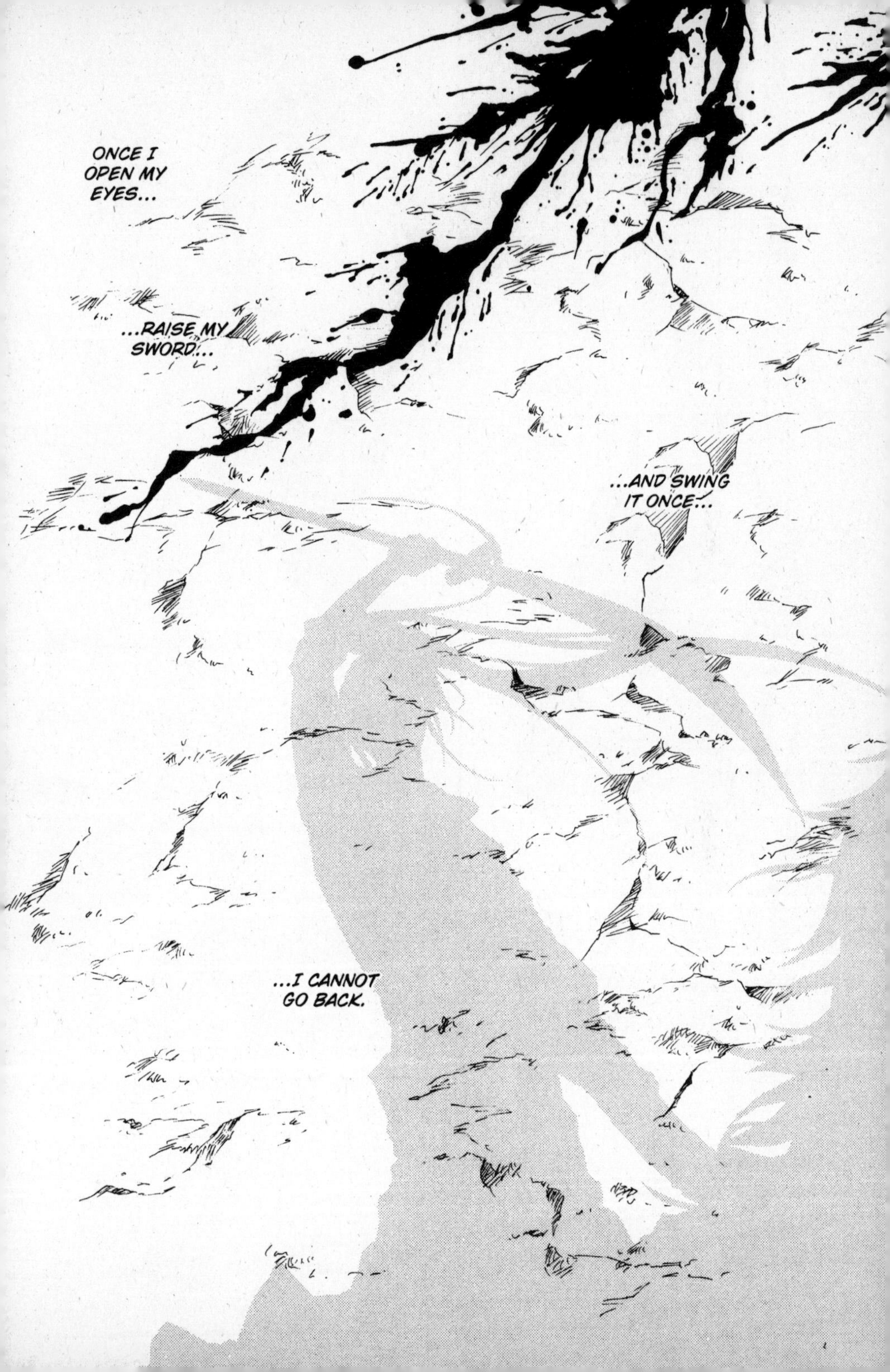
ONCE I OPEN MY EYES...
...RAISE MY SWORD...
...AND SWING IT ONCE...
...I CANNOT GO BACK.

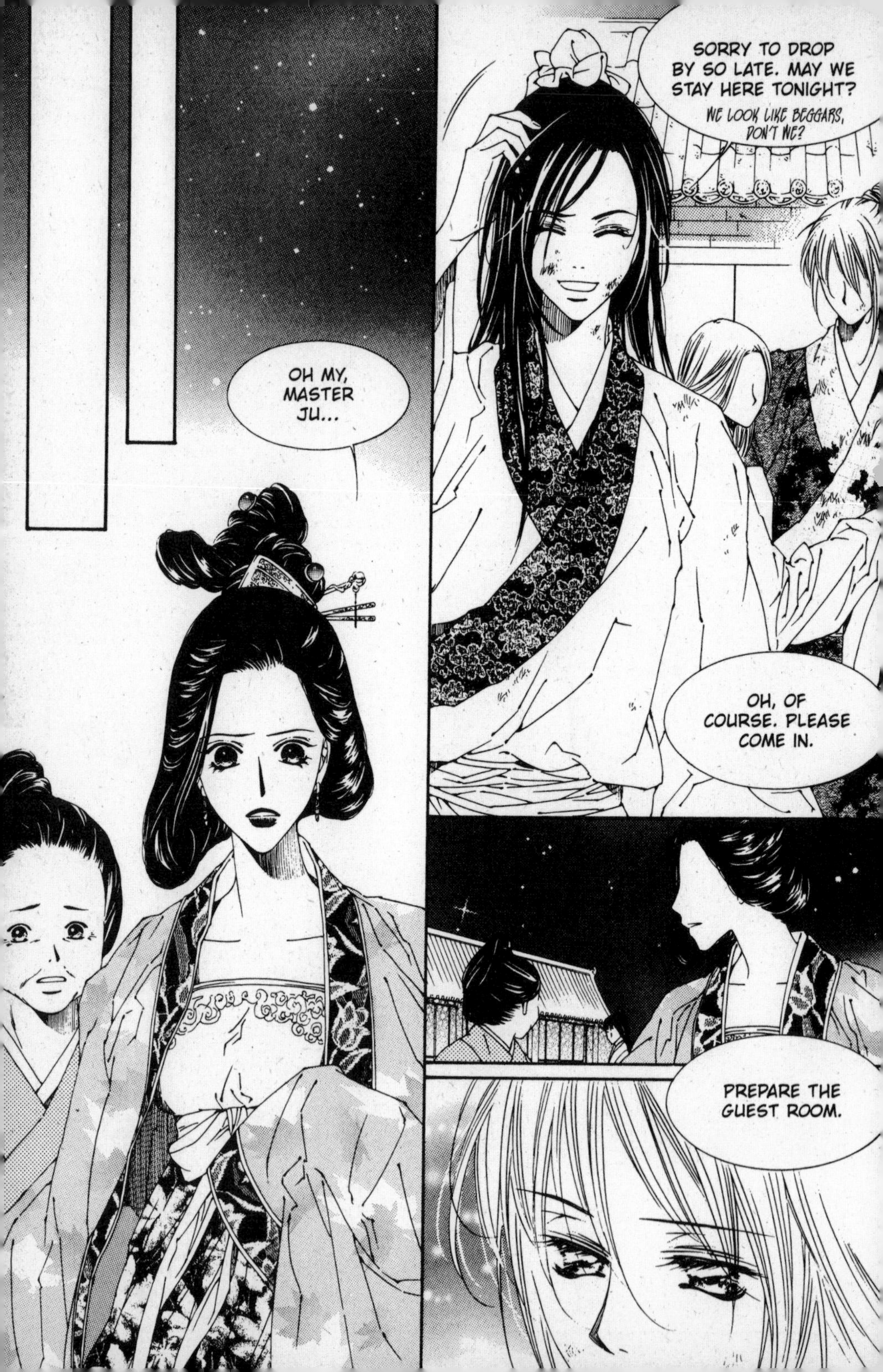
OH MY, MASTER JU...
SORRY TO DROP BY SO LATE. MAY WE STAY HERE TONIGHT?
WE LOOK LIKE BEGGARS, DON'T WE?
OH, OF COURSE. PLEASE COME IN.
PREPARE THE GUEST ROOM.

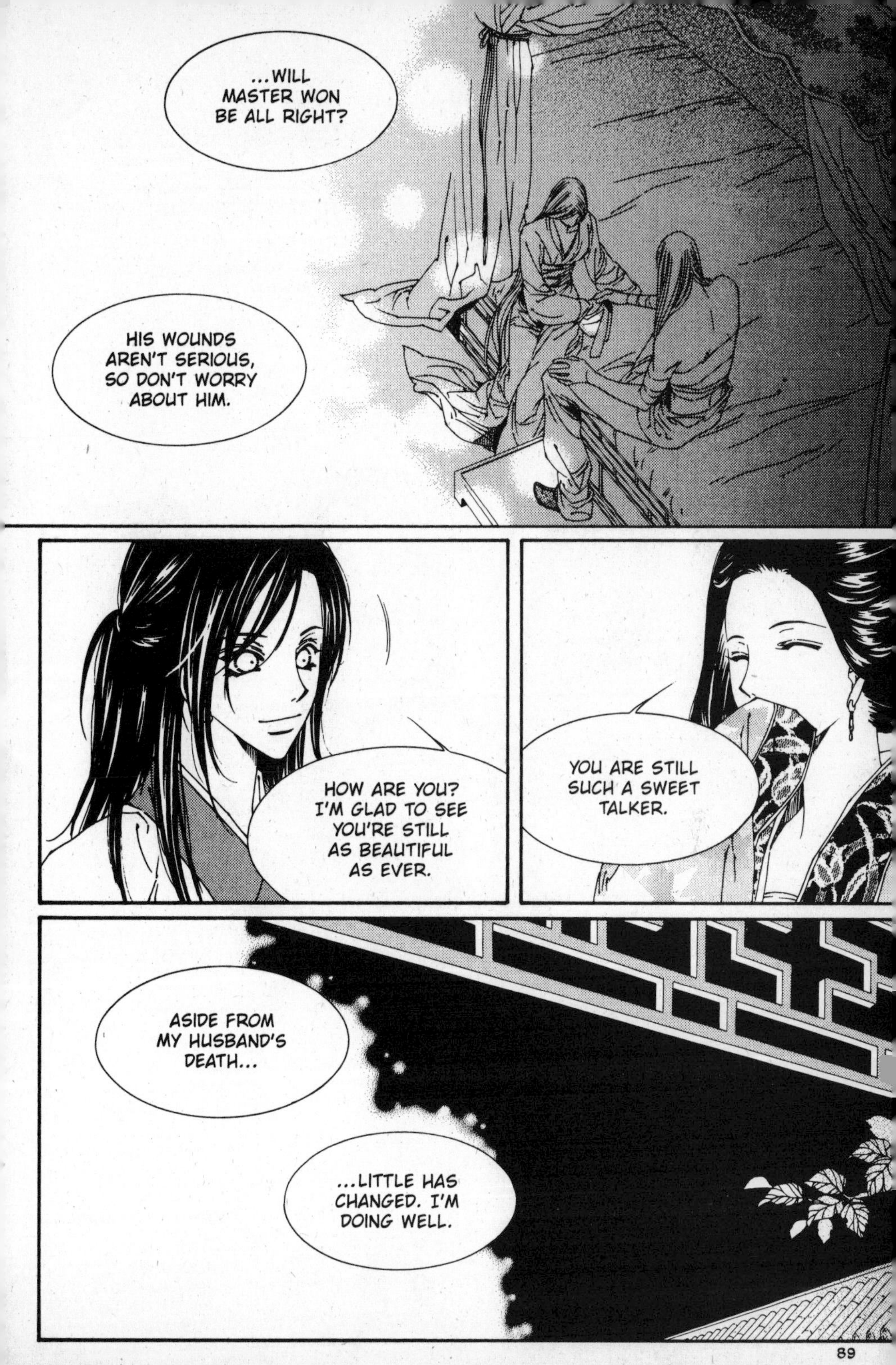
...WILL MASTER WON BE ALL RIGHT?
HIS WOUNDS AREN'T SERIOUS, SO DON'T WORRY ABOUT HIM.
HOW ARE YOU? I'M GLAD TO SEE YOU'RE STILL AS BEAUTIFUL AS EVER.
YOU ARE STILL SUCH A SWEET TALKER.
ASIDE FROM MY HUSBAND'S DEATH...
...LITTLE HAS CHANGED. I'M DOING WELL.

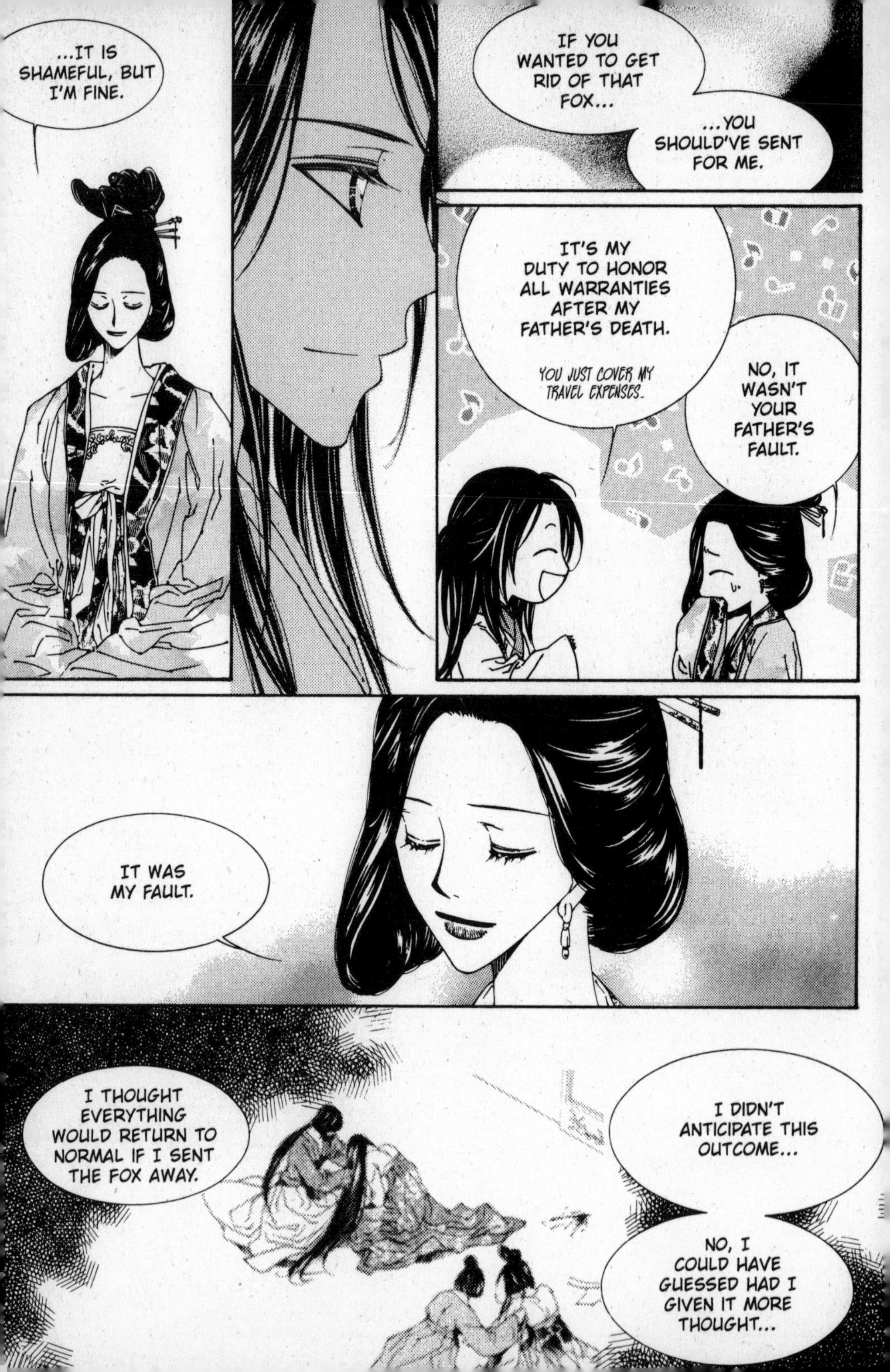
...IT IS SHAMEFUL, BUT I'M FINE.
IF YOU WANTED TO GET RID OF THAT FOX...
...YOU SHOULD'VE SENT FOR ME.
IT'S MY DUTY TO HONOR ALL WARRANTIES AFTER MY FATHER'S DEATH.
YOU JUST COVER MY TRAVEL EXPENSES.
NO, IT WASN'T YOUR FATHER'S FAULT.
IT WAS MY FAULT.
I THOUGHT EVERYTHING WOULD RETURN TO NORMAL IF I SENT THE FOX AWAY.
I DIDN'T ANTICIPATE THIS OUTCOME...
NO, I COULD HAVE GUESSED HAD I GIVEN IT MORE THOUGHT...

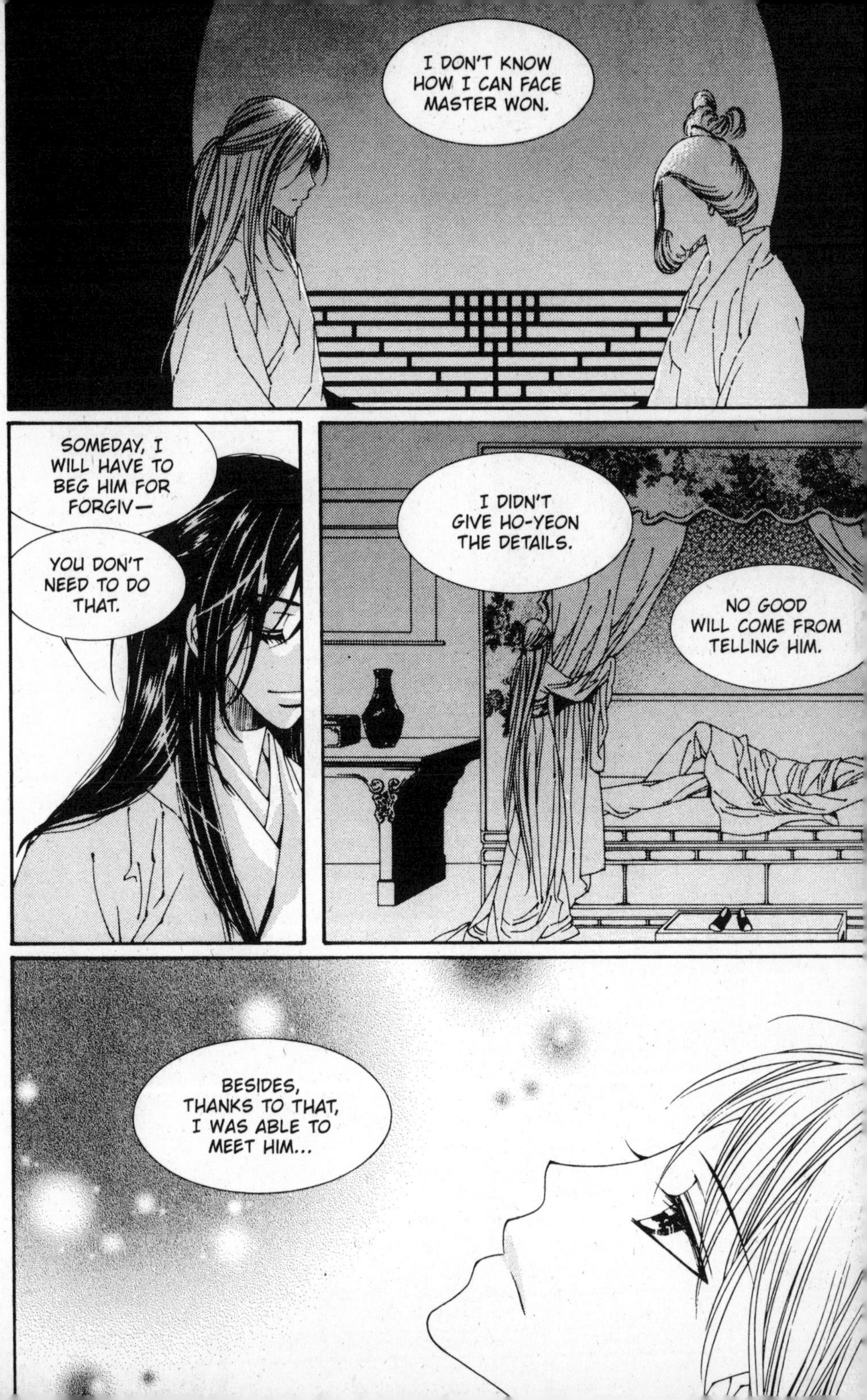
I DON'T KNOW HOW I CAN FACE MASTER WON.
SOMEDAY, I WILL HAVE TO BEG HIM FOR FORGIV—
YOU DON'T NEED TO DO THAT.
I DIDN'T GIVE HO-YEON THE DETAILS.
NO GOOD WILL COME FROM TELLING HIM.
BESIDES, THANKS TO THAT, I WAS ABLE TO MEET HIM...

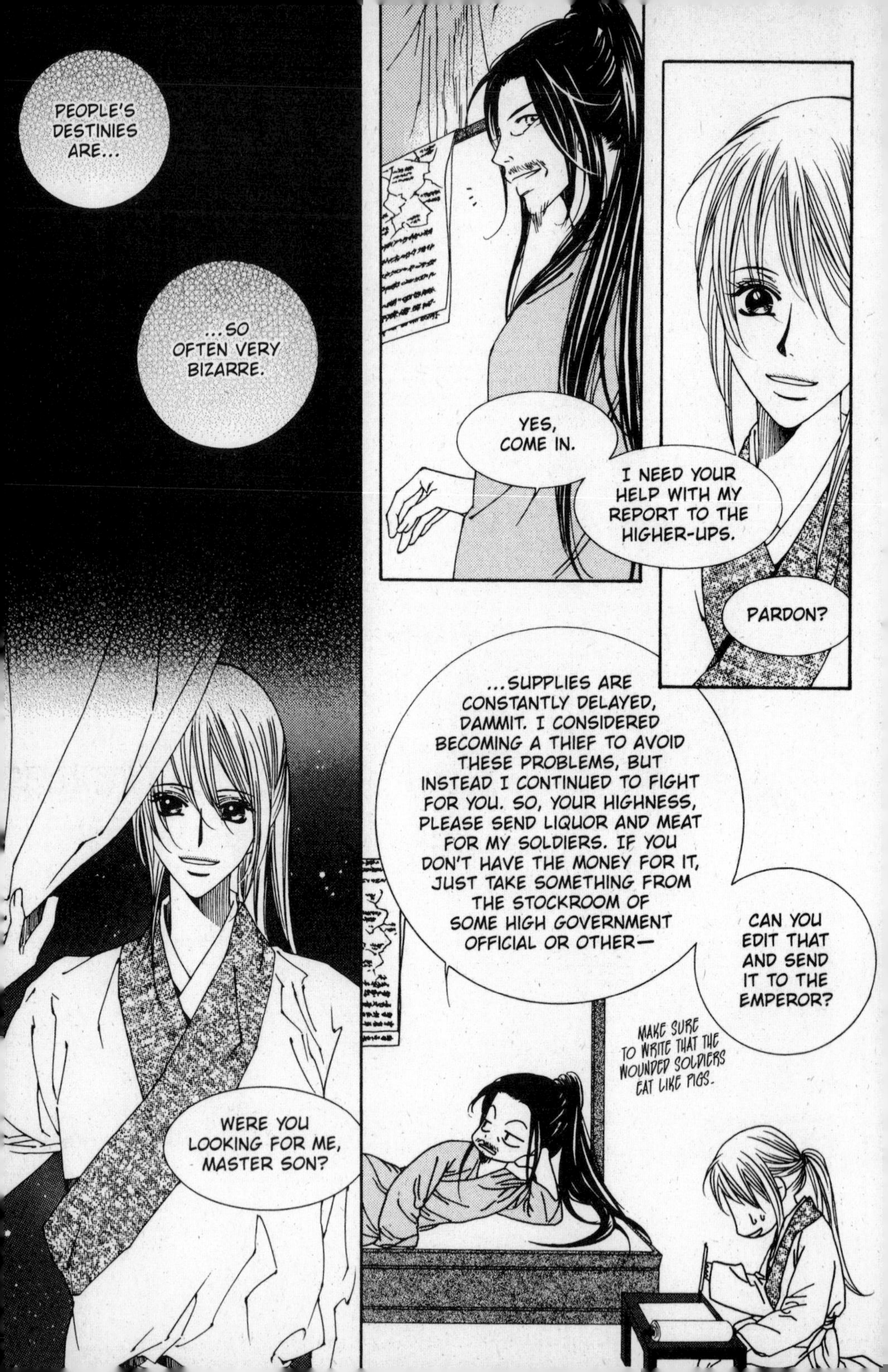
PEOPLE'S DESTINIES ARE...
...SO OFTEN VERY BIZARRE.
WERE YOU LOOKING FOR ME, MASTER SON?
YES, COME IN.
I NEED YOUR HELP WITH MY REPORT TO THE HIGHER-UPS.
PARDON?
...SUPPLIES ARE CONSTANTLY DELAYED, DAMMIT. I CONSIDERED BECOMING A THIEF TO AVOID THESE PROBLEMS, BUT INSTEAD I CONTINUED TO FIGHT FOR YOU. SO, YOUR HIGHNESS, PLEASE SEND LIQUOR AND MEAT FOR MY SOLDIERS. IF YOU DON'T HAVE THE MONEY FOR IT, JUST TAKE SOMETHING FROM THE STOCKROOM OF SOME HIGH GOVERNMENT OFFICIAL OR OTHER—
CAN YOU EDIT THAT AND SEND IT TO THE EMPEROR?
MAKE SURE TO WRITE THAT THE WOUNDED SOLDIERS EAT LIKE PIGS.

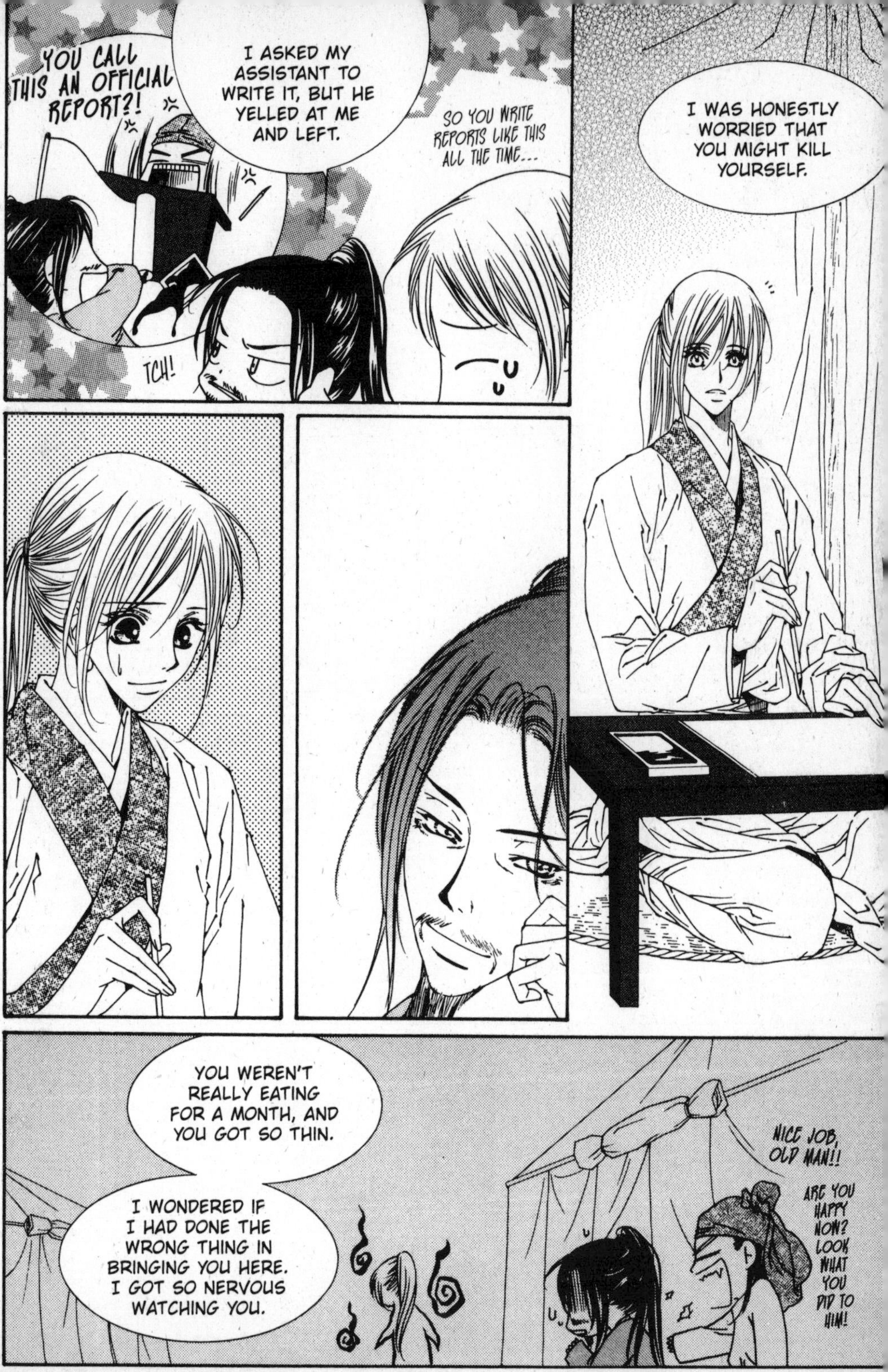
YOU CALL THIS AN OFFICIAL REPORT?!
I ASKED MY ASSISTANT TO WRITE IT, BUT HE YELLED AT ME AND LEFT.
SO YOU WRITE REPORTS LIKE THIS ALL THE TIME...
TCH!
I WAS HONESTLY WORRIED THAT YOU MIGHT KILL YOURSELF.
YOU WEREN'T REALLY EATING FOR A MONTH, AND YOU GOT SO THIN.
I WONDERED IF I HAD DONE THE WRONG THING IN BRINGING YOU HERE. I GOT SO NERVOUS WATCHING YOU.
NICE JOB, OLD MAN!!
ARE YOU HAPPY NOW? LOOK WHAT YOU DID TO HIM!

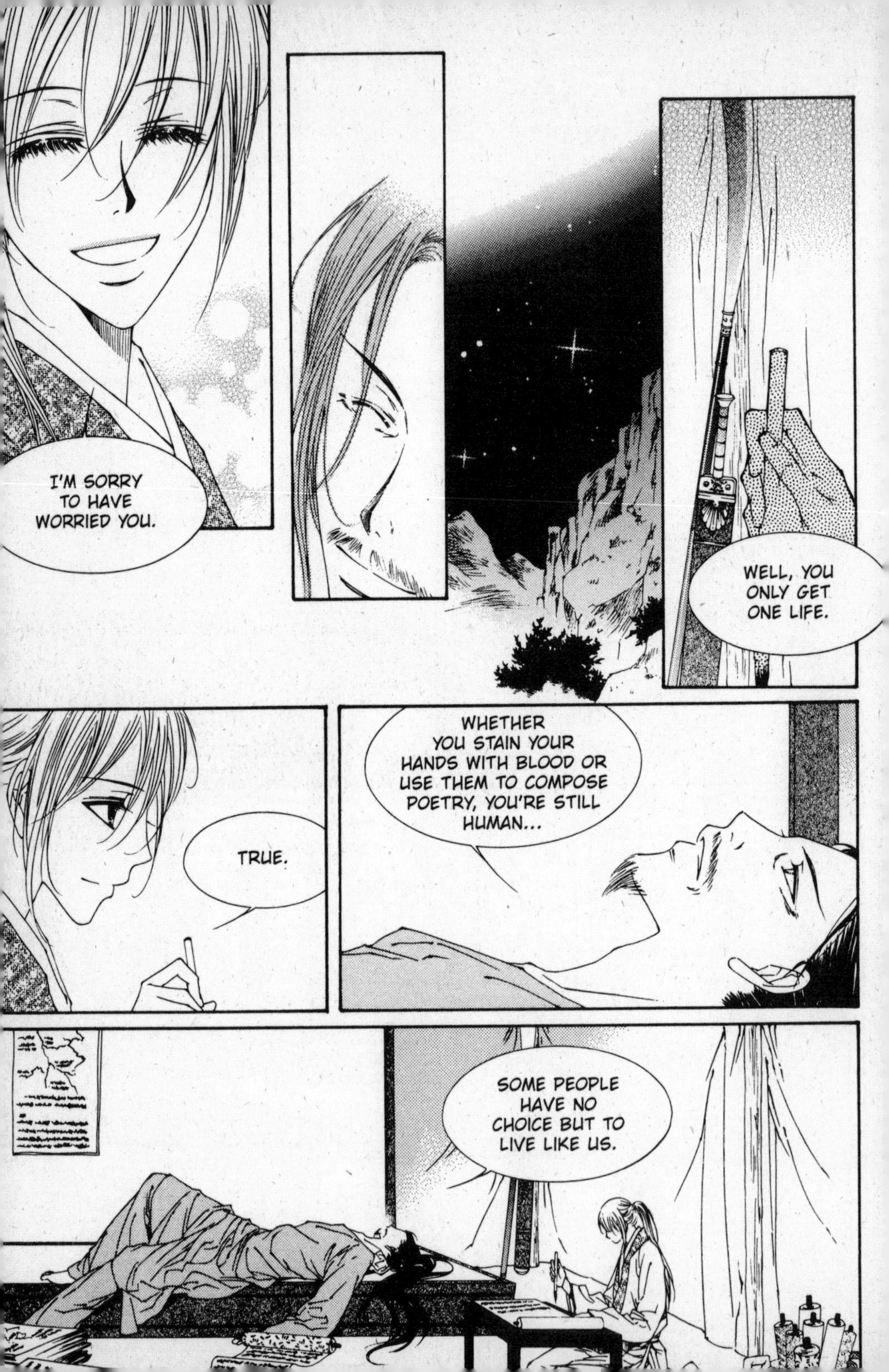
I'M SORRY TO HAVE WORRIED YOU.
WELL, YOU ONLY GET ONE LIFE.
TRUE.
WHETHER YOU STAIN YOUR HANDS WITH BLOOD OR USE THEM TO COMPOSE POETRY, YOU'RE STILL HUMAN...
SOME PEOPLE HAVE NO CHOICE BUT TO LIVE LIKE US.

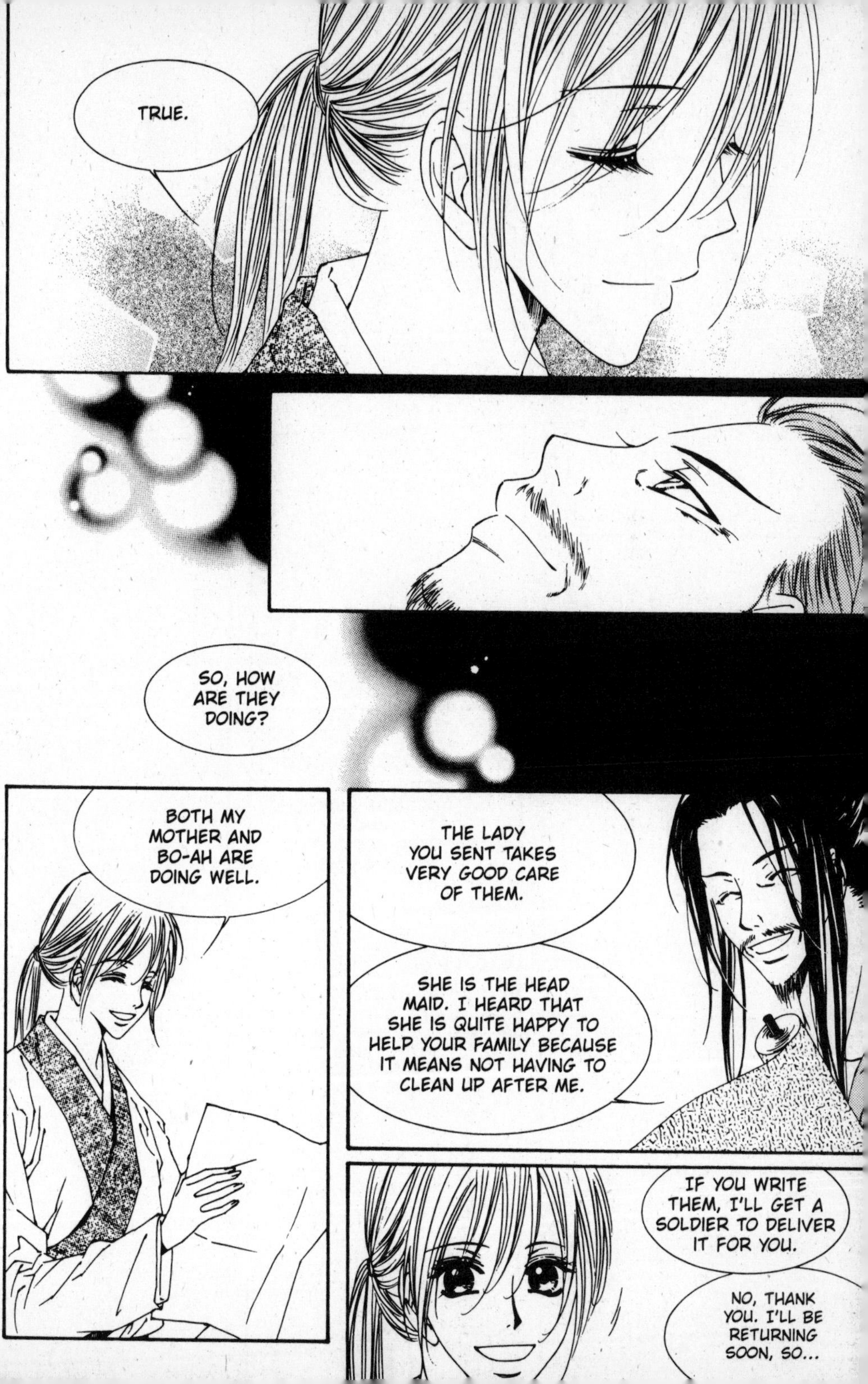
TRUE.
SO, HOW ARE THEY DOING?
BOTH MY MOTHER AND BO-AH ARE DOING WELL.
THE LADY YOU SENT TAKES VERY GOOD CARE OF THEM.
SHE IS THE HEAD MAID. I HEARD THAT SHE IS QUITE HAPPY TO HELP YOUR FAMILY BECAUSE IT MEANS NOT HAVING TO CLEAN UP AFTER ME.
IF YOU WRITE THEM, I'LL GET A SOLDIER TO DELIVER IT FOR YOU.
NO, THANK YOU. I'LL BE RETURNING SOON, SO...

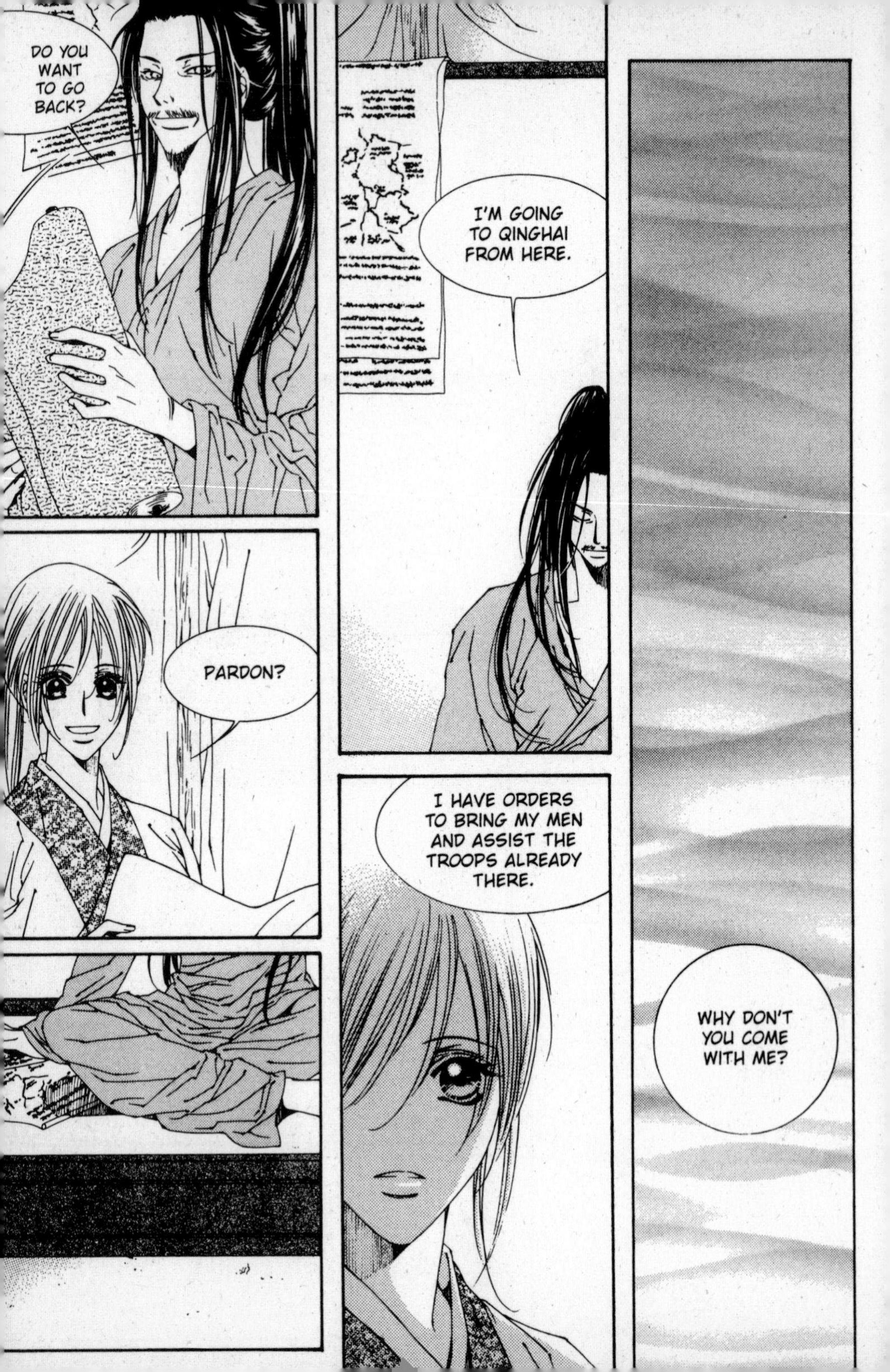
DO YOU WANT TO GO BACK?
PARDON?
I'M GOING TO QINGHAI FROM HERE.
I HAVE ORDERS TO BRING MY MEN AND ASSIST THE TROOPS ALREADY THERE.
WHY DON'T YOU COME WITH ME?

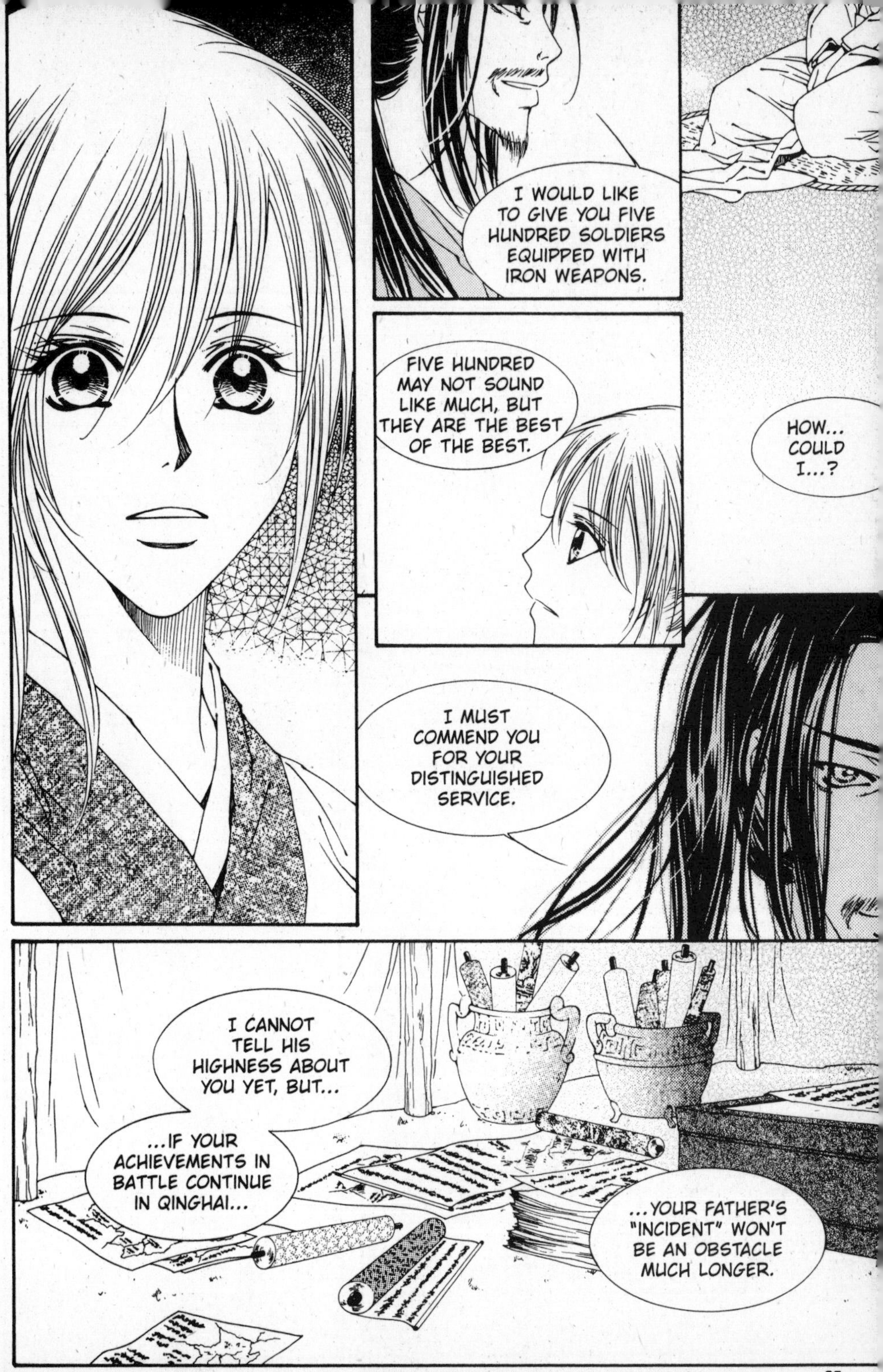
I WOULD LIKE TO GIVE YOU FIVE HUNDRED SOLDIERS EQUIPPED WITH IRON WEAPONS.
FIVE HUNDRED MAY NOT SOUND LIKE MUCH, BUT THEY ARE THE BEST OF THE BEST.
HOW... COULD I...?
I MUST COMMEND YOU FOR YOUR DISTINGUISHED SERVICE.
I CANNOT TELL HIS HIGHNESS ABOUT YOU YET, BUT...
...IF YOUR ACHIEVEMENTS IN BATTLE CONTINUE IN QINGHAI...
...YOUR FATHER'S "INCIDENT" WON'T BE AN OBSTACLE MUCH LONGER.

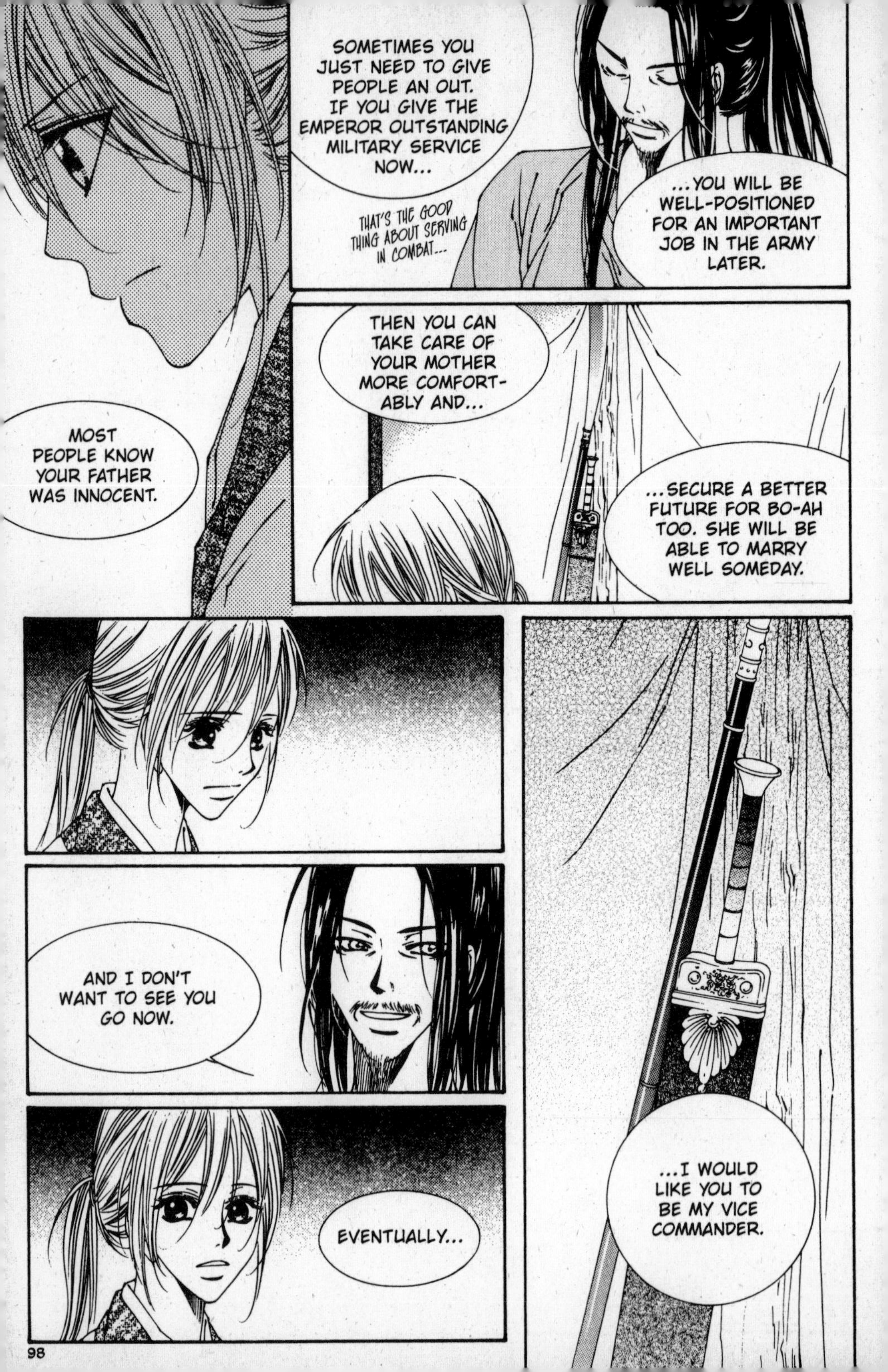
SOMETIMES YOU JUST NEED TO GIVE PEOPLE AN OUT. IF YOU GIVE THE EMPEROR OUTSTANDING MILITARY SERVICE NOW...
THAT'S THE GOOD THING ABOUT SERVING IN COMBAT...
...YOU WILL BE WELL-POSITIONED FOR AN IMPORTANT JOB IN THE ARMY LATER.
THEN YOU CAN TAKE CARE OF YOUR MOTHER MORE COMFORT-ABLY AND...
...SECURE A BETTER FUTURE FOR BO-AH TOO. SHE WILL BE ABLE TO MARRY WELL SOMEDAY.
MOST PEOPLE KNOW YOUR FATHER WAS INNOCENT.
AND I DON'T WANT TO SEE YOU GO NOW.
EVENTUALLY...
...I WOULD LIKE YOU TO BE MY VICE COMMANDER.

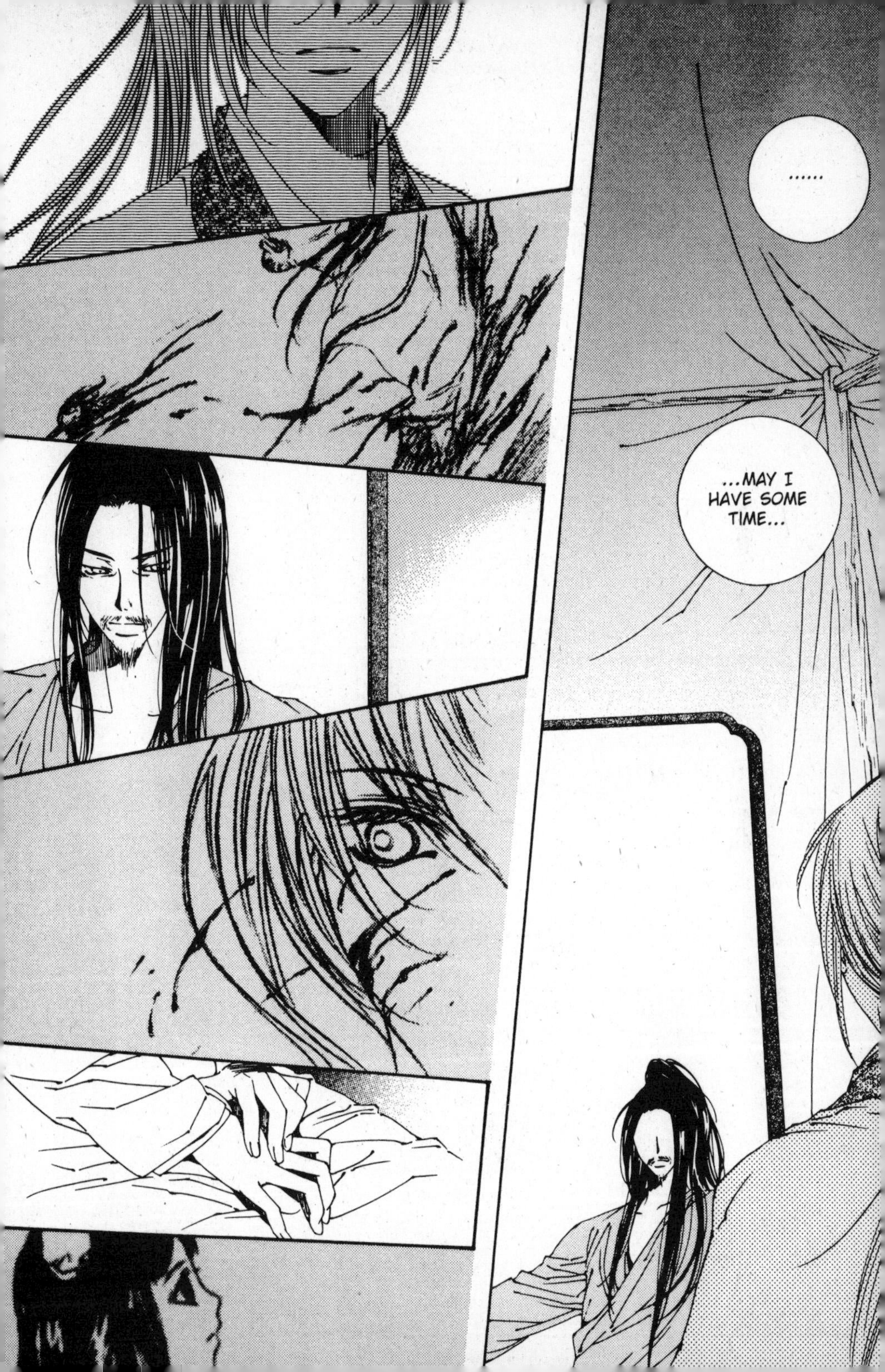
......
...MAY I HAVE SOME TIME...

...TO THINK ABOUT IT...?

YOU MUST NEVER EVEN CONSIDER USING YOUR CRUEL TALENTS TO GAIN WEALTH.

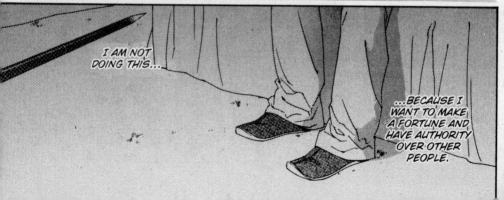

I AM NOT DOING THIS...

...BECAUSE I WANT TO MAKE A FORTUNE AND HAVE AUTHORITY OVER OTHER PEOPLE.

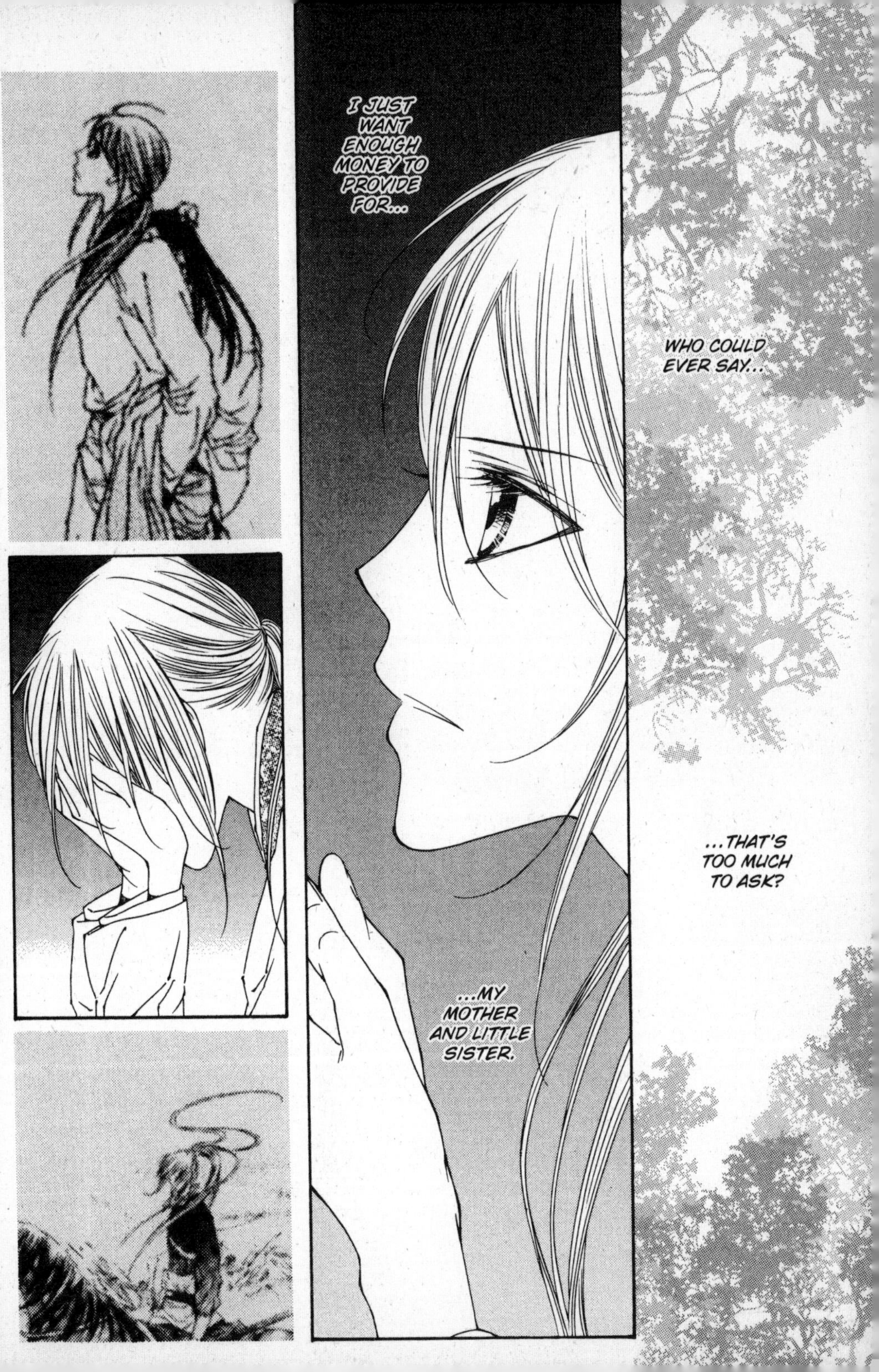
I JUST WANT ENOUGH MONEY TO PROVIDE FOR...
...MY MOTHER AND LITTLE SISTER.
WHO COULD EVER SAY...
...THAT'S TOO MUCH TO ASK?

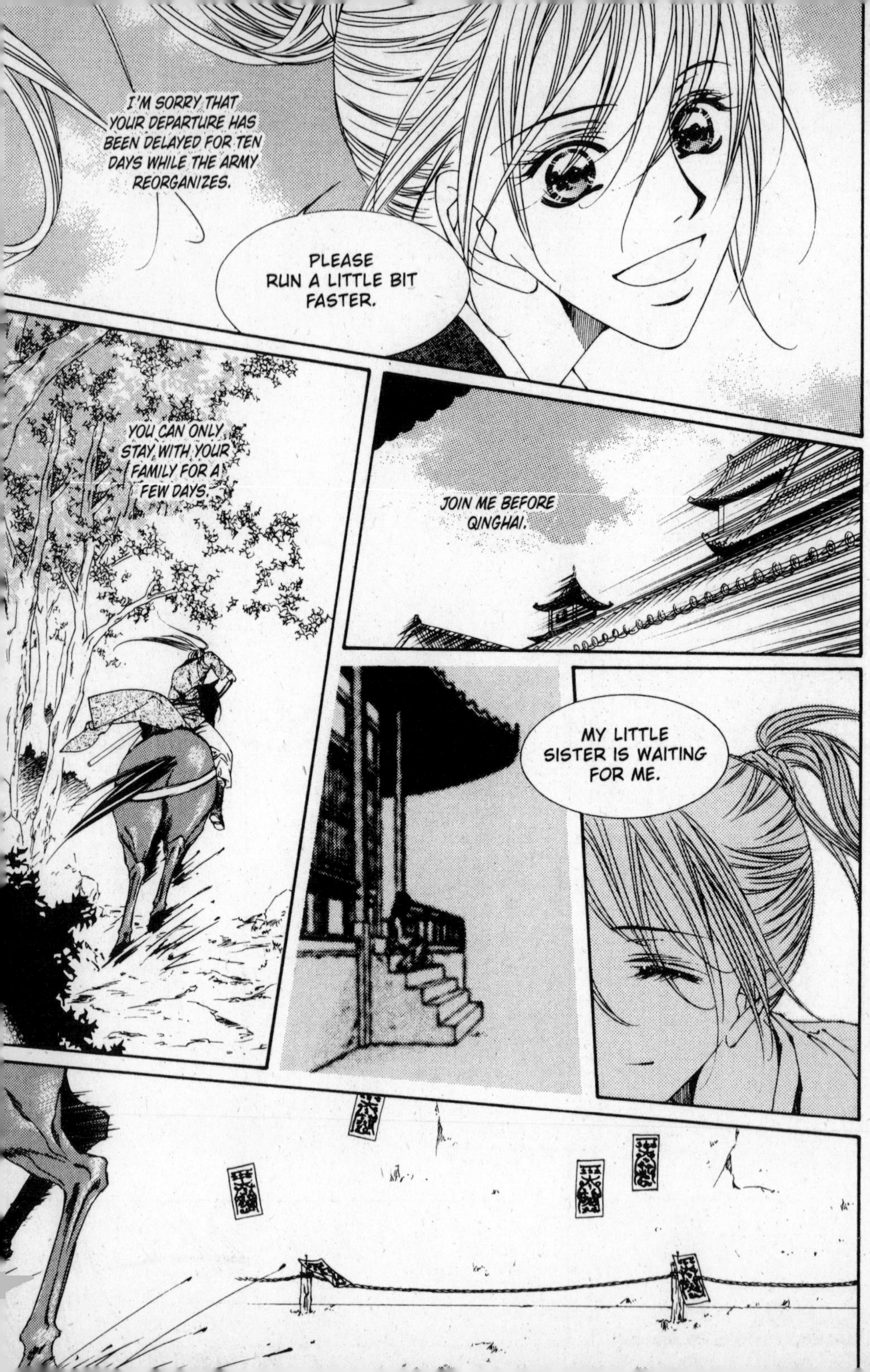
I'M SORRY THAT YOUR DEPARTURE HAS BEEN DELAYED FOR TEN DAYS WHILE THE ARMY REORGANIZES.
PLEASE RUN A LITTLE BIT FASTER.
YOU CAN ONLY STAY WITH YOUR FAMILY FOR A FEW DAYS.
JOIN ME BEFORE QINGHAI.
MY LITTLE SISTER IS WAITING FOR ME.

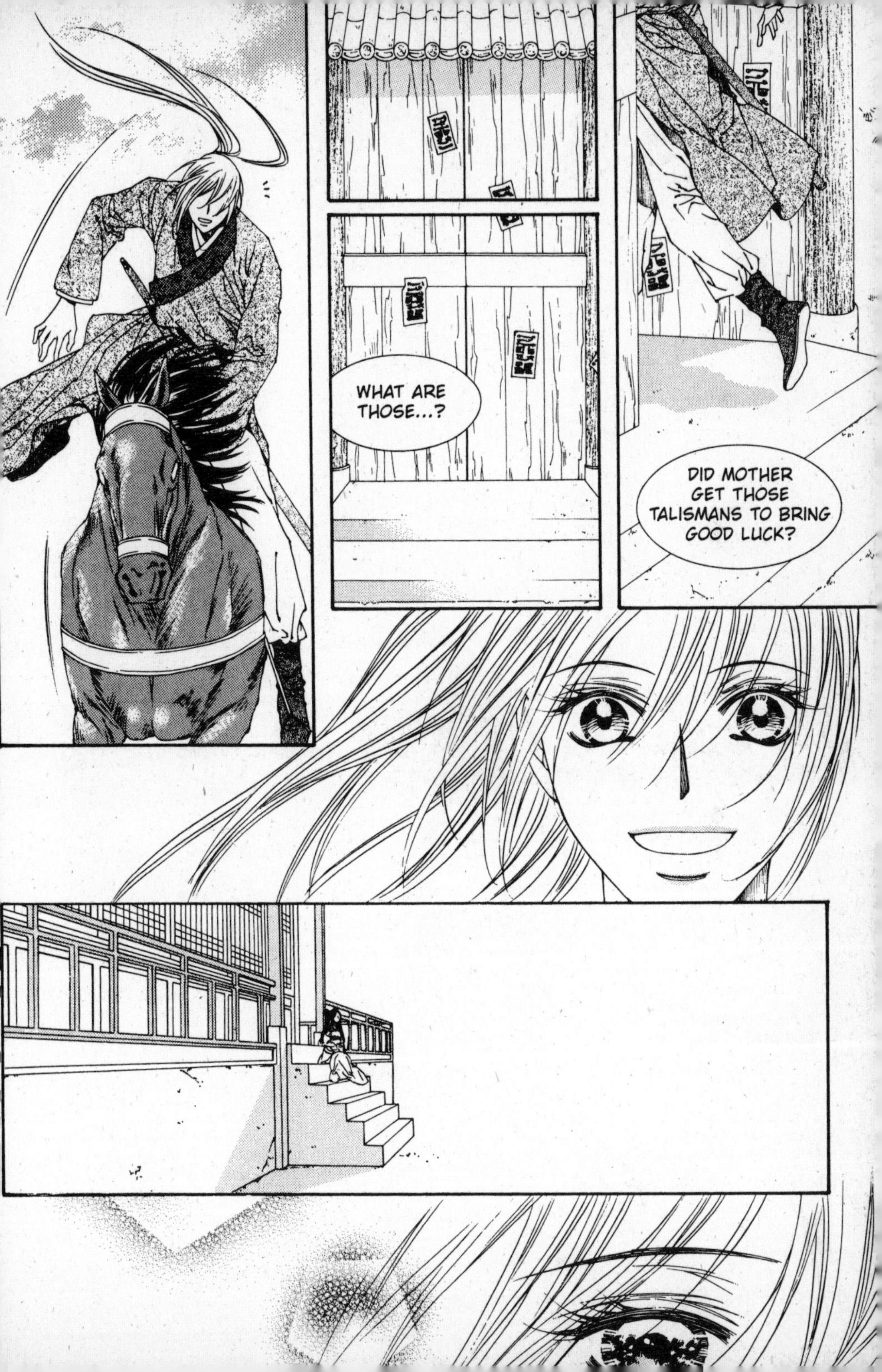
WHAT ARE THOSE...?
DID MOTHER GET THOSE TALISMANS TO BRING GOOD LUCK?

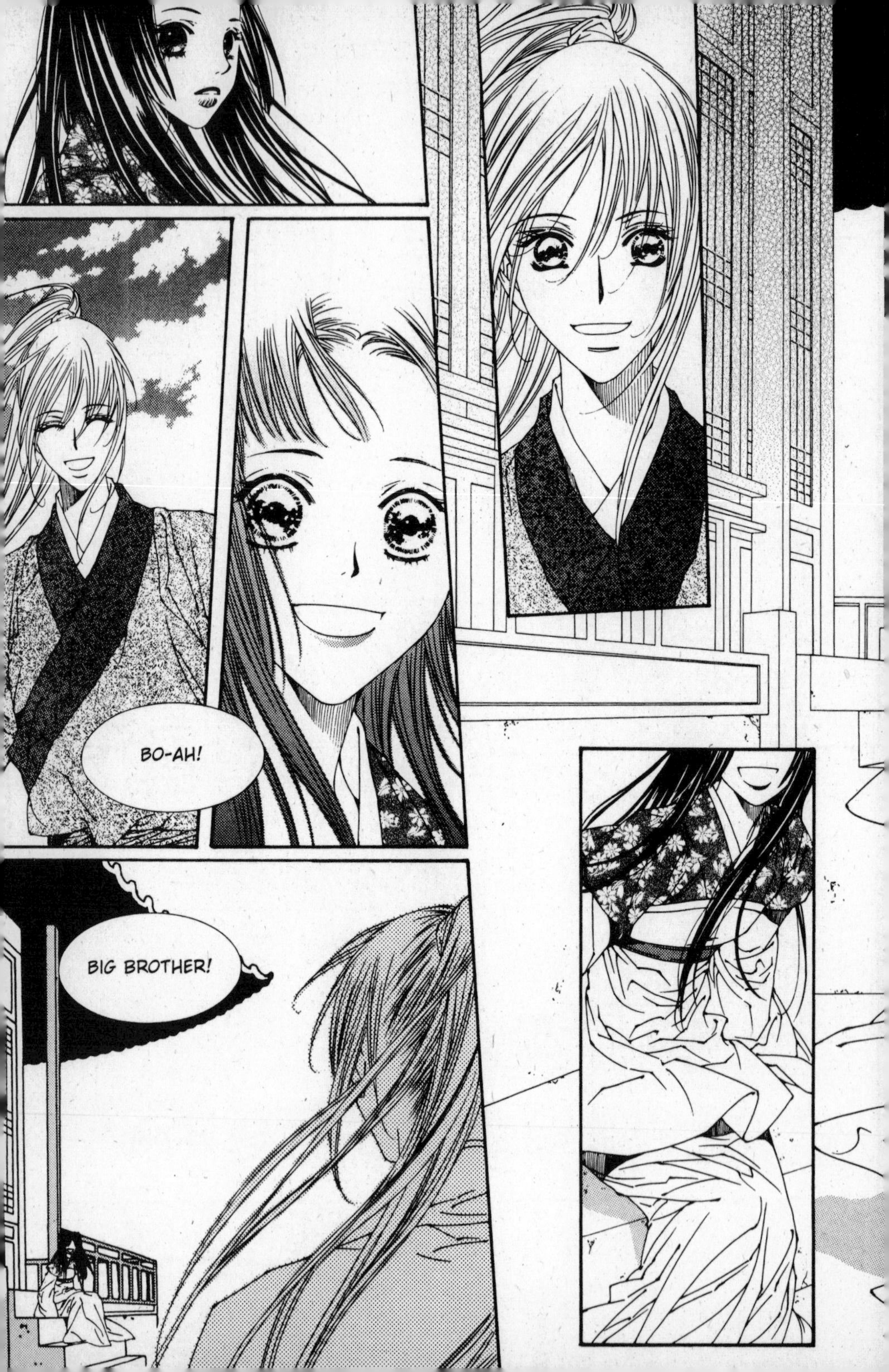
BO-AH!
BIG BROTHER!

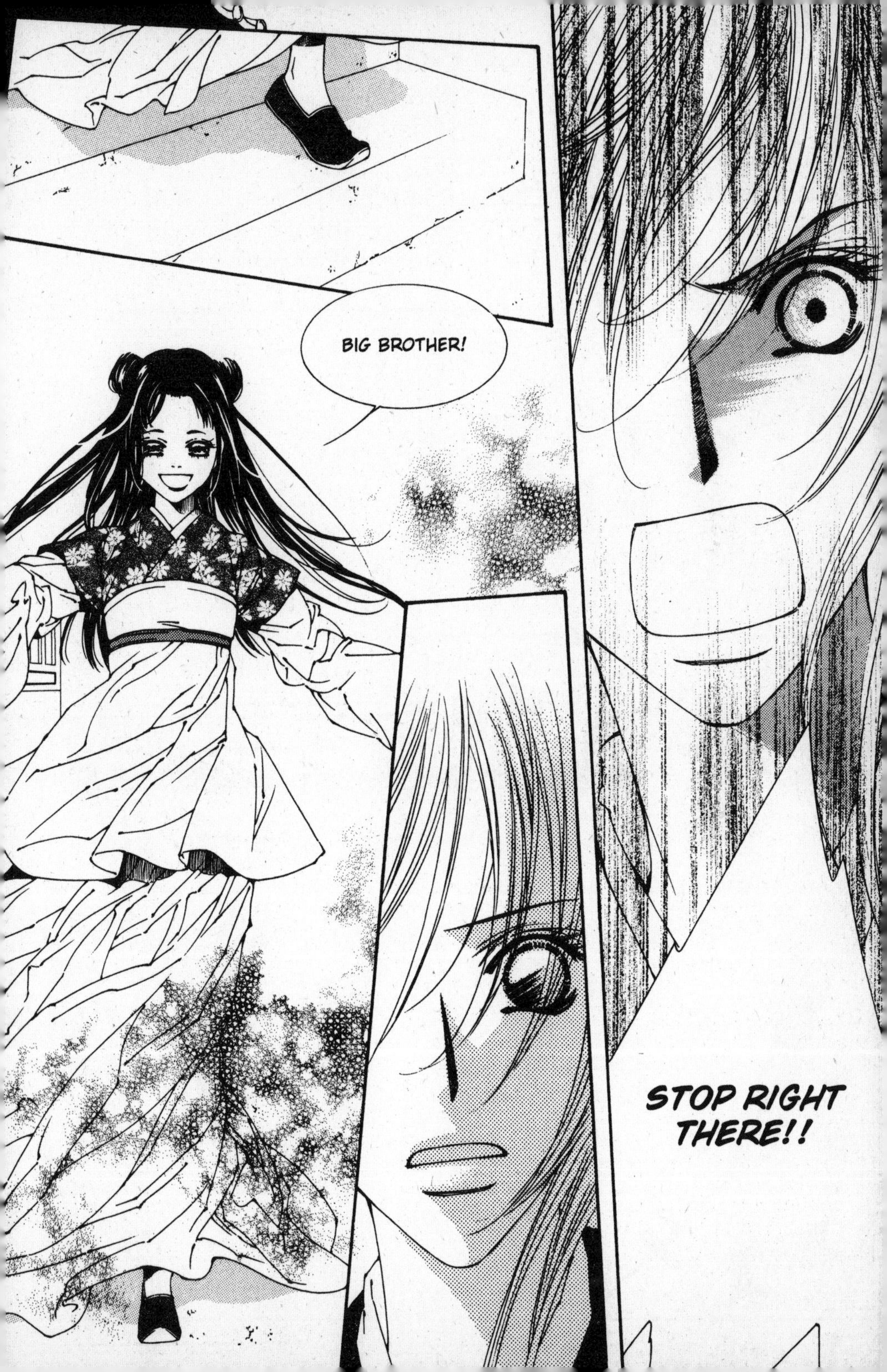
BIG BROTHER!
STOP RIGHT THERE!!

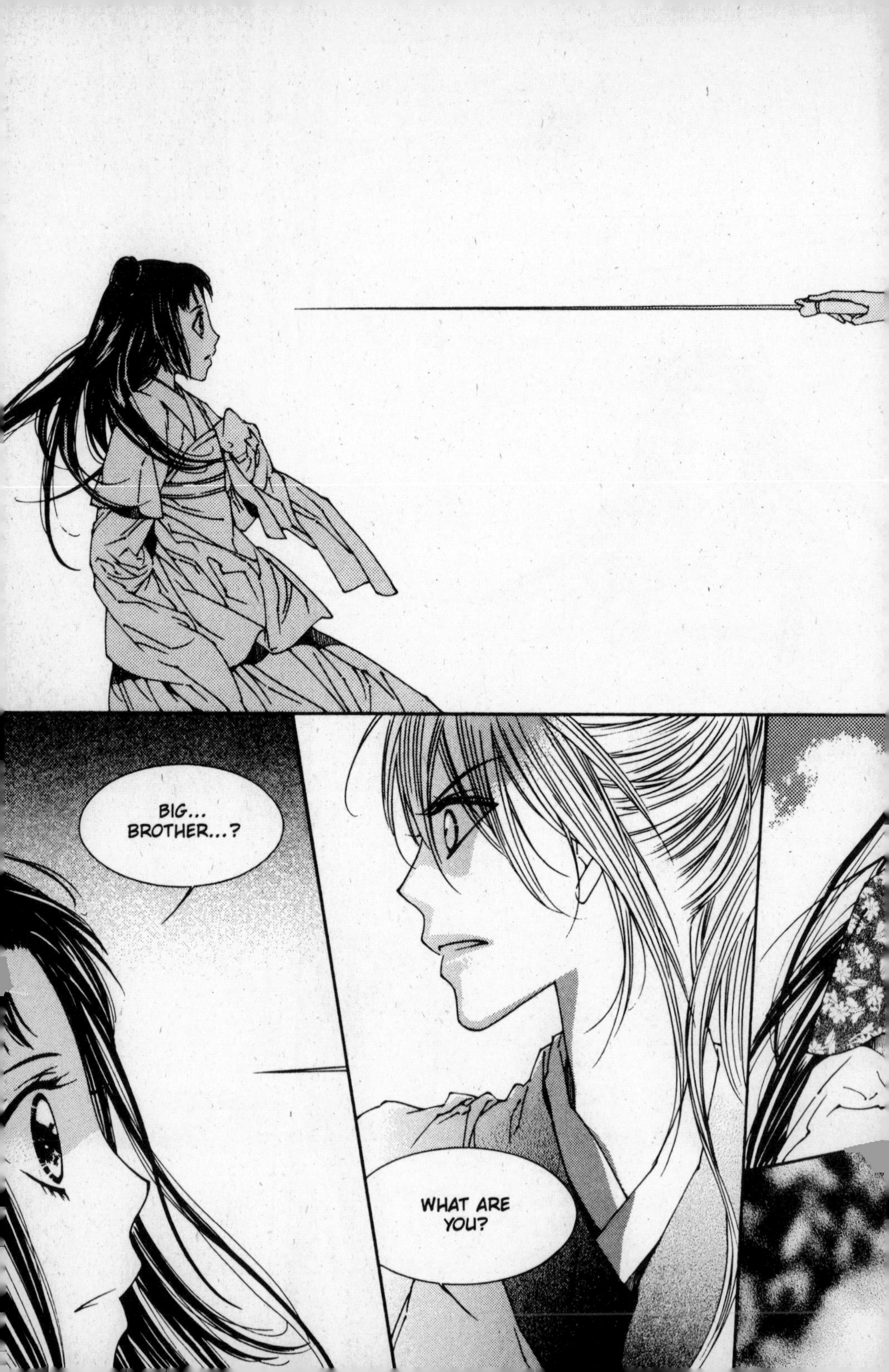
BIG... BROTHER...?
WHAT ARE YOU?

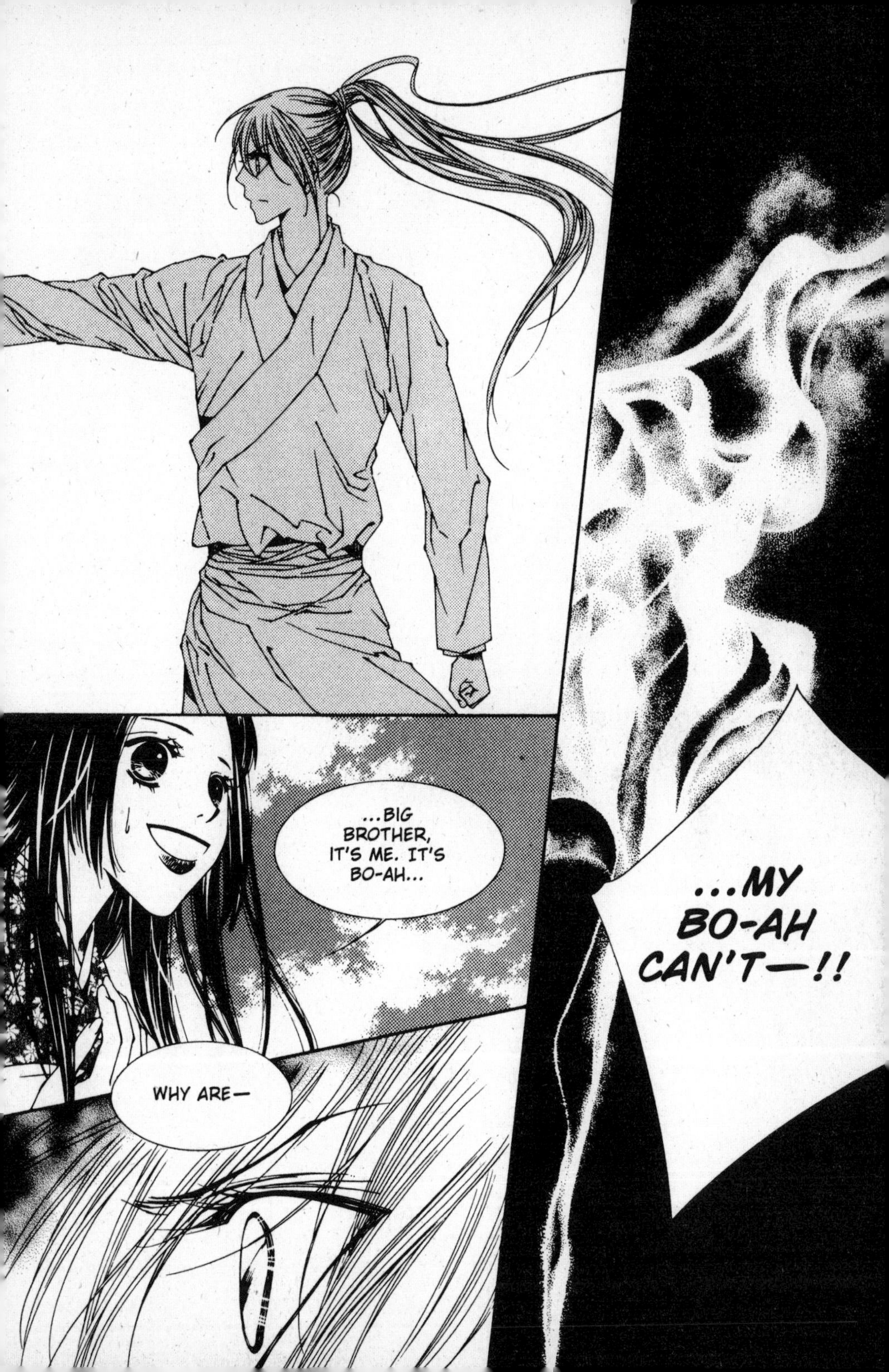
...BIG BROTHER, IT'S ME. IT'S BO-AH...
WHY ARE—
...MY BO-AH CAN'T—!!

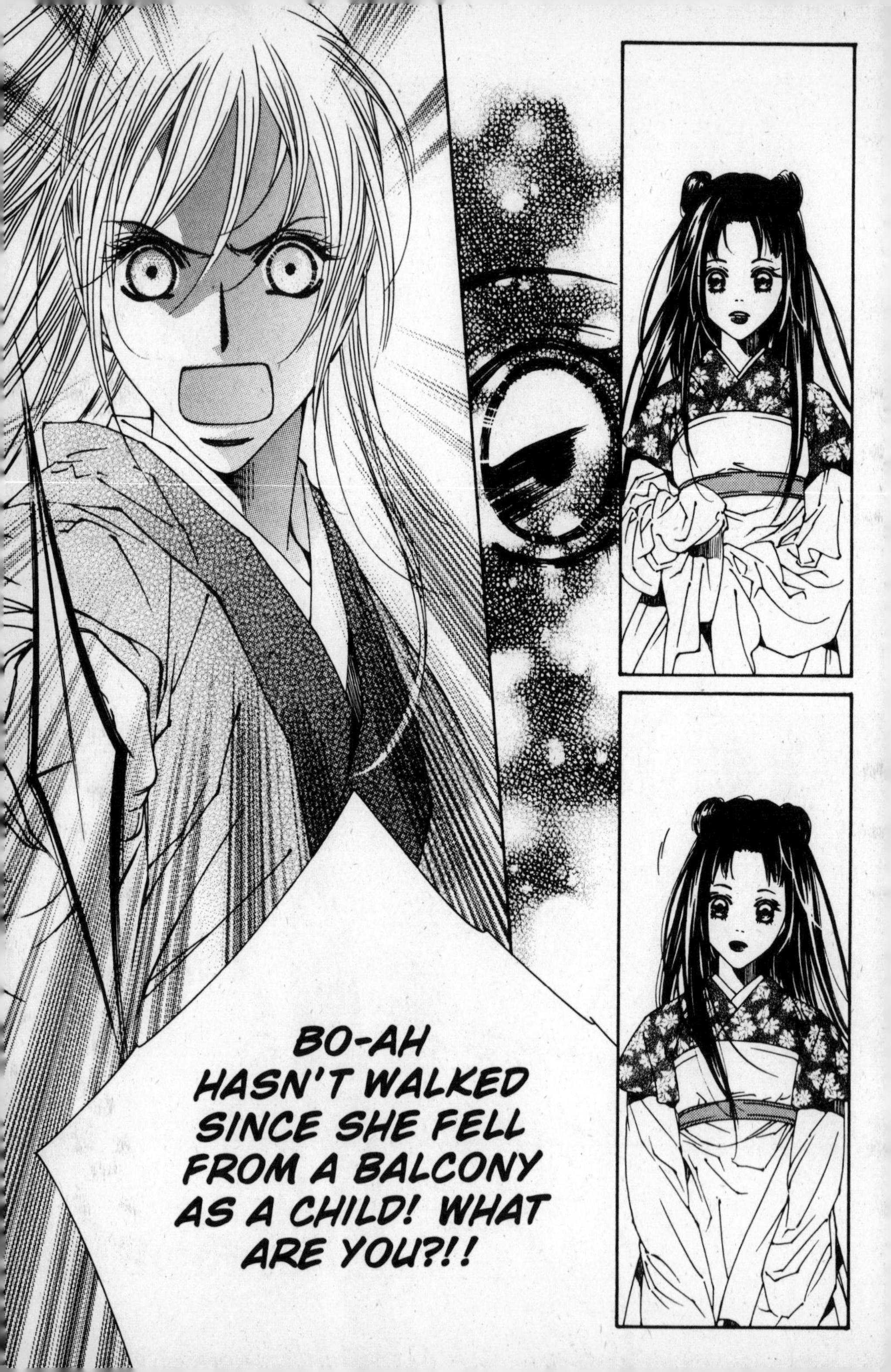
BO-AH HASN'T WALKED SINCE SHE FELL FROM A BALCONY AS A CHILD! WHAT ARE YOU?!!

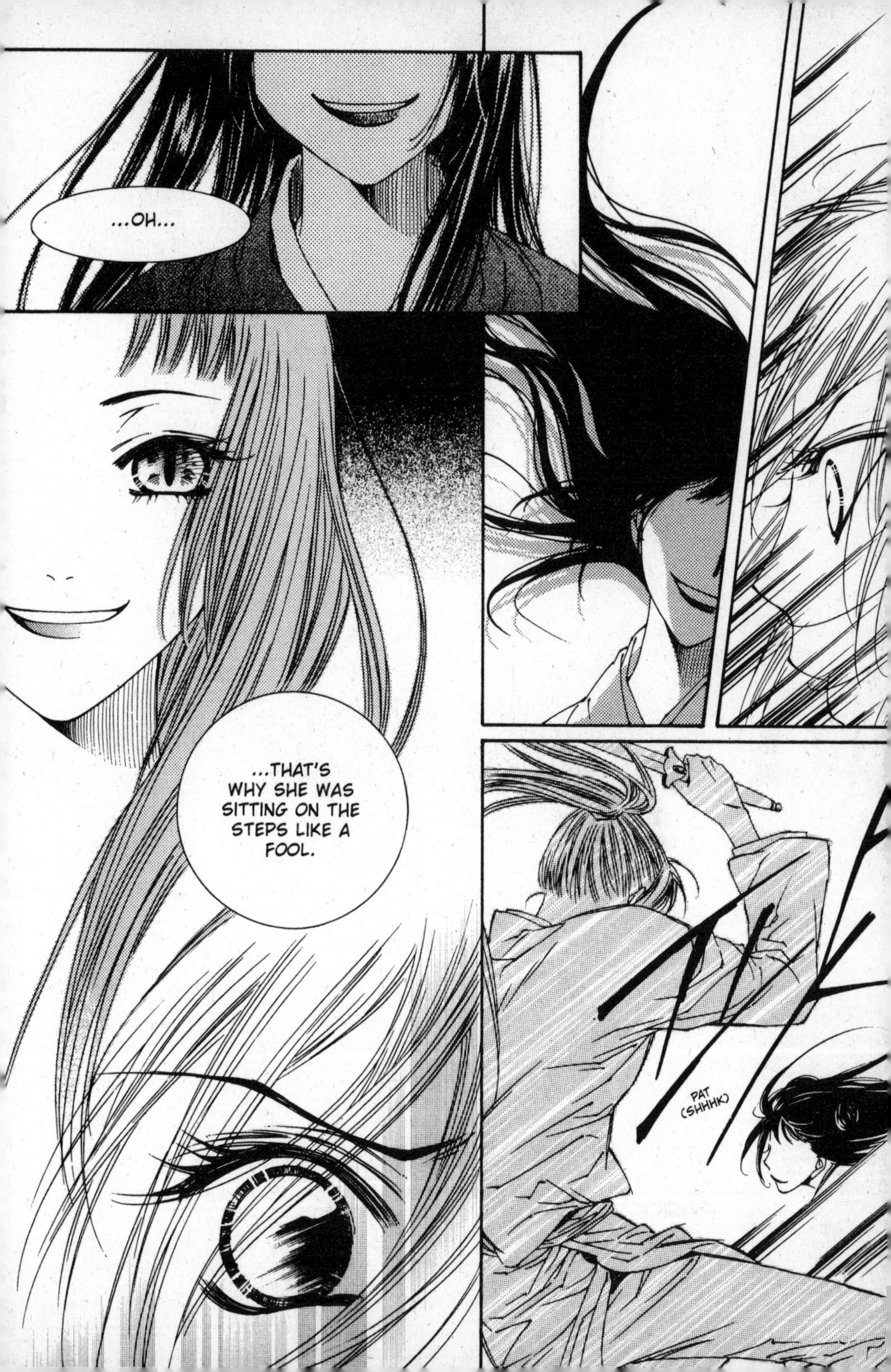
...OH...
...THAT'S WHY SHE WAS SITTING ON THE STEPS LIKE A FOOL.
PAT (SHHHK)

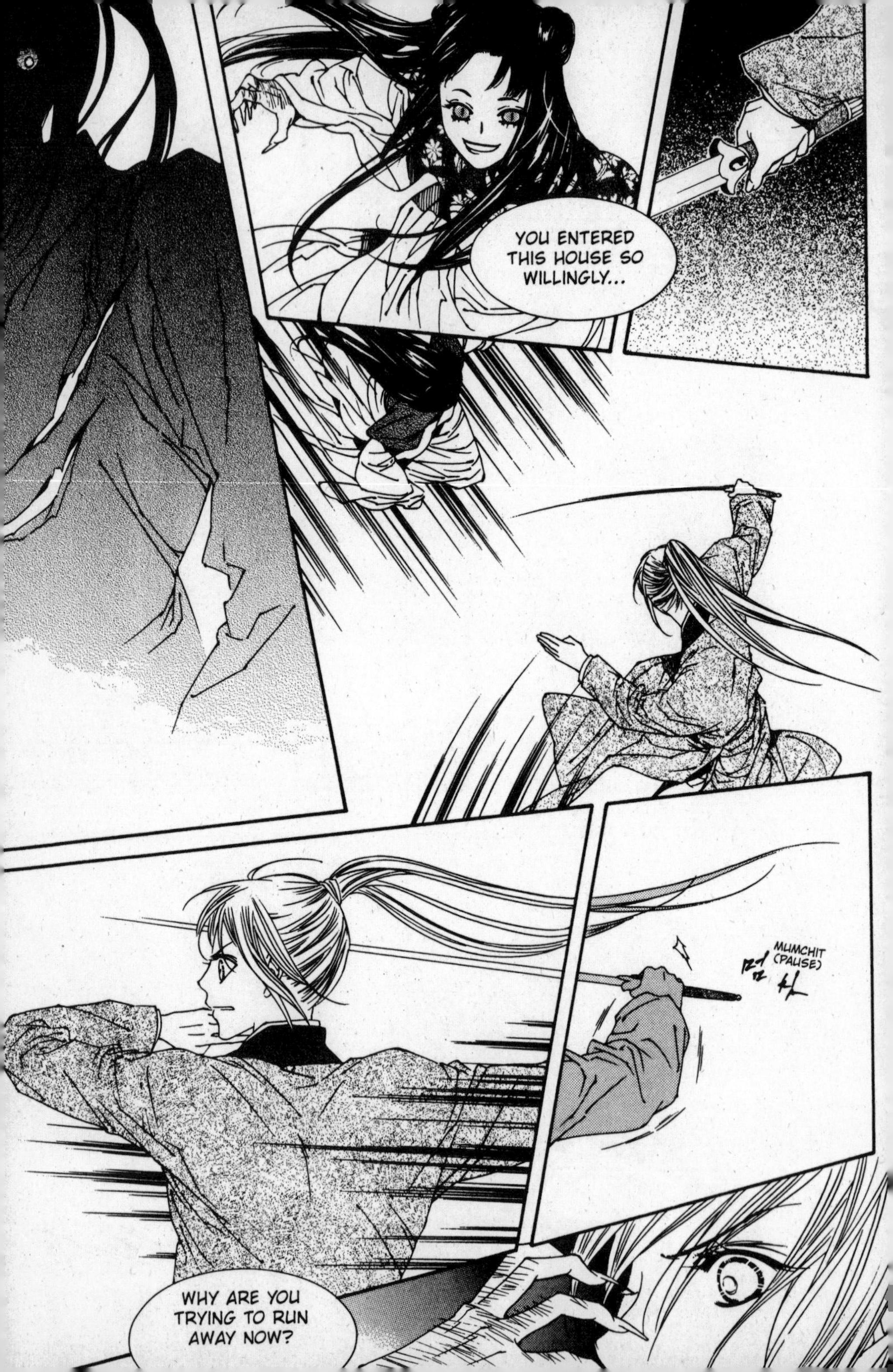
YOU ENTERED THIS HOUSE SO WILLINGLY...
MUMCHIT (PAUSE)
WHY ARE YOU TRYING TO RUN AWAY NOW?

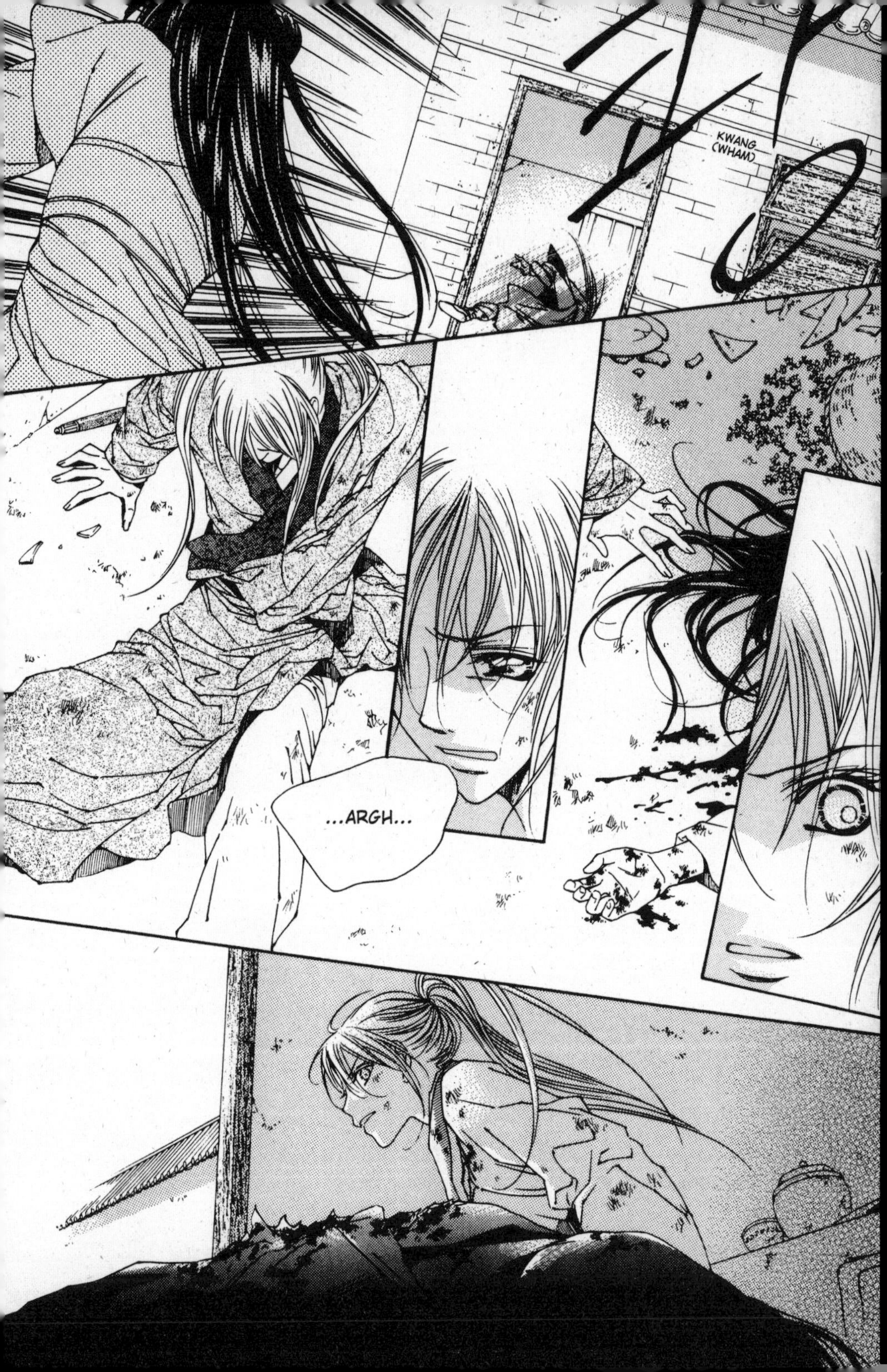
KWANG (WHAM)
...ARGH...

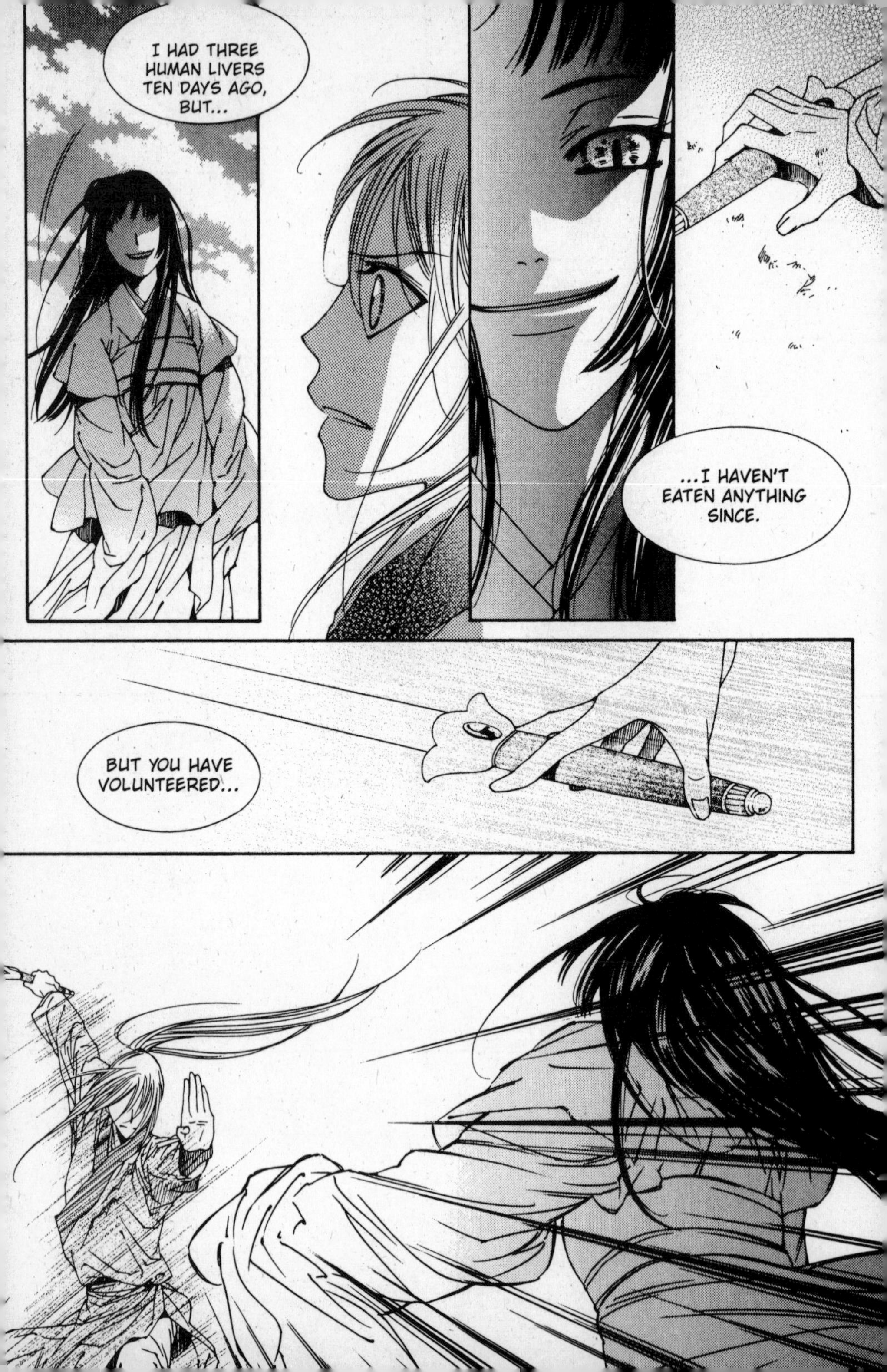
I HAD THREE HUMAN LIVERS TEN DAYS AGO, BUT...
...I HAVEN'T EATEN ANYTHING SINCE.
BUT YOU HAVE VOLUNTEERED...

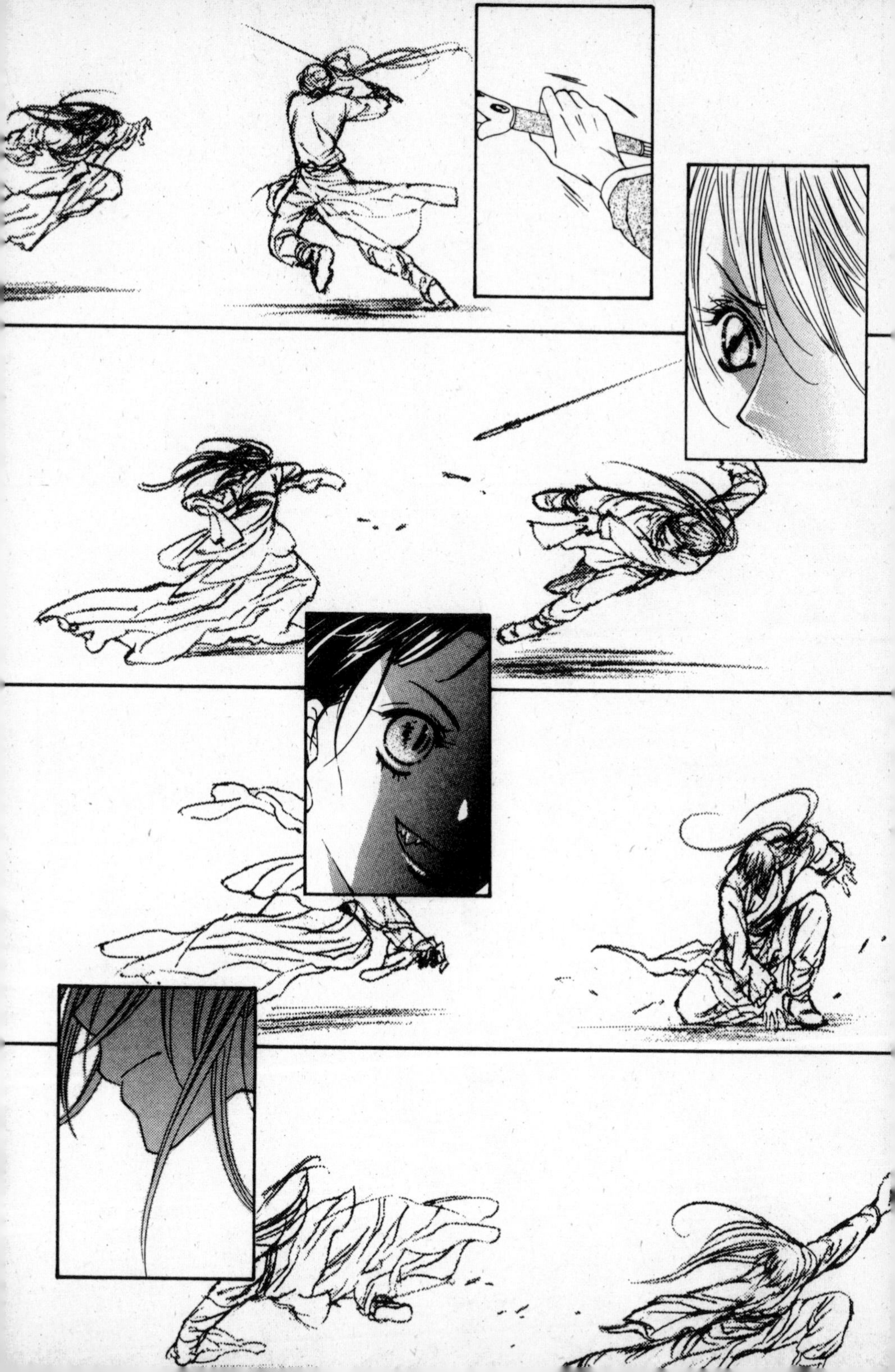

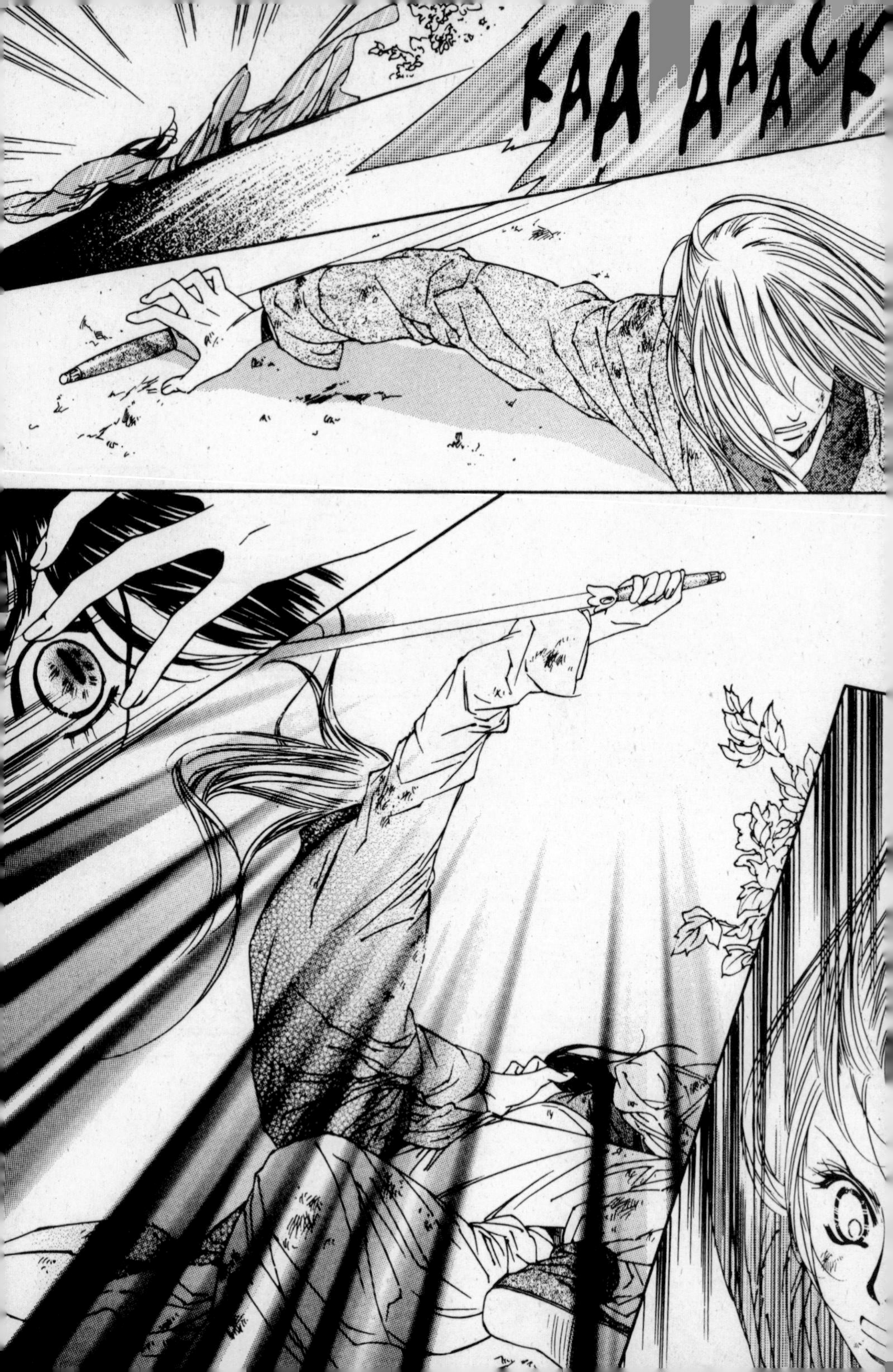
KAAAAAACK

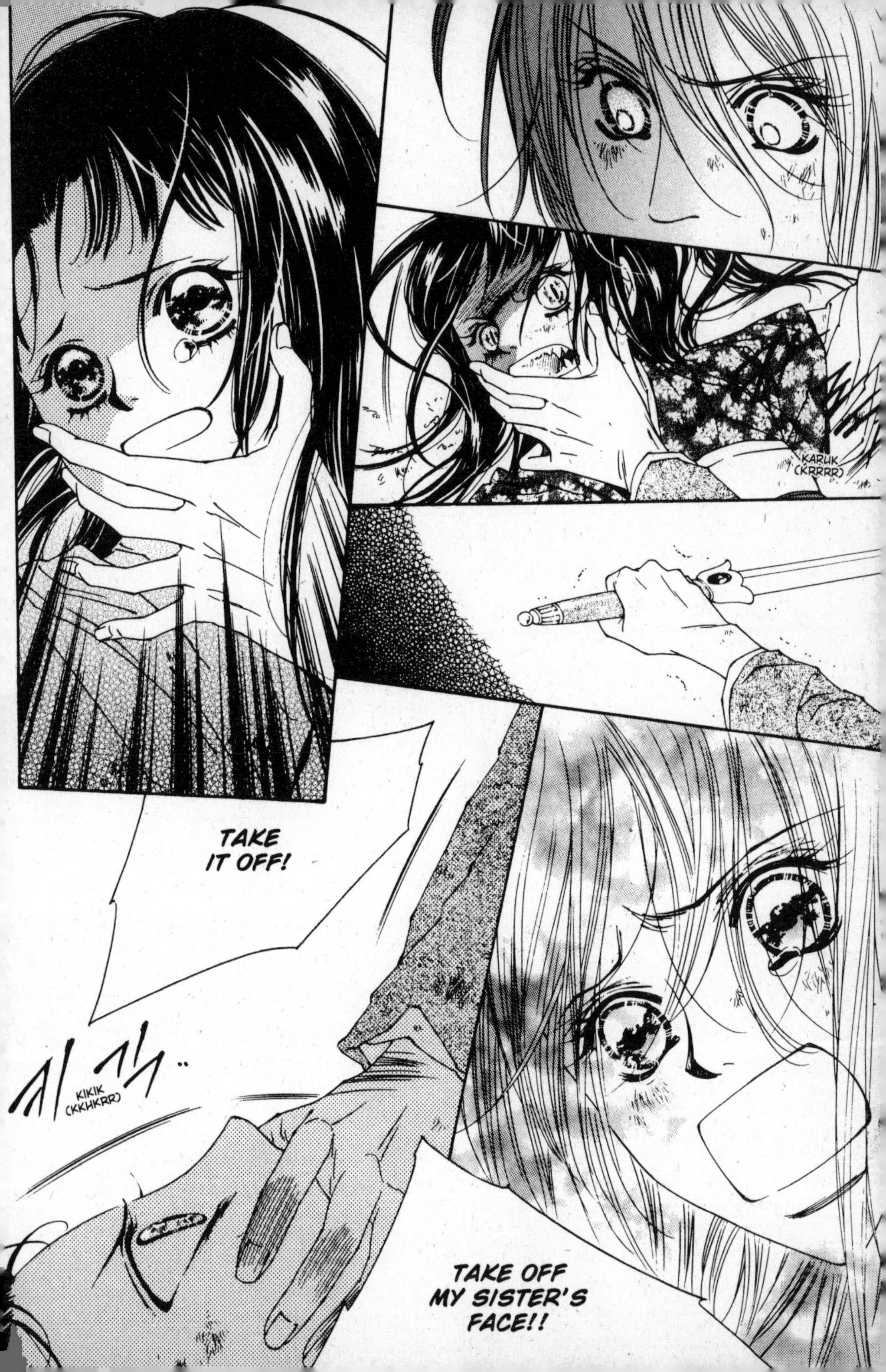
KARUK (KRRRR)
TAKE IT OFF!
KIKIK (KKHKRR)
TAKE OFF MY SISTER'S FACE!!

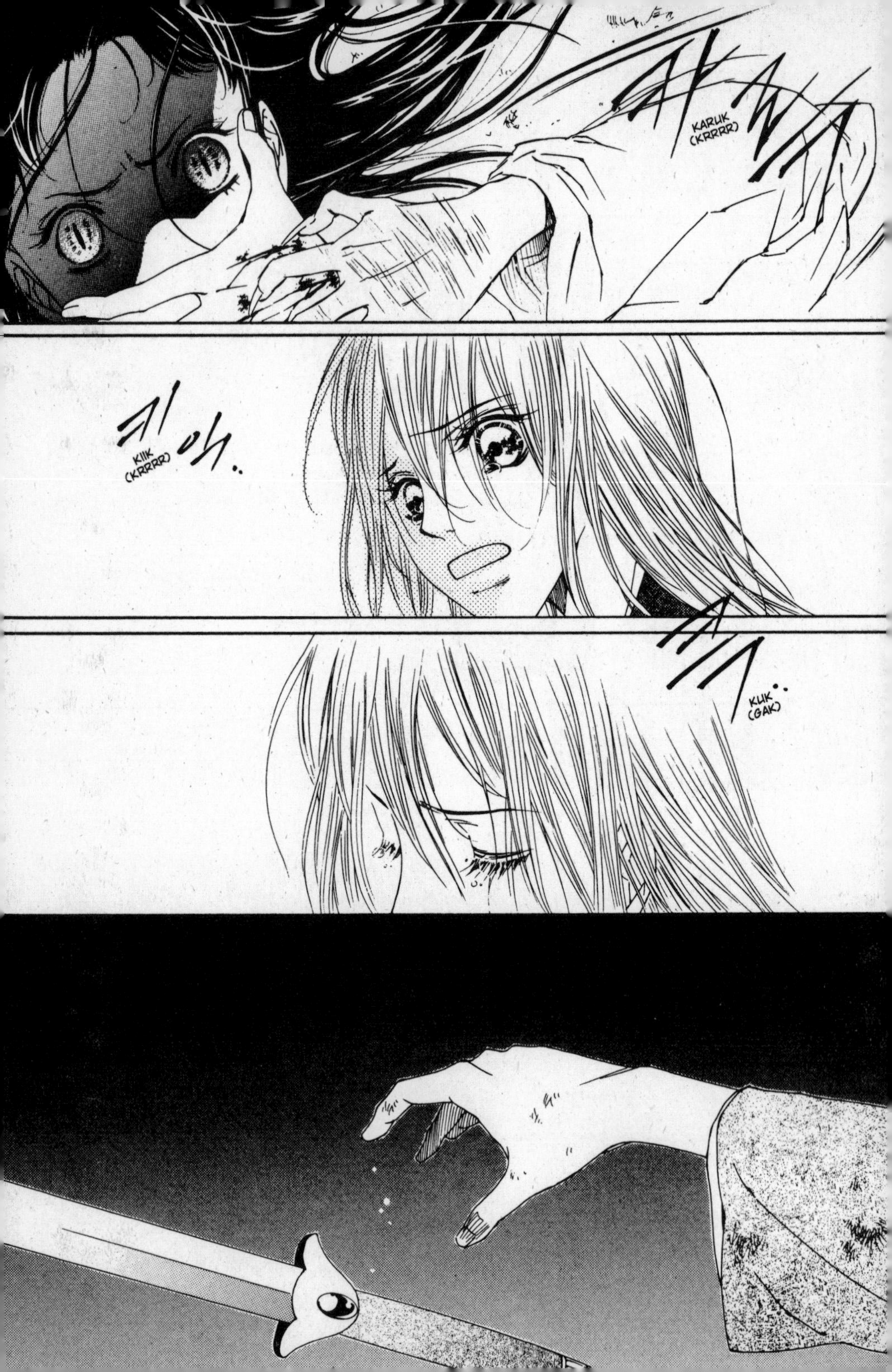
KARUK
(KRRRR)
KIIK
(KRRRR)
KUK..
(GAK)

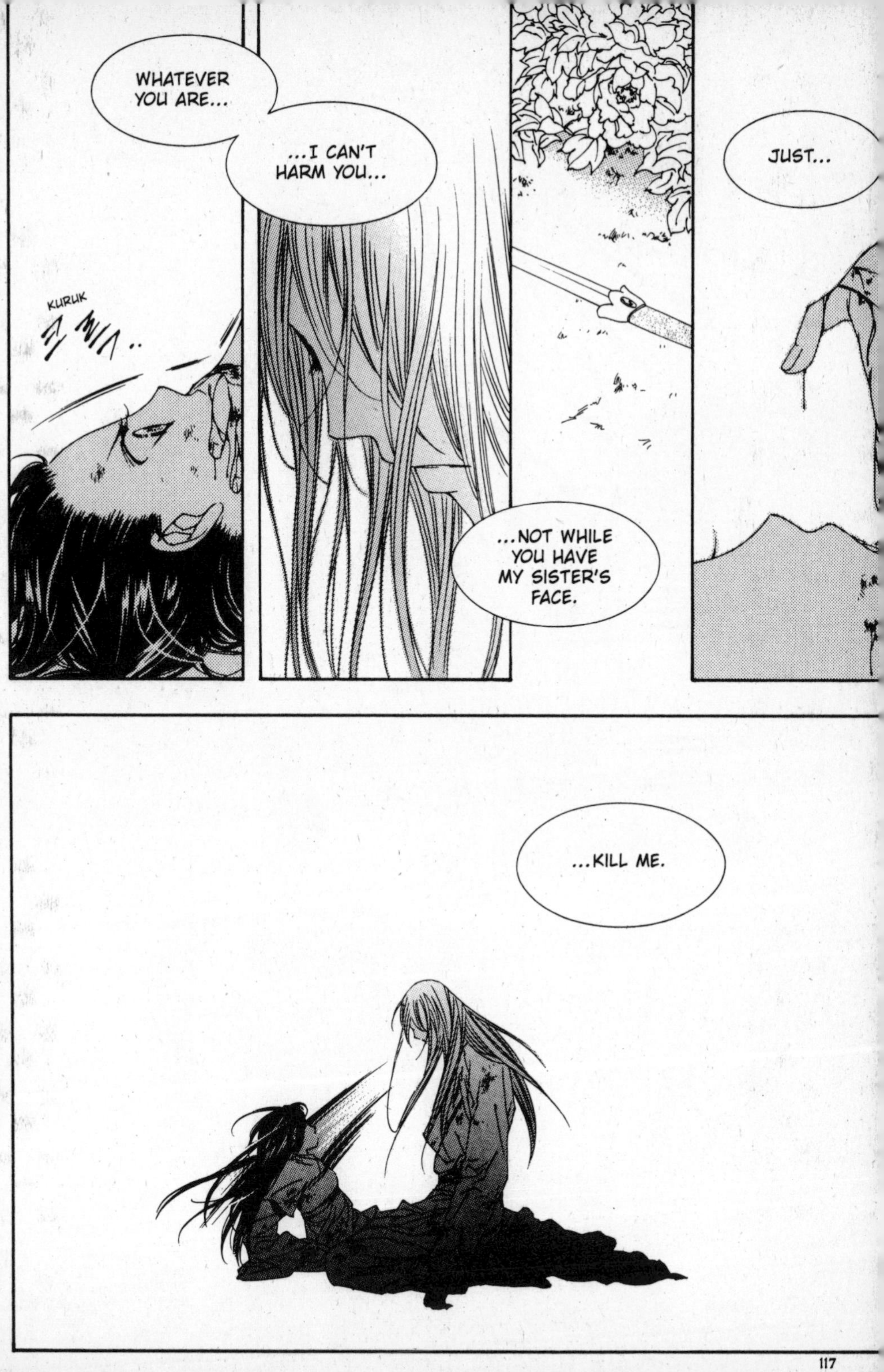
WHATEVER YOU ARE...
KURUK
...I CAN'T HARM YOU...
...NOT WHILE YOU HAVE MY SISTER'S FACE.
JUST...
...KILL ME.

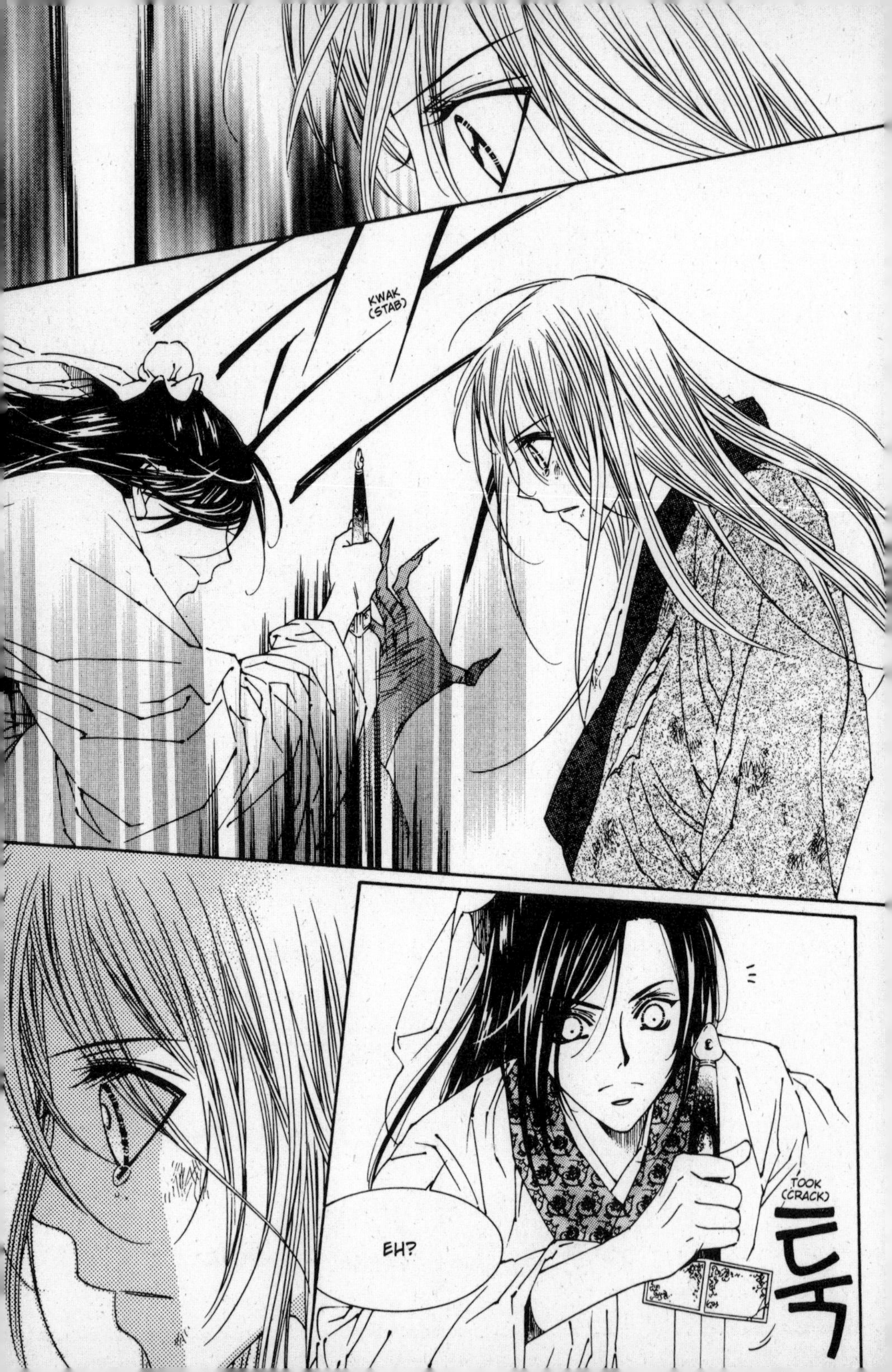
KWAK (STAB)
TOOK (CRACK)
EH?

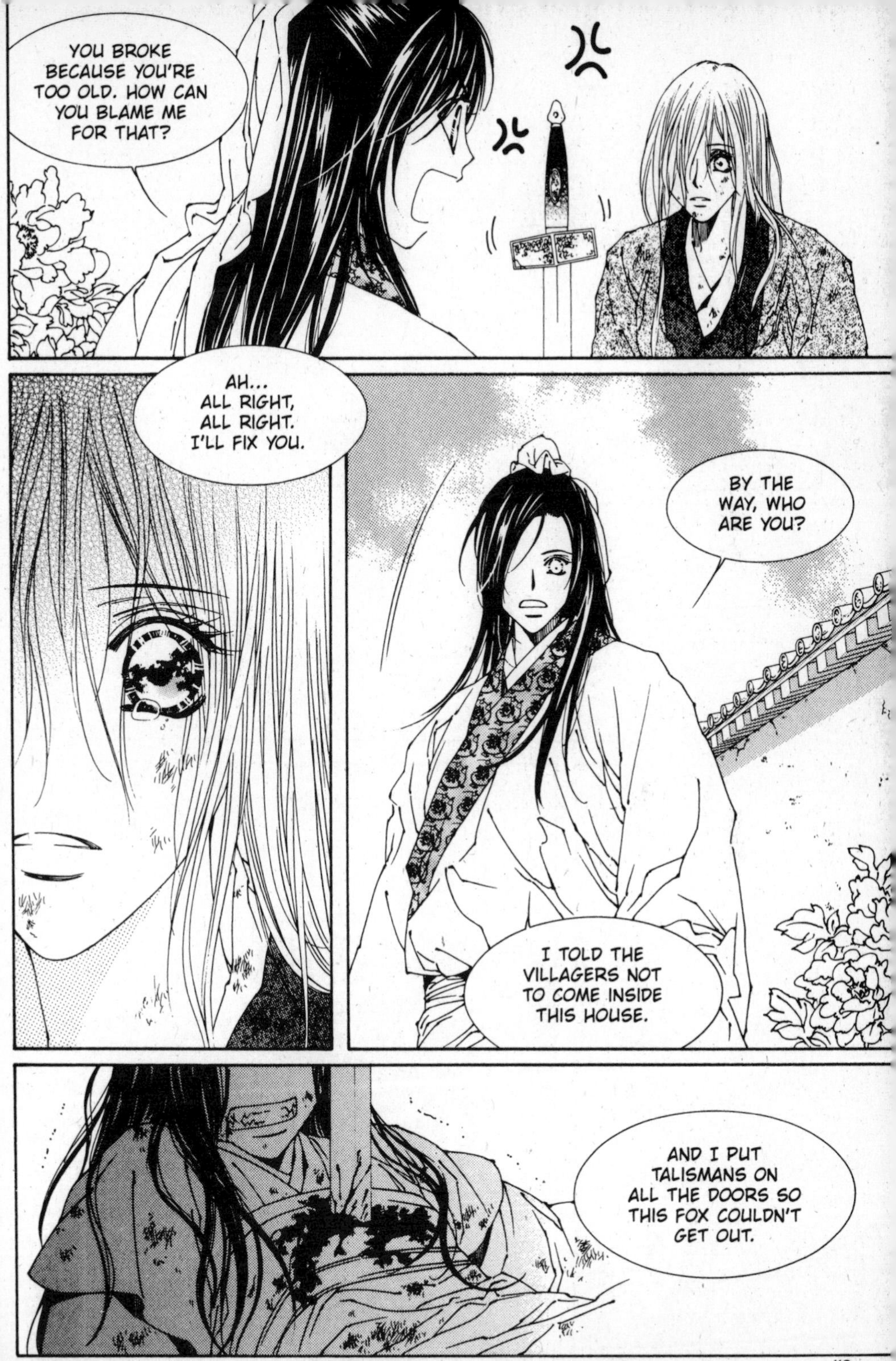
YOU BROKE BECAUSE YOU'RE TOO OLD. HOW CAN YOU BLAME ME FOR THAT?
AH... ALL RIGHT, ALL RIGHT. I'LL FIX YOU.
BY THE WAY, WHO ARE YOU?
I TOLD THE VILLAGERS NOT TO COME INSIDE THIS HOUSE.
AND I PUT TALISMANS ON ALL THE DOORS SO THIS FOX COULDN'T GET OUT.

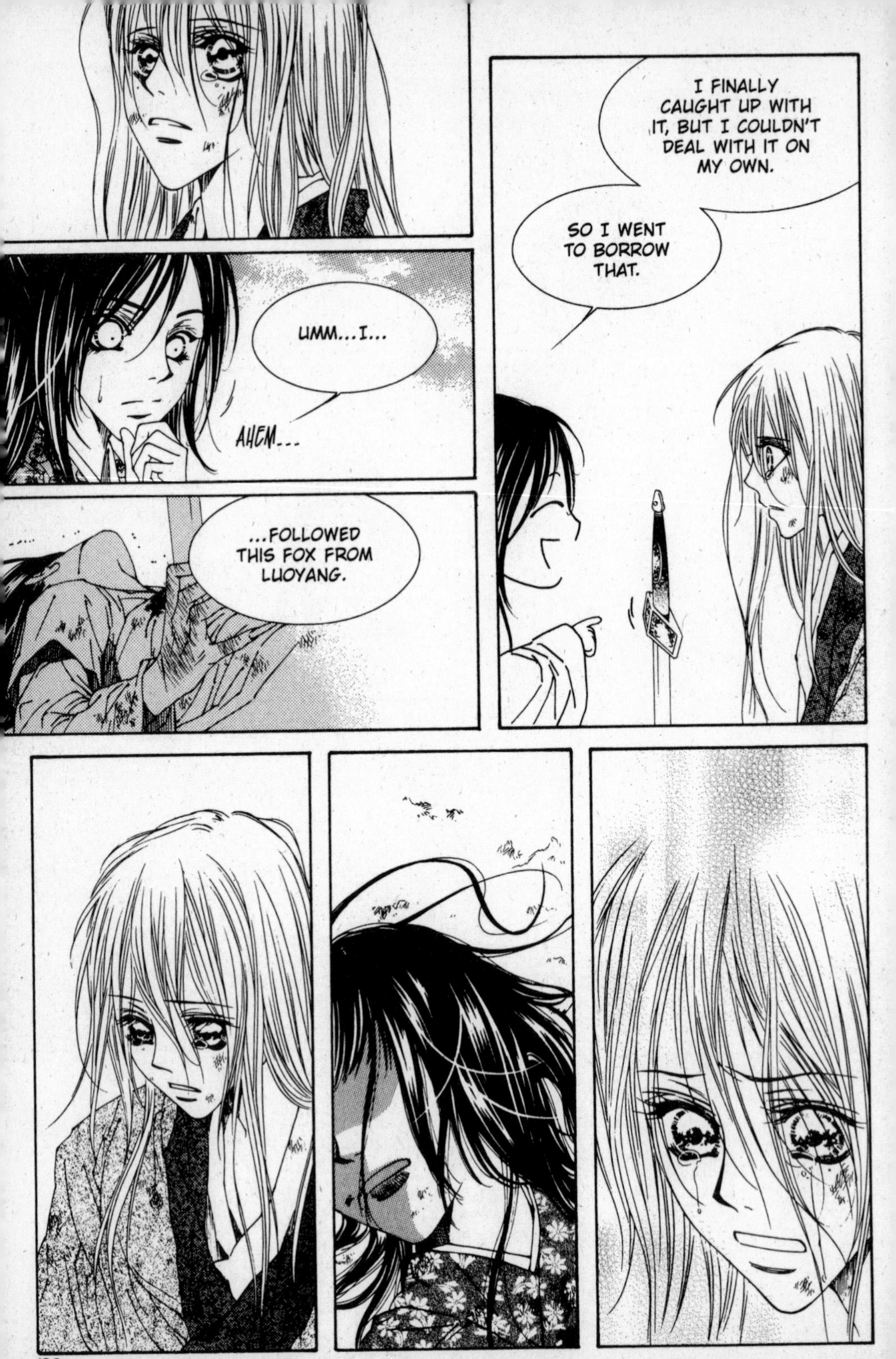
UMM...I...
AHEM...
...FOLLOWED THIS FOX FROM LUOYANG.
I FINALLY CAUGHT UP WITH IT, BUT I COULDN'T DEAL WITH IT ON MY OWN.
SO I WENT TO BORROW THAT.

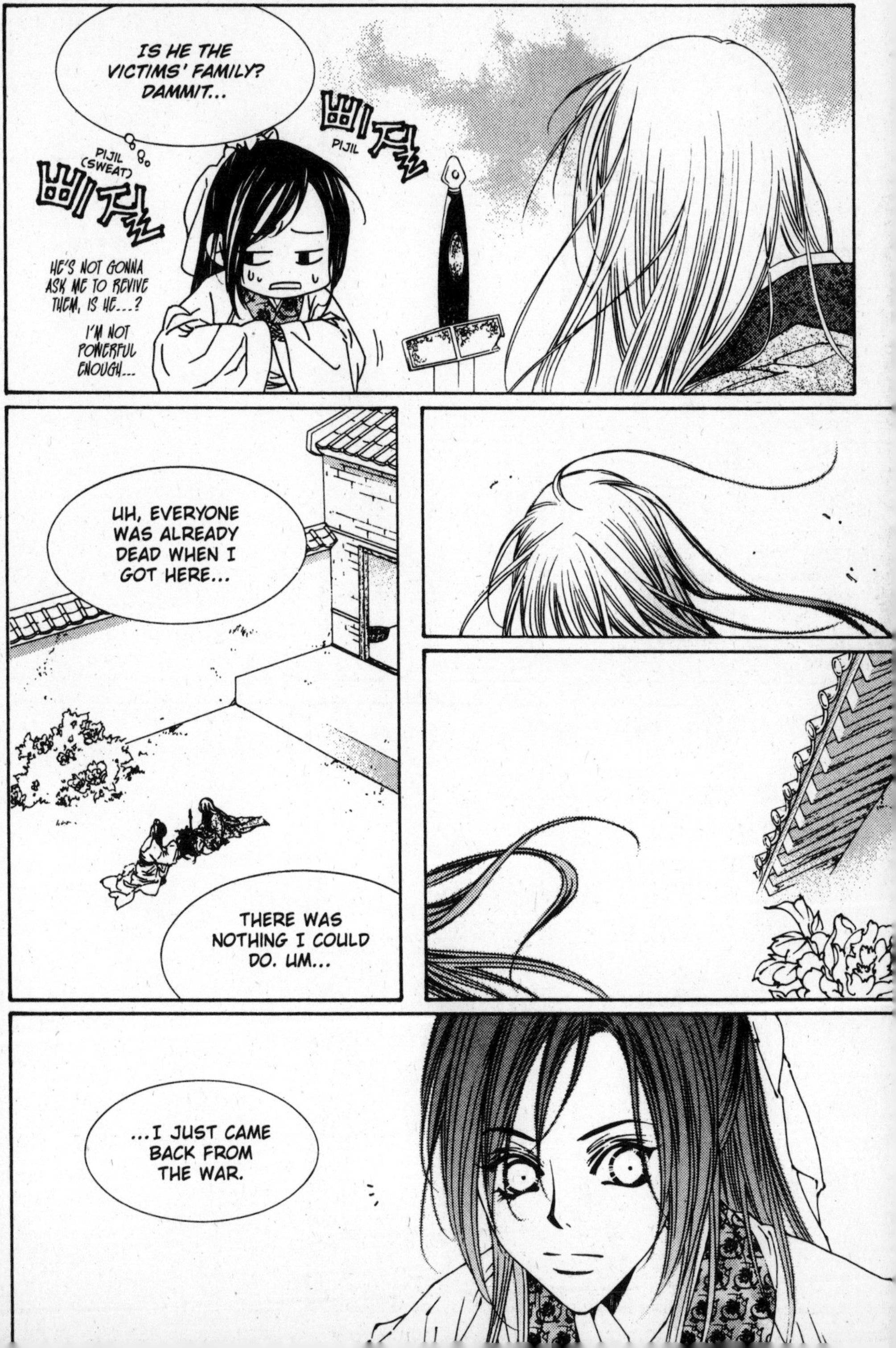
IS HE THE VICTIMS' FAMILY? DAMMIT...
PIJIL (SWEAT)
삐질
PIJIL
삐질
HE'S NOT GONNA ASK ME TO REVIVE THEM, IS HE...?
I'M NOT POWERFUL ENOUGH...
UH, EVERYONE WAS ALREADY DEAD WHEN I GOT HERE...
THERE WAS NOTHING I COULD DO. UM...
...I JUST CAME BACK FROM THE WAR.

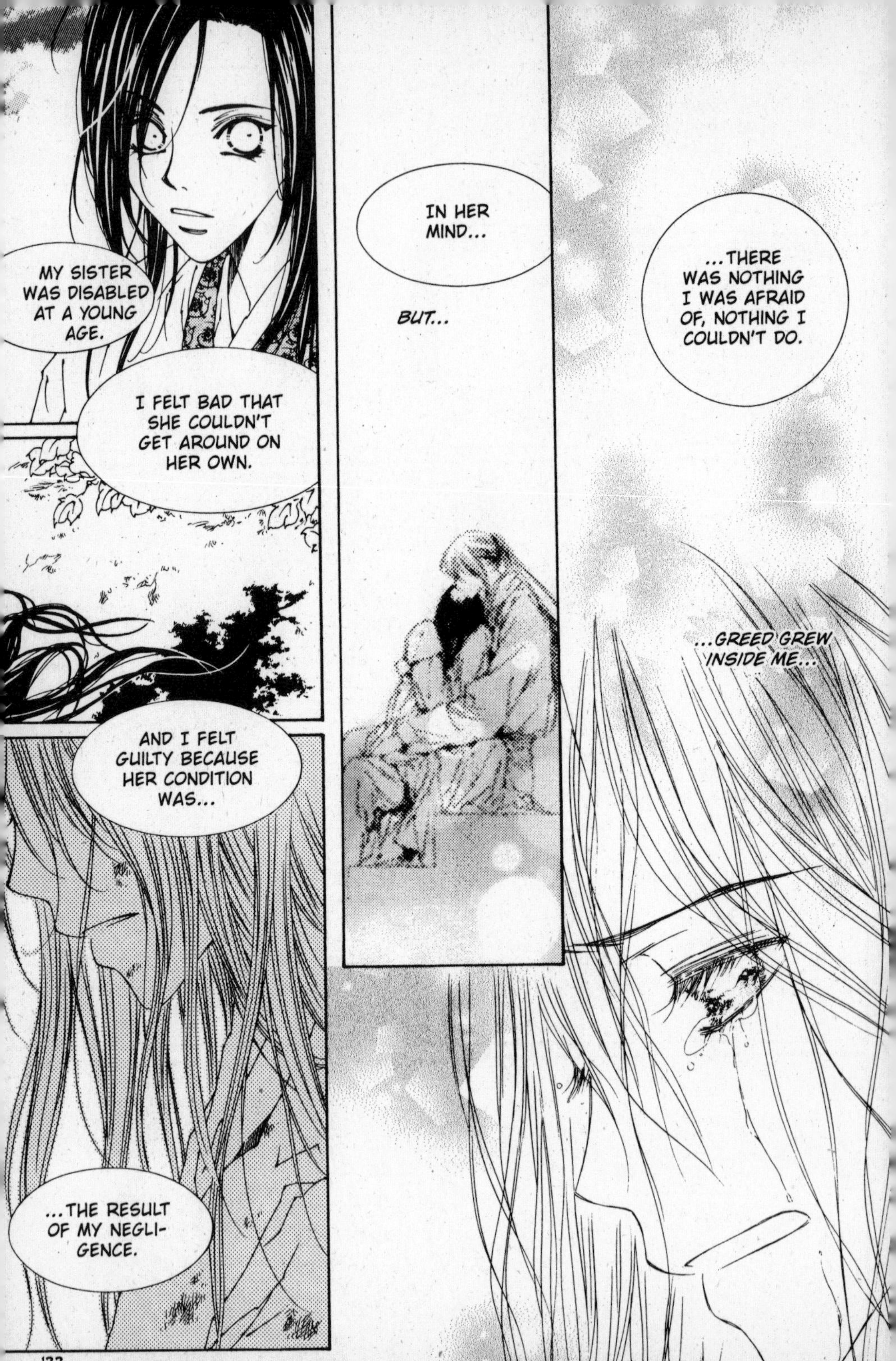
MY SISTER WAS DISABLED AT A YOUNG AGE.
I FELT BAD THAT SHE COULDN'T GET AROUND ON HER OWN.
AND I FELT GUILTY BECAUSE HER CONDITION WAS...
...THE RESULT OF MY NEGLI-GENCE.
IN HER MIND...
BUT...
...THERE WAS NOTHING I WAS AFRAID OF, NOTHING I COULDN'T DO.
...GREED GREW INSIDE ME...

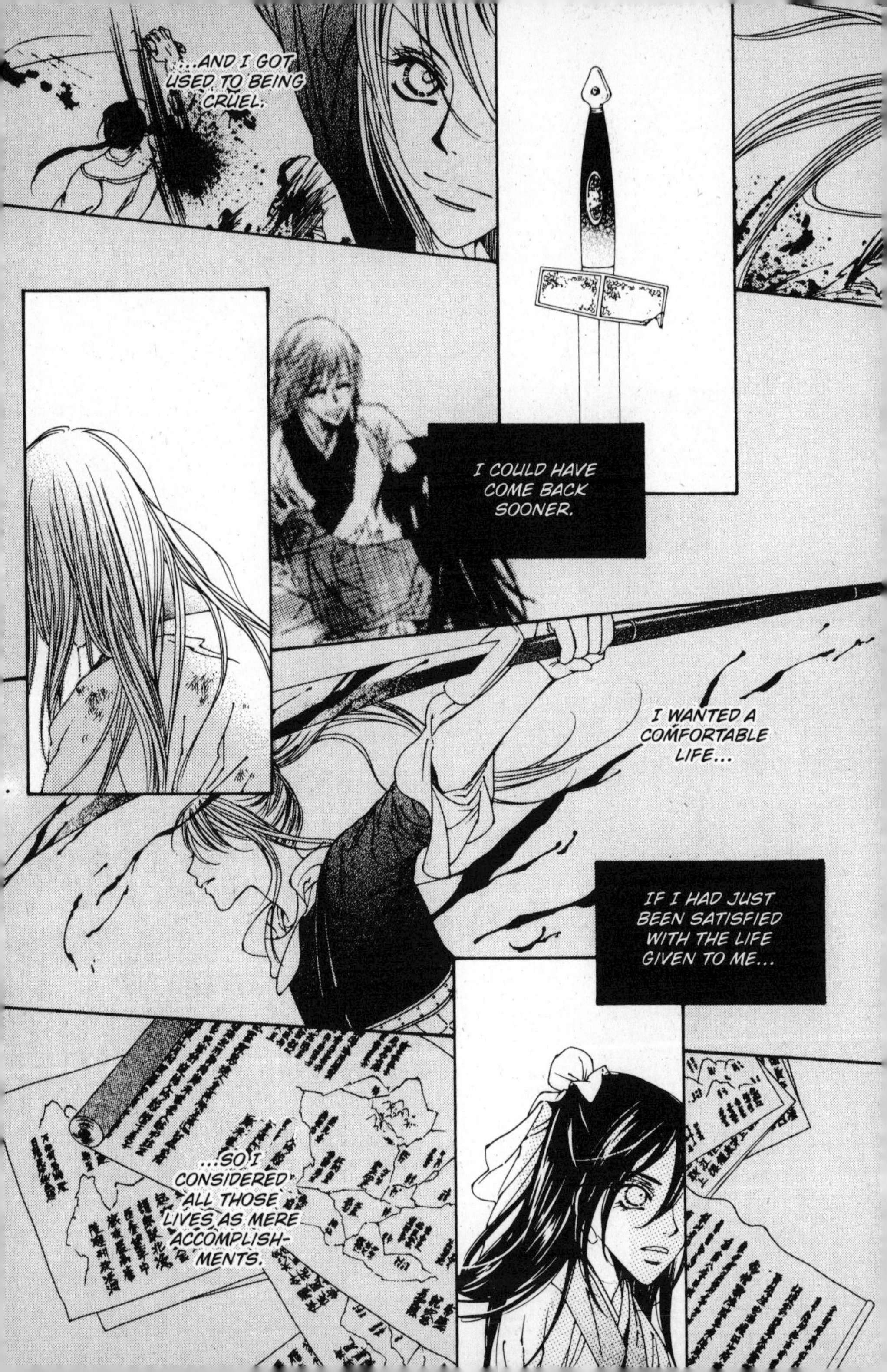
...AND I GOT USED TO BEING CRUEL.
I COULD HAVE COME BACK SOONER.
I WANTED A COMFORTABLE LIFE...
IF I HAD JUST BEEN SATISFIED WITH THE LIFE GIVEN TO ME...
...SO I CONSIDERED ALL THOSE LIVES AS MERE ACCOMPLISH-MENTS.

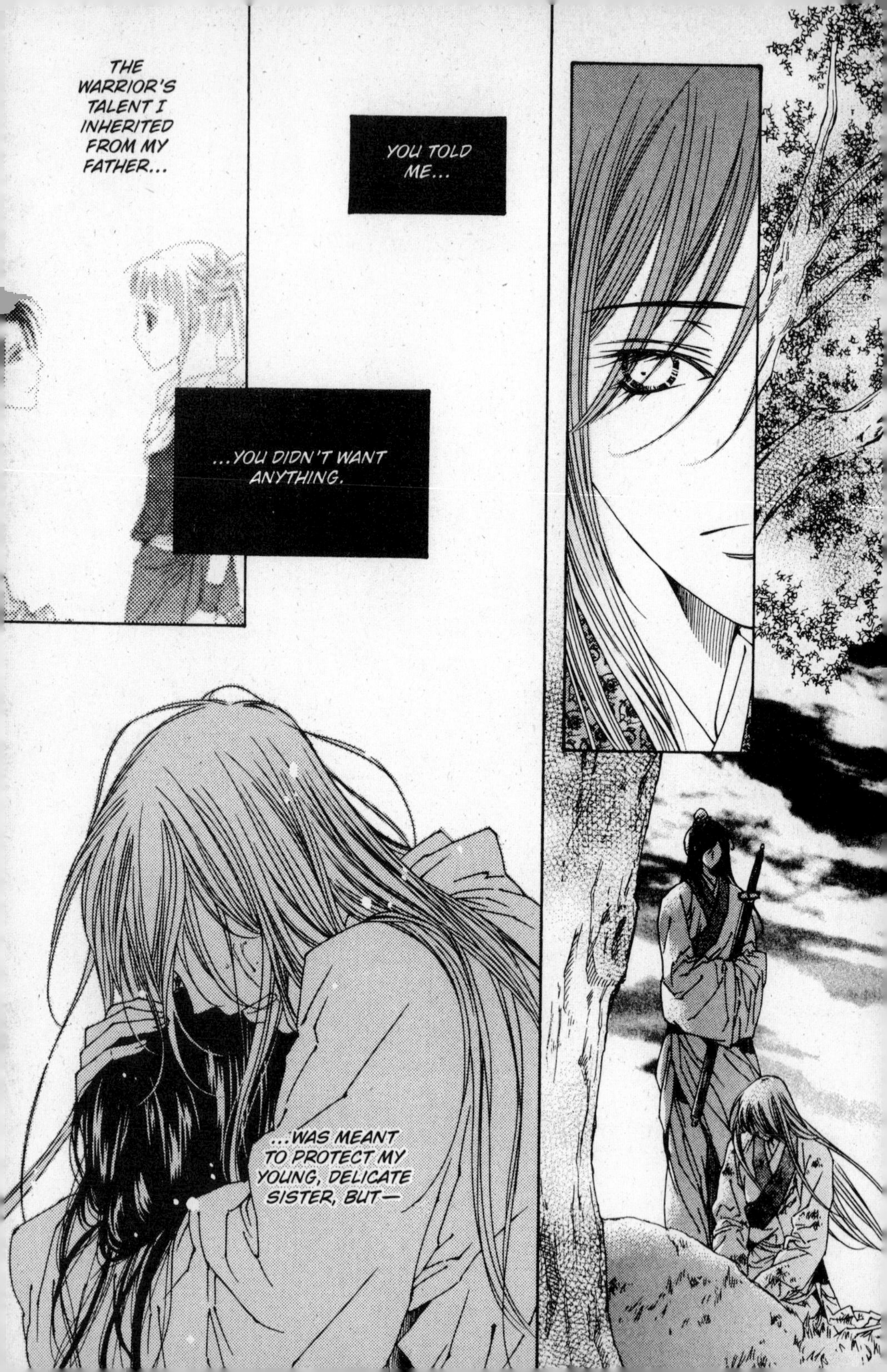
THE WARRIOR'S TALENT I INHERITED FROM MY FATHER...
YOU TOLD ME...
...YOU DIDN'T WANT ANYTHING.
...WAS MEANT TO PROTECT MY YOUNG, DELICATE SISTER, BUT—

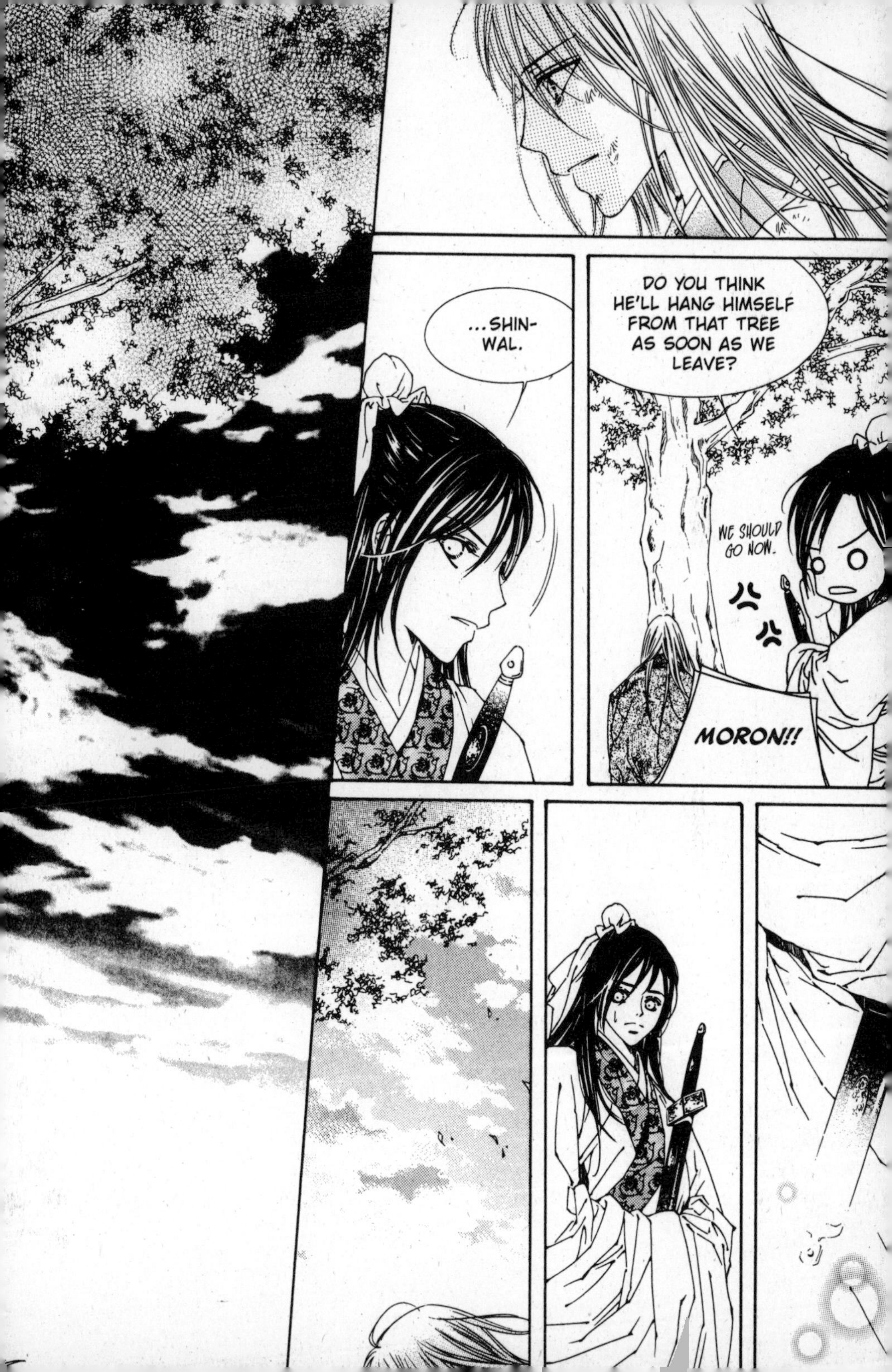
...SHIN-
WAL.
DO YOU THINK HE'LL HANG HIMSELF FROM THAT TREE AS SOON AS WE LEAVE?
WE SHOULD GO NOW.
MORON!!

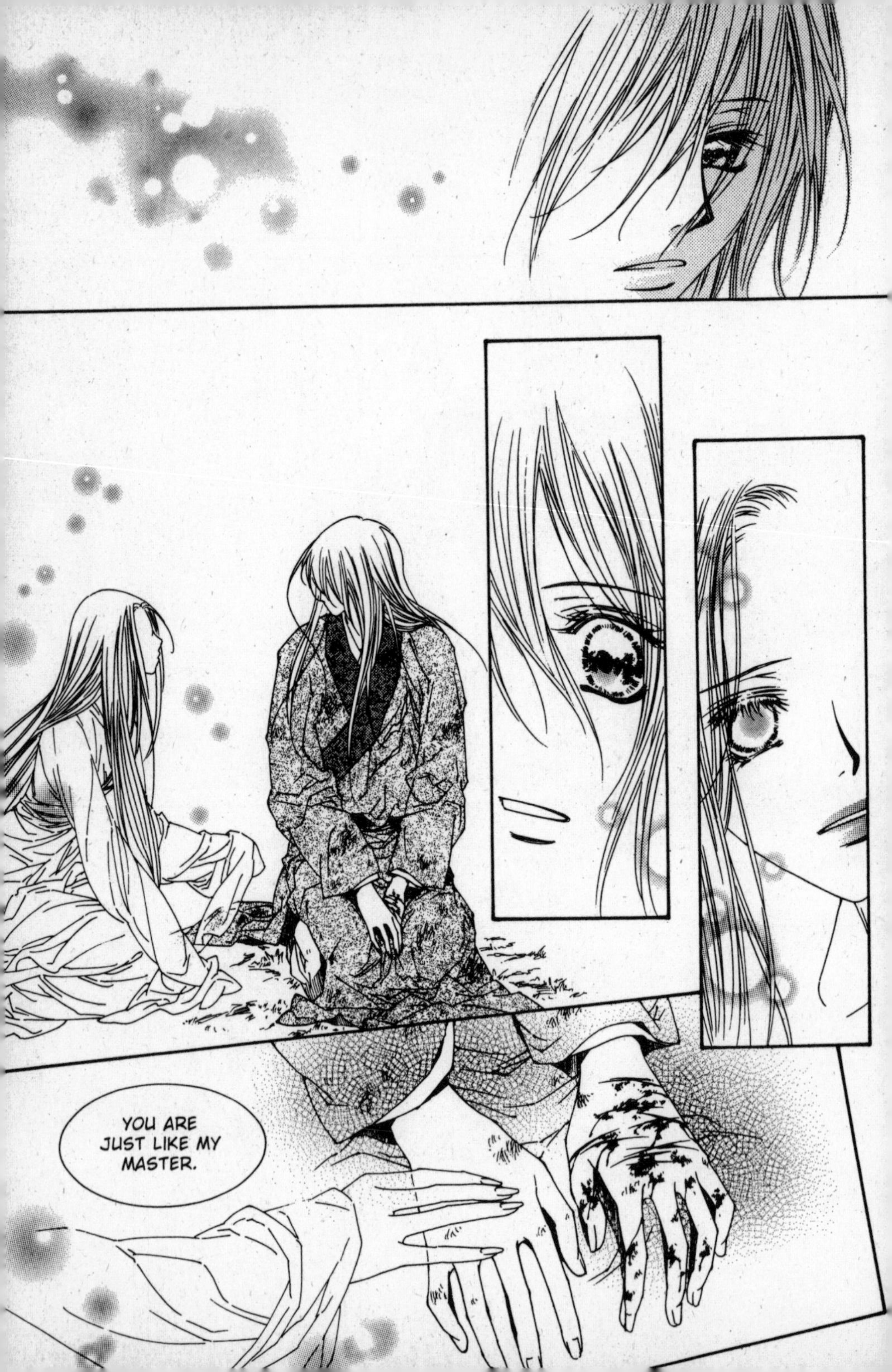
YOU ARE JUST LIKE MY MASTER.

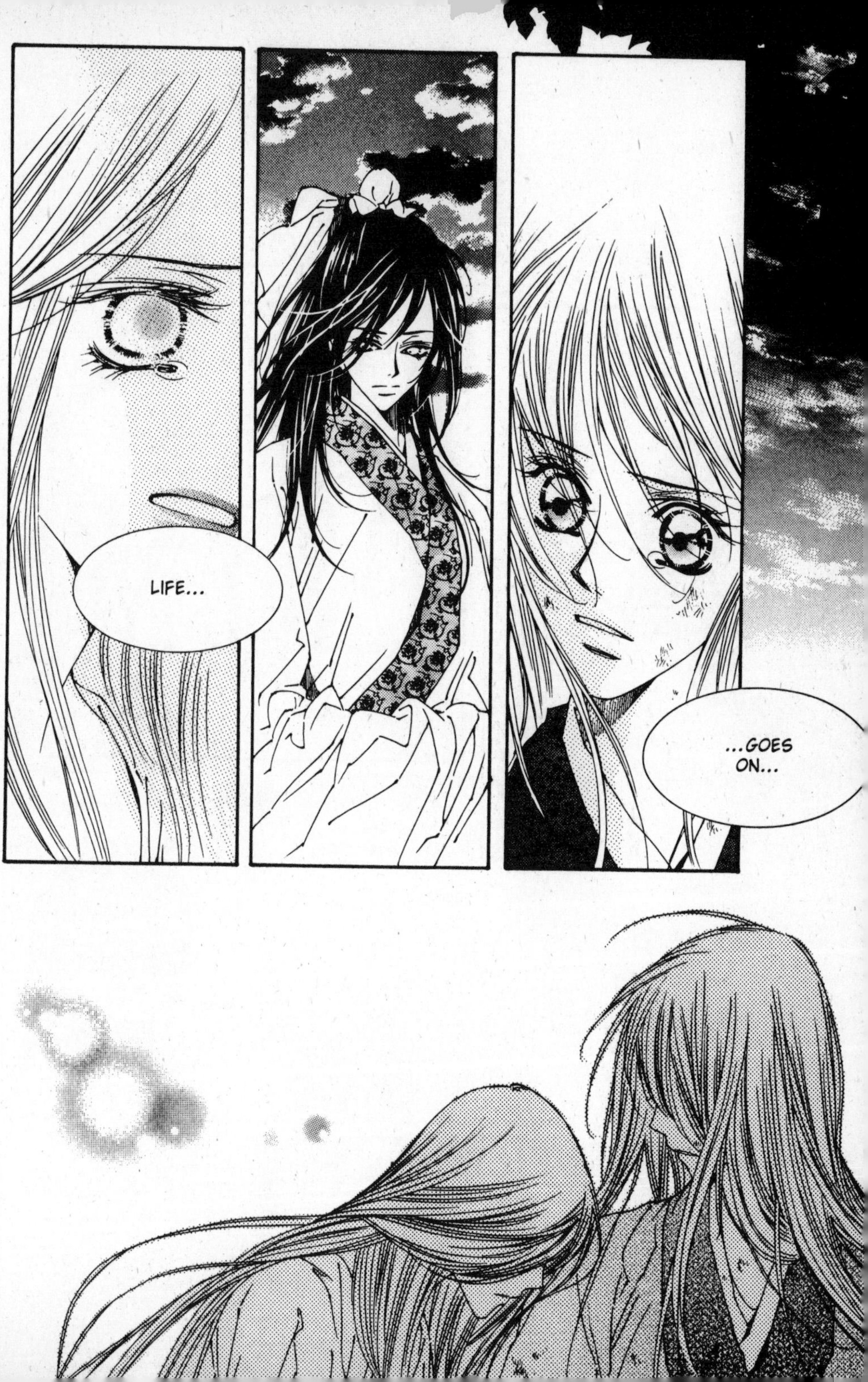
LIFE...
...GOES ON...

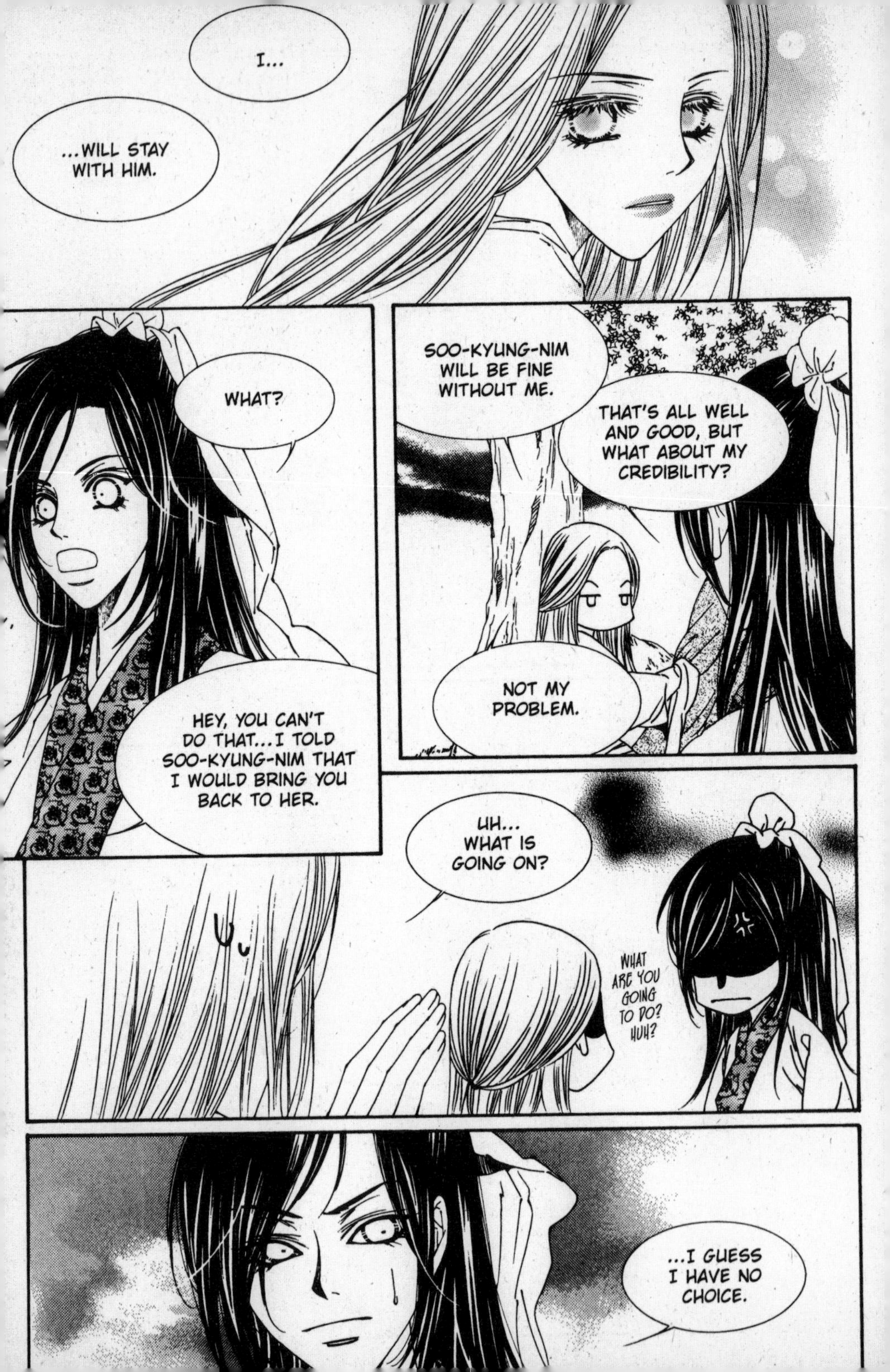
I...
...WILL STAY WITH HIM.
WHAT?
HEY, YOU CAN'T DO THAT...I TOLD SOO-KYUNG-NIM THAT I WOULD BRING YOU BACK TO HER.
SOO-KYUNG-NIM WILL BE FINE WITHOUT ME.
THAT'S ALL WELL AND GOOD, BUT WHAT ABOUT MY CREDIBILITY?
NOT MY PROBLEM.
UH... WHAT IS GOING ON?
WHAT ARE YOU GOING TO DO? HUH?
...I GUESS I HAVE NO CHOICE.

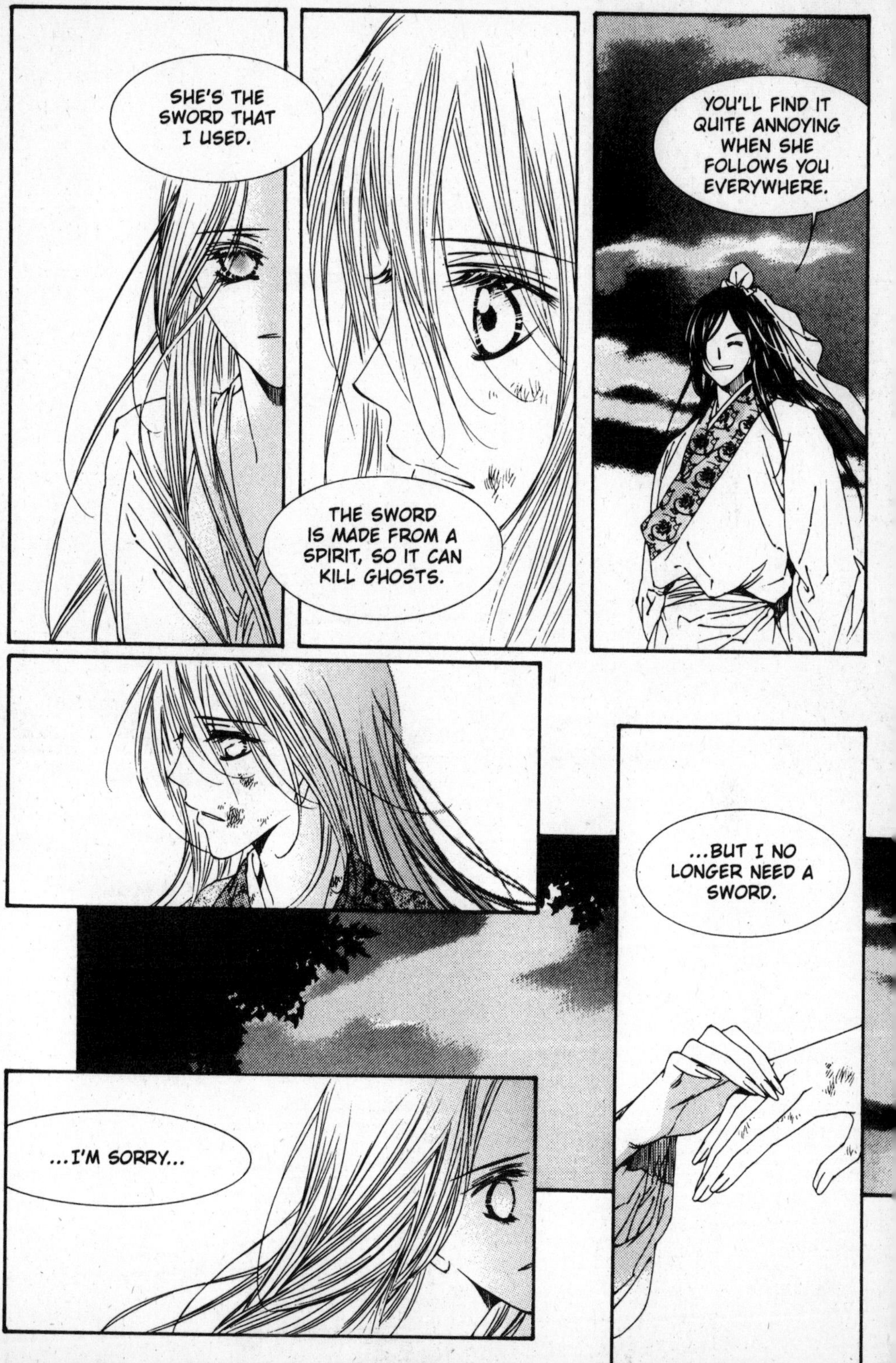
SHE'S THE SWORD THAT I USED.
THE SWORD IS MADE FROM A SPIRIT, SO IT CAN KILL GHOSTS.
YOU'LL FIND IT QUITE ANNOYING WHEN SHE FOLLOWS YOU EVERYWHERE.
...I'M SORRY...
...BUT I NO LONGER NEED A SWORD.

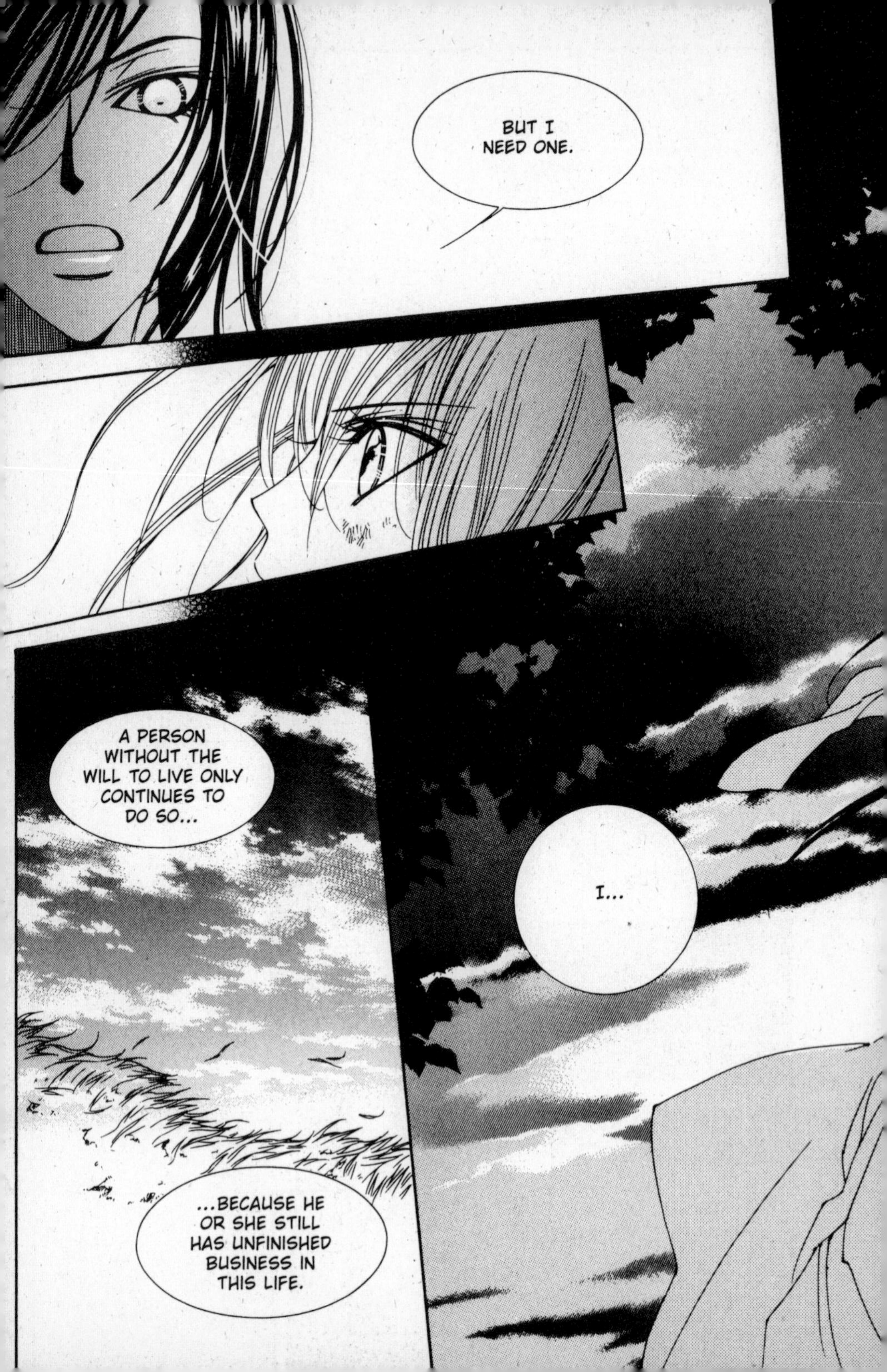
BUT I NEED ONE.
A PERSON WITHOUT THE WILL TO LIVE ONLY CONTINUES TO DO SO...
...BECAUSE HE OR SHE STILL HAS UNFINISHED BUSINESS IN THIS LIFE.
I...

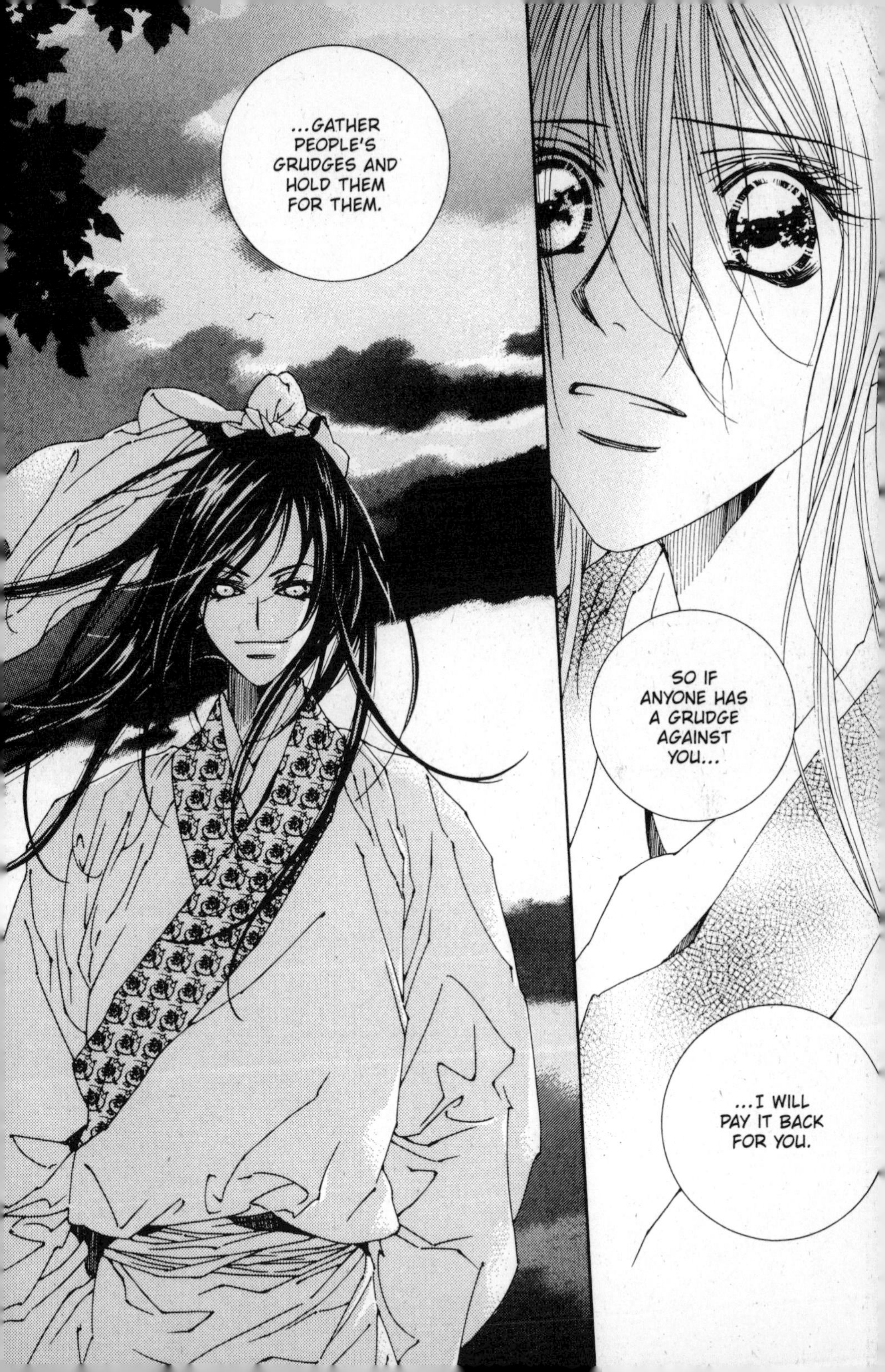
...GATHER PEOPLE'S GRUDGES AND HOLD THEM FOR THEM.
SO IF ANYONE HAS A GRUDGE AGAINST YOU...
...I WILL PAY IT BACK FOR YOU.

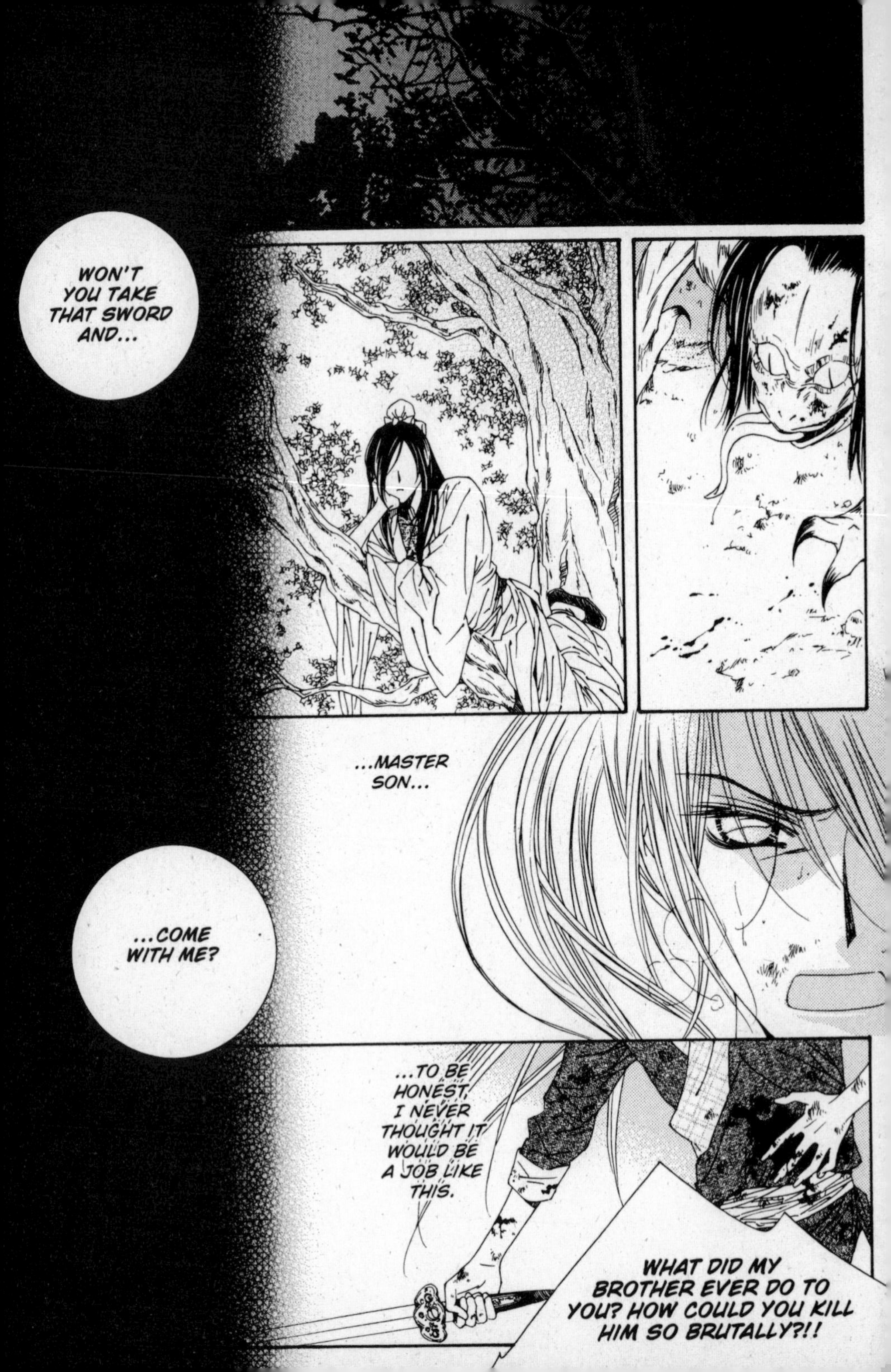
WON'T YOU TAKE THAT SWORD AND...
...MASTER SON...
...COME WITH ME?
...TO BE HONEST, I NEVER THOUGHT IT WOULD BE A JOB LIKE THIS.
WHAT DID MY BROTHER EVER DO TO YOU? HOW COULD YOU KILL HIM SO BRUTALLY?!!

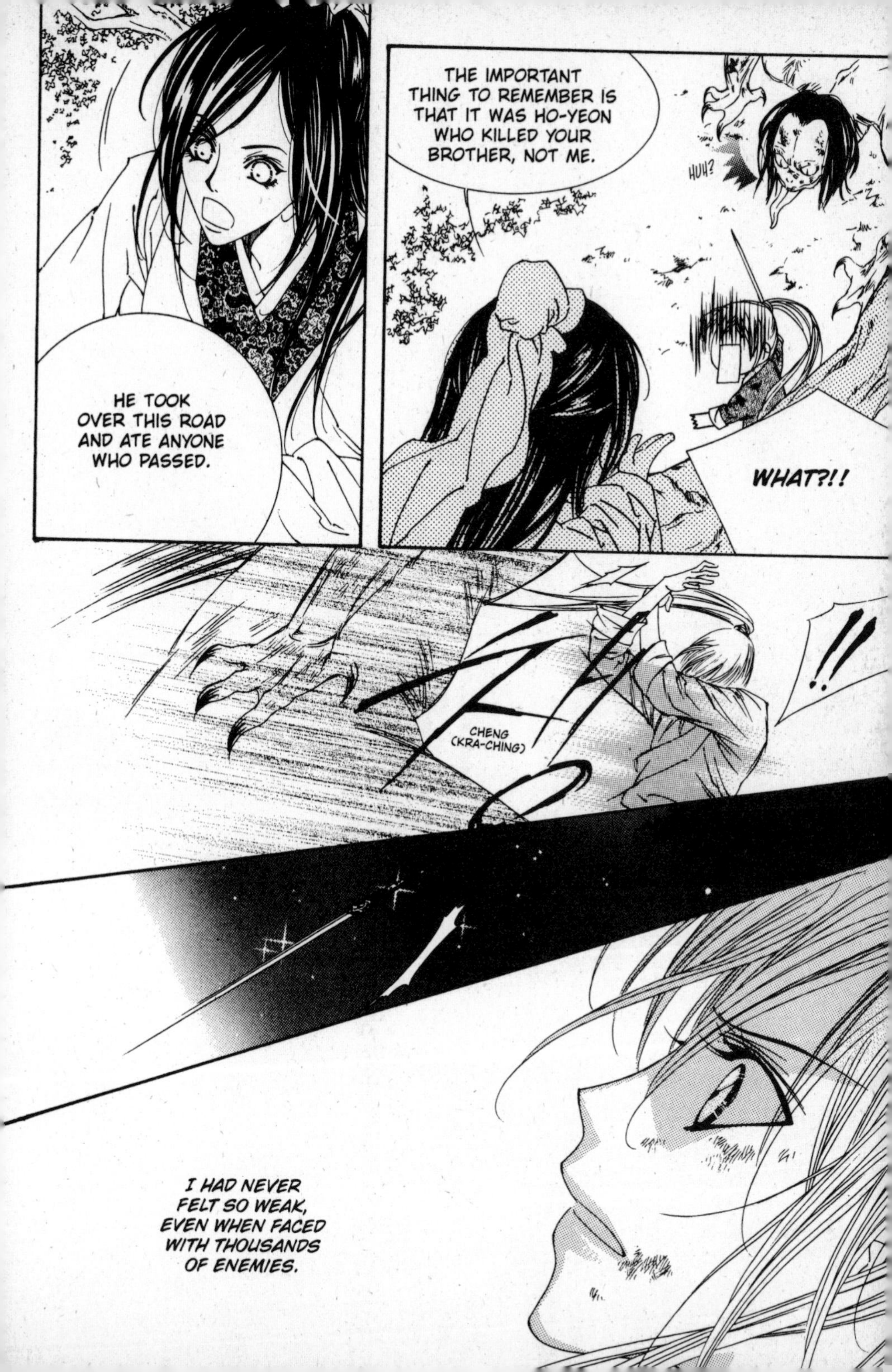
HE TOOK OVER THIS ROAD AND ATE ANYONE WHO PASSED.
THE IMPORTANT THING TO REMEMBER IS THAT IT WAS HO-YEON WHO KILLED YOUR BROTHER, NOT ME.
HUH?
WHAT?!!
CHENG (KRA-CHING)
!!
I HAD NEVER FELT SO WEAK, EVEN WHEN FACED WITH THOUSANDS OF ENEMIES.

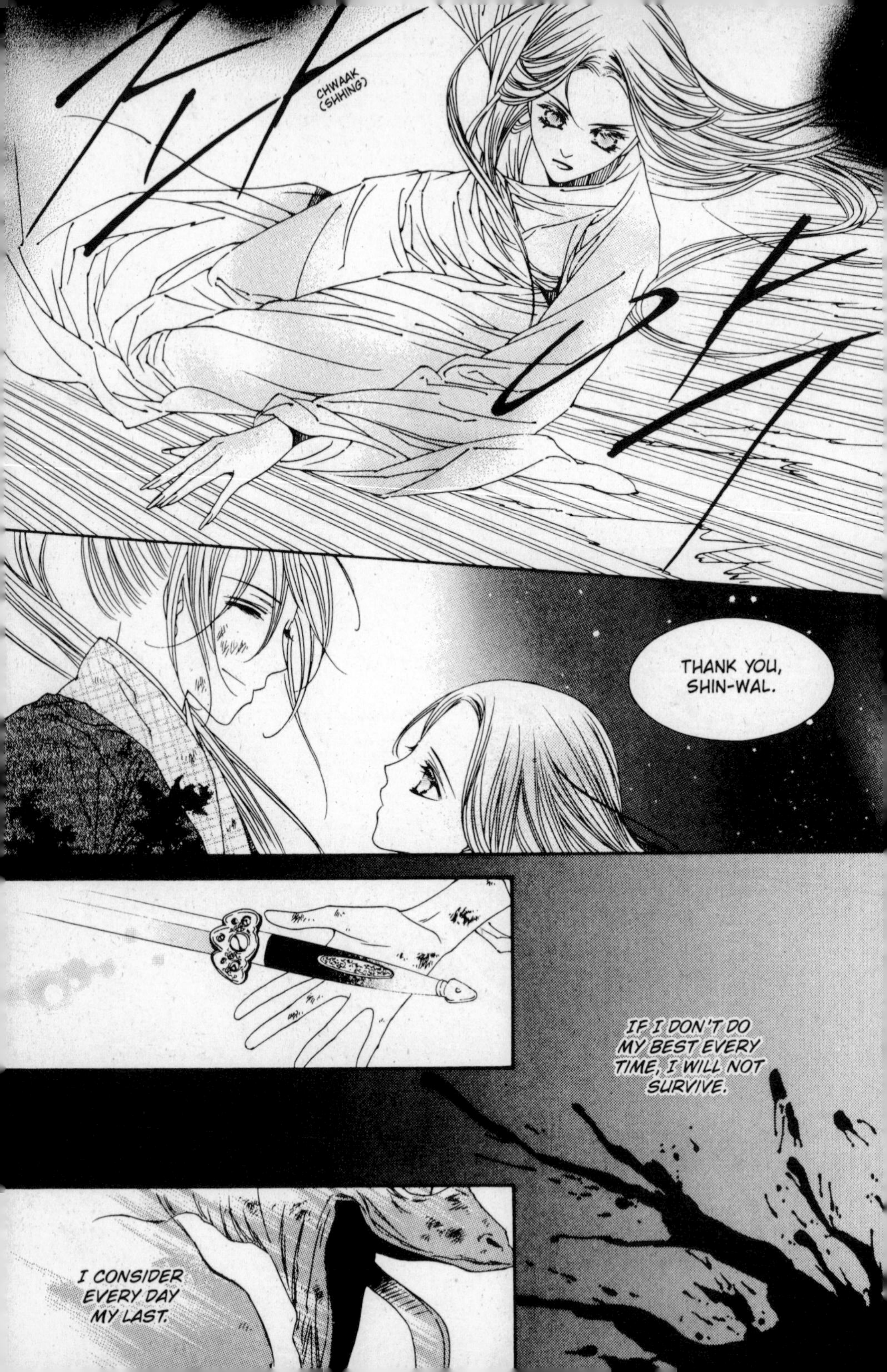
CHWAAK
(SHHING)
THANK YOU, SHIN-WAL.
IF I DON'T DO MY BEST EVERY TIME, I WILL NOT SURVIVE.
I CONSIDER EVERY DAY MY LAST.

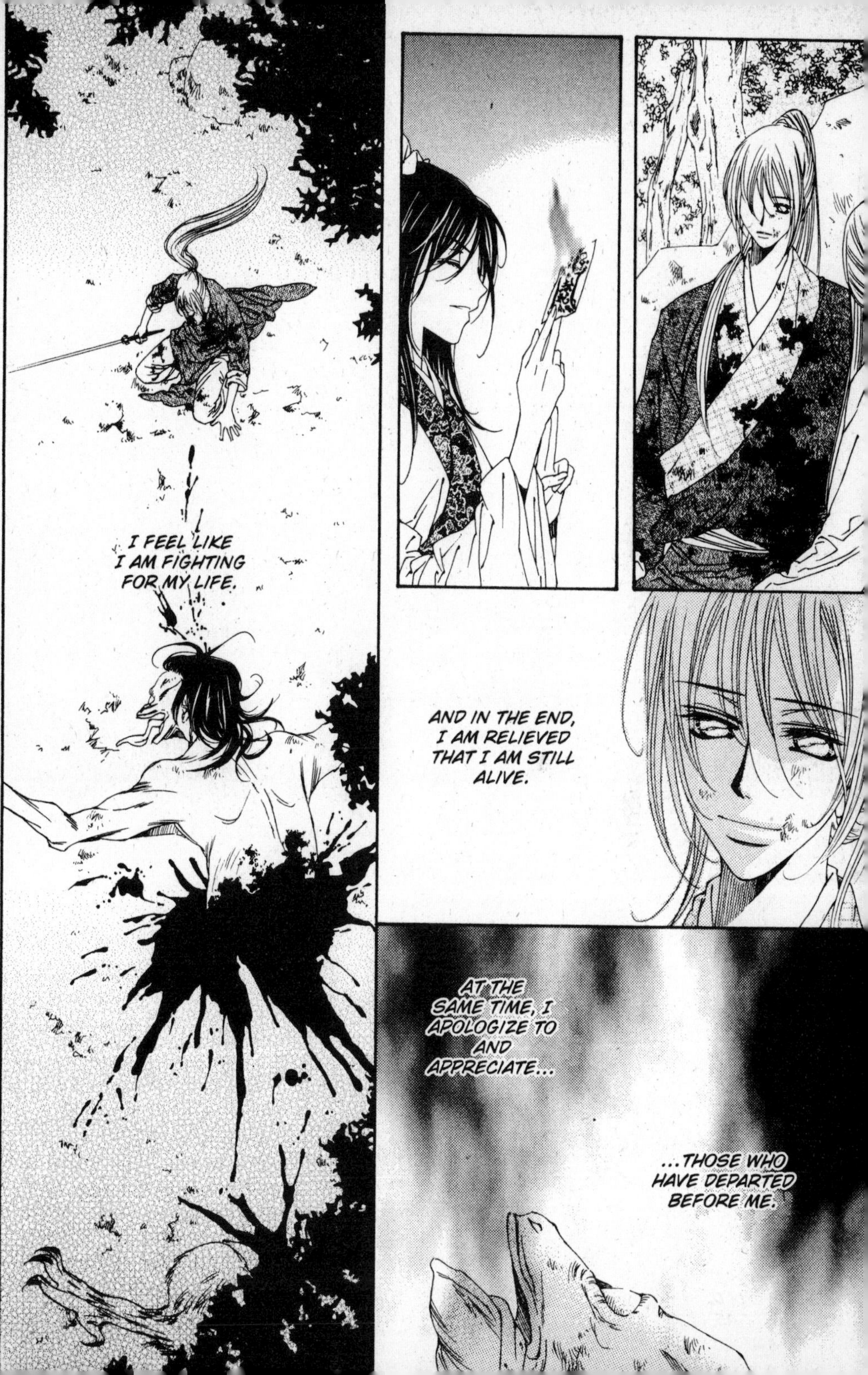
I FEEL LIKE I AM FIGHTING FOR MY LIFE.
AND IN THE END, I AM RELIEVED THAT I AM STILL ALIVE.
AT THE SAME TIME, I APOLOGIZE TO AND APPRECIATE...
...THOSE WHO HAVE DEPARTED BEFORE ME.

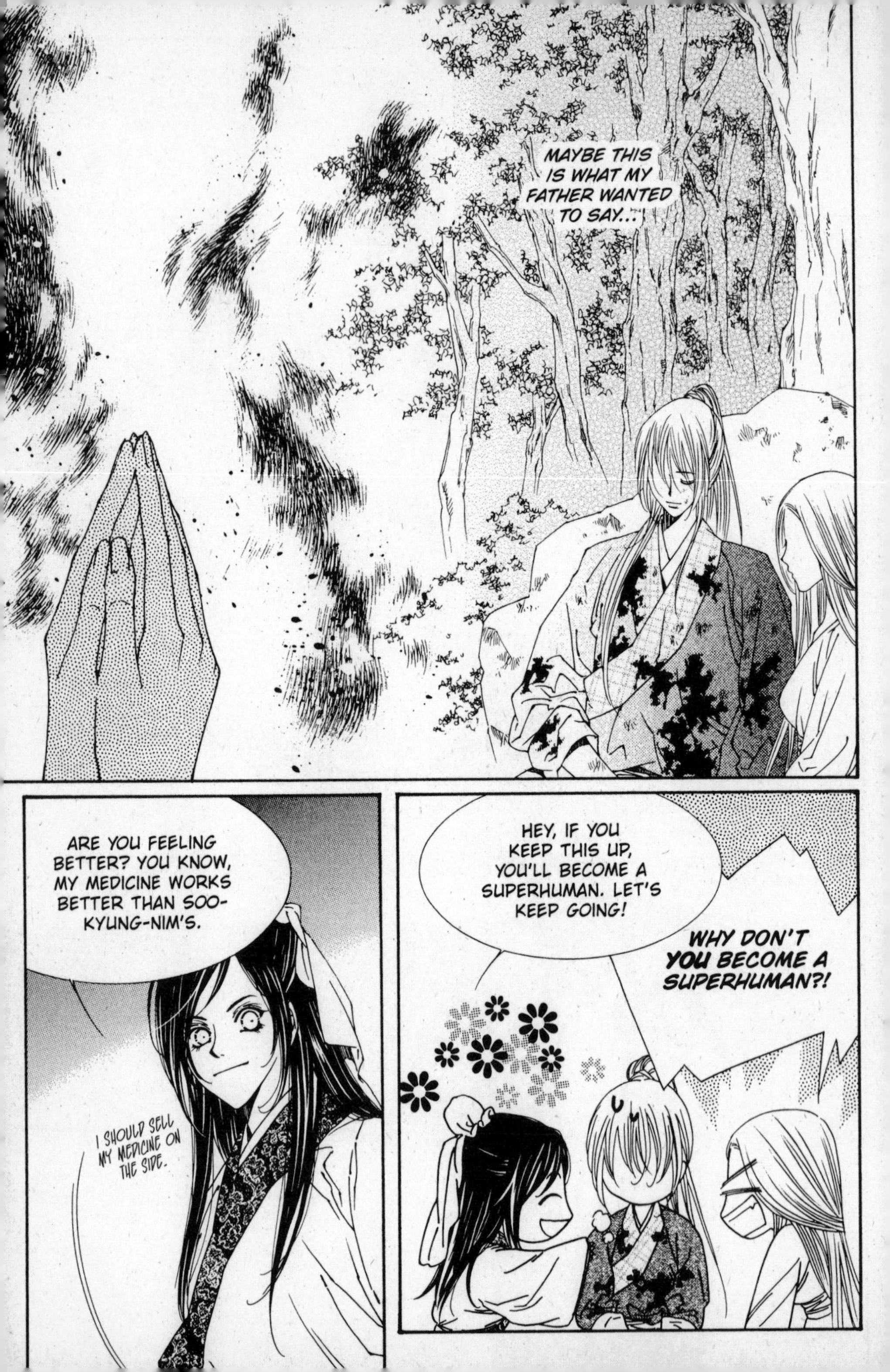

MAYBE THIS IS WHAT MY FATHER WANTED TO SAY...
ARE YOU FEELING BETTER? YOU KNOW, MY MEDICINE WORKS BETTER THAN SOO-KYUNG-NIM'S.
I SHOULD SELL MY MEDICINE ON THE SIDE.
HEY, IF YOU KEEP THIS UP, YOU'LL BECOME A SUPERHUMAN. LET'S KEEP GOING!
WHY DON'T YOU BECOME A SUPERHUMAN?!

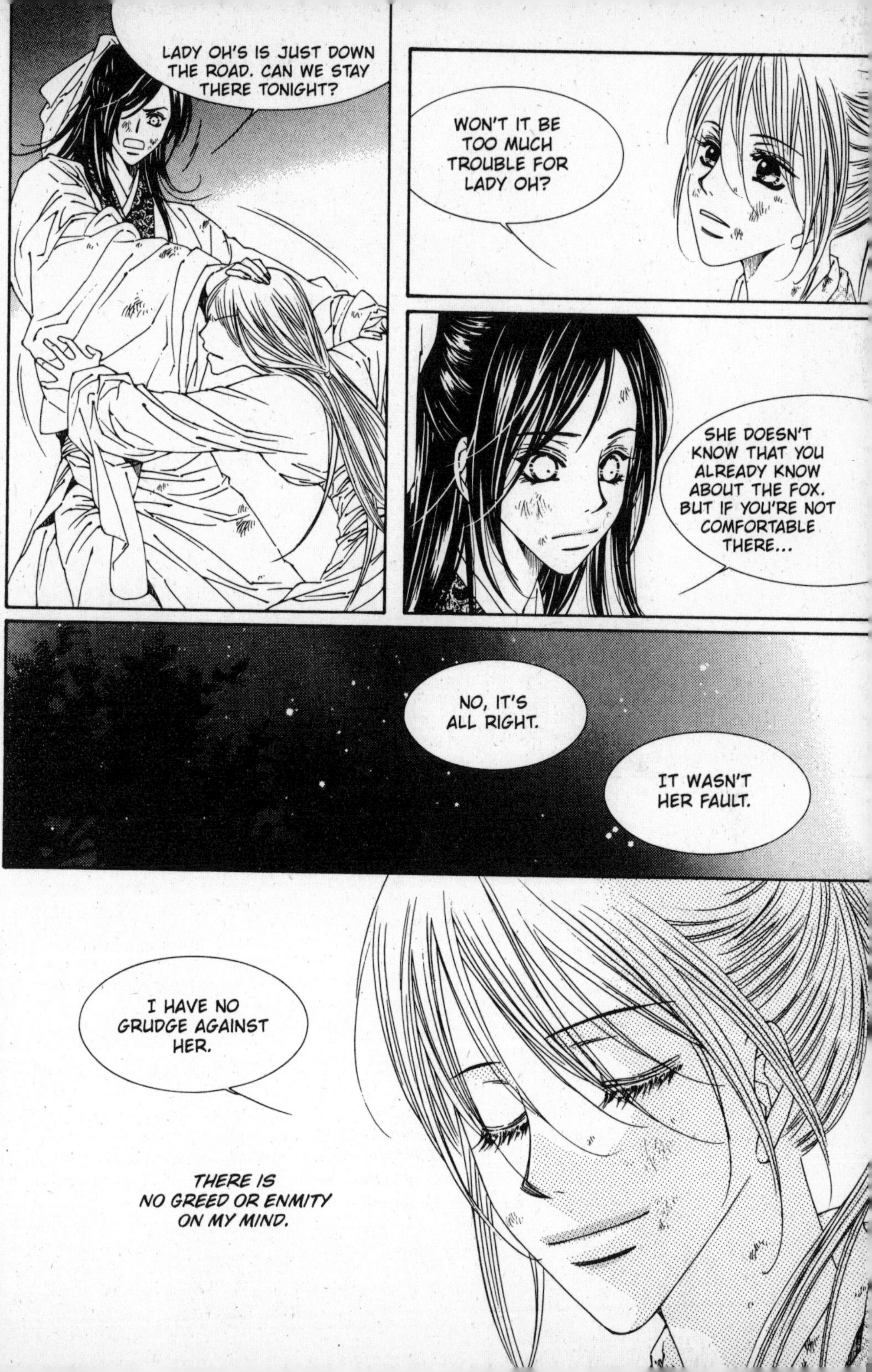
LADY OH'S IS JUST DOWN THE ROAD. CAN WE STAY THERE TONIGHT?
WON'T IT BE TOO MUCH TROUBLE FOR LADY OH?
SHE DOESN'T KNOW THAT YOU ALREADY KNOW ABOUT THE FOX. BUT IF YOU'RE NOT COMFORTABLE THERE...
NO, IT'S ALL RIGHT.
IT WASN'T HER FAULT.
I HAVE NO GRUDGE AGAINST HER.
THERE IS NO GREED OR ENMITY ON MY MIND.

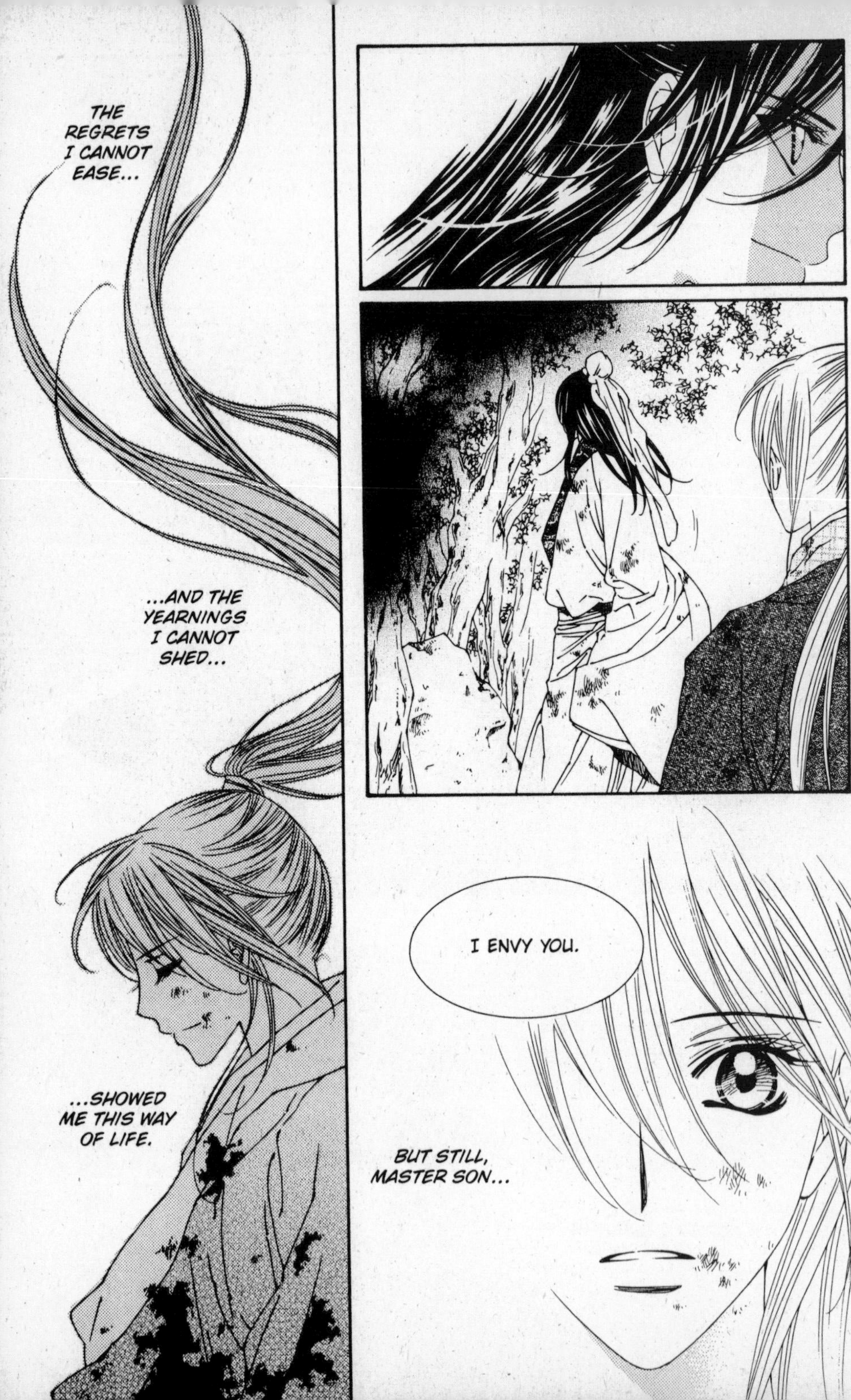
THE REGRETS I CANNOT EASE...
...AND THE YEARNINGS I CANNOT SHED...
...SHOWED ME THIS WAY OF LIFE.
I ENVY YOU.
BUT STILL, MASTER SON...

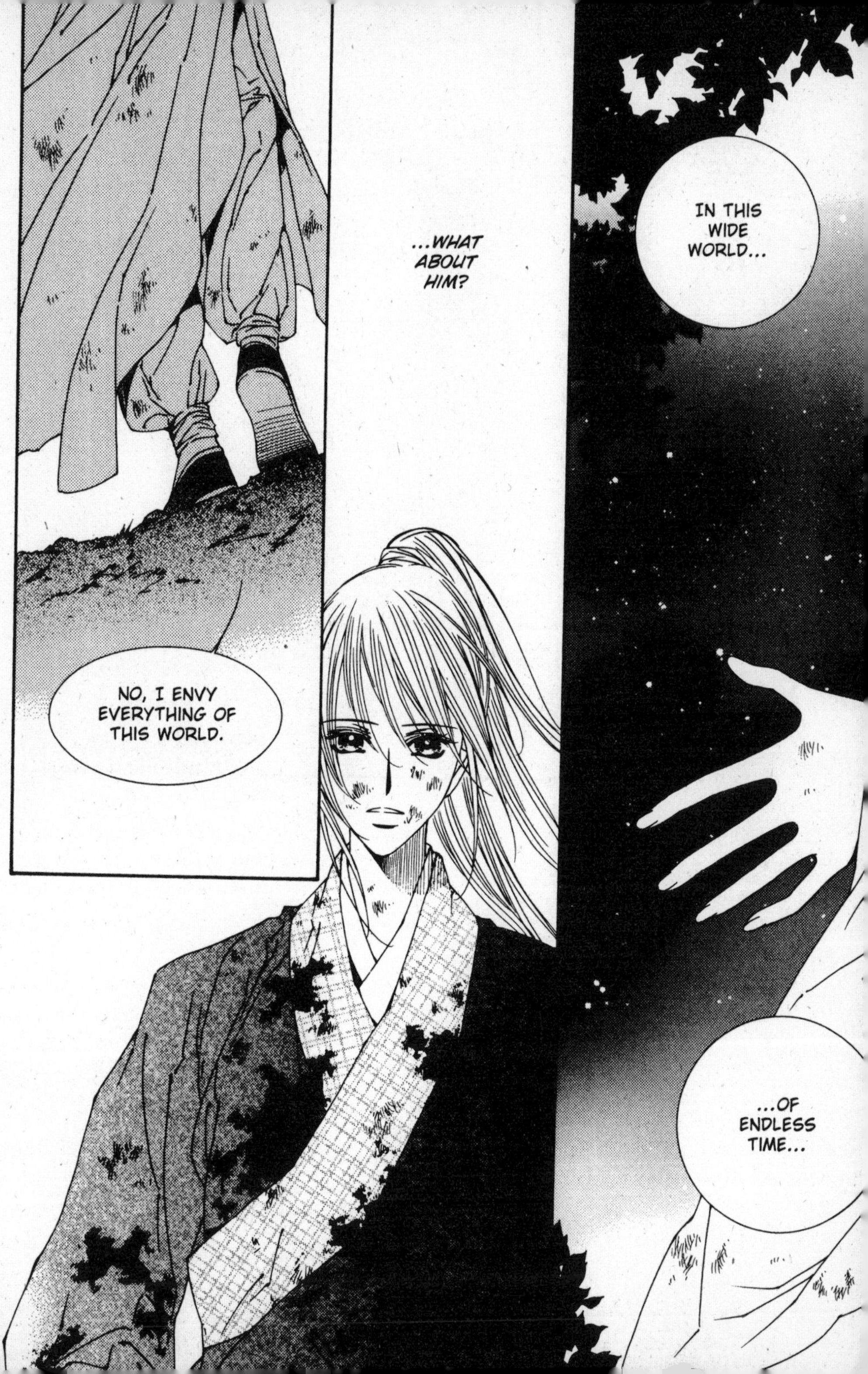
NO, I ENVY EVERYTHING OF THIS WORLD.
...WHAT ABOUT HIM?
IN THIS WIDE WORLD...
...OF ENDLESS TIME...

...I HAVE NOWHERE TO GO.
WHAT ABOUT HIM...
...HIS HEAVY, SAD FOOTSTEPS...
THE END OF CHAPTER THIRTEEN

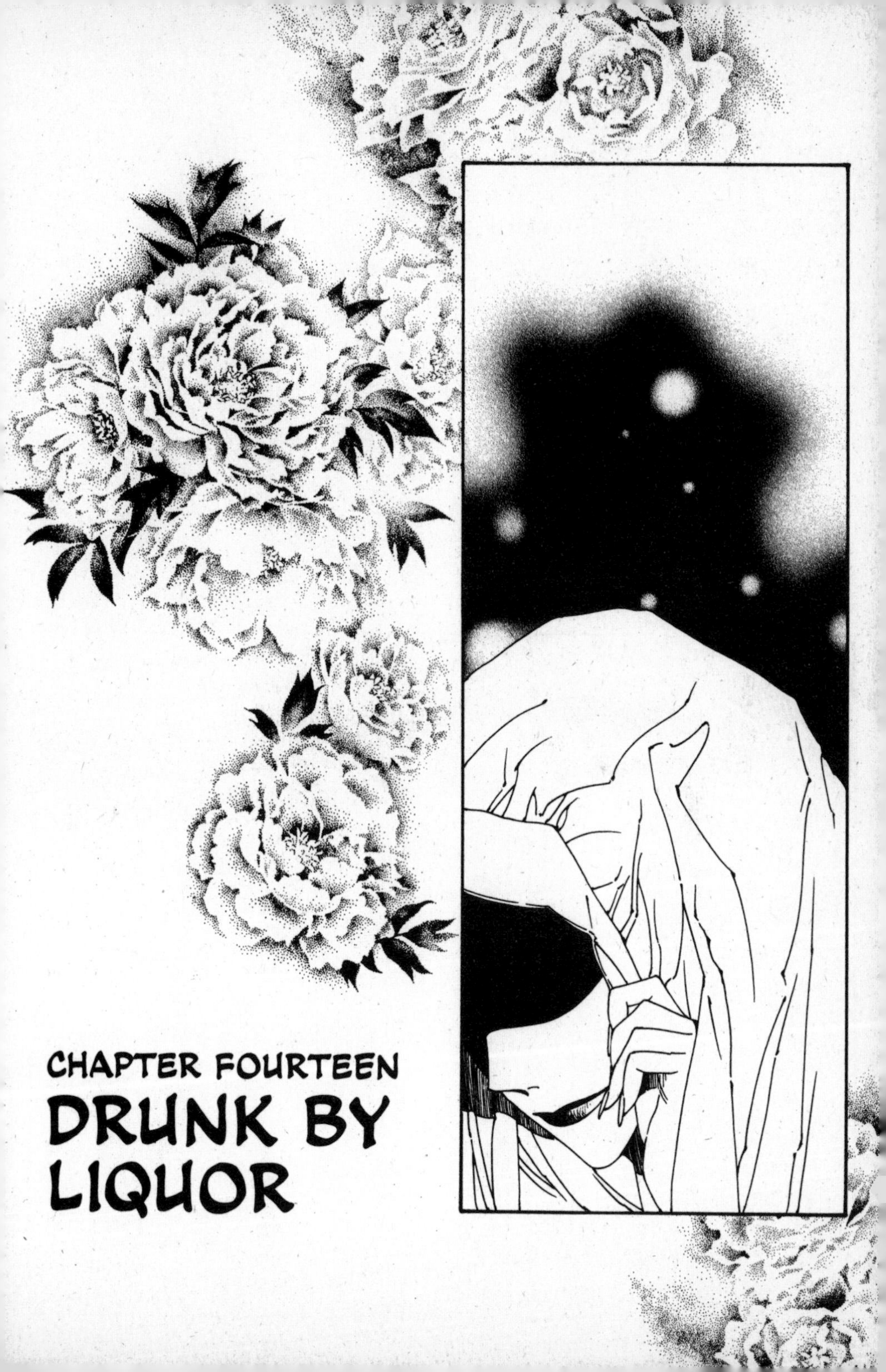

CHAPTER FOURTEEN

DRUNK BY LIQUOR

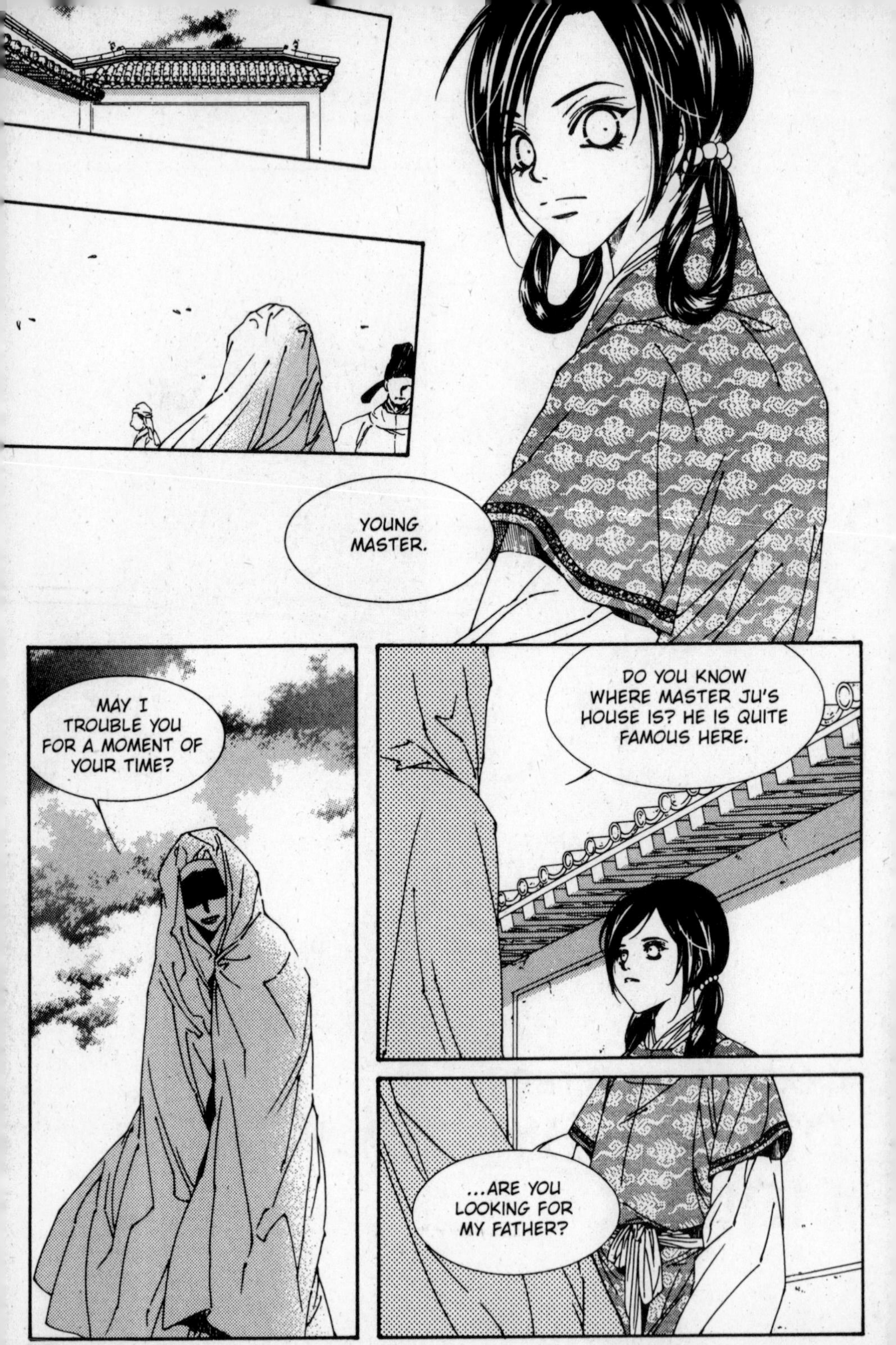
YOUNG MASTER.
MAY I TROUBLE YOU FOR A MOMENT OF YOUR TIME?
DO YOU KNOW WHERE MASTER JU'S HOUSE IS? HE IS QUITE FAMOUS HERE.
...ARE YOU LOOKING FOR MY FATHER?

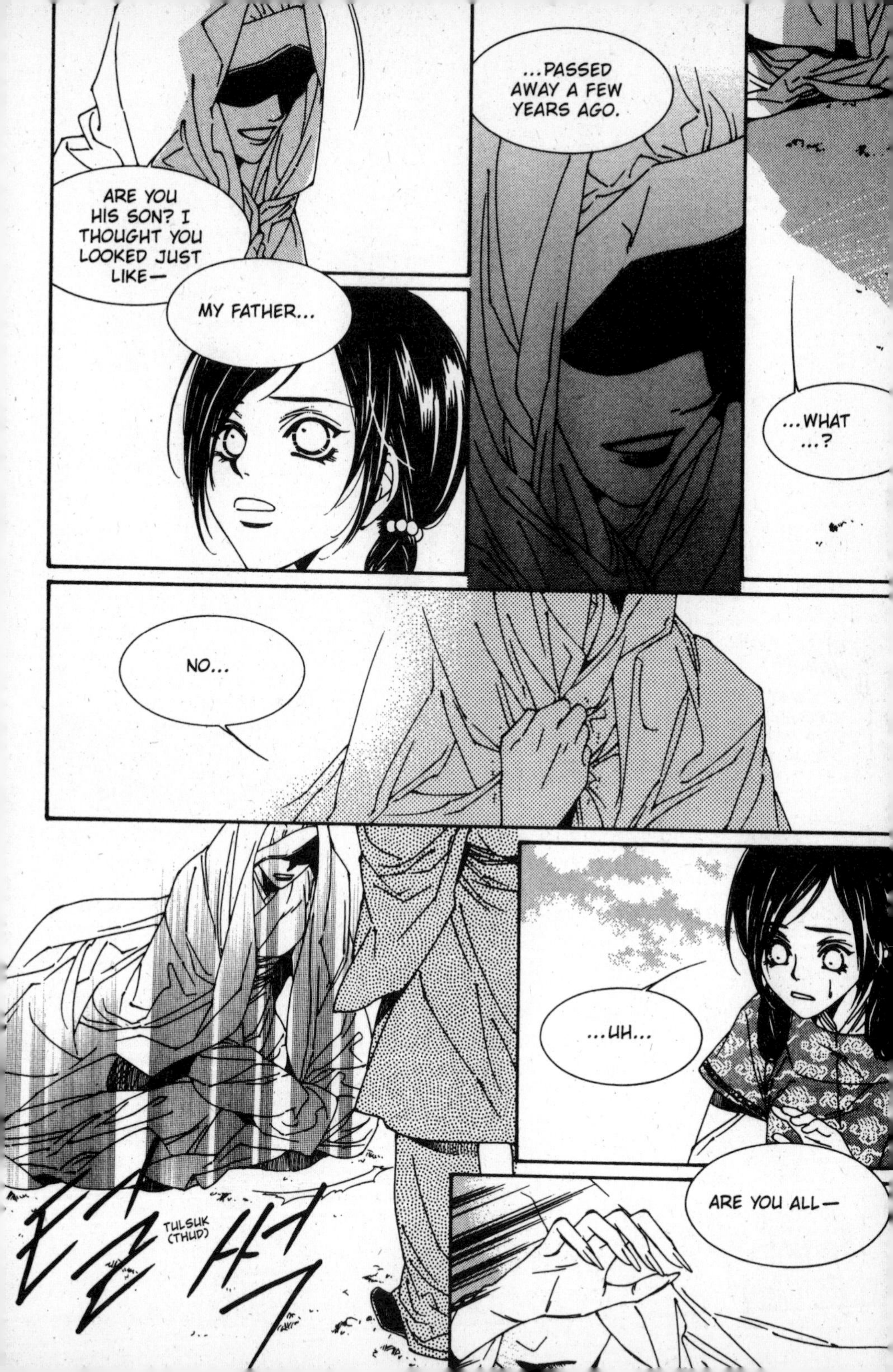
ARE YOU HIS SON? I THOUGHT YOU LOOKED JUST LIKE—
MY FATHER...
...PASSED AWAY A FEW YEARS AGO.
...WHAT ...?
NO...
TULSUK (THUD)
...UH...
ARE YOU ALL—

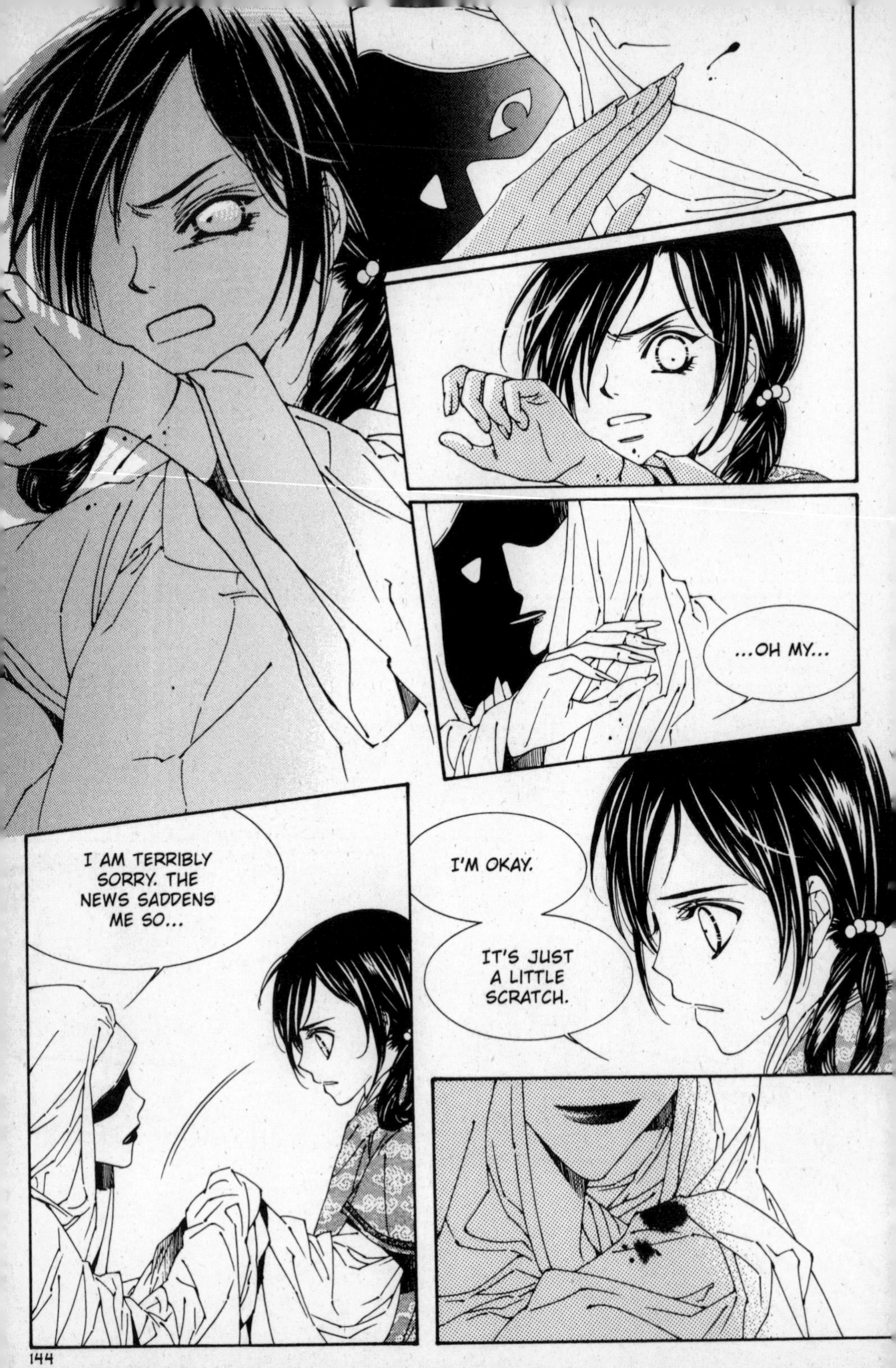
...OH MY...
I AM TERRIBLY SORRY. THE NEWS SADDENS ME SO...
I'M OKAY.
IT'S JUST A LITTLE SCRATCH.

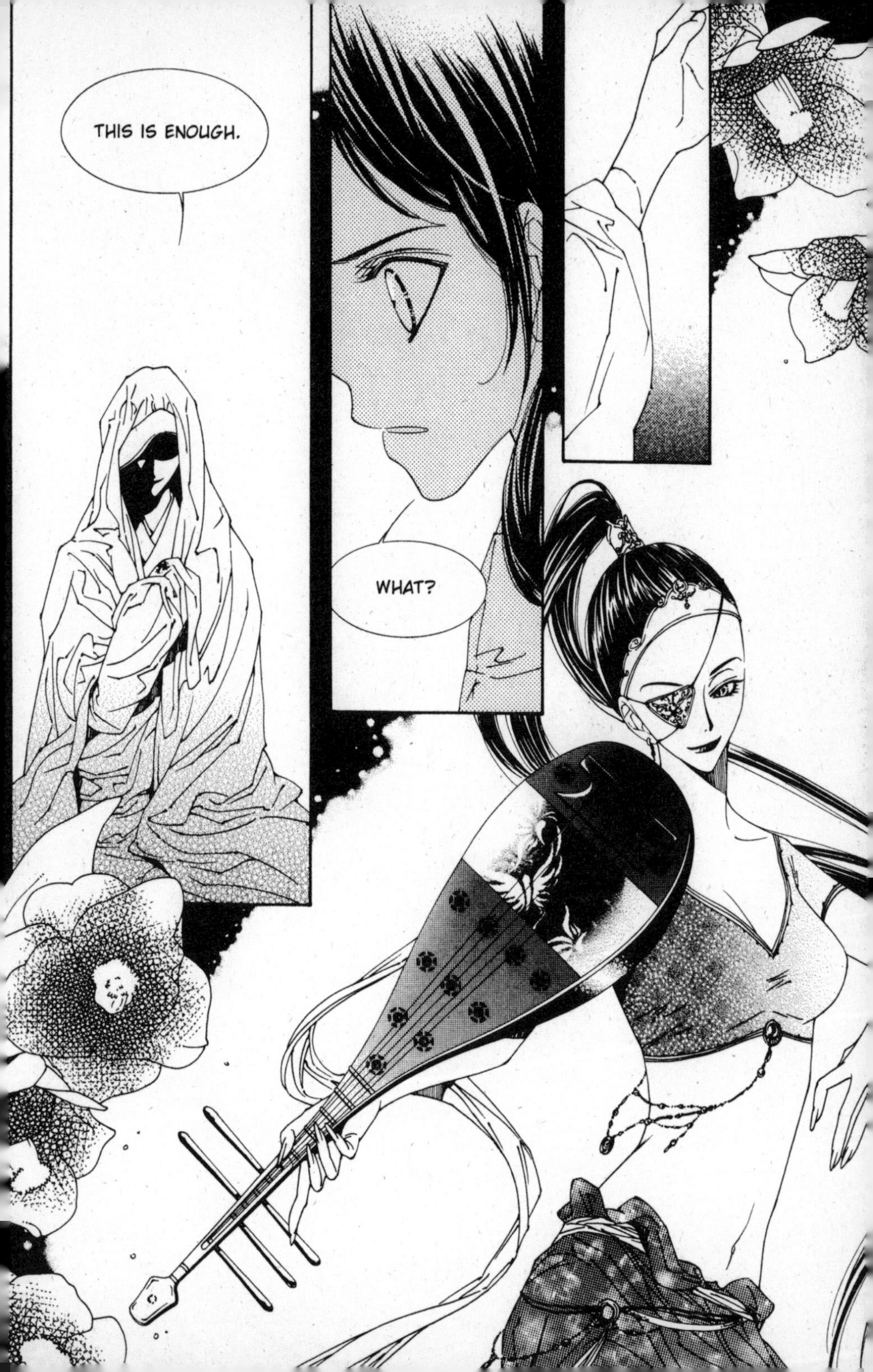
THIS IS ENOUGH.
WHAT?

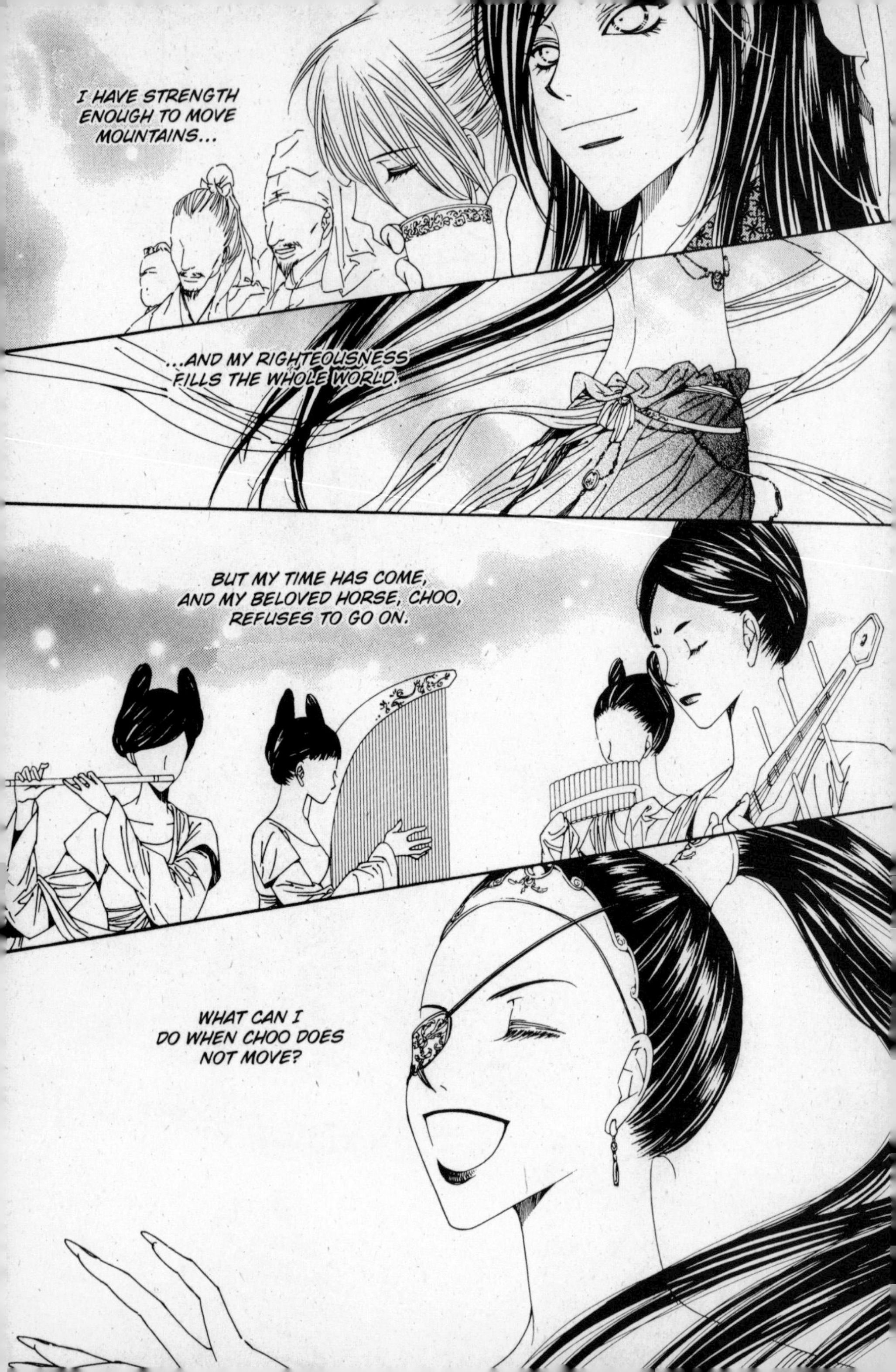
I HAVE STRENGTH ENOUGH TO MOVE MOUNTAINS...
...AND MY RIGHTEOUSNESS FILLS THE WHOLE WORLD.
BUT MY TIME HAS COME, AND MY BELOVED HORSE, CHOO, REFUSES TO GO ON.
WHAT CAN I DO WHEN CHOO DOES NOT MOVE?

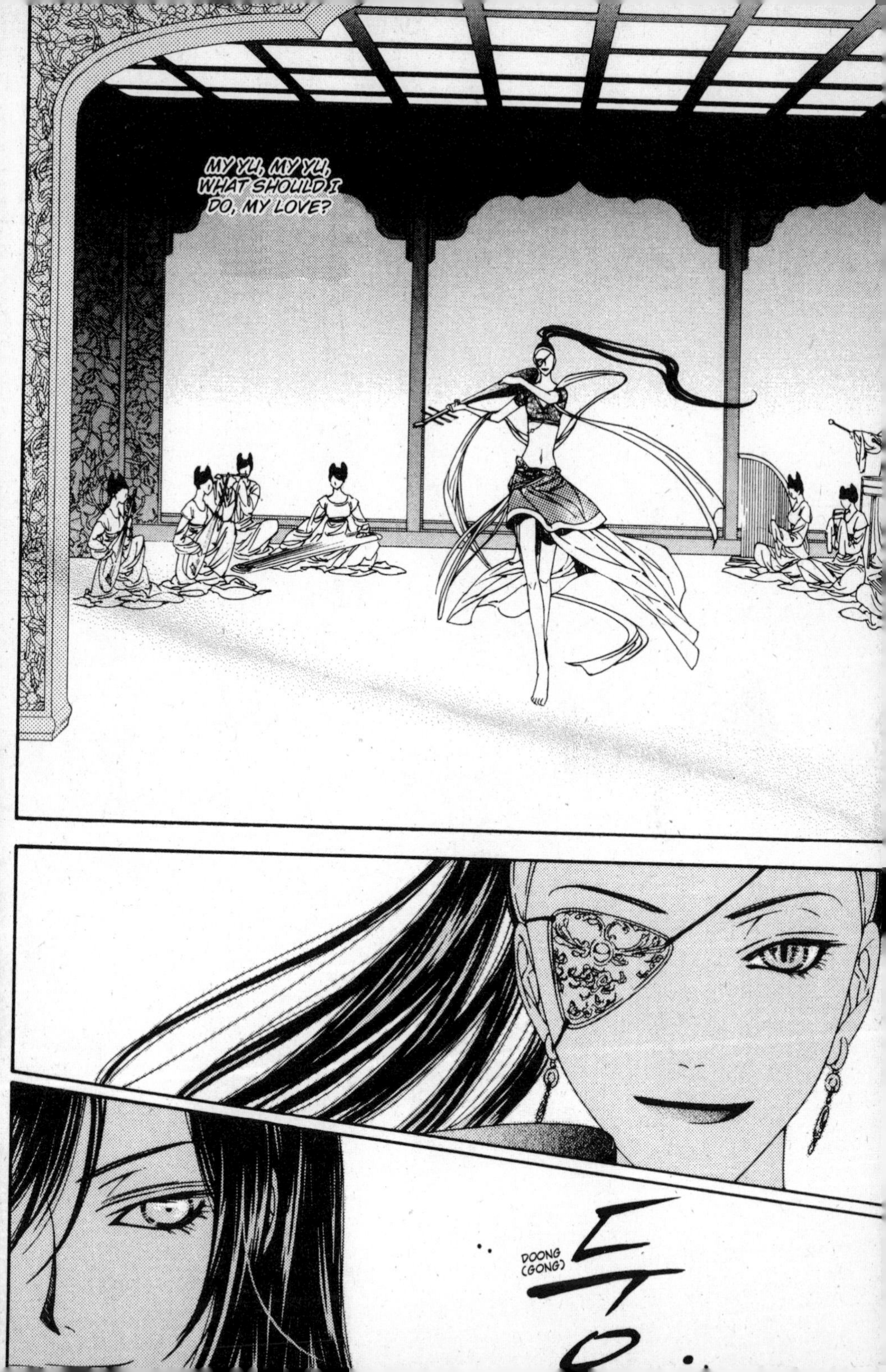

MY YU, MY YU, WHAT SHOULD I DO, MY LOVE?
DOONG (GONG)

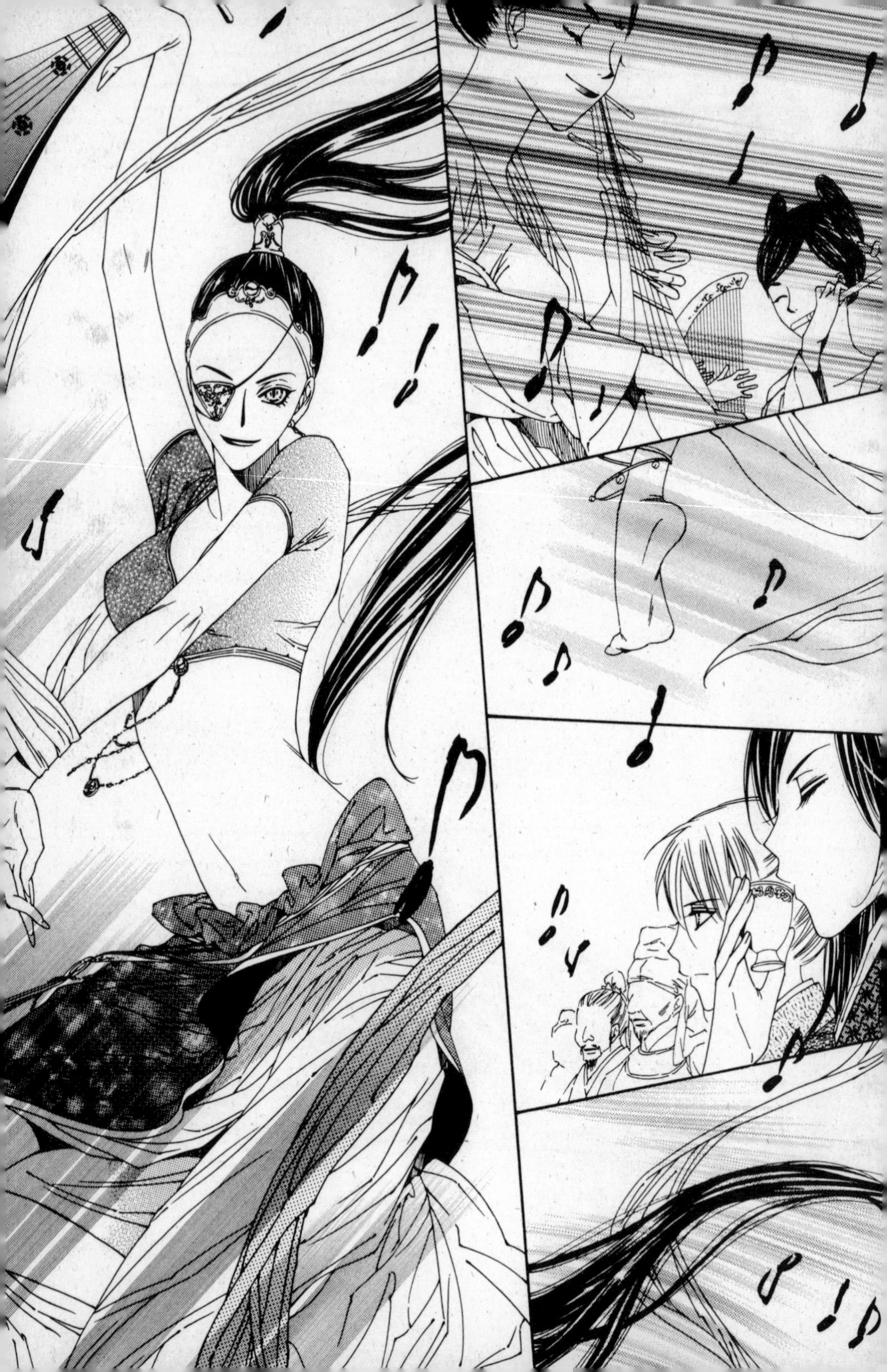

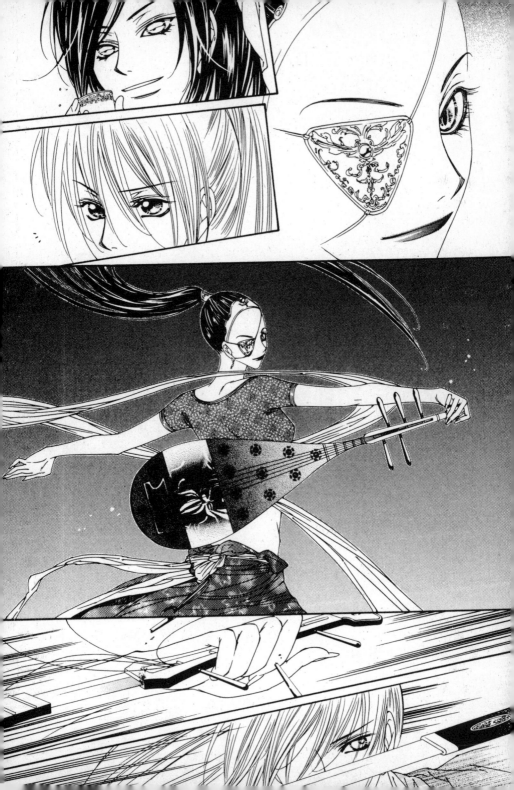

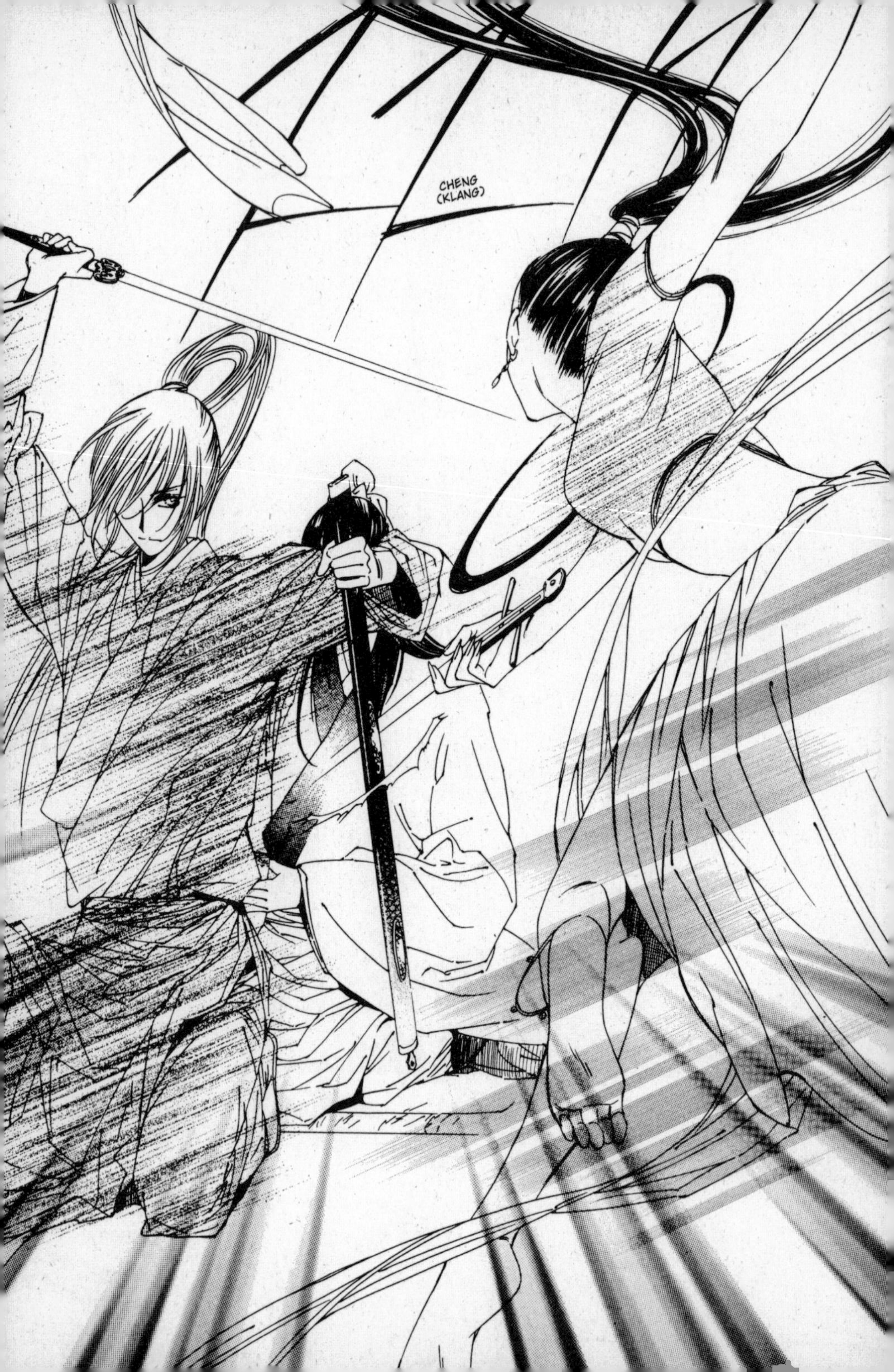
CHENG
(KLANG)

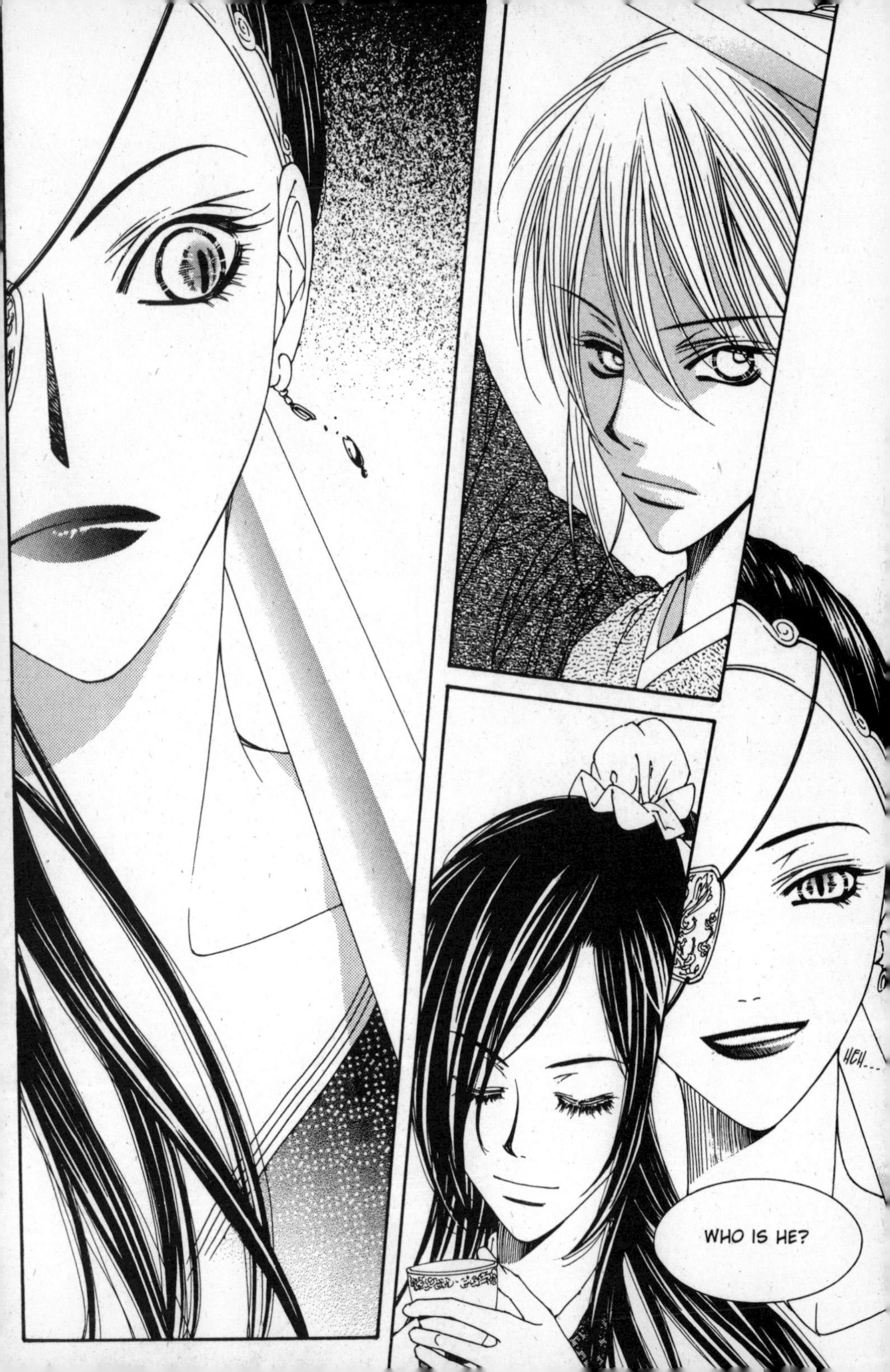
HEH...
WHO IS HE?

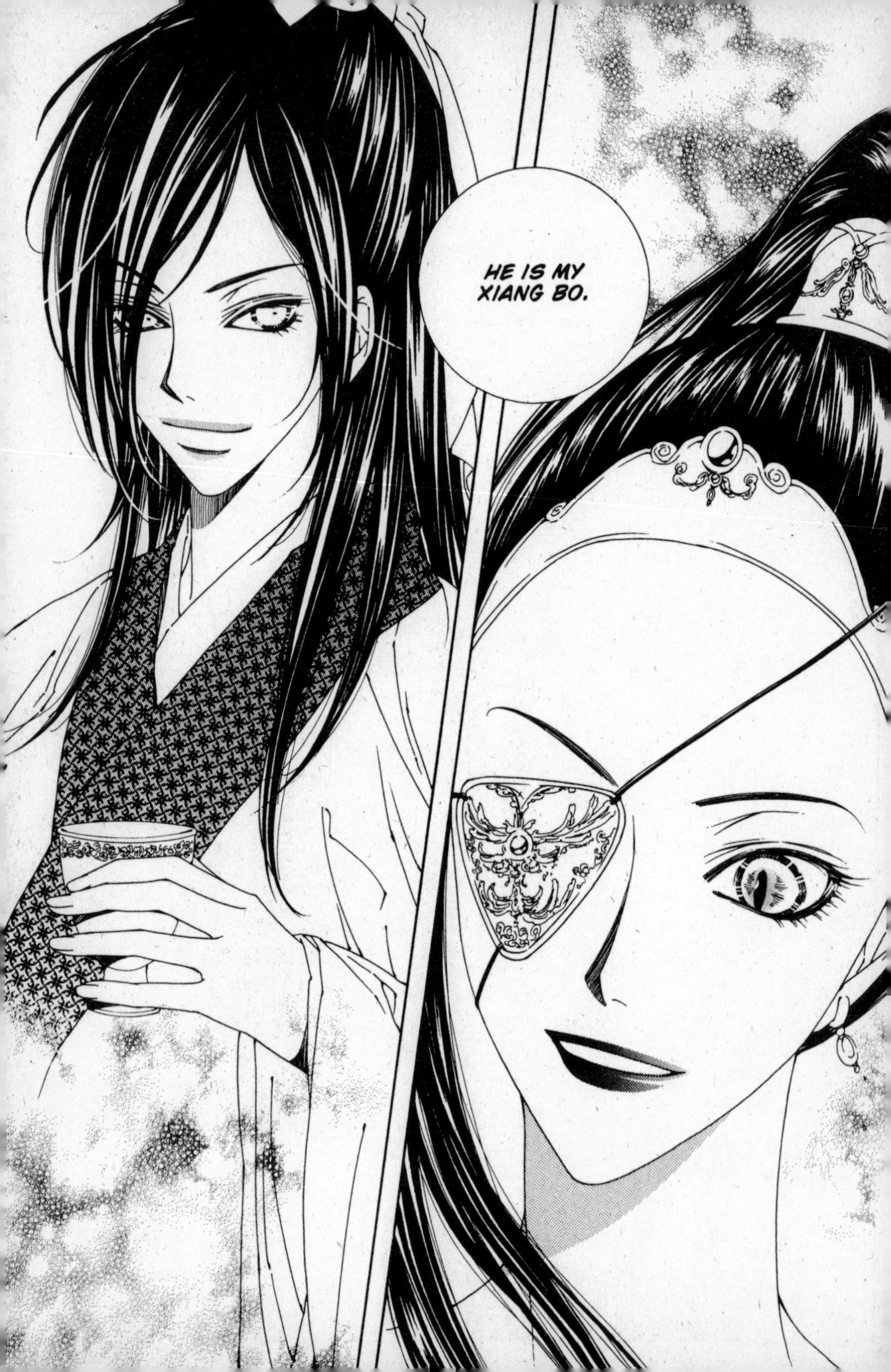
HE IS MY XIANG BO.

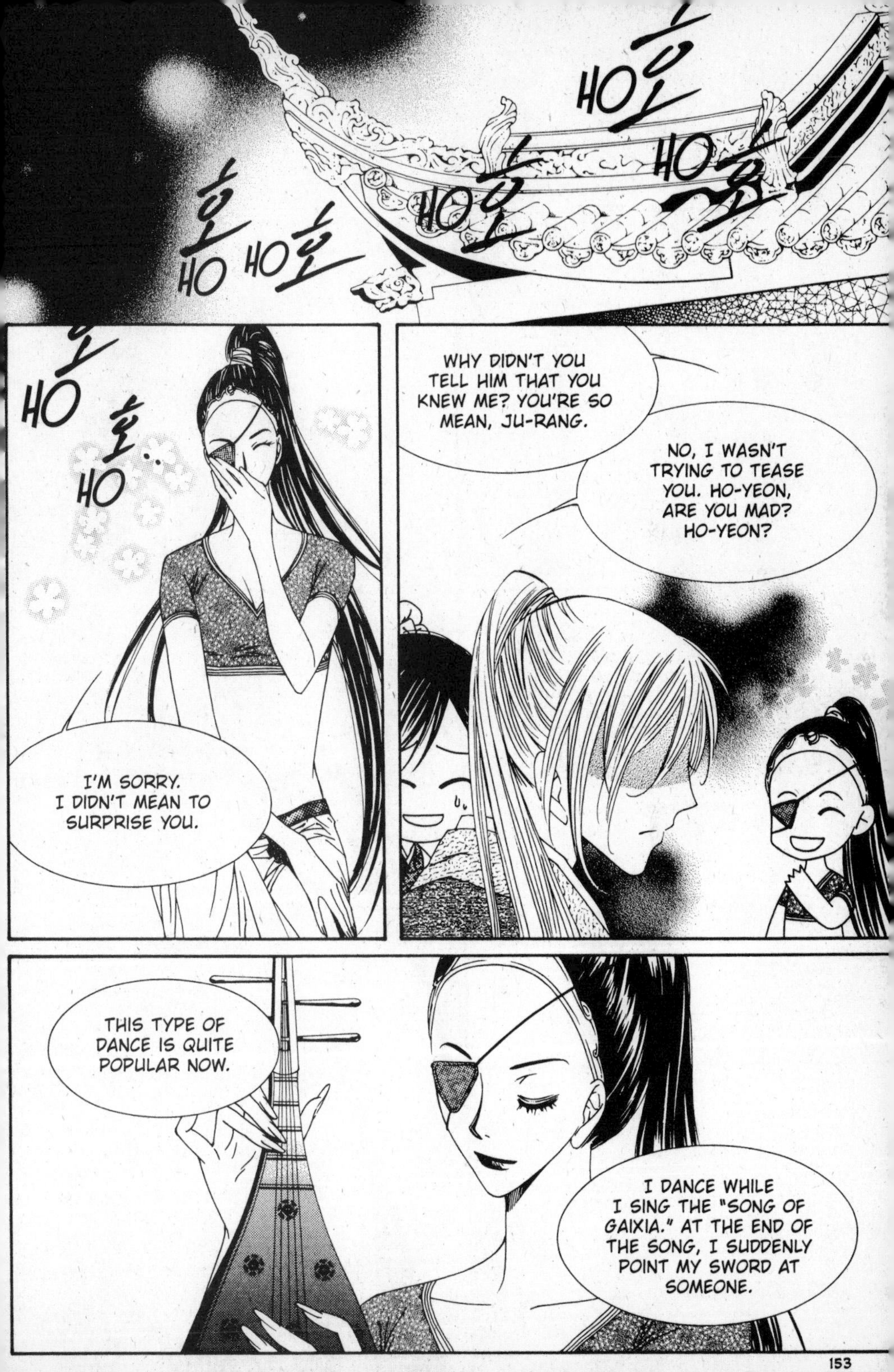

HO 호 HO 호
HO 호 HO 효
HO 호
HO 호
HO 호..
WHY DIDN'T YOU TELL HIM THAT YOU KNEW ME? YOU'RE SO MEAN, JU-RANG.
NO, I WASN'T TRYING TO TEASE YOU. HO-YEON, ARE YOU MAD? HO-YEON?
I'M SORRY. I DIDN'T MEAN TO SURPRISE YOU.
THIS TYPE OF DANCE IS QUITE POPULAR NOW.
I DANCE WHILE I SING THE "SONG OF GAIXIA." AT THE END OF THE SONG, I SUDDENLY POINT MY SWORD AT SOMEONE.

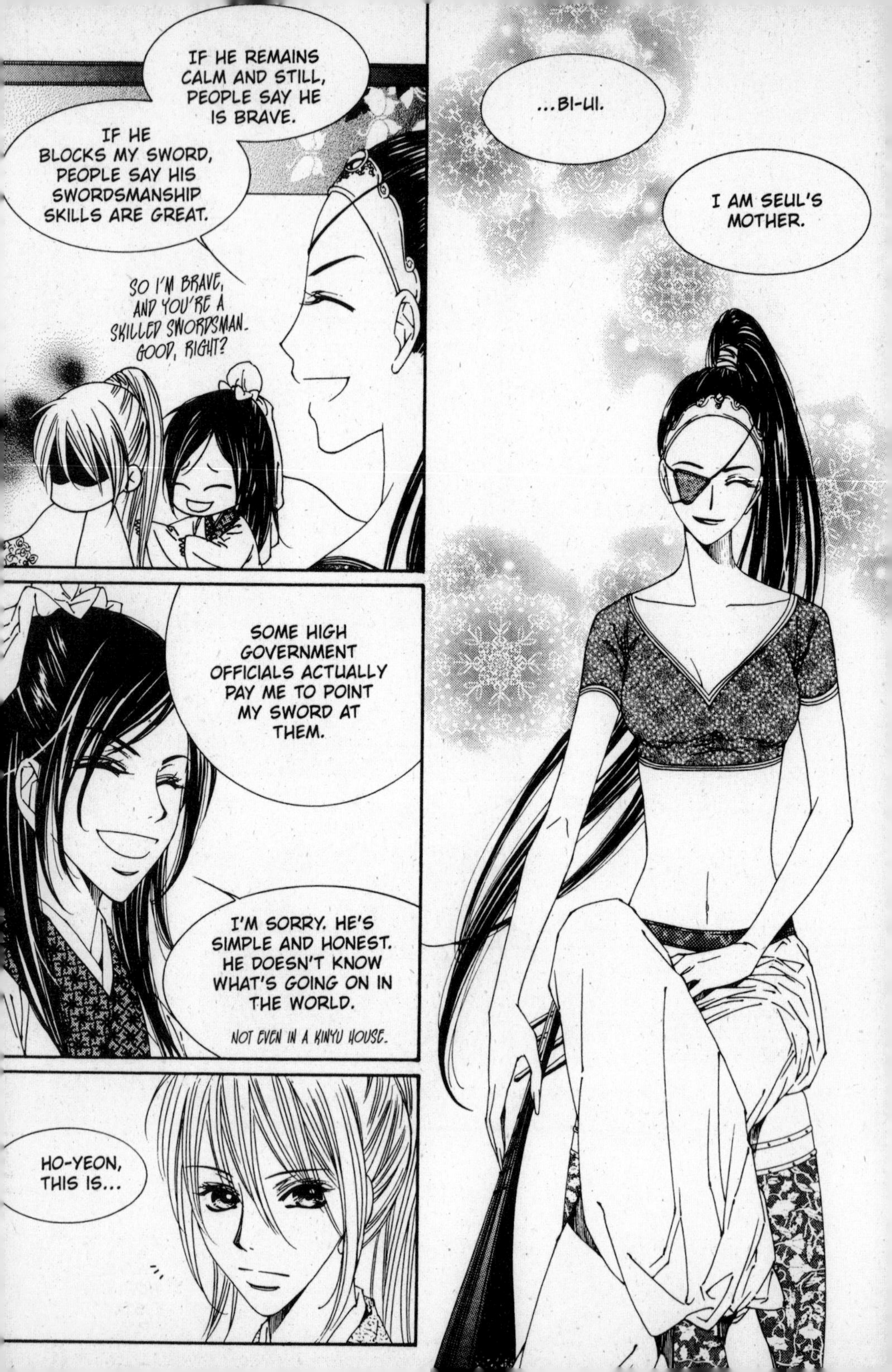
IF HE REMAINS CALM AND STILL, PEOPLE SAY HE IS BRAVE.
IF HE BLOCKS MY SWORD, PEOPLE SAY HIS SWORDSMANSHIP SKILLS ARE GREAT.
SO I'M BRAVE, AND YOU'RE A SKILLED SWORDSMAN. GOOD, RIGHT?
SOME HIGH GOVERNMENT OFFICIALS ACTUALLY PAY ME TO POINT MY SWORD AT THEM.
I'M SORRY. HE'S SIMPLE AND HONEST. HE DOESN'T KNOW WHAT'S GOING ON IN THE WORLD.
NOT EVEN IN A KINYU HOUSE.
HO-YEON, THIS IS...
...BI-UI.
I AM SEUL'S MOTHER.

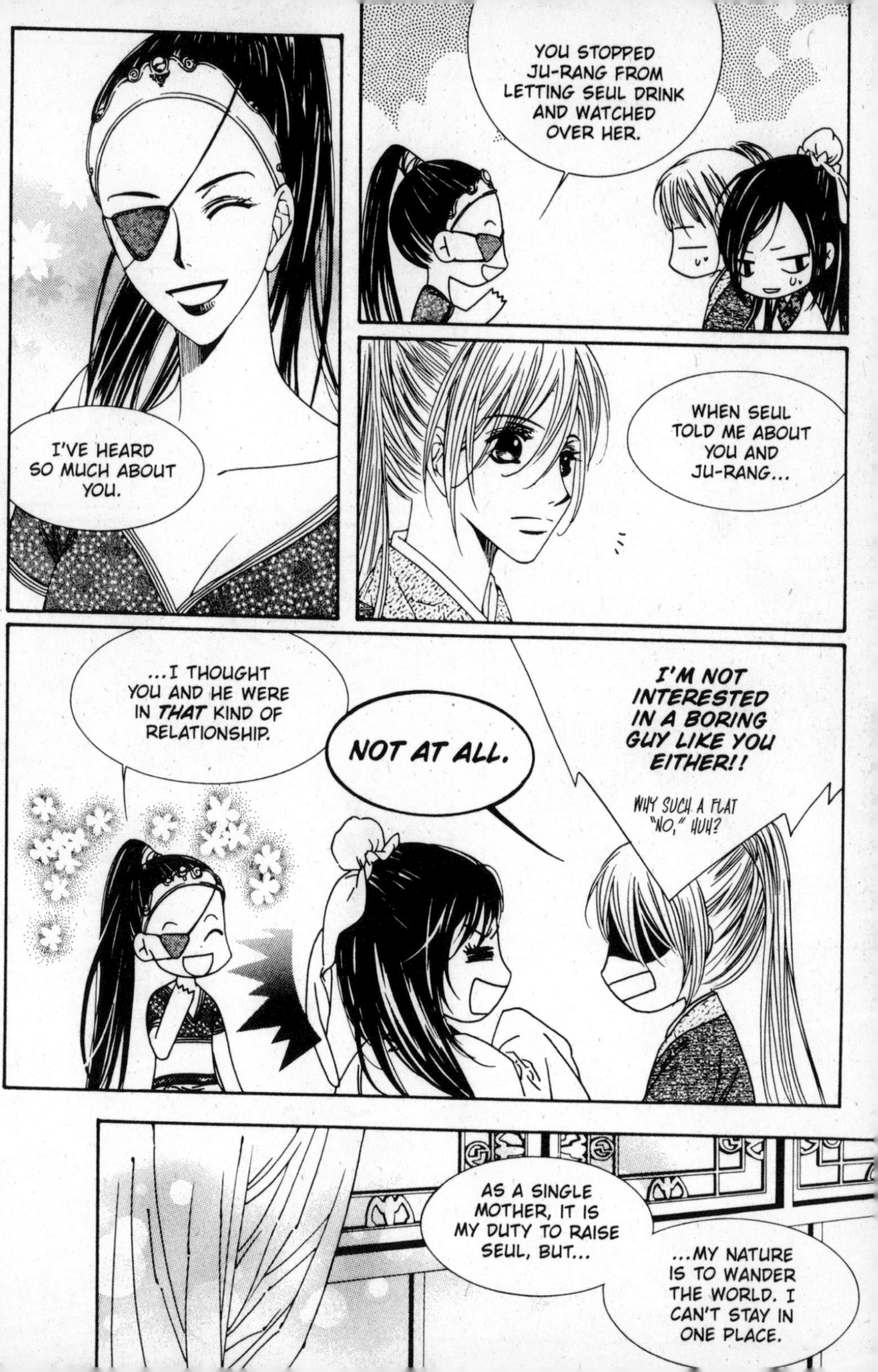
I'VE HEARD SO MUCH ABOUT YOU.
YOU STOPPED JU-RANG FROM LETTING SEUL DRINK AND WATCHED OVER HER.
WHEN SEUL TOLD ME ABOUT YOU AND JU-RANG...
...I THOUGHT YOU AND HE WERE IN THAT KIND OF RELATIONSHIP.
NOT AT ALL.
I'M NOT INTERESTED IN A BORING GUY LIKE YOU EITHER!!
WHY SUCH A FLAT "NO," HUH?
AS A SINGLE MOTHER, IT IS MY DUTY TO RAISE SEUL, BUT...
...MY NATURE IS TO WANDER THE WORLD. I CAN'T STAY IN ONE PLACE.

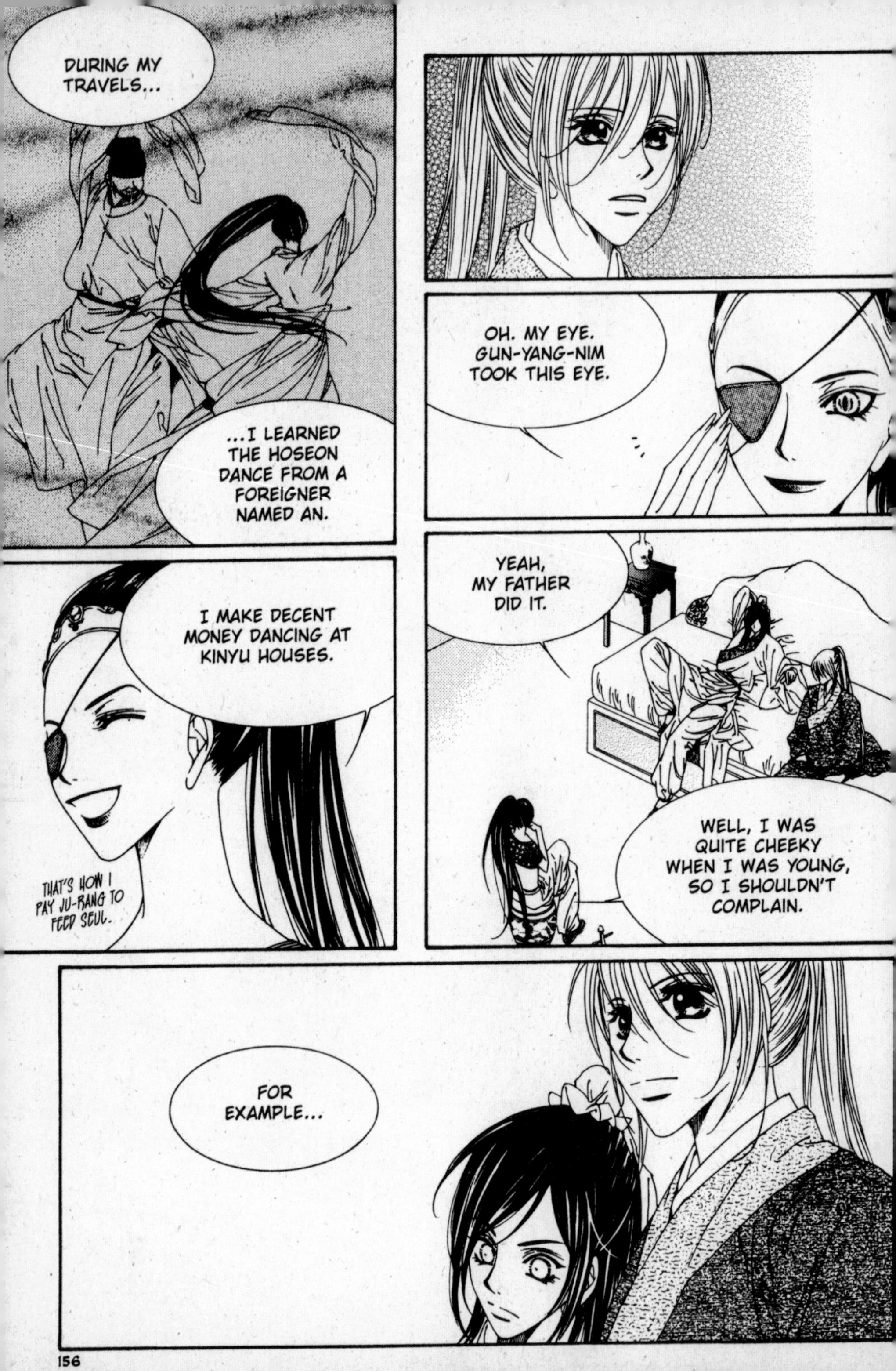

DURING MY TRAVELS...
...I LEARNED THE HOSEON DANCE FROM A FOREIGNER NAMED AN.
OH. MY EYE. GUN-YANG-NIM TOOK THIS EYE.
I MAKE DECENT MONEY DANCING AT KINYU HOUSES.
THAT'S HOW I PAY JU-RANG TO FEED SEUL.
YEAH, MY FATHER DID IT.
WELL, I WAS QUITE CHEEKY WHEN I WAS YOUNG, SO I SHOULDN'T COMPLAIN.
FOR EXAMPLE...

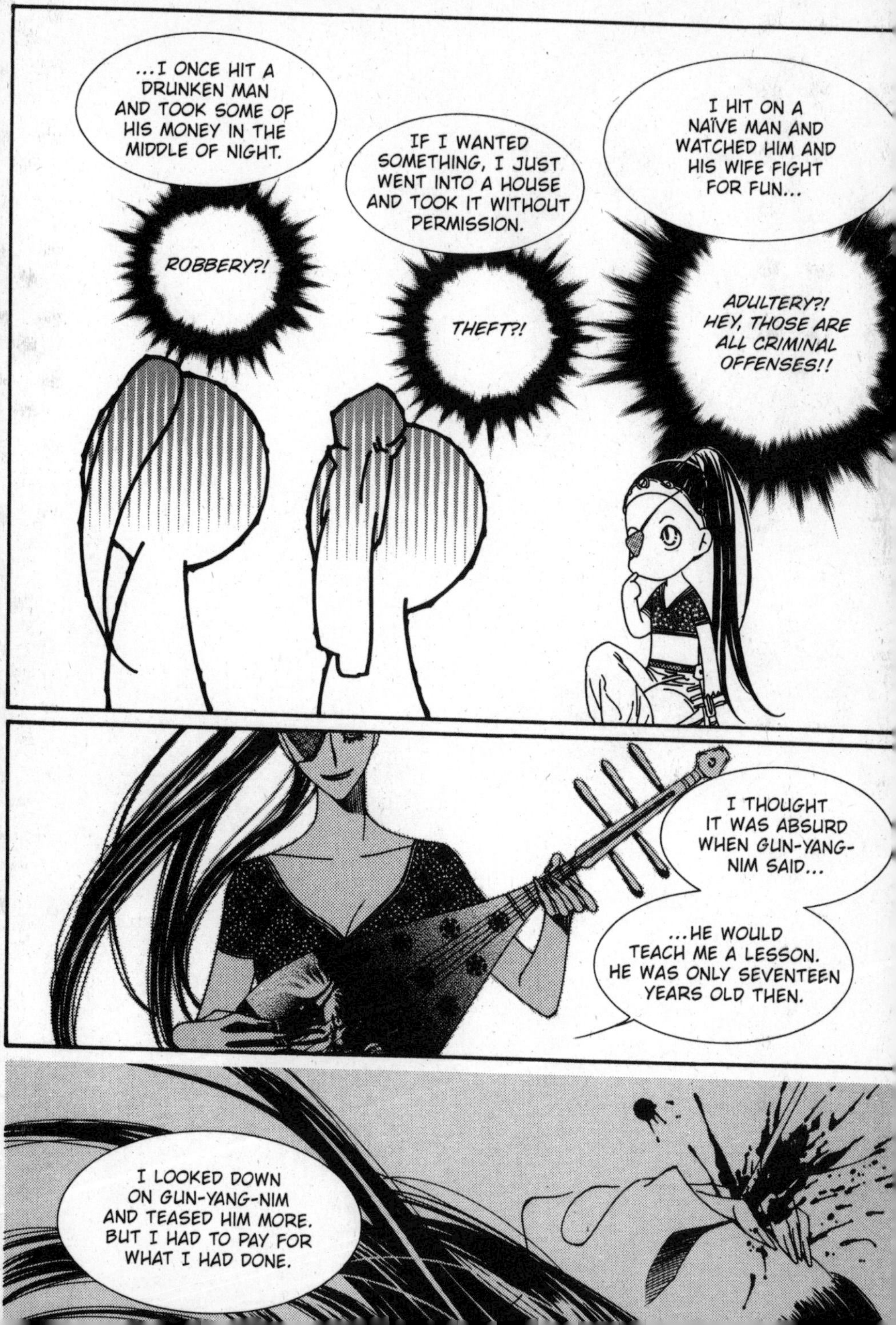
...I ONCE HIT A DRUNKEN MAN AND TOOK SOME OF HIS MONEY IN THE MIDDLE OF NIGHT.
ROBBERY?!
IF I WANTED SOMETHING, I JUST WENT INTO A HOUSE AND TOOK IT WITHOUT PERMISSION.
THEFT?!
I HIT ON A NAÏVE MAN AND WATCHED HIM AND HIS WIFE FIGHT FOR FUN...
ADULTERY?! HEY, THOSE ARE ALL CRIMINAL OFFENSES!!
I THOUGHT IT WAS ABSURD WHEN GUN-YANG-NIM SAID...
...HE WOULD TEACH ME A LESSON. HE WAS ONLY SEVENTEEN YEARS OLD THEN.
I LOOKED DOWN ON GUN-YANG-NIM AND TEASED HIM MORE. BUT I HAD TO PAY FOR WHAT I HAD DONE.

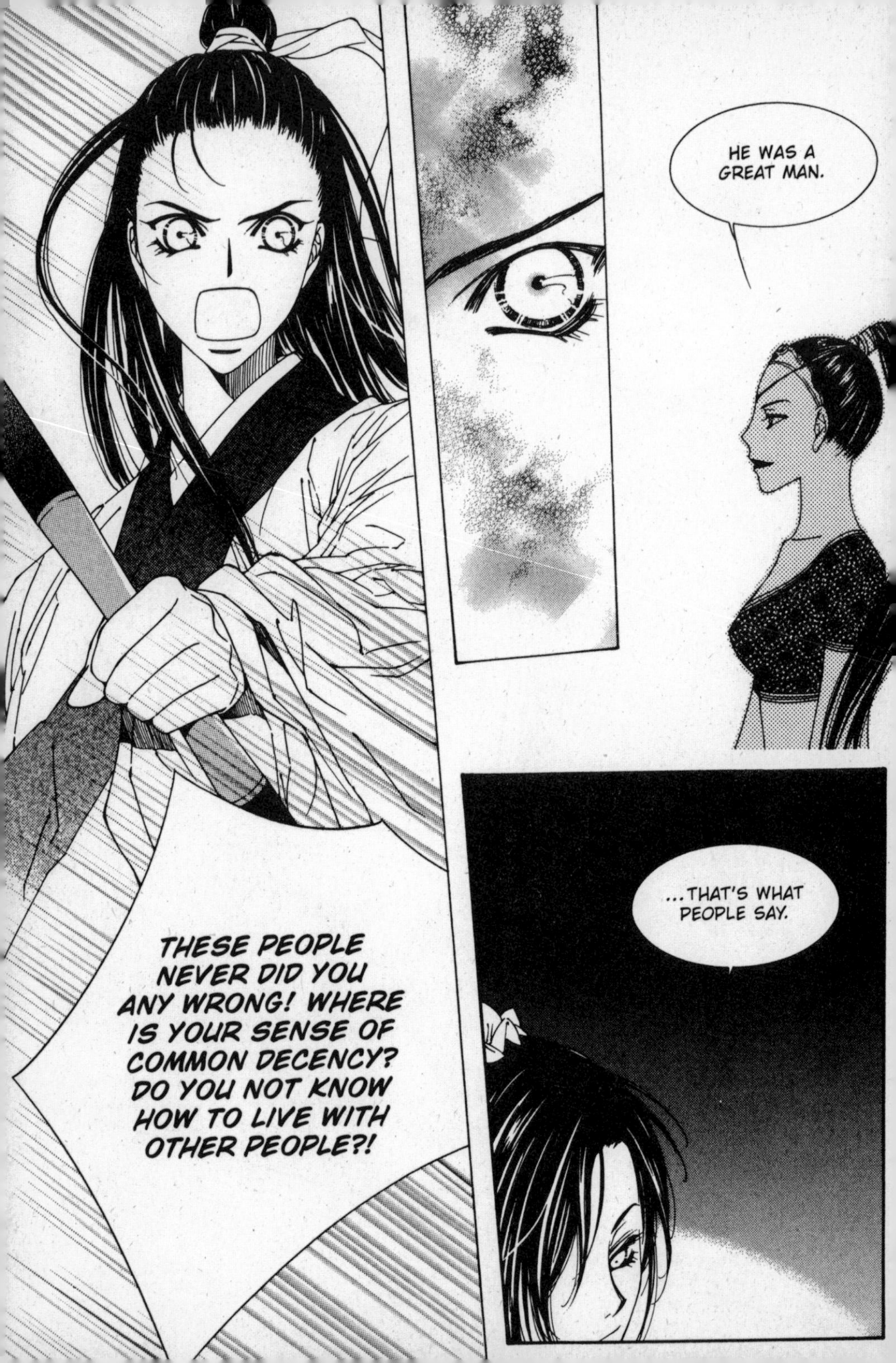
THESE PEOPLE NEVER DID YOU ANY WRONG! WHERE IS YOUR SENSE OF COMMON DECENCY? DO YOU NOT KNOW HOW TO LIVE WITH OTHER PEOPLE?!
HE WAS A GREAT MAN.
...THAT'S WHAT PEOPLE SAY.

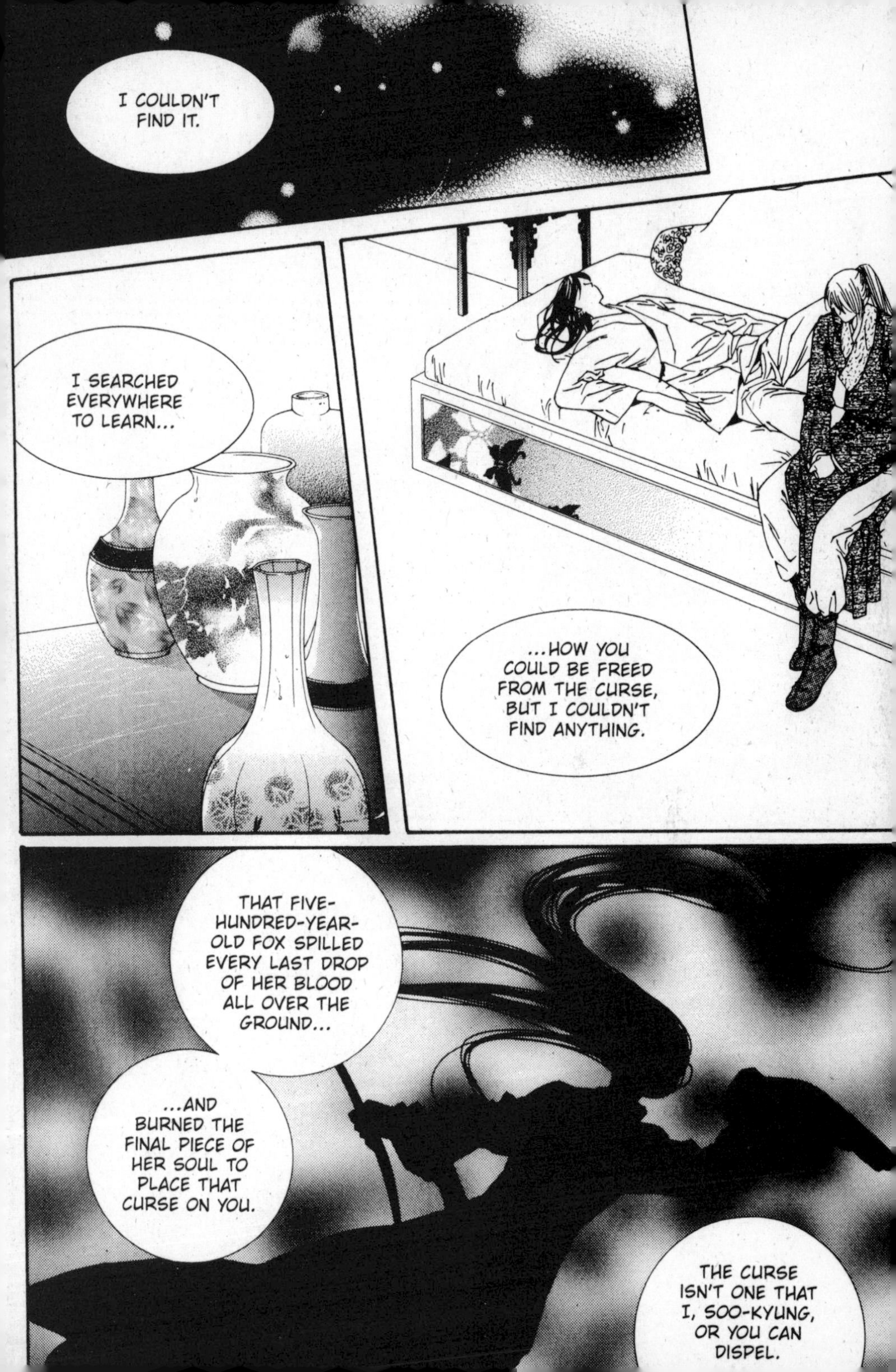
I COULDN'T FIND IT.
I SEARCHED EVERYWHERE TO LEARN...
...HOW YOU COULD BE FREED FROM THE CURSE, BUT I COULDN'T FIND ANYTHING.
THAT FIVE-HUNDRED-YEAR-OLD FOX SPILLED EVERY LAST DROP OF HER BLOOD ALL OVER THE GROUND...
...AND BURNED THE FINAL PIECE OF HER SOUL TO PLACE THAT CURSE ON YOU.
THE CURSE ISN'T ONE THAT I, SOO-KYUNG, OR YOU CAN DISPEL.

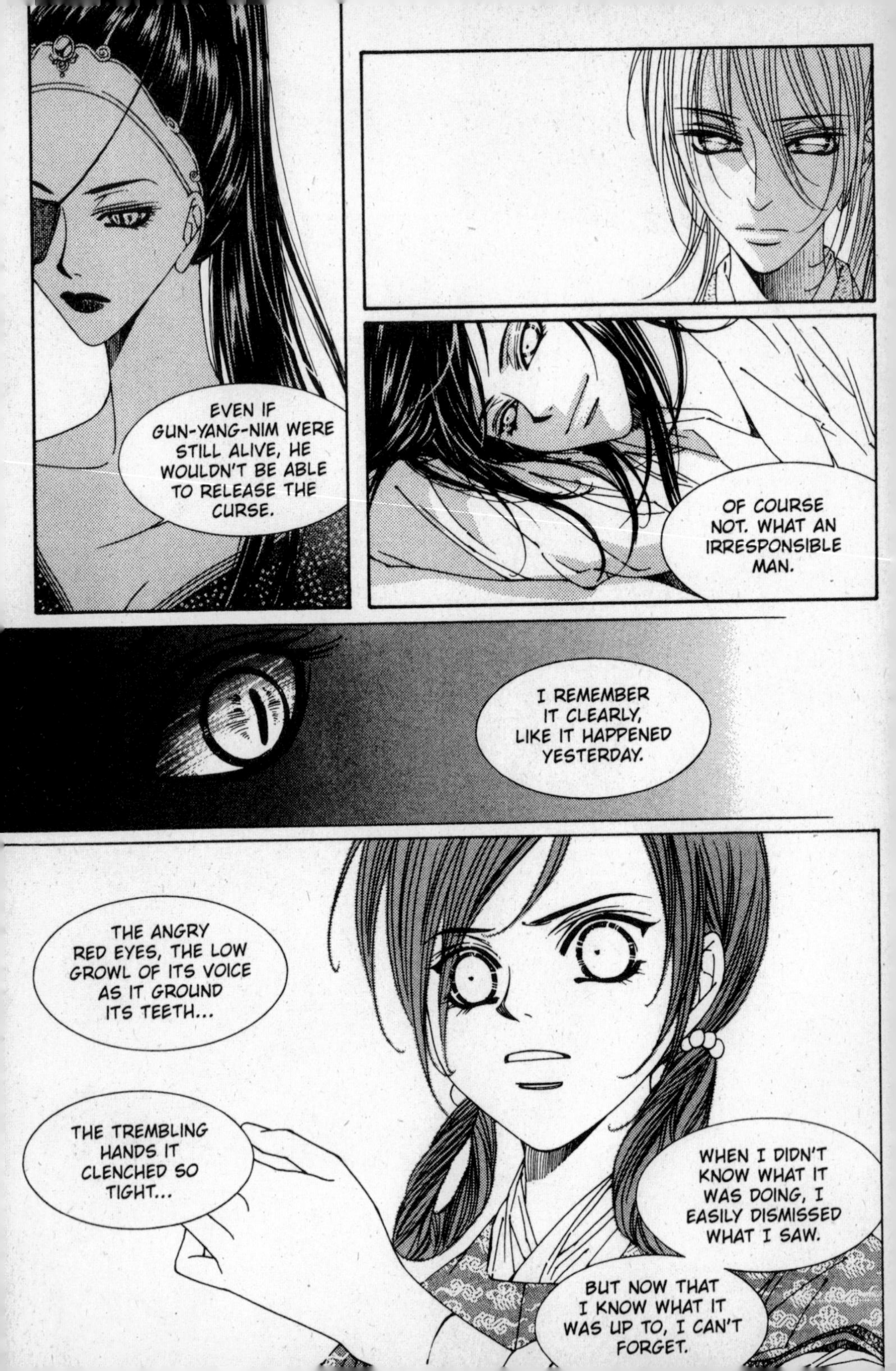
EVEN IF GUN-YANG-NIM WERE STILL ALIVE, HE WOULDN'T BE ABLE TO RELEASE THE CURSE.
OF COURSE NOT. WHAT AN IRRESPONSIBLE MAN.
I REMEMBER IT CLEARLY, LIKE IT HAPPENED YESTERDAY.
THE ANGRY RED EYES, THE LOW GROWL OF ITS VOICE AS IT GROUND ITS TEETH...
THE TREMBLING HANDS IT CLENCHED SO TIGHT...
WHEN I DIDN'T KNOW WHAT IT WAS DOING, I EASILY DISMISSED WHAT I SAW.
BUT NOW THAT I KNOW WHAT IT WAS UP TO, I CAN'T FORGET.

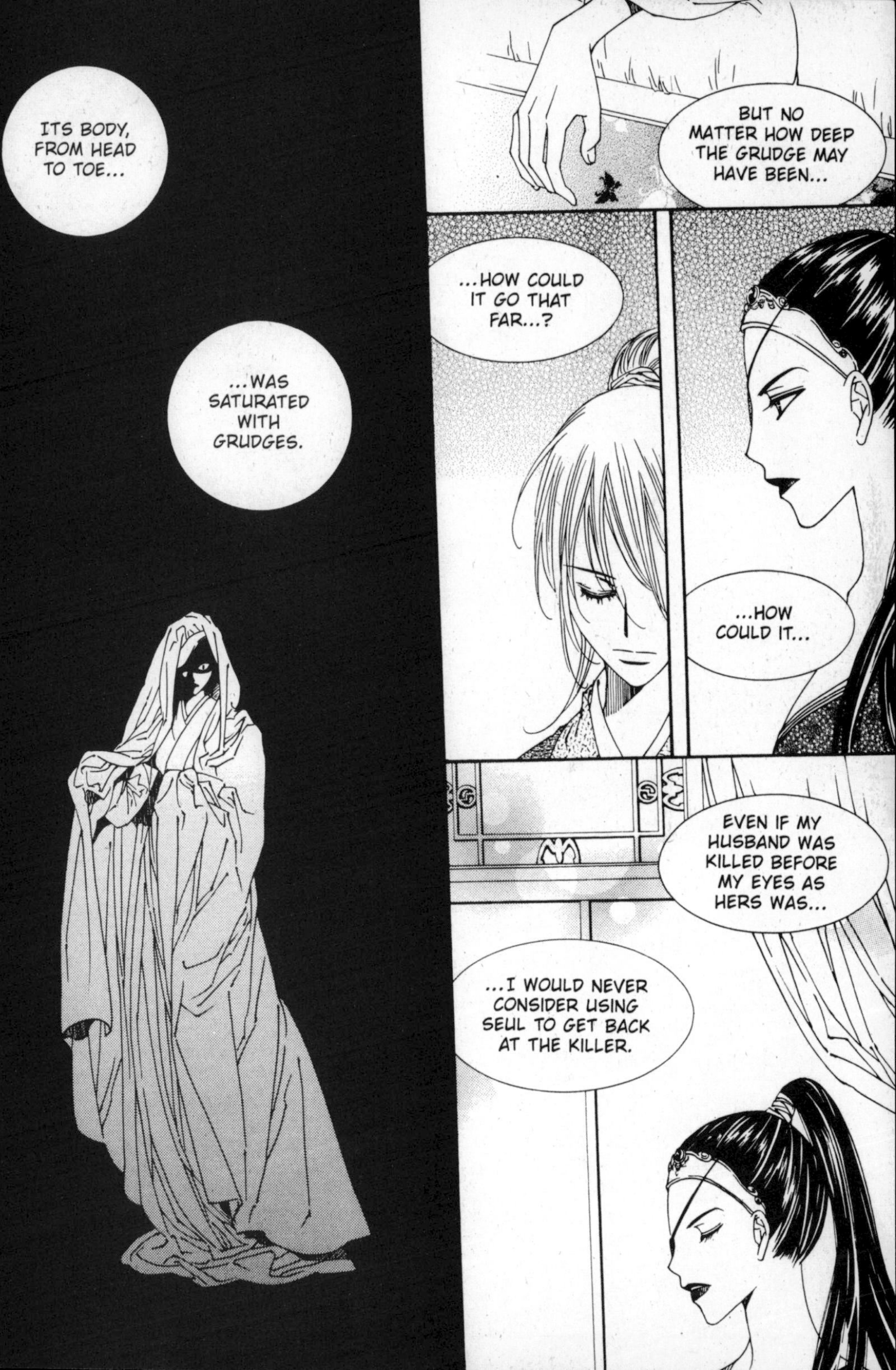
ITS BODY, FROM HEAD TO TOE...
...WAS SATURATED WITH GRUDGES.
BUT NO MATTER HOW DEEP THE GRUDGE MAY HAVE BEEN...
...HOW COULD IT GO THAT FAR...?
...HOW COULD IT...
EVEN IF MY HUSBAND WAS KILLED BEFORE MY EYES AS HERS WAS...
...I WOULD NEVER CONSIDER USING SEUL TO GET BACK AT THE KILLER.

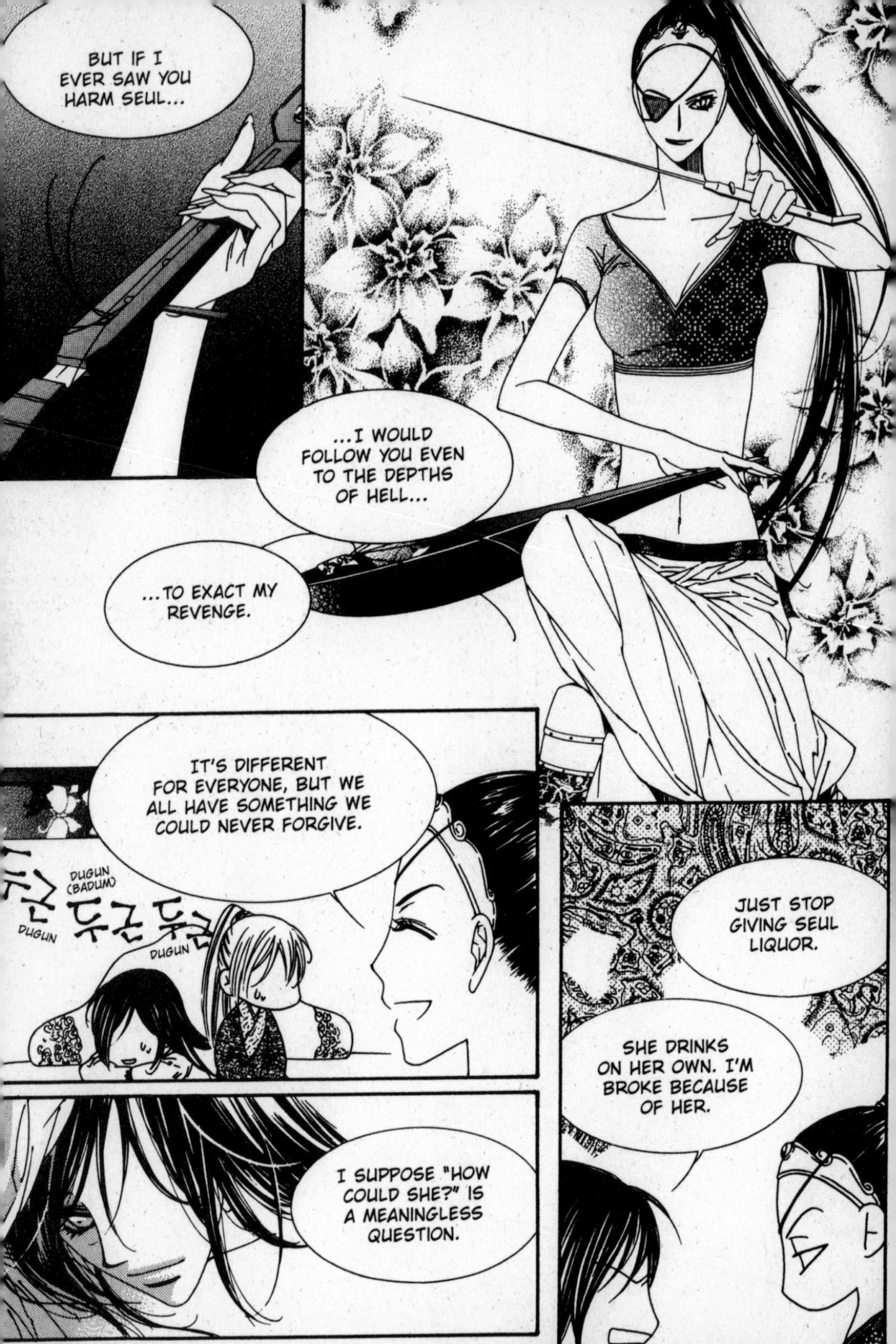
BUT IF I EVER SAW YOU HARM SEUL...
...I WOULD FOLLOW YOU EVEN TO THE DEPTHS OF HELL...
...TO EXACT MY REVENGE.
IT'S DIFFERENT FOR EVERYONE, BUT WE ALL HAVE SOMETHING WE COULD NEVER FORGIVE.
두근 두근 두근
DUGUN (BADUM)
DUGUN
DUGUN
I SUPPOSE "HOW COULD SHE?" IS A MEANINGLESS QUESTION.
JUST STOP GIVING SEUL LIQUOR.
SHE DRINKS ON HER OWN. I'M BROKE BECAUSE OF HER.

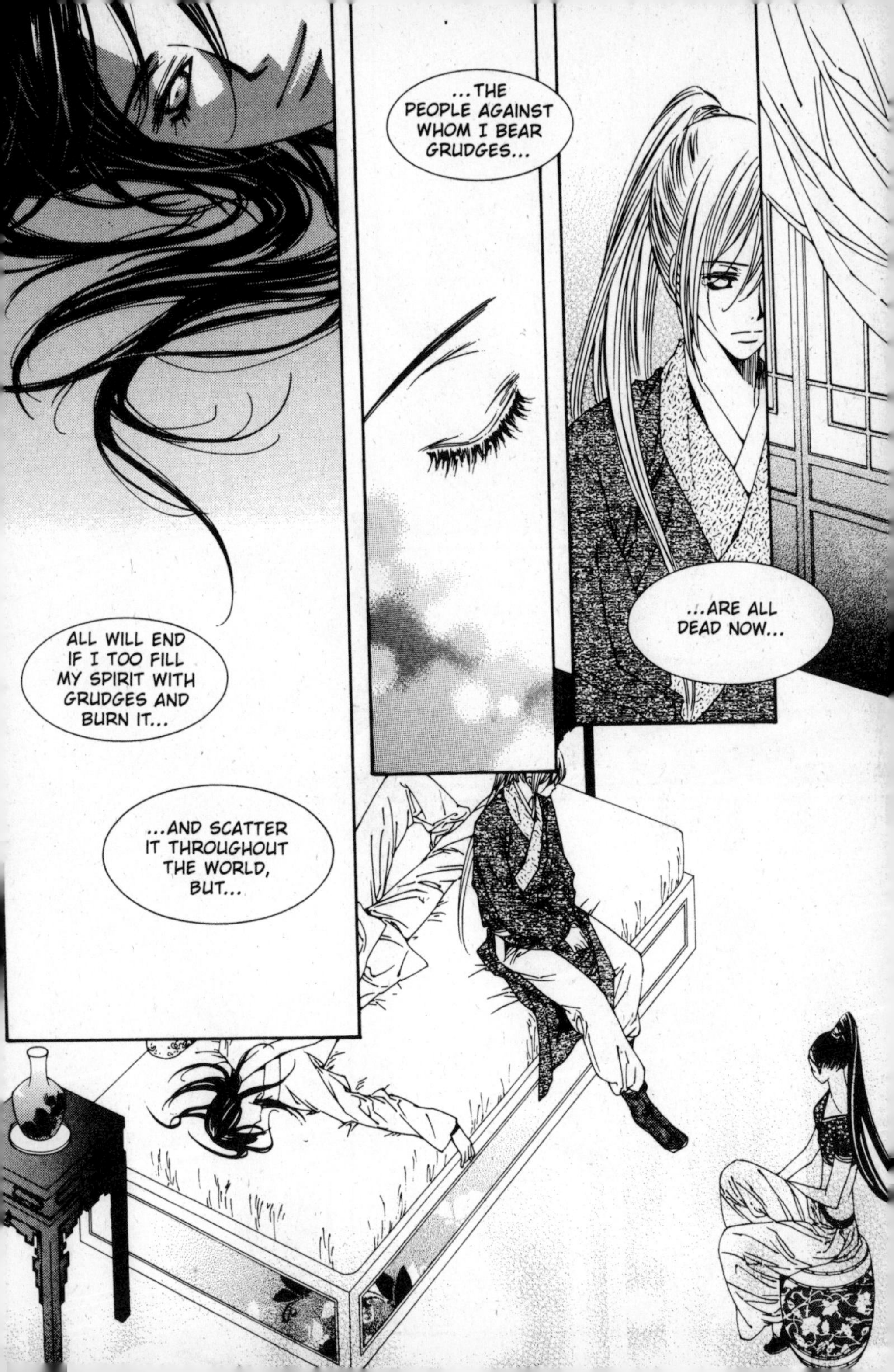
ALL WILL END IF I TOO FILL MY SPIRIT WITH GRUDGES AND BURN IT...
...AND SCATTER IT THROUGHOUT THE WORLD, BUT...
...THE PEOPLE AGAINST WHOM I BEAR GRUDGES...
...ARE ALL DEAD NOW...

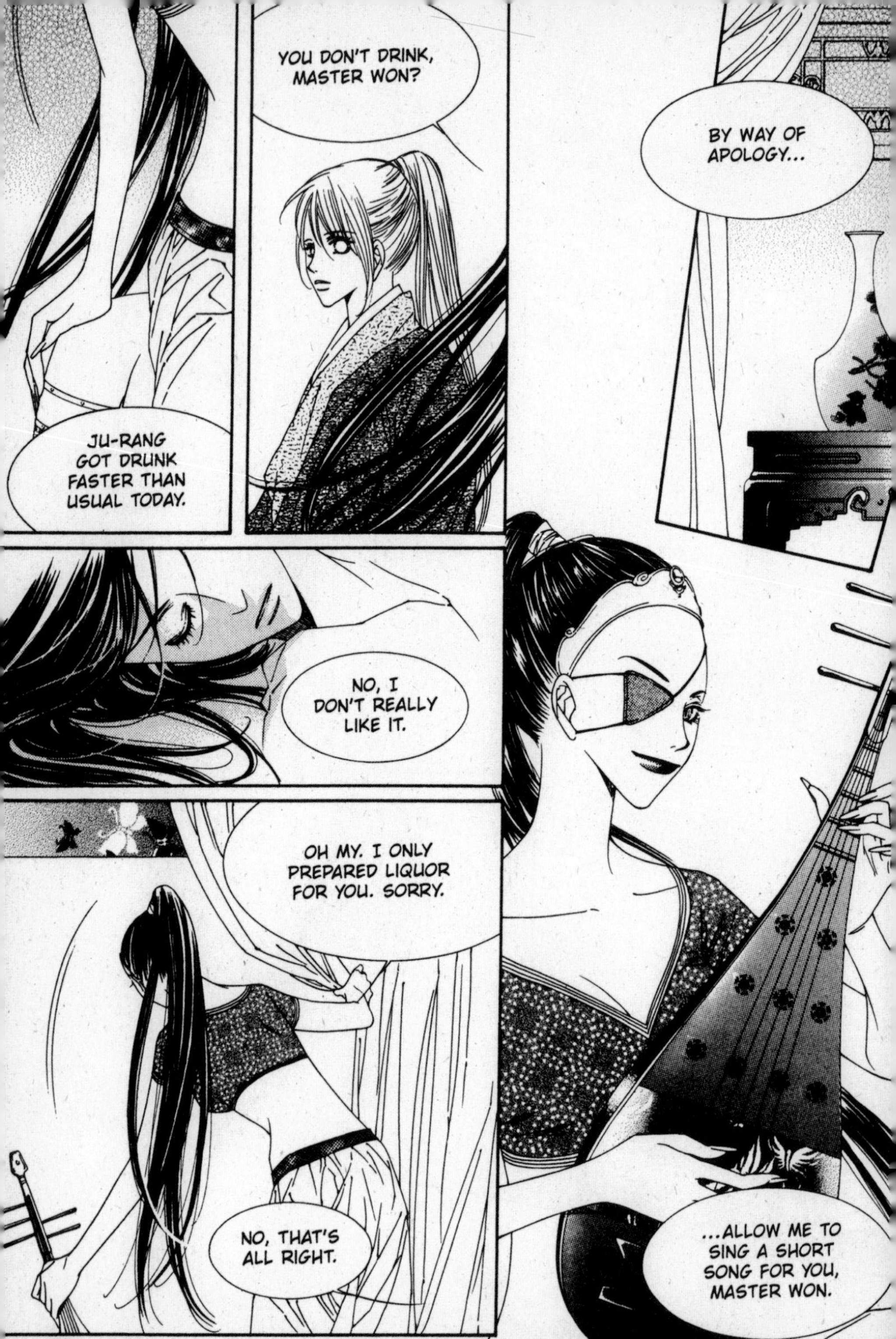

JU-RANG GOT DRUNK FASTER THAN USUAL TODAY.
YOU DON'T DRINK, MASTER WON?
NO, I DON'T REALLY LIKE IT.
OH MY. I ONLY PREPARED LIQUOR FOR YOU. SORRY.
NO, THAT'S ALL RIGHT.
BY WAY OF APOLOGY...
...ALLOW ME TO SING A SHORT SONG FOR YOU, MASTER WON.

THE HAN RIVER FLOWS
RAPIDLY AS A WHITE SEAGULL
SKIMS THE WATER.

DEEP INTO THE SPRING
THE GREENS GROW GREENER
AS IF DYEING MY CLOTHES.

LIFE IS BUSY AND TIME
FLIES, I GROW OLD BEFORE
I REALIZE.

THE SETTING SUN
WATCHES FOREVER THE FISHING
BOAT AS IT SAILS HOME.

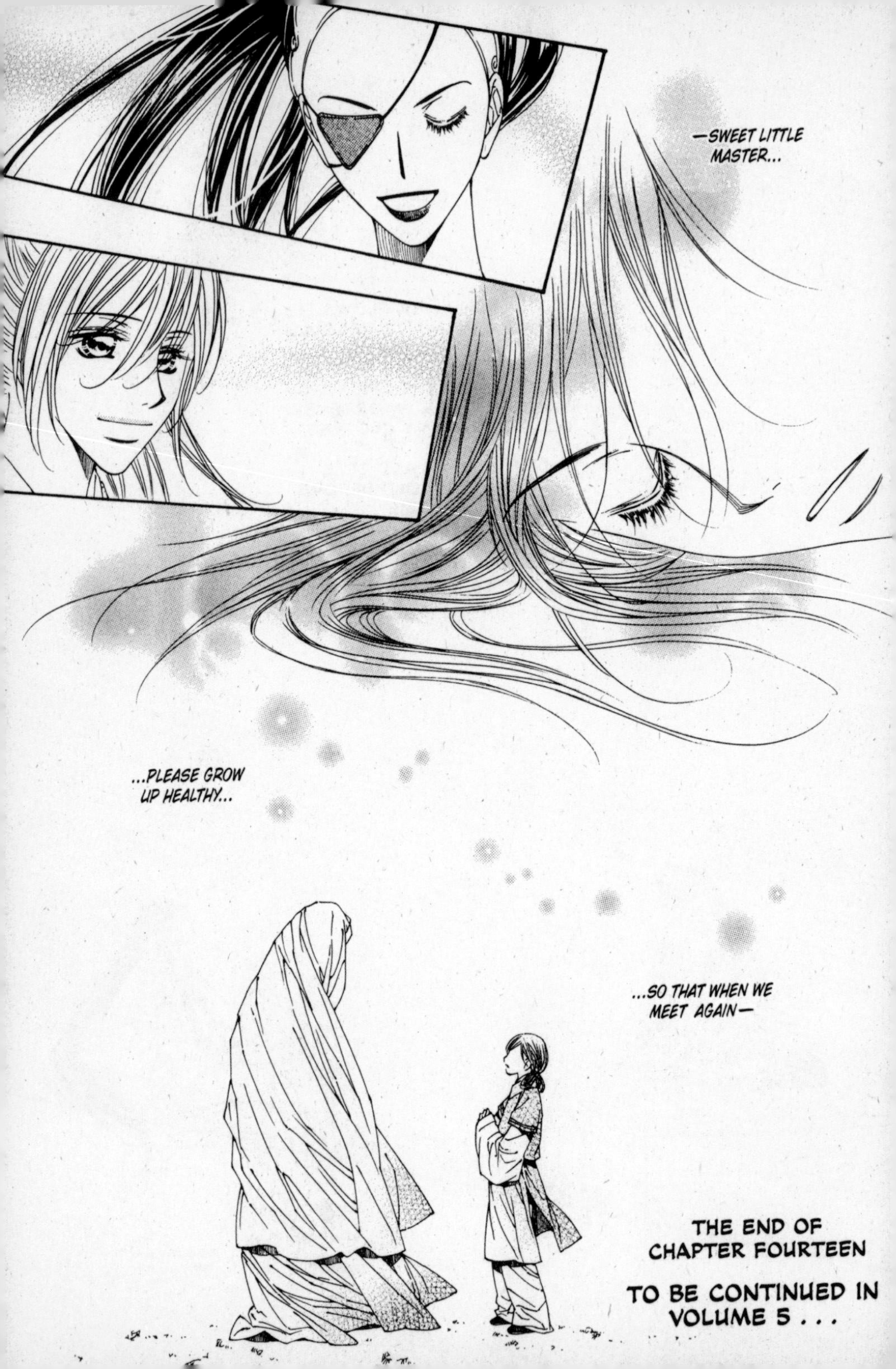
—SWEET LITTLE MASTER...
...PLEASE GROW UP HEALTHY...
...SO THAT WHEN WE MEET AGAIN—
THE END OF CHAPTER FOURTEEN
TO BE CONTINUED IN VOLUME 5 . . .

TIME AND AGAIN

Afterword

CHAPTER TWELVE

I KNOW THAT VERY WELL.

...WELL THEN, SHALL WE GO?

HEY, WAIT! ARE YOU LEAVING? WHAT ABOUT TAKING BACK THE JUG?

AREN'T YOU BEING KIND OF IRRESPONSIBLE? HEY!

SIGH...

I TOOK THE BASIC STORY FROM THE KOREAN BOOK HAEDONGYASEO, BUT EVEN IN CHINA, THERE ARE MANY, MANY STORIES ABOUT PEOPLE GAINING FORTUNE FROM AN OBJECT THEY ACQUIRE BY CHANCE. IT'S LIKE AN OLD LOTTERY STORY. IN MOST OF THE TALES, THE PEOPLE BECOME HAPPIER AFTER THEY GET RICH. BUT I DON'T THINK YOU CAN BE HAPPY JUST BECAUSE YOU'RE RICH ALL OF A SUD- DEN. ACTUALLY, EIGHTY PER- CENT OF LOTTERY WINNERS SAY THEY WEREN'T HAPPIER AFTER WINNING.

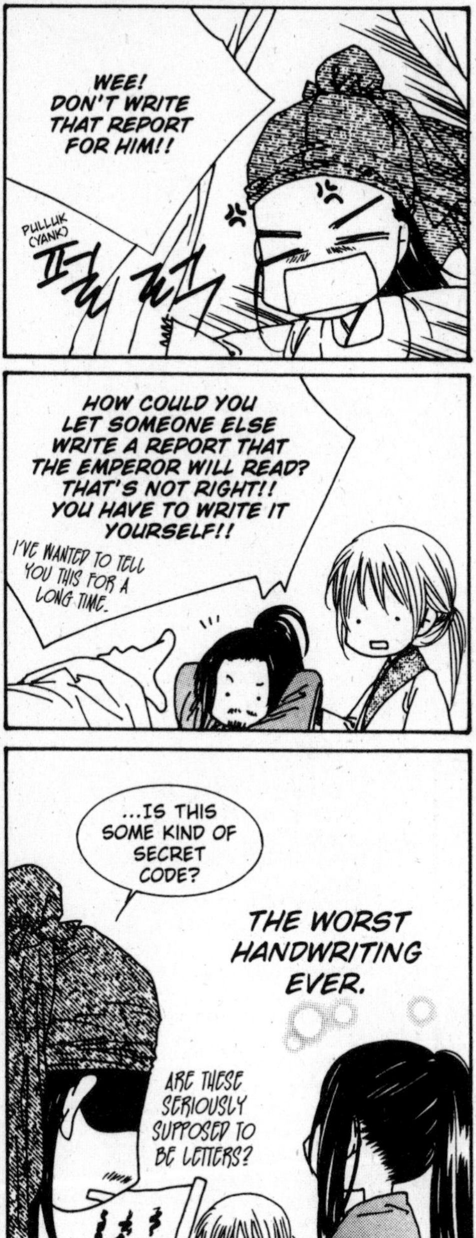
WEE! DON'T WRITE THAT REPORT FOR HIM!!
PULLUK (YANK)
HOW COULD YOU LET SOMEONE ELSE WRITE A REPORT THAT THE EMPEROR WILL READ? THAT'S NOT RIGHT!! YOU HAVE TO WRITE IT YOURSELF!!
I'VE WANTED TO TELL YOU THIS FOR A LONG TIME.
...IS THIS SOME KIND OF SECRET CODE?
THE WORST HANDWRITING EVER.
ARE THESE SERIOUSLY SUPPOSED TO BE LETTERS?
THE EMPEROR TOLD ME THAT HE COULDN'T READ MY WRITING.
MASTER SON IS A TYPICAL MILITARY OFFICER-TYPE.

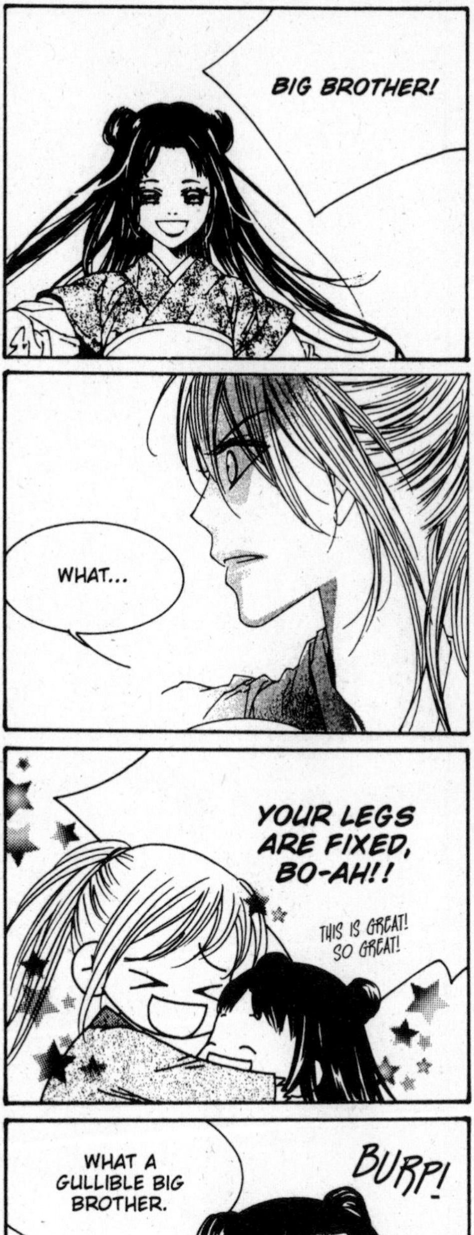
BIG BROTHER!
WHAT...
YOUR LEGS ARE FIXED, BO-AH!!
THIS IS GREAT! SO GREAT!
WHAT A GULLIBLE BIG BROTHER.
BURP!
IF I WERE HO-YEON, THIS WOULD'VE BEEN MY REACTION.

WOULD YOU COME TO THE YOU REGION WITH ME?
JOLJOLJOL (FOLLOW)
쫄 쫄 쫄
COME TO QINGHAI WITH ME.
JOLJOLJOL
쫄 쫄 쫄
WHY DON'T YOU COME WITH ME?
JOLJOLJOL
쫄 쫄 쫄
MOST BAD THINGS HAPPEN TO YOU WHEN YOU JUST GO ALONG WITH WHAT OTHER PEOPLE SAY, RIGHT?
INCLUDING YOU.
YOU WERE KID-NAPPED WHEN YOU WERE YOUNG, WEREN'T YOU?

DURING THE TANG DYNASTY, PEONIES WERE AS POPULAR AS DESIGNER PURSES ARE TODAY. THERE IS A LINE FROM BUY FLOWERS *BY BAI JUYI WHICH READS: "THE PRICE OF ONE PEONY TREE IS AS MUCH AS THE TAXES PAID BY TEN FARMERS." ALSO, THERE IS THE LINE FROM* PEONIES *BY IN SEO THAT SAYS: "100,000 FAMILIES WENT BANKRUPT BECAUSE OF PEONIES." BUT NO ONE WAS INTERESTED IN WHITE PEONIES. THAT'S NOT SURPRISING SINCE DAZZLING THINGS WERE POPULAR IN THE TANG DYNASTY. I THINK THE PEONY TREND IS QUITE ELEGANT.*

I BORROWED THE KOREAN FOLK STORY OF "THE FOX SISTER AND HER THREE BROTHERS" FOR HO-YEON'S STORY. IN THE ORIGINAL STORY, THE THREE BROTHERS ATTACK THE FOX WHO LOOKED JUST LIKE THEIR SISTER WITHOUT ANY HESITATION. I THOUGHT THE BROTHERS WERE SO COLD.

ACCORDING TO A CHINESE BOOK CALLED XUANZHONG-JI, *A FOX CAN TRANSFORM INTO A WOMAN WHEN IT LIVES MORE THAN FIFTY YEARS, AND CAN TRANSFORM INTO A BEAUTIFUL WOMAN OR A MAN WHEN IT REACHES ONE HUNDRED YEARS. A THOUSAND-YEAR-OLD FOX CAN EVEN COMMUNICATE WITH HEAVEN, SO IT'S CALLED A "HEAVEN FOX." A FOX WITH NINE TAILS IS DIFFERENT FROM REGULAR FOXES. IT WAS CONSIDERED A HOLY ANIMAL. THE WORLD OF FOXES IS MORE COMPLICATED THAN I THOUGHT.*

CHAPTER FOURTEEN

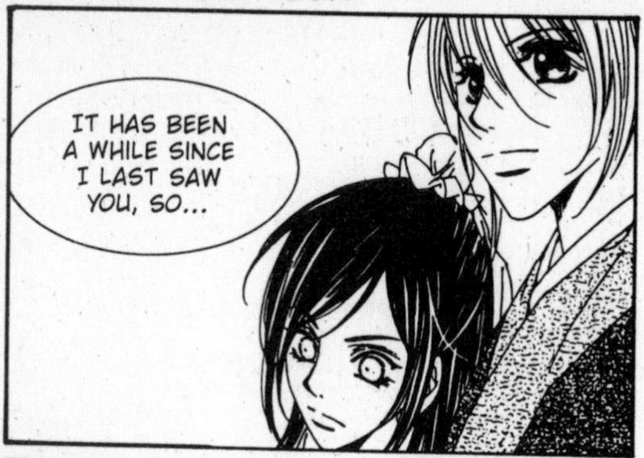
IT HAS BEEN A WHILE SINCE I LAST SAW YOU, SO...

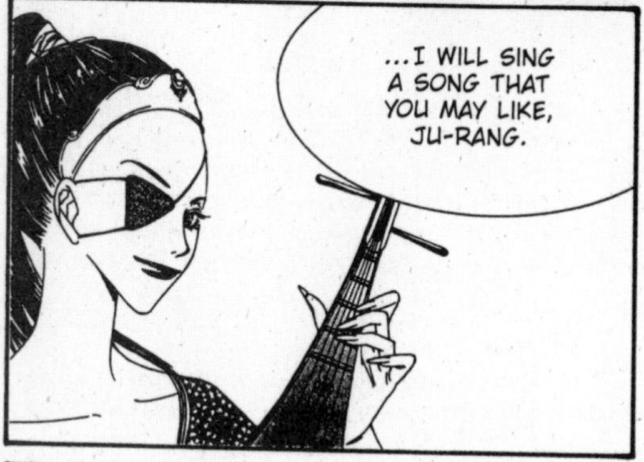
...I WILL SING A SONG THAT YOU MAY LIKE, JU-RANG.

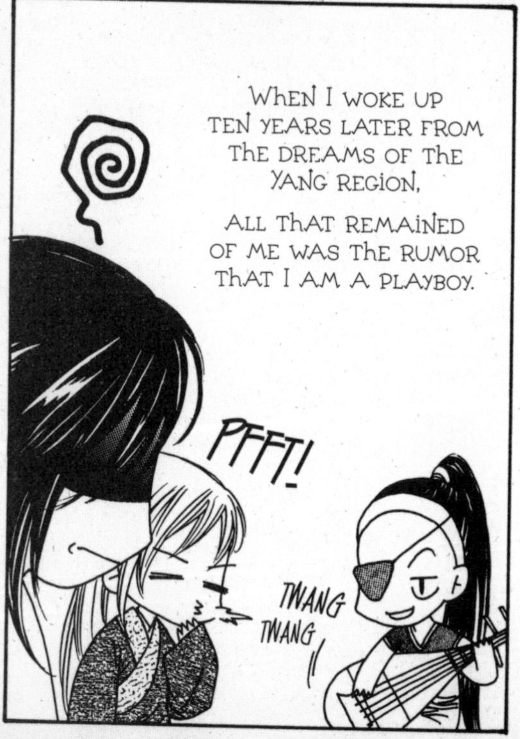
WHEN I WOKE UP TEN YEARS LATER FROM THE DREAMS OF THE YANG REGION,
ALL THAT REMAINED OF ME WAS THE RUMOR THAT I AM A PLAYBOY.
PFFT!
TWANG
TWANG

HOSEON DANCE: IT LOOKS LIKE AN ARABIAN DANCE HIGHLIGHTED BY FAST TURNS. WHEN LUSHAN AN, WHOSE SPECIALTY WAS HOSEON DANCE, DANCED IN FRONT OF EMPEROR XUAN-ZONG OF TANG DYNASTY, PEOPLE SAID THEY COULDN'T SEE HIS FEET BECAUSE HE WAS AS FAST AS THE WIND. IT SEEMS THE DANCE WAS POPULAR BACK THEN, BUT THERE IS NO RECORD OF THE EXACT MOVES. HOW DISAP-POINTING...

DANSUJIBYUK: THE LITERAL MEANING IS "THE HABIT OF CUTTING SLEEVES." EM-PEROR AI OF HAN WAS IN LOVE WITH A LOWER OFFICIAL NAMED DONG XIAN (HE WAS PROBABLY YOUNGER), SO THE TWO MEN OFTEN SLEPT TOGETHER. ONE DAY, DONG XIAN FELL ASLEEP ON TOP OF THE EMPEROR'S SLEEVE. RATHER THAN DISTURB HIS LOVER, THE EMPEROR CUT HIS SLEEVE. THAT'S HOW THE EXPRESSION CAME INTO BEING.

THE SONG BI-UI SINGS FOR HO-YEON IS THE POEM CALLED "HAN RIVER" BY DU MU. UP UNTIL THE LAST MINUTE, I COULDN'T DECIDE WHICH ONE TO USE, THAT ONE OR THE POEM BELOW. THE POEM BELOW IS CALLED "KYUNHEE," AND I ONLY USED IT FOR THIS EXTRA PAGE AT THE END. BUT THE POET WASN'T EVEN ALIVE DUR-ING THE TIME THIS BOOK TAKES PLACE. HE WAS BORN IN 803. (AHEM.) PLEASE UNDERSTAND ME.

"BECAUSE THE POWER OF WARRIORS BEGAN TO WANE,
I FREQUENTED BARS AND THE BEAUTIES OF CHO.
WHEN I WOKE UP TEN YEARS LATER FROM THE DREAMS OF THE YANG REGION,
ALL THAT REMAINED OF ME WAS THE RUMOR THAT I AM A PLAYBOY."

TRANSLATION NOTES

In Asian history and culture, a certain value was placed on a person's given name, so it was considered rude to use it too often. Thus, when a person married or reached a certain age, he or she would be given another name to be used more commonly. This is why Yoo Ju and Wee Won refer to each other as Baek-On Ju and Ho-Yeon Won respectively.

Page 36
Yuan was the ancient currency used in China and Korea.

Boryong literally means "the treasure of dragon," which is a fitting name for the liquor.

A *kinyu* was similar to a Japanese *geisha*. These women would entertain their guests with dance, song, recitation, and conversation.

Page 128
The Korean suffix *-nim* is used to convey respect, similar to *-san* or *-sama* in Japanese.

Page 146
The song Bi-Ui sings during her dance is the famous **"Song of Gaixia,"** written in 202 BC during the Chu-Han Contention. As Chinese rulers battled for supremacy after the fall of the Qin Dynasty, General Xiang Yu led the Chu army against invading Han forces in the Battle of Gaixia. Outnumbered and low on supplies, many of Xiang Yu's soldiers deserted him, and those who remained fell into despair. Deeply depressed, Xiang Yu composed and sang the *Song of Gaixia*. Shortly thereafter, his beloved concubine, Consort Yuji, committed suicide. The next morning, he rallied his dwindling troops to face the Han Army and was ultimately defeated.

Page 152
Xiang Bo: Fan Zeng, advisor to Emperor Gaozu of the Han Dynasty, plotted to have the emperor killed during the Feast at Hong Gate, a meeting between the emperor and his long-time rival, Xiang Yu, around 205 BC. Summoning Xiang Yu's cousin, Xiang Zhuang, Fan Zeng asked the young man to perform a sword dance as part of the entertainment, during which Xiang Zhuang was to stab the emperor. Sensing danger, Xiang Yu's uncle, Xiang Bo, began to dance as well, protecting Emperor Gaozu with his artful swords.

Page 153
The suffix *-rang* is used to refer to someone else's son in a familiar way, similar to saying "son of" whomever.

A totally new Arabian nights, where Scheherazade is a guy!

Everyone knows the story of Scheherazade and her wonderful tales from the Arabian Nights. For one thousand and one nights, the stories that she created entertained the mad Sultan and eventually saved her life. In this version, Scheherazade is a guy who disguises himself as a woman to save his sister from the mad Sultan. When he puts his life on the line, what kind of strange and unique stories will he tell? This new twist on one of the greatest classical tales might just keep you awake for another ONE THOUSAND AND ONE NIGHTS!

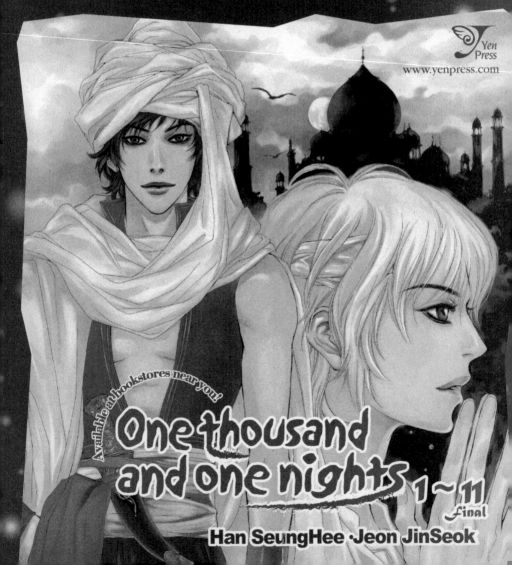

Yen Press
www.yenpress.com

Available at bookstores near you!

One thousand and one nights 1~11 final

Han SeungHee · Jeon JinSeok

Yen Press

www.yenpress.com

THE MOST BEAUTIFUL FACE, THE PERFECT BODY,
AND A SINCERE PERSONALITY...THAT'S WHAT HYE-MIN HWANG HAS.
NATURALLY, SHE'S THE CENTER OF EVERYONE'S ATTENTION.
EVERY BOY IN SCHOOL LOVES HER, WHILE EVERY GIRL HATES HER OUT OF JEALOUSY.
EVERY SINGLE DAY, SHE HAS TO ENDURE TORTURES AND HARDSHIPS FROM THE GIRLS.

A PRETTY FACE COMES WITH A PRICE.

THERE IS NOTHING MORE SATISFYING THAN GETTING THEM BACK.
WELL, EXCEPT FOR ONE PROBLEM . . . HER SECRET CRUSH, JUNG-YUN.
BECAUSE OF HIM, SHE HAS TO HIDE HER CYNICAL AND DARK SIDE
AND DAILY PUT ON AN INNOCENT FACE. THEN ONE DAY, SHE FINDS OUT
THAT HE DISLIKES HER ANYWAY!! WHAT?! THAT'S IT! NO MORE NICE GIRL!
AND THE FIRST VICTIM OF HER RAGE IS A PLAYBOY SHE JUST MET, MA-HA.

vol.**1~9**
FINAL

Cynical Orange

Yun JiUn

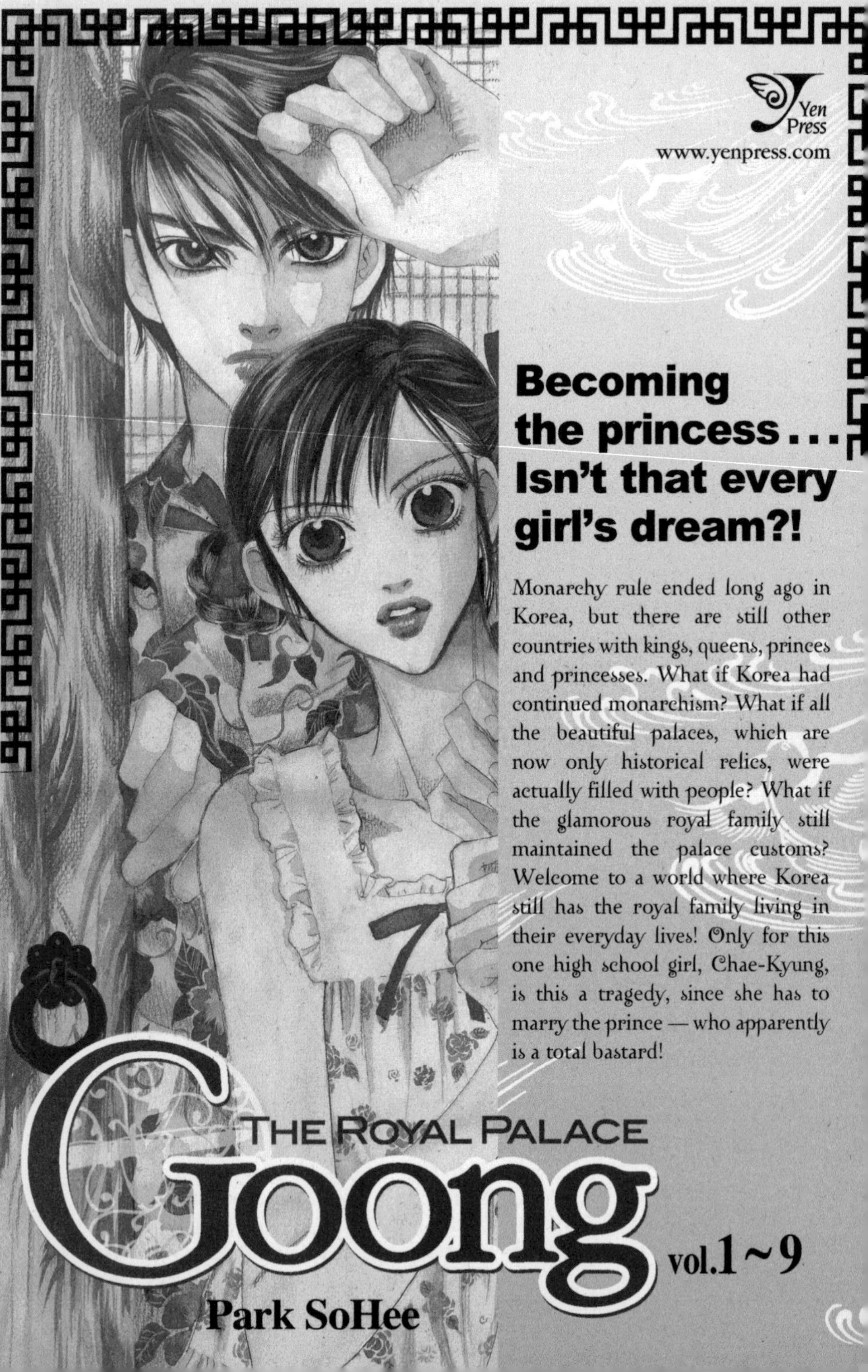

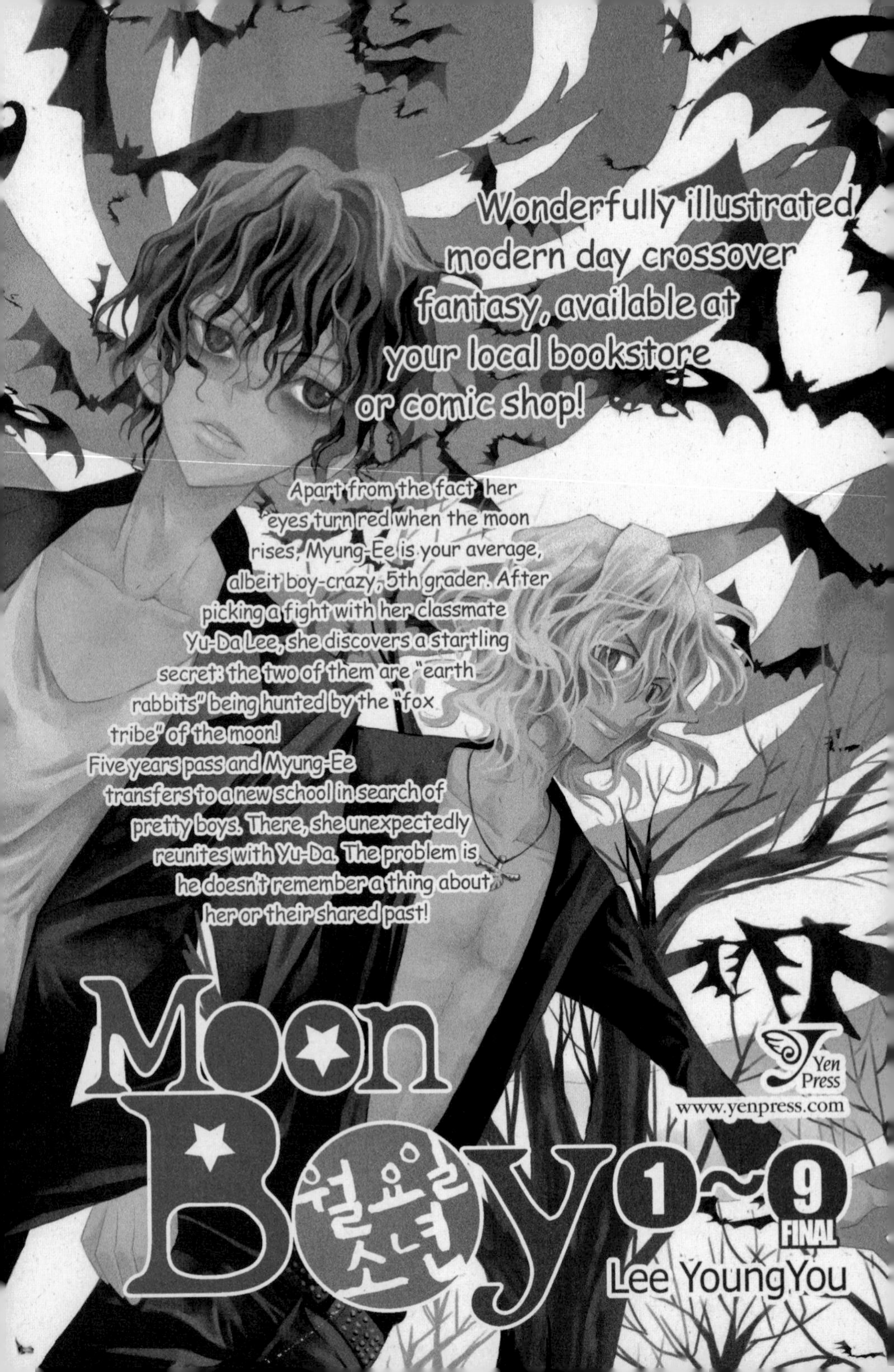
Wonderfully illustrated modern day crossover fantasy, available at your local bookstore or comic shop!
Apart from the fact her eyes turn red when the moon rises, Myung-Ee is your average, albeit boy-crazy, 5th grader. After picking a fight with her classmate Yu-Da Lee, she discovers a startling secret: the two of them are "earth rabbits" being hunted by the "fox tribe" of the moon! Five years pass and Myung-Ee transfers to a new school in search of pretty boys. There, she unexpectedly reunites with Yu-Da. The problem is he doesn't remember a thing about her or their shared past!
Moon Boy
월요일 소년
1~9
FINAL
Lee YoungYou
Yen Press
www.yenpress.com

Sometimes, just being a teenager is hard enough.

Da-Eh, an aspiring manhwa artist who lives with her father and her little brother, comes across Sun-Nam, a softie whose ultimate goal is simply to become a "Tough guy." Whenever these two meet, trouble follows. Meanwhile, Ta-Jun, the hottest guy in town, finds himself drawn to the one girl that his killer smile does not work on–Da-Eh. With their complicated family history hanging on their shoulders, watch how these three teenagers find their way out into the world!

Available at bookstores near you!

HISSING

1~6
COMPLETE

Kang EunYoung

TIME AND AGAIN ④

JIUN YUN

Translation: HyeYoung Im   •   English Adaptation: J. Torres

Lettering: Abigail Blackman

Time and Again, vol. 4 © 2007 by YUN Ji-un, DAEWON C.I. Inc. All rights reserved. First published in Korea in 2007 by DAEWON C.I. Inc. English translation rights in USA, Canada, UK and Commonwealth arranged by Daewon C.I. Inc. through TOPAZ Agency Inc.

Translation © 2010 by Hachette Book Group, Inc.

Yen Press
Hachette Book Group
237 Park Avenue, New York, NY 10017

www.HachetteBookGroup.com
www.YenPress.com

Yen Press is an imprint of Hachette Book Group, Inc.
The Yen Press name and logo are trademarks of Hachette Book Group, Inc.

First Yen Press Edition: November 2010

ISBN: 978-0-7595-3061-4

10 9 8 7 6 5 4 3 2 1

BVG

Printed in the United States of America